PLAYBOY'S
SILVERSTEIN AROUND THE WORLD

SHEL SILVERSTEIN

A FIRESIDE BOOK
PUBLISHED BY SIMON & SCHUSTER

NEW YORK   LONDON   TORONTO   SYDNEY

FIRESIDE
Rockefeller Center
1230 Avenue of the Americas
New York, NY 10020

FIRESIDE and colophon are registered trademarks
of Simon & Schuster, Inc.

For information regarding special discounts for bulk purchases,
please contact Simon & Schuster Special Sales at 1-800-456-6798
or business@simonandschuster.com.

Design by Carrmichael
Introduction photo credits: initial photo by Don Bronstein; all others by Larry Moyer

Manufactured in the United States of America

1 3 5 7 9 10 8 6 4 2

Library of Congress Cataloging-in-Publication Data is available.

ISBN-13: 978-0-7432-9024-1
ISBN-10:   0-7432-9024-0

These essays were originally published individually by *Playboy* magazine.

CONTENTS

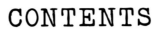

FOREWORD

BY HUGH M. HEFNER

Shel Silverstein was one of the most creative individuals I've ever known. His contributions to *Playboy* are legendary—and, as you can see in this book, his work stands the test of time. Shel was a true Renaissance man. He was a person of multiple talents that went beyond the art and humor I initially saw in him. Shel began his career as a cartoonist, but he went on to greater glory. He became an author of bestselling children's books, a songwriter, poet and playwright. He became our house humorist. And, most important to me, he became a confidant and one of my closest friends.

I remember well the first time I met him. It was in Chicago in 1956. A veteran who had just returned to the States from military duty in Japan, he had heard word about a new, upstart magazine named *Playboy*. He decided to take his drawings to the *Playboy* office at 11 East Superior. He left a portfolio of his drawings with my secretary, but I didn't get around to looking at it right away. After a couple of weeks Shel came back to the office and demanded his cartoons back. He didn't think we were going to buy any of them. I asked him to wait while I looked them over. I went through his portfolio—there were maybe fifteen drawings in it—and I took out eight and put them on my desk. "Let's see, what's that?" I asked him. "Five hundred, six hundred dollars?" Shel nodded his head. "I suppose you could use it now," I said. "Yeah," he said. So I took out a checkbook from my desk and wrote Shel a check. I sensed some uncertainty on his part. Maybe it was because I needed a shave and was wearing my pajamas. Shel didn't think the magazine was going to last or that the check would even clear. It was quarter to five on a Friday afternoon and the banks were closed. Shel took off in disbelief, found a currency exchange someplace, and cashed the check right away. We always got a kick about that in later years. How implausible it all seems now.

Everything begins with Shel's travels. I think it was through the work you'll see in this volume that he started to define himself. He wasn't sure about what he wanted to do with his life. He knew he wanted to revisit Japan, and I asked him to send back drawings from the trip, and to include himself as a character in them. I envisioned something along the lines of the travel letters Ernest Hemingway submitted to *Esquire*—a sort of personal diary that would be dispatched from around the globe. Shel was uncomfortable in that role. He didn't want to include himself, but I persisted. And I'm glad I did. What we got back in those drawings was narrative storytelling of a very personal manner. We saw Shel establish himself as a character.

What is clear in those cartoons is Shel's humanity. During the Cold War, he went into the belly of the beast, traveling to Red Square in Moscow. Right from the beginning Shel established a rapport with people wherever he went.

In some cases, what artists do on paper has nothing to do with their personal lives. But that's not the case with Shel. He was Uncle Shelby. He was the dreamer. He was his work. What comes through in the drawings is from the heart. What you'll see here is the expression of a great talent and a great friend.

Hugh M. Hefner
Los Angeles
September 2006

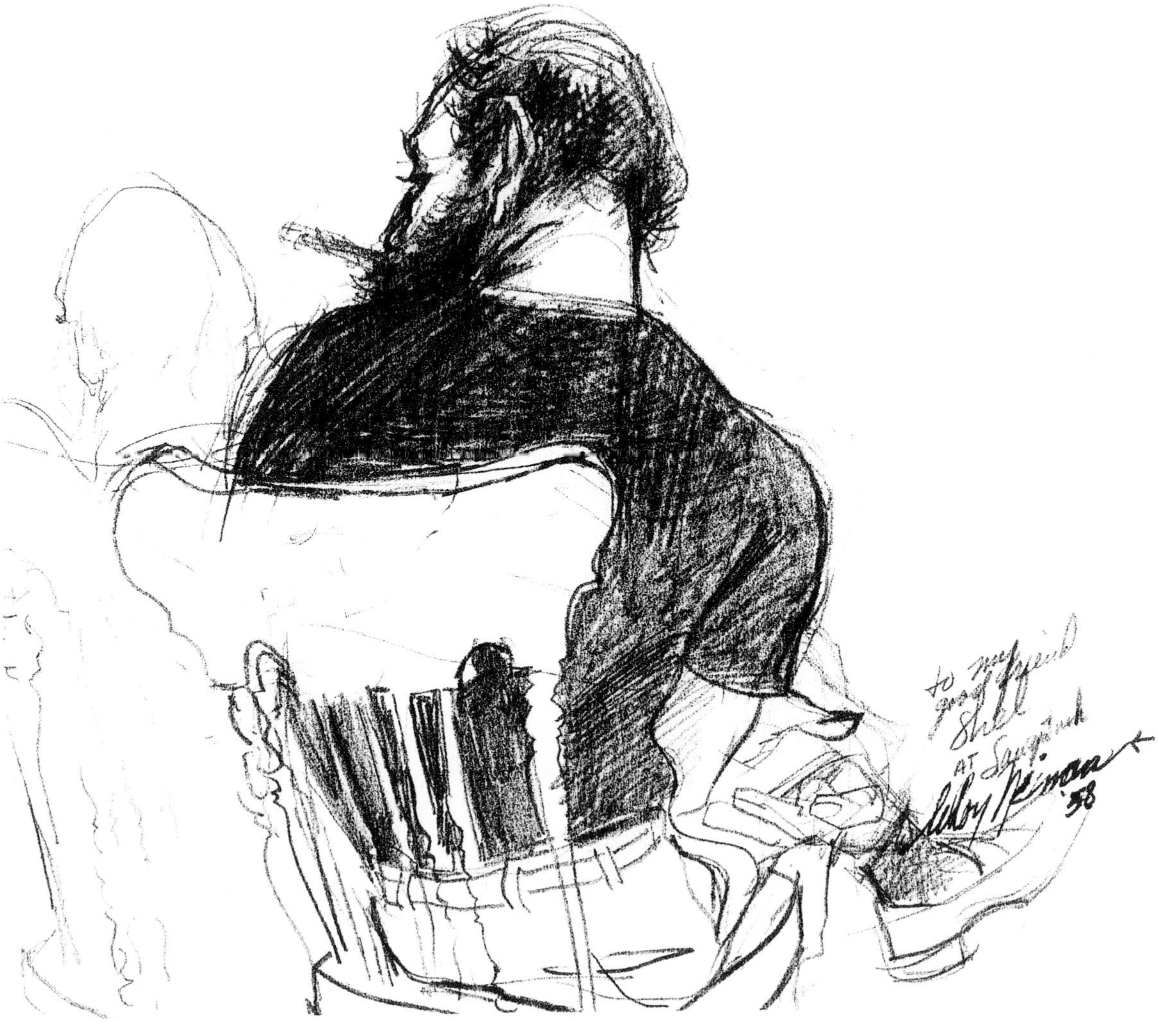
to my good friend
Shel
AT
LeRoy Neiman
'58

INTRODUCTION | BY MITCH MYERS

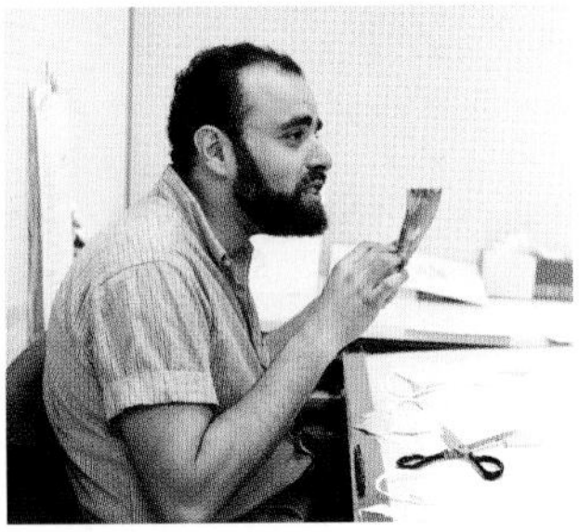

This book is for Hef. Who else could have come up with such a dream job for Shel? He got to travel the globe—expenses paid—and send artistic impressions of his exotic experiences back home to be published in a popular new magazine with a growing circulation that would make him a star. Hef gave Shel the opportunity to have a good time, indulge his inner child and his outer adult, and, for heaven's sake—get laid as much as possible!

Shel Silverstein is known throughout the world as a children's author who wrote and illustrated a number of memorable books that have charmed readers of all ages. His reputation as a writer of children's books began with the auspicious rise in popularity of *The Giving Tree*, which was first published in 1964. His literary fame grew further with storybooks like *The Missing Piece* and timeless poetry collections like *A Light in the Attic* and *Where the Sidewalk Ends*.

At the same time, Shel was a wry, sometimes bawdy songwriter who wrote hits for Johnny Cash ("A Boy Named Sue"), the Irish Rovers ("The Unicorn"), and Doctor Hook and the Medicine Show ("Sylvia's Mother" and "The Cover of the Rolling Stone"). He made a number of records under his own name, including offbeat albums like *I'm So Good That I Don't Have to Brag* and *Freakin' at the Freakers Ball*.

In Nashville, Shel enjoyed friendships with essential American artists like Bobby Bare, Waylon Jennings, Kris Kristofferson, John Hartford and Chet Atkins. He composed songs for films like "I'm Checkin' Out," performed by Meryl Streep in Mike Nichols's *Postcards from the Edge*. He wrote the songs for *Ned Kelly* starring Mick Jagger, and Marianne Faithfull covered "The Ballad of Lucy Jordan," which was featured in *Thelma & Louise*.

Shel was also an accomplished playwright, with credits that include *The Lady or the Tiger Show*, *Gorilla* and his one-man opus, *The Devil and Billy Markham*. He co-wrote the screenplay *Things Change* with David Mamet.

What is often overlooked is that Shel came to prominence in the 1950s as a cartoonist for *Playboy*. More than an illustrator, he was a creative talent—and eager to be a part of the team. Almost immediately, he assumed the role of roving ambassador for the up-and-coming magazine. This esteemed assignment was due in no small part to his unique friendship with *Playboy* editor in chief, Hugh M. Hefner.

Along with other early players—including artist LeRoy Neiman, businessman Victor Lownes and restaurateur John Dante—Shel was part of Hefner's inner circle, hanging out at the old *Playboy* offices and frequenting the adult playground situated at 1340 North State Parkway in Chicago: the Playboy Mansion.

"Hef was in his pajamas when I met him," Shel recalled in 1986. "I had really thought at the time that I was meeting a guy who just woke up, which is a legitimate concern, you know? That same day I met LeRoy Neiman, who was wearing ragged shorts and was barefoot, and I thought—this is an interesting place."

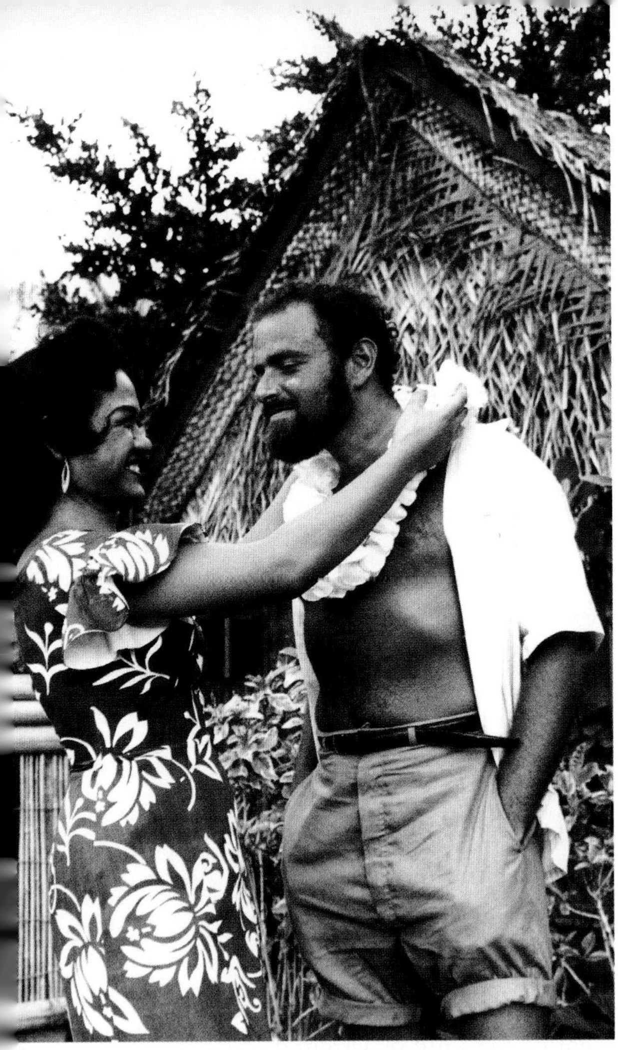

Surrounded by celebrities, intellectuals, jazzmen, comedians and beautiful women, the *Playboy* elite enjoyed a very special camaraderie while the magazine became a cultural fountainhead. Shel was the true bohemian of the bunch, and one of the few to remain a lifelong bachelor.

Playboy's *Silverstein Around the World* is a series of illustrated comic travelogues—a legacy of the relationship between Shel and Hef and a by-product of the social revolution led by *Playboy* in the 1950s and 1960s. The bond that these men shared was profound, and their alliance transcended all trappings of success. Shel's affiliation with *Playboy* made him a local hero in Chicago, and his stature as a Renaissance man grew along with the fortunes of the magazine.

Before Shel turned up at *Playboy,* he served in the army. He worked for the military newspaper *Stars and Stripes* while stationed in Japan during the Korean War. His series of sardonic cartoons about army life for *Stars and Stripes* were quite popular among the enlisted men. He collected and published these works as his first book, *Take Ten,* which is also known as *Grab Your Socks.*

Returning to his hometown of Chicago, Shel made his way as an illustrator, successfully placing small cartoons in *Sports Illustrated* and *Look* magazine. He would later rework the *Look* illustration for the cover of his book *Now Here's My Plan: A Book of Futilities.*

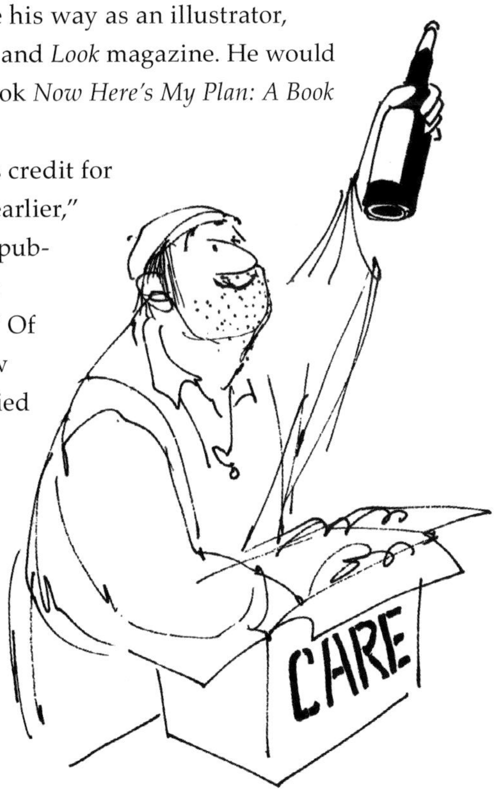
CARE

Art Paul, the original art director for *Playboy,* takes credit for introducing Shel to Hefner in 1956. "I met Shel a little earlier," says Art. "He came to the office after he had a cartoon published in *Look* magazine. It was just one of those classic cartoons, with the single caption 'Now here's my plan.' Of course, I was impressed. I saw his other stuff and knew Hef had to see them. I got them together and they carried the thing—they got close, the both of them—through the years."

"That was the beginning of a lifelong personal and professional relationship," says Hefner. "I didn't have a lot of close personal friends working for the magazine but Shel became one of my closest

friends, and so did LeRoy. Shel started hanging around the office a lot and he really became part of the cadre of friends—and our resident humorist."

His *Playboy* debut came in August 1956. According to Art Paul, Shel and his cartoons were introduced in memorable fashion. "The first thing of Shel's that appeared in *Playboy* was an insert," Art recalls. "He was presented wonderfully in the sense that it wasn't overdone. There wasn't a lot of shouting about having a new cartoonist, but there was a great deal of attention gathered by the way we presented his first bit of work—and it was a four-page insert. They were inserts on yellow paper and had one cartoon on each page. Each cartoon was a little gem."

LeRoy Neiman was there from the earliest beginnings of *Playboy*, and he remembers the camaraderie between himself, Shel and Hefner. He also remembers Hefner's eye for talent—and his ability to bring that talent into the fold.

"When Shel came back from the army he had that book, *Grab Your Socks*, which was really very different. Nobody had ever seen anything like that," says Neiman. "And Hef was not only interested in snaring you, he was interested in tying you down—we all knew that by the talent around. He had me, and he had Jack Cole, who was the best watercolor cartoonist that's ever been. Later Harvey Kurtzman came in. Boy, those cartoonists—Hef had the eye to pick these guys out. But Shel had something special."

Despite his early strides with *Playboy*, things didn't happen fast enough for Shel. He decided to return to Japan, where his celebrity had led to better treatment than he was getting in Chicago. "I had been in Japan and I'd been a star," Silverstein recalled.

"Now I was nothing. I had already sold stuff to *Playboy* and felt very good about it—and even that wasn't enough."

Shel told Hefner his travel plans, and Hef responded with a tempting offer. In 1986, Shel remembered it this way: "I decided to go back to Japan, and Hef said, 'What are you going to do?' I said, 'I'm going back to live there.' He said, 'While you're there, draw some stuff for us. Send it back.' And I said, 'That's not why I'm going back. I don't know what I'd draw.' And he said, 'Well, you'll think of it,' and he paid for my boat ticket over there. I agonized greatly about it because I couldn't see what I would draw about that would be good for *Playboy*. I never wanted to do the sexy stuff. I wasn't going to do that there. I didn't think they'd want general gags or subtle stuff. I didn't want to draw about myself."

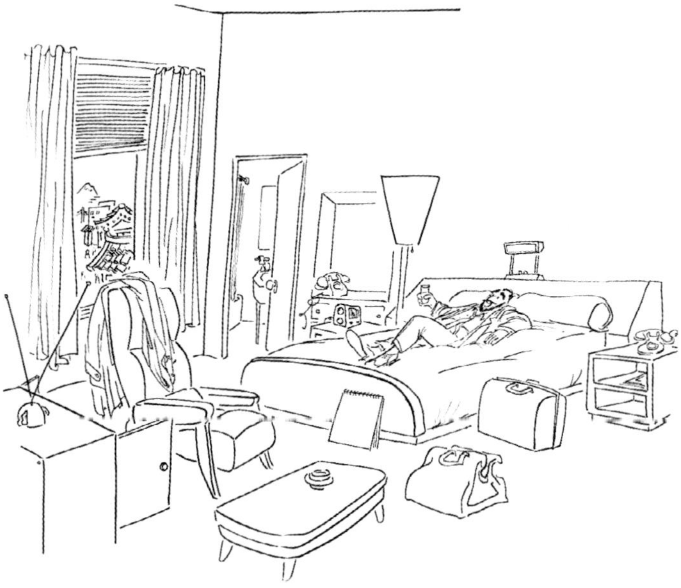

"By God, the Orient!"

As Hef described in this book's Foreword, he was inspired by what Ernest Hemingway had done—sending articles in letter form back to *Esquire*. "It was the notion that Shel would be our traveling representative, sending back recollections in the form of cartoons," says Hefner. "I wanted him, therefore, to include himself in the cartoons. But Shel didn't *want* to include himself. He really didn't think they would work. I said, 'Well, you try it. If it doesn't work, okay—but let's see.'"

Let's see, indeed.

The adventures began in May 1957 with "Return to Tokyo" and ended in the summer of 1968 with the two-part comic epic "Silverstein Among the Hippies." Over the course of eleven years there were twenty-three episodes.

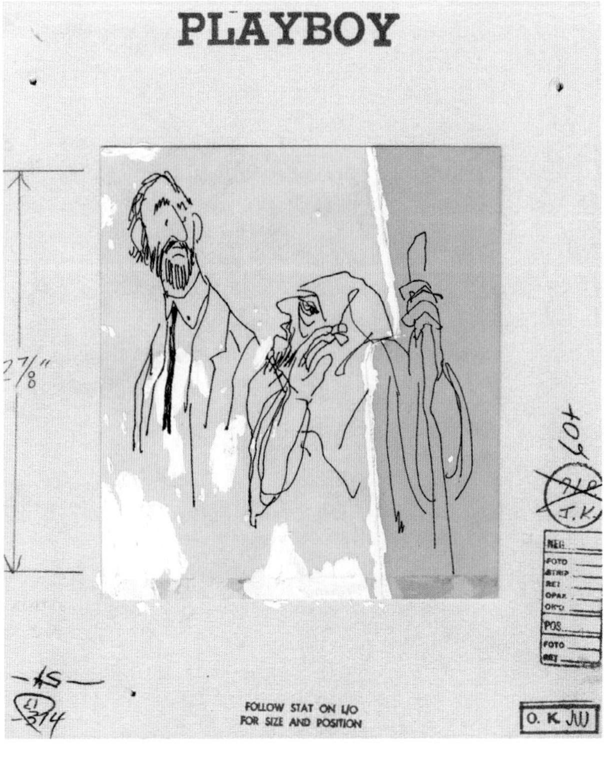
PLAYBOY
2 7/8"
FOLLOW STAT ON I/O
FOR SIZE AND POSITION
O. K.

This wasn't all Shel did with *Playboy*—for his was a lifetime association. Early on, he authored the magazine's film-oriented parlor-game book, *Teevee Jeebies*. Through the years he contributed poems, fables, songs, stories, a hilarious three-part "History of *Playboy*" and many other comic illustrations. His work graced the pages of *Playboy* from the 1950s through the 1990s—and

" WHY CAN'T YOU OUTSIDERS LEAVE US ALONE! ALL WE WANT
IS TO REMAIN <u>INCONSPICUOUS</u>! "

then again posthumously in 2001. The only other *Playboy* contributor to appear in every decade—besides Hefner himself—is LeRoy Neiman, who enjoyed his own long-running travel feature, "Man at His Leisure."

The direction of Shel's travel series was not charted in advance—it was determined by a world of events and his whimsy. Some cartoons in "Return to Tokyo" felt like an extension of his work in *Stars and Stripes*, but Hef was pleased with the illustrated visit and encouraged Shel to continue his wandering ways, resulting in a quick succession of trips to places like Scandinavia, London, Russia, Paris, Italy and Spain.

In addition to his other responsibilities at *Playboy*, Hef was the magazine's first cartoon editor. In the beginning he was himself a cartoonist and he had an affinity with his illustrators. Although Shel was given free rein as to the topics, drawings and humor, Hef still offered up a number of suggestions, and according to Shel's friend Larry Moyer, "Shel thought that Hef was the best cartoon editor around."

One way that this collection differs from Silverstein's other illustrated work is the premise of featuring himself as the central character. Despite Shel's initial reservations, Hefner's editorial directive had been astute, and the majority of the series showcased Shel in a variety of comic situations.

"It's almost impossible to separate what Shel got out of this experience of putting himself into it and what came out of it afterward," says Hefner. "It's all about the relationship between him and the reader. That personal perception made this stuff so special. He humanized the relationship between the peoples of the various cultures and various countries so that it wasn't a continual 'them and us.' Because in the 1950s and throughout the Cold War, there was a real 'them and us' mentality—even as there is today."

Demystifying indigenous cultures, foreign lands and odd social scenarios, Shel depicted himself as a wandering Everyman. He lampooned the sad-but-true stereotypes of the American tourist and maintained unusually sharp insights into human nature. Shel's ironic perspective also captured the sexual ethos of the time.

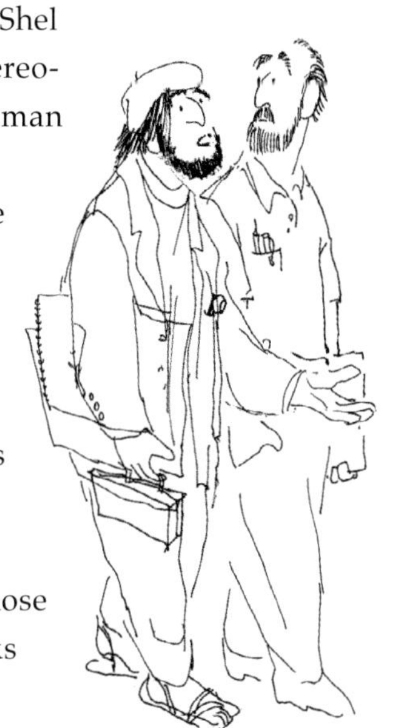

"There are two kinds of artists," says LeRoy Neiman. "There's the introspective artist who asks himself 'How do *I* feel?' and 'What do *I* think about this?' Then you have the person who's aware of *everything*—everything in the room, everything—wherever they go. They care about everything. That doesn't mean that they don't care about themselves, but they are *observers*. Observing is an incredible thing. To sit in a sidewalk café for an hour and observe people passing by is one thing—but to observe *all the time* is something else. *Everything*."

Another difference between these *Playboy* portfolios and Shel's other illustrations is the use of color overlays on his inimitable pen-and-ink drawings. For those wondering why his trademark black-and-white style was not used, it was thanks to the pragmatic sensibilities of Art Paul.

"Hef commissioned Shel to travel around and send back these autobiographical, humoresque tales," says Paul. "The layouts for these were six, seven, eight pages of text. The problem was that the magazine as a whole needed color, and it had little advertising at that time. It needed a color punch and this seemed to be an opportunity. I knew it wouldn't make Shel happy, and I would have preferred to leave it all black and white, too. But then these color blocks became part of the identity that went with his travel cartoons. He really wanted something pure and simpler. So, that was unfortunate. I think I can take the blame for it."

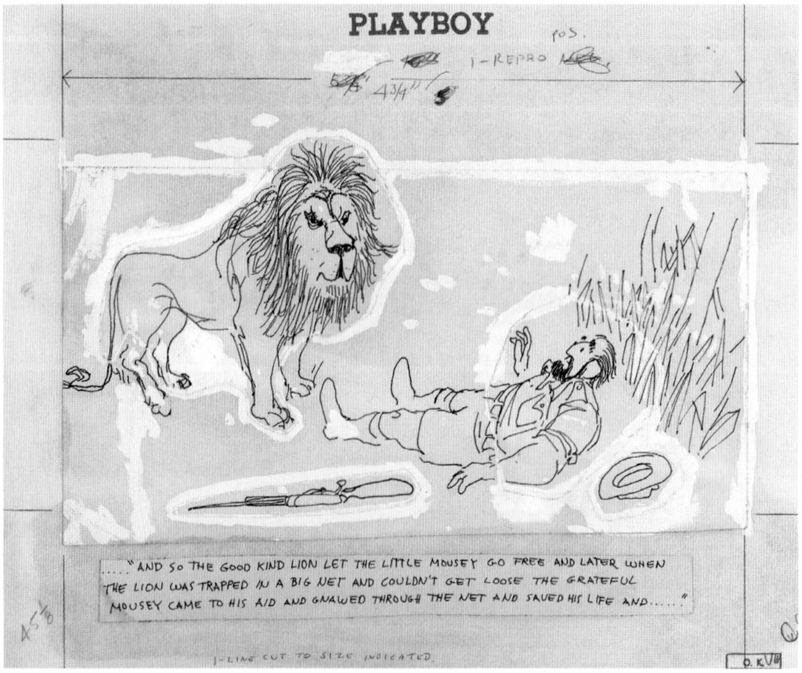
PLAYBOY
....."AND SO THE GOOD KIND LION LET THE LITTLE MOUSEY GO FREE AND LATER WHEN THE LION WAS TRAPPED IN A BIG NET AND COULDN'T GET LOOSE THE GRATEFUL MOUSEY CAME TO HIS AID AND GNAWED THROUGH THE NET AND SAVED HIS LIFE AND....."

The use of color did become part of Shel's travel pieces. Some of the episodes were color-coded—red for Russia, blue for Switzerland, etc. But looking back, even Hugh Hefner concurred with Art Paul's mea culpa. "I wish in retrospect that I hadn't had Arthur add the color to the series," said Hef. "I think Shel would have been much happier. Pure black and white, that's the way it should have been."

PLAYBOY'S
shel silverstein
around the world

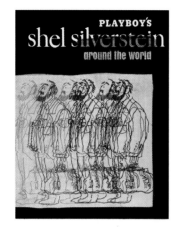

Shel's early creativity was informed by an extensive artistic groundswell. A perpetual houseguest at the Playboy Mansion, he began painting and drawing (and traveling) with LeRoy Neiman. He also became friendly with two young comics, Lenny Bruce and Bill Cosby. He spent a lot of time at Chicago clubs like the Gate of Horn and was tight with folksinger Bob Gibson. Maintaining an apartment in Manhattan, Shel hung out with radio great Jean Shepherd and playwright Herb Gardner. The sexual mystique of *Playboy* reflected his lifestyle, and his adventurous spirit knew no bounds.

Another element unique to these early illustrations is Shel's use of detailing, which serves as a contrast from the minimal leanings of his later work. His black-and-white drawings already had a distinctive line style, and his vision seemed particularly inspired by the romantic climes of Europe and the bohemian milieu of Greenwich Village. Elaborate depictions of the Left Bank in Paris and the ruins of the Colosseum in Rome indicate that he was stimulated as an illustrator and still evolving artistically.

Along with illustrations and dialogue, the series included photographs of Shel in action, intending to prove that he'd actually visited the places rendered in his cartoons. Inevitably, there would be a shot of Shel drawing on his sketch pad surrounded by curious locals who were often, coincidentally, eager-looking young women. But Shel met all sorts of people in his travels, including Larry Moyer, who became a lifelong friend and served as his photographer on several excursions.

PLAYBOY

"I met Shel in 1957 in Moscow in Red Square," Moyer remembers. "I looked over and I see this guy sketching. You never see anybody sketching in Red Square, especially in 1957. He was drawing a Red Army soldier, and when he got to the bottom of the page there wasn't enough room for his boots. So he just crunched up the boots in the drawing. That's how we met, in front of the Kremlin."

Of course, with *Playboy*, sexuality was to be celebrated, and Shel explored this subject with deft and self-effacing humor. Satirizing his man-on-the-make persona, he portrayed the battle of the sexes in almost futile terms. Shel was more interested in the human aspects of the sexual revolution—wanting it more than getting it, looking more than touching, and highlighting "no" as one of the most discouraging words to be heard in any language.

According to Moyer, Shel's method for gathering material was straightforward. "We were looking for bad girls and good food. That was the bottom line," Moyer recalls. "We'd go to a place we didn't know too much about. Before we could start doing stuff he would have to learn something about the joint. We would hang out for two or three weeks. Then Shel would sketch frantically for a few days and I would shoot a shitload of pictures—and always get Shel with a broad. That was the thing. The shot had to have some broads in there, and the better-looking the better!"

In addition to his ribald pursuits, Shel's journeys were a mix of typical sightseeing and unorthodox stunts. In London he visited pubs and Trafalgar Square; in Switzerland it was mountain climbing. He was fearless, and hunted big game while on safari in Africa, felling a water buffalo. His momentous trip to Spain was split into two episodes: After learning flamenco and suggesting siestas with the señoritas, Shel put on a matador's suit and fought a bull, only to be gored (slightly) in the process.

The most significant moment in his travels occurred during the trip to Africa. He'd been traveling from country to country, and after a successful safari expedition in Uganda, Shel and photographer Pat Morin were in a traffic accident—a head-to-head collision with a truck. The pair were badly injured and left alone on the side of the road in the jungle, only to be rescued by a tourist couple that happened to be driving by.

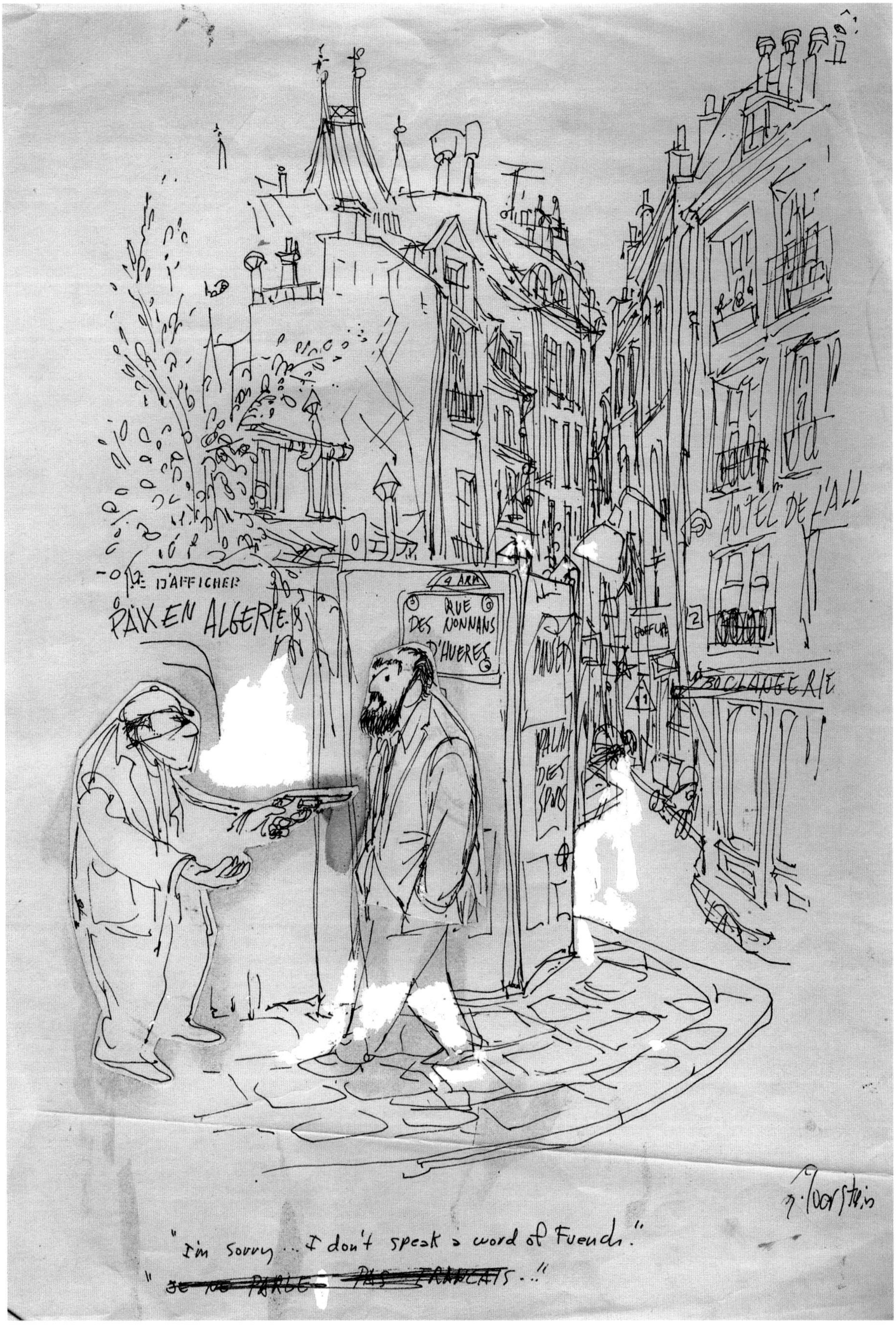
D'AFFICHER
PAIX EN ALGERIE
4 ARR
RUE DES NONNANS D'HUERES
HOTEL DE L'ALL
BOULANGERIE
PALAIS DES SPORTS
"I'm sorry... I don't speak a word of French."
"~~JE NE PARLE PAS FRANCAIS~~..!"

Upon his return from Africa, Shel stayed closer to home, documenting a number of adventures in the U.S. and Mexico before making a return trip to London. He toured the newly added states of Alaska (where he panned for gold) and Hawaii (where he tried to get lei'd), and explored conventional tourist destinations like Miami and Hollywood. Profiling the scenes in Greenwich Village and Haight-Ashbury may have been convenient—Shel kept homes in both locales—but his incisive takes on the beat generation in 1960 and the hippie culture in 1968 were right on time.

Despite the allure of the Playboy Mansion in Chicago, Shel made New York City his main residence for years. "Shel was different," says Vic Lownes. "He was very independent. The headquarters of *Playboy* were in Chicago but he stayed in Greenwich Village. Although he would make extensive visits to the Mansion, this was where he liked to be—in his part of town."

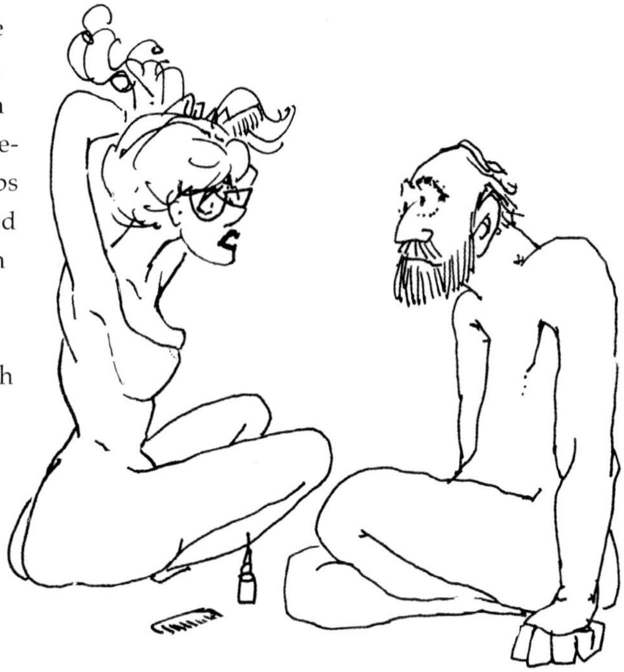

Shel's bohemian aesthetic brought him to the nexus of the beatnik scene. He was familiar with the folk community that gathered in Washington Square Park, and he was well known at the coffeehouses near Bleecker and MacDougal. Friendships with wannabe poets, artists and writers enhanced his comic portrayals in "Silverstein in Greenwich Village," and he parodied the elements of "cool" with great insight.

After his trips to the forty-ninth and fiftieth states, Shel went back to his own beginnings and fulfilled a lifelong dream of being on the playing field with the Chicago White Sox. As a teenager, Shel had worked as a beer-and-hot-dog vendor at Comiskey Park, and he remained a fan of the South Siders. Of course, it was only spring training in Sarasota, Florida, but the thrill of it all cannot be denied. Similar in spirit to the amateur sporting efforts of George Plimpton, Shel's workouts with the White Sox led him to meet stars like Nellie Fox and Luis Aparicio—but it was too bad he didn't get a chance to play with his idol, Minnie Miñoso, who'd recently been traded.

Hugh Hefner remembers Shel's passion for his hometown team. "There's an illustration with the cartoon in Russia where someone says to him, 'Just think of it, comrade—under the Communist system of equal distribution, once every eight years the White Sox would *win the pennant*!' "

One of the best-remembered episodes was Shel's 1963 visit to the Sunny Rest Lodge in Palmerton, Pennsylvania. The ten-page extravaganza, "Silverstein in a Nudist Camp," put a brave new spin on the *Playboy* lifestyle—with Shel at the forefront. While *Playboy* had an illustrious history of revealing the female form, his bare-assed

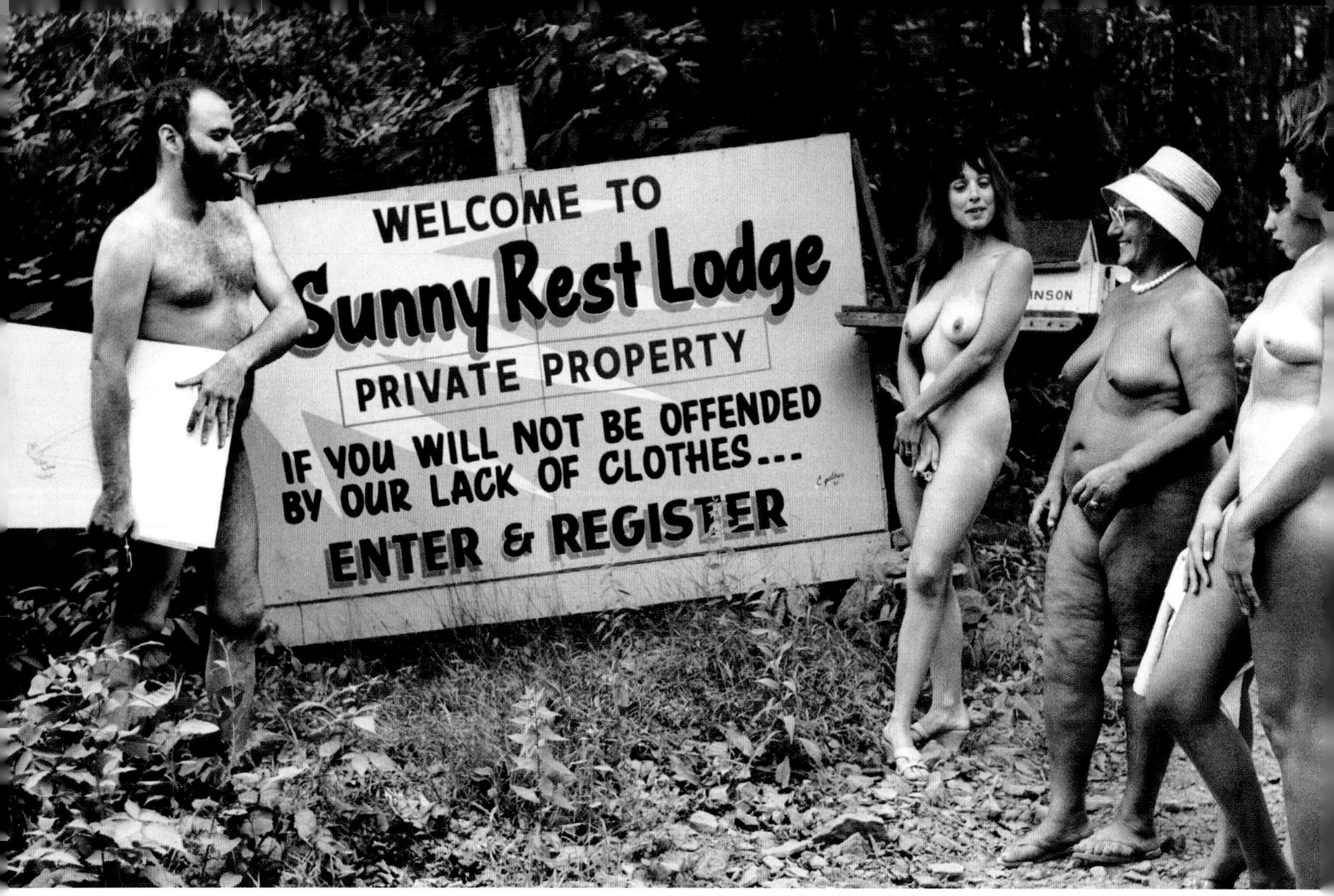
WELCOME TO
Sunny Rest Lodge
PRIVATE PROPERTY
IF YOU WILL NOT BE OFFENDED
BY OUR LACK OF CLOTHES...
ENTER & REGISTER

appearance was rare, if not unusual, for the magazine. Larry Moyer suggested they visit a nudist camp and brought him to Sunny Rest—and he served as the feature's photographer.

"A lot of people don't want to be photographed at a nudist camp, because there are a lot of secretaries and bank tellers, that kind of thing," says Moyer. "So, to guarantee the layouts for the story, we brought models along for that particular job. It was so great being in a nudist camp that we didn't want to put our clothes on again after that. We drove all the way back to New York in this convertible naked—me and Shel and the three models that we brought with us. I think when we crossed the George Washington Bridge, we knew, 'Well, maybe we better put some clothes on.' Reluctantly!"

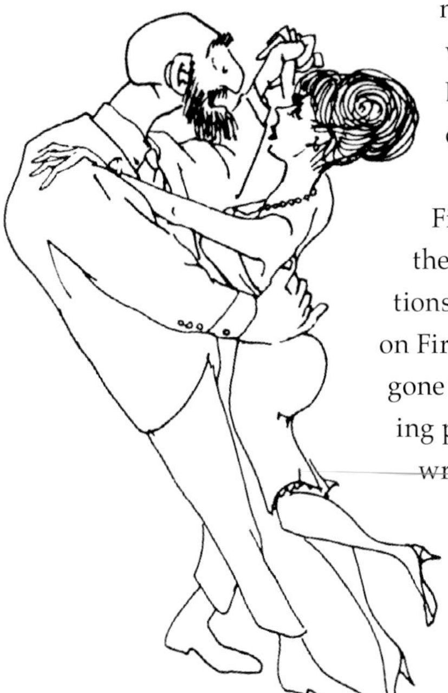

Their summer visit to the Cherry Grove district of Fire Island was edgier still, as Shel and Larry mingled with the island's vacationing gay population. Using his illustrations to challenge and exploit sexual stereotypes, "Silverstein on Fire Island" comically ventured where no (straight) man had gone before. "When we were on Fire Island, nobody was making passes at us," Moyer says. "So we started thinking—what's wrong with *us*?"

"One thing I have to say about Shel," Moyer adds. "He was one of the funniest guys I ever knew—and it

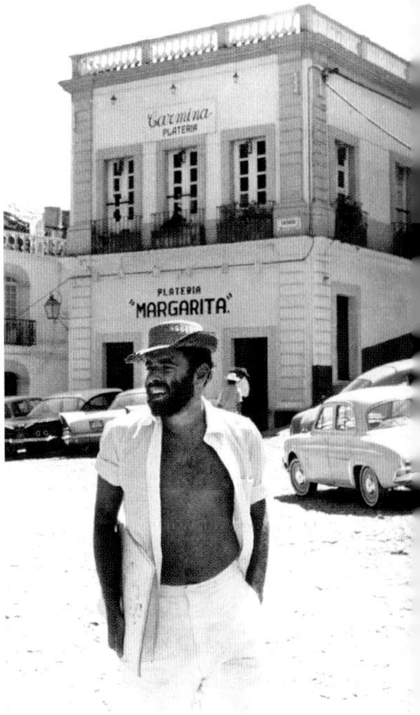
PLATERIA
"MARGARITA"

was never at anybody's expense. A lot of humor is based on putting other people down. I don't remember one time Shel ever put anybody down in his work—and that's something."

By the latter 1960s, Shel was gaining status as a children's author and a songwriter—and his career was still intertwined with the popularity of *Playboy*. With his return to swinging London in 1967, it was obvious that times had changed—his reputation now preceded him and the magazine was a household word. He was still sketching in Trafalgar Square and schmoozing guards at Buckingham Palace, but he was also spotted lunching with Twiggy and gambling at the Playboy Club's chic London casino.

In the summer of 1968, *Playboy* published the two-part classic "Silverstein Among the Hippies." The hippie episodes turned out to be the last of his travel series, but they also showcased Shel at his creative best. With the pages saturated in psychedelic coloring, his illustrations were fluid, bold and sure-handed. He was already familiar with the San Francisco scene and had a houseboat in Sausalito. Amid frolicking spoofs on free love and hippie drug culture, he made some of his most succinct social commentaries. The progressive *Playboy* philosophy had merged with the idealistic values of the Love Generation—and it looked a lot like Shel Silverstein.

Other than a retrospective article in 1971, this was the conclusion of "Silverstein Around the World." There were further adventures left undocumented, including trips to Tahiti and Thailand and a return to Japan, but numerous artistic endeavors took his attention away from *Playboy* and

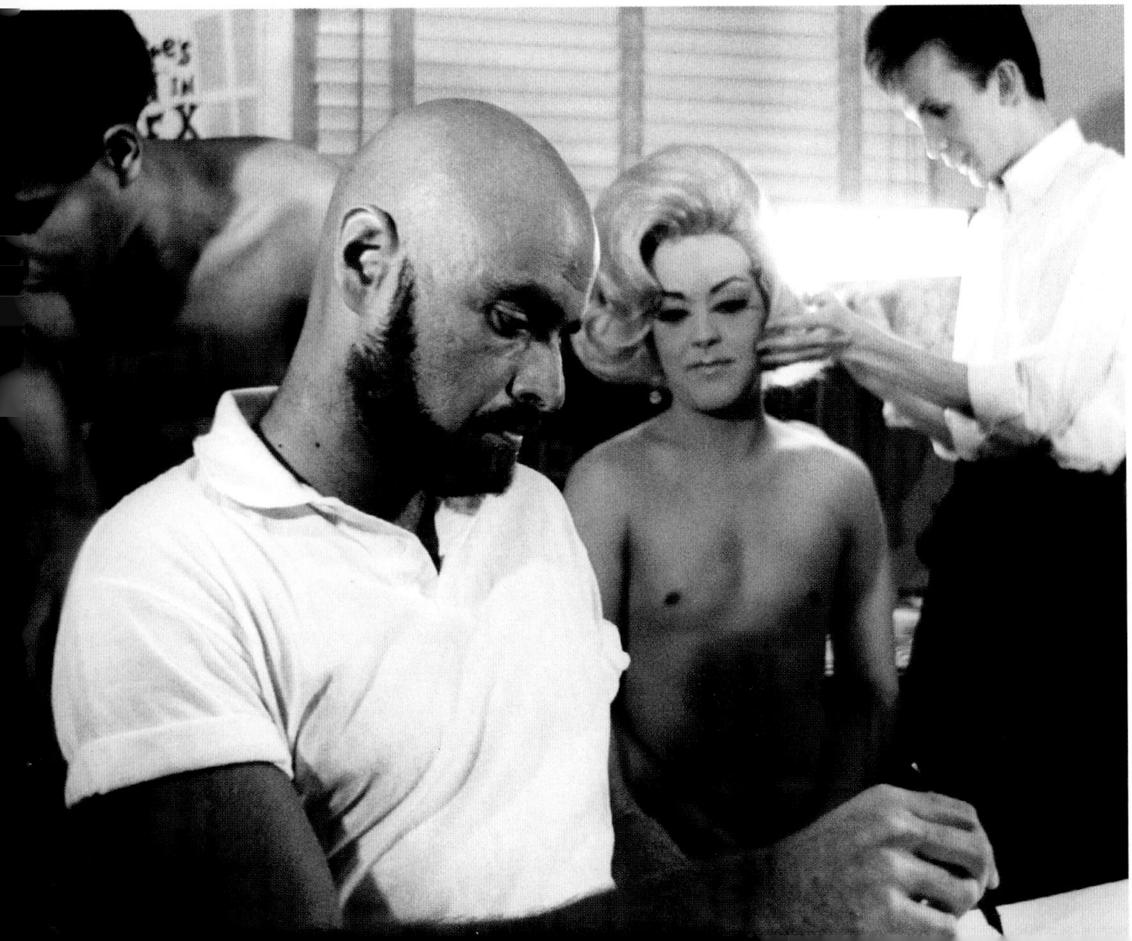

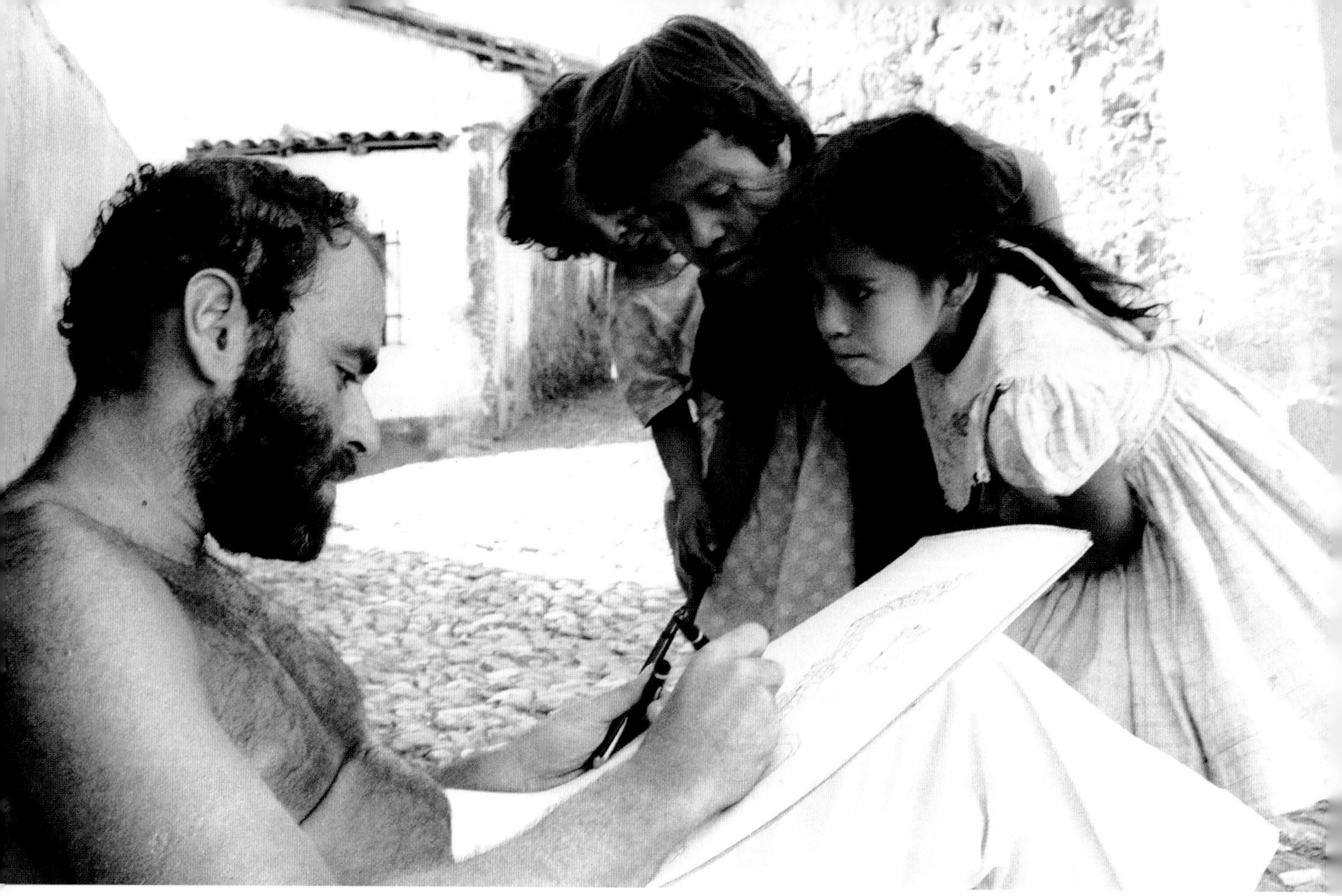

Shel's contributions to the magazine became more sporadic. Never again would his work be so overtly autobiographical.

Shel remained productive until his death in 1999. He was still drawing, writing songs, composing poems, making records and putting on plays. There was a collection of adult illustrations, *Different Dances*, and his poetry book *Falling Up* became yet another bestseller. He worked on a collection of illustrated spoonerisms for more than twenty-five years, called *Runny Babbit*, which was published posthumously.

Looking back, Shel told Hugh Hefner, "I find that the things of value to me have become quite clear—that the times of closeness with real friends is becoming the most valuable thing of all. So the travel for me has almost no value anymore. Seeing what? They're only places with people like myself. If you want to show me a mountain, I've seen some high mountains, and I've seen what men can do with the pyramids. I've seen the tropics and so what? If I've created an image of a world traveler and adventurer, and the fact is I fucking want to sit down and grow roses with Suzie-Q—*I'm gonna do it.*"

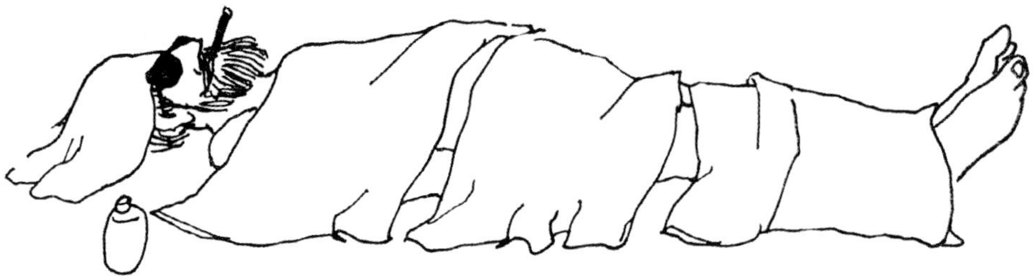

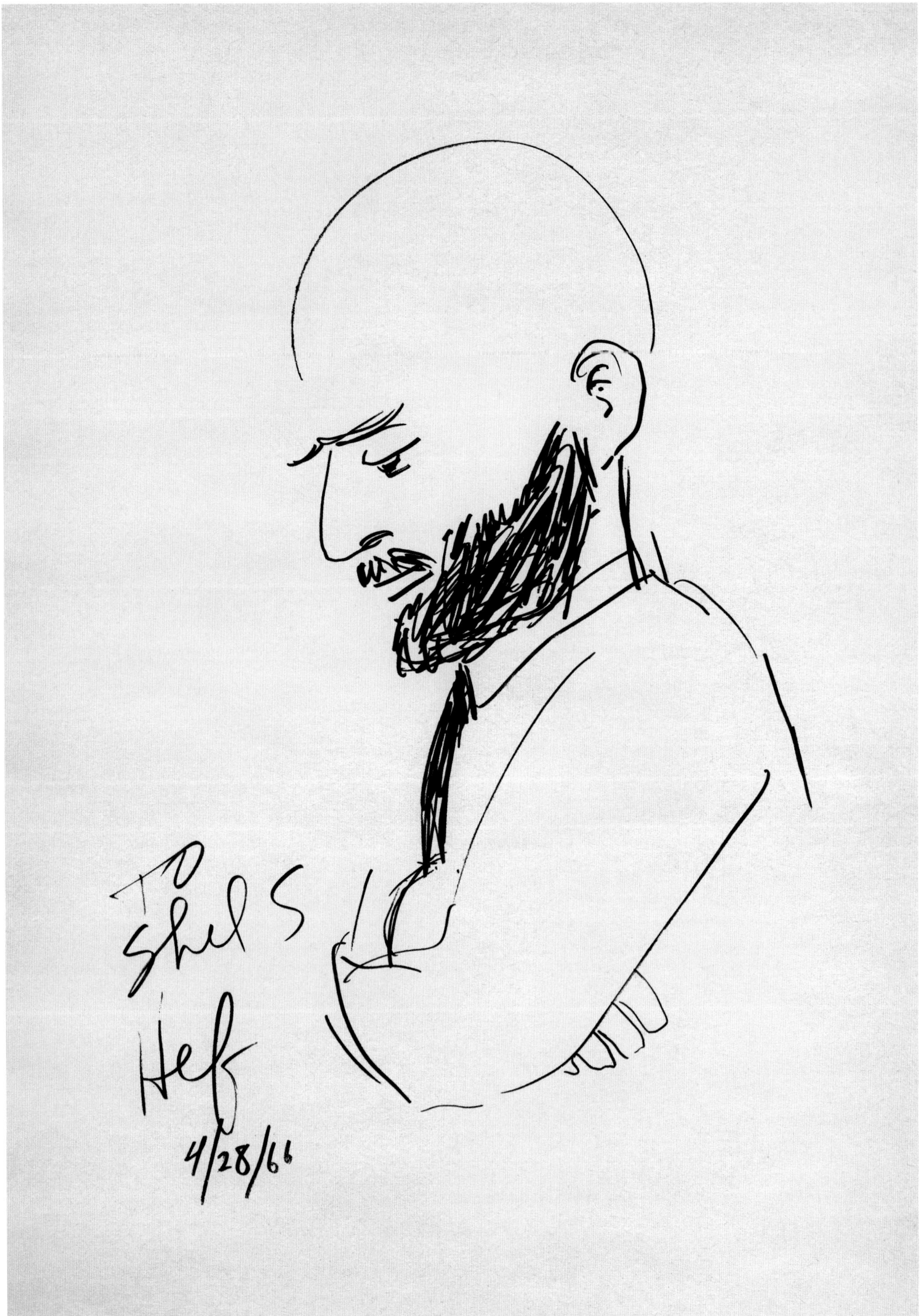
To
Shel S
Hef
4/28/66

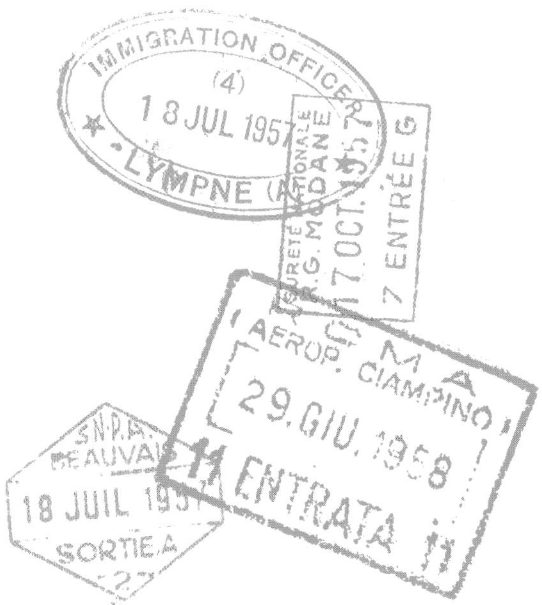
IMMIGRATION OFFICER
(4)
18 JUL 1957
LYMPNE
17 OCT
7 ENTRÉE G
AEROP. CIAMPINO
29.GIU.1958
ENTRATA
BEAUVAIS
18 JUIL
SORTIE A

RETURN TO TOKYO

MAY 1957

cartoonist silverstein takes a sentimental journey

Schickless Shel Silverstein, the brilliant, bearded cartoonist whose work appears regularly in PLAYBOY, served most of a two year army hitch with the staff of the *Pacific Stars and Stripes,* bringing a bit of satirical sunlight into the dark days of the Korean occupation. The indigestion that followed the GIs' bouts with army chow was alleviated to some extent when they'd open the pages of *S&S* and see a Silverstein mess sergeant admonishing his underlings with, "OK, who's been sneaking meat into the hamburger?" And every joe who ever received a dressing-down from the military police could chuckle sardonically over the drawing in which one surly MP whispered to another, "Psst . . . Merry Christmas!" Shel has confessed that the enthusiastic reception given his cartoons by fellow GIs was the second nicest experience of his life. The first was being stationed in Japan.

Sitting in front of his drawing board in our offices, Shel has often leaned back in his chair and reminisced about the Land of the Rising Sun. "In Japan, it's different," he has said on more than one occasion, never bothering to define *it.* "You're treated like a very special fellow in Japan—especially by the women. The country really looks like those old Japanese prints. I love the place. I love everything about it—the people, the culture, the way it looks, the way it sounds, the way it smells. I'm going to go back some day."

Shel Silverstein has done just that, as the first stop in a trip around the world for PLAYBOY. He took his sketchbook with him, at our suggestion, and we received these impressions of a revisited Tokyo just a few days before this issue went to press.

RETURN TO TOKYO

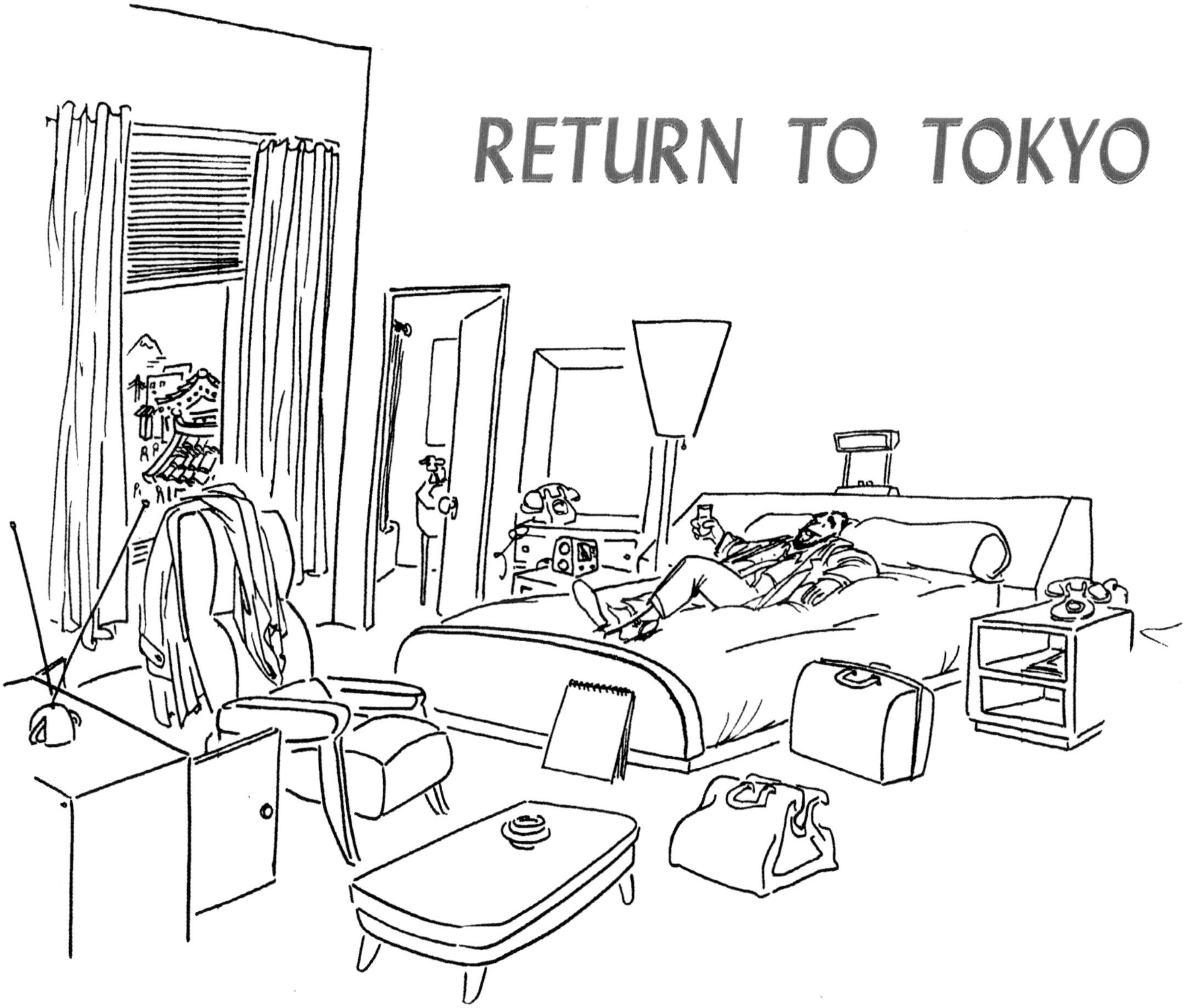

"By God, the Orient!"

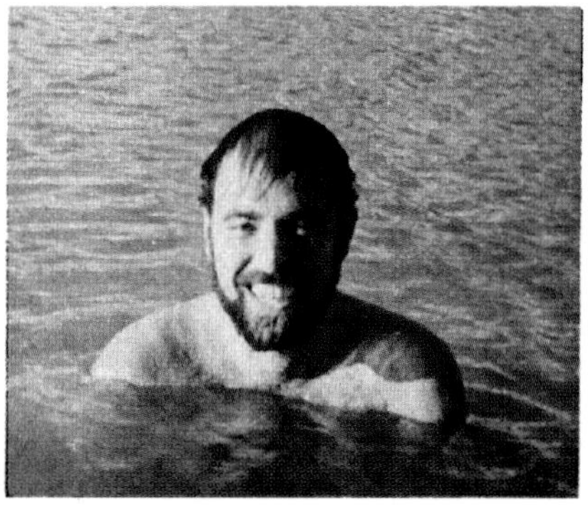

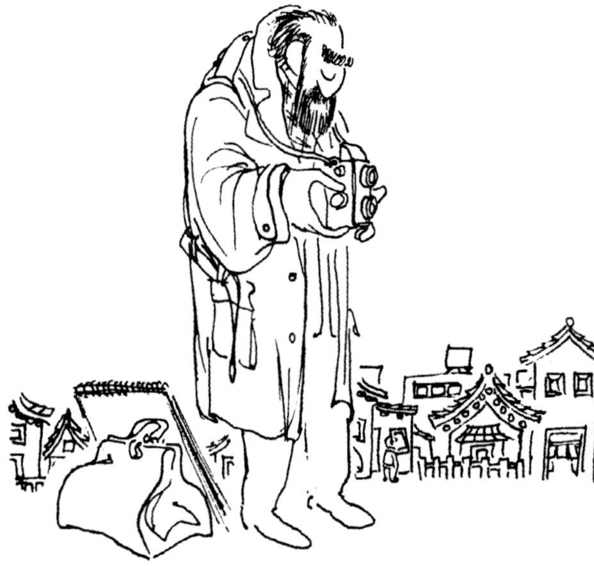

SILVERSTEIN *continued*

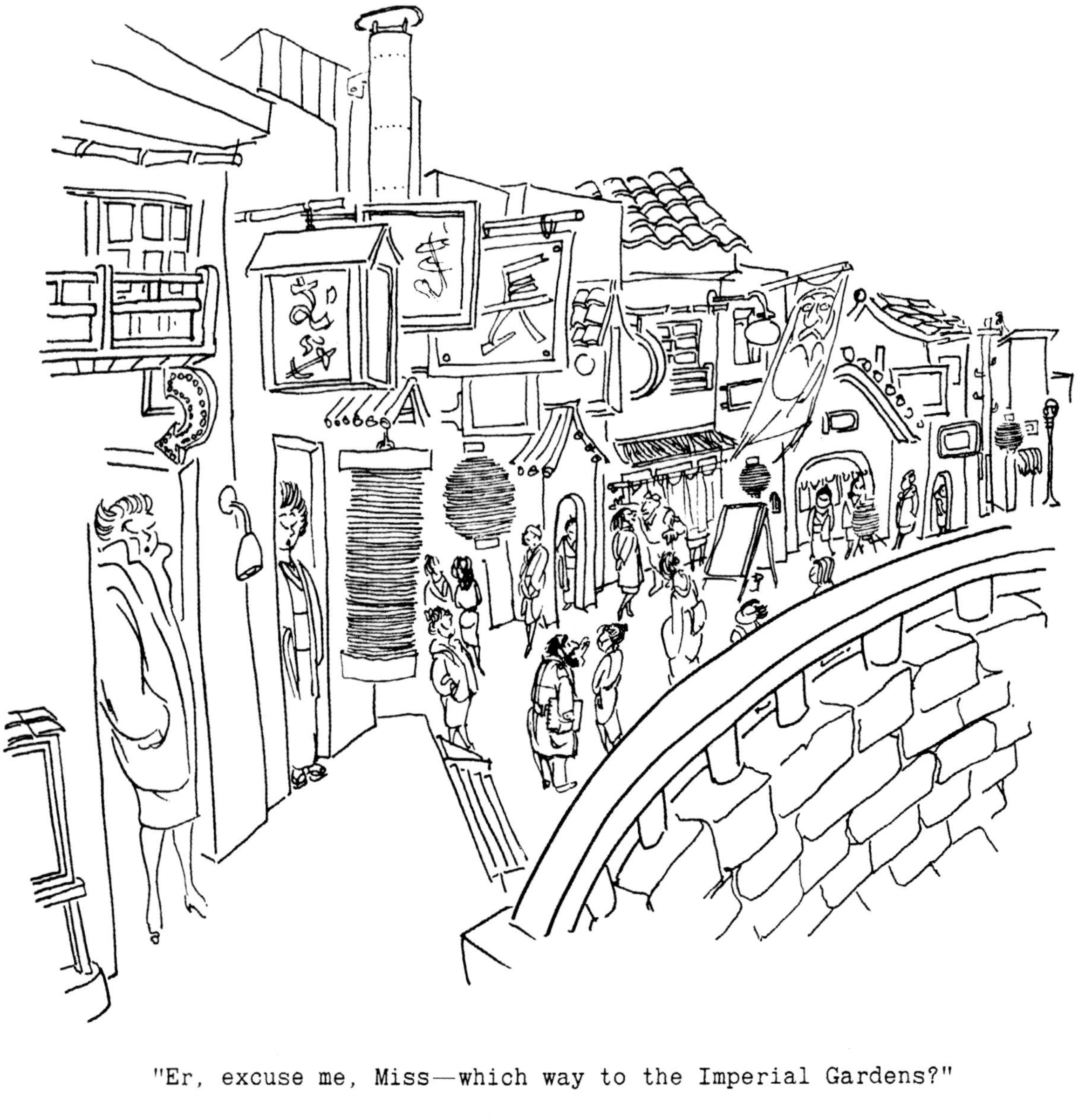

"Er, excuse me, Miss—which way to the Imperial Gardens?"

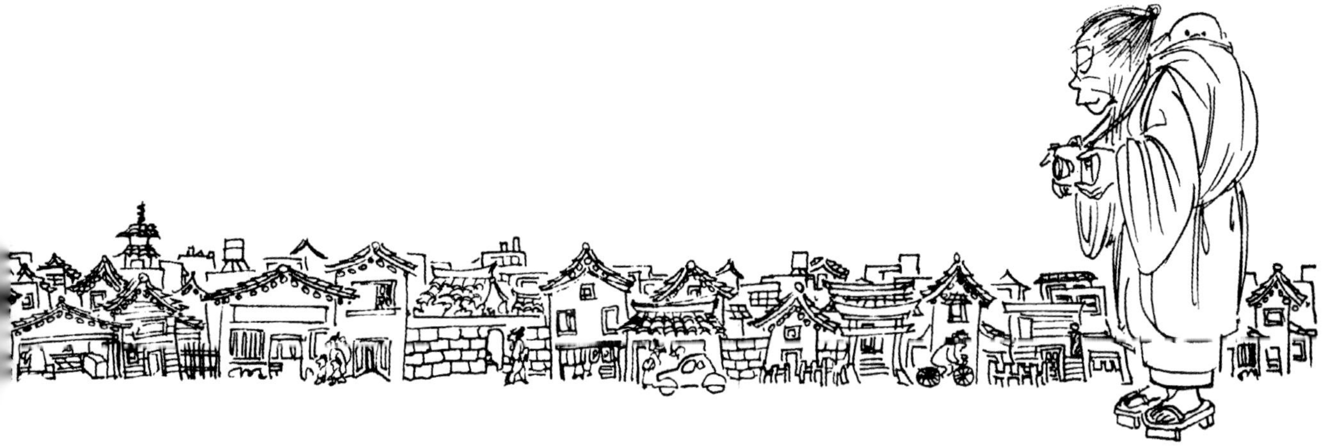

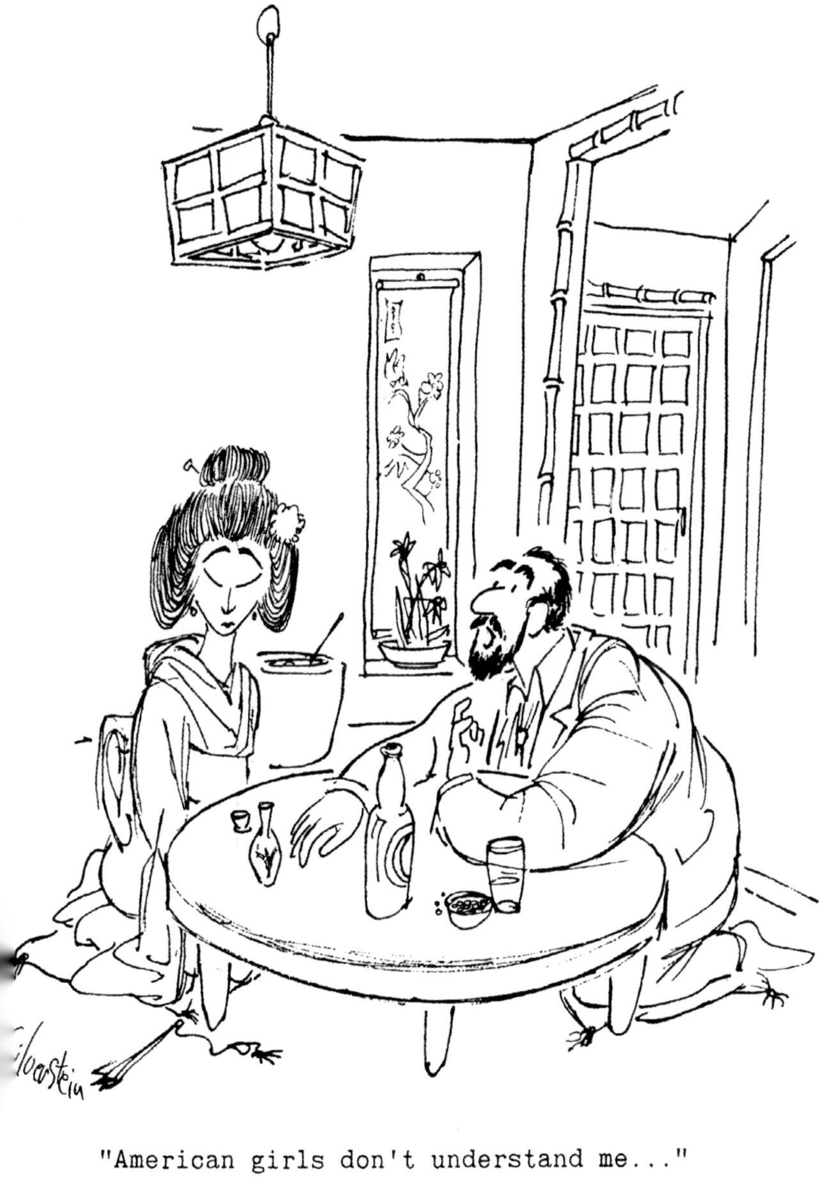

"American girls don't understand me..."

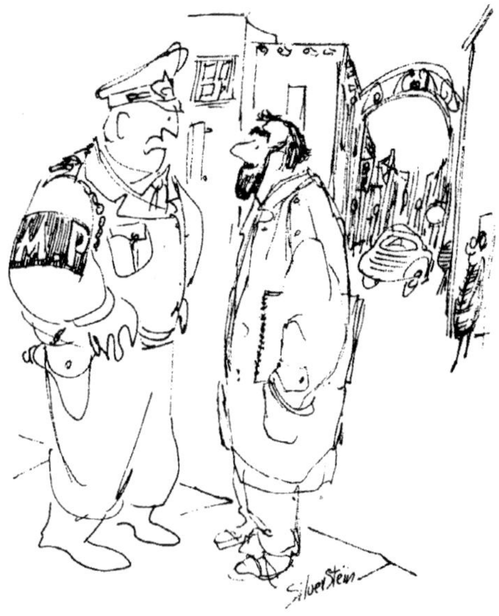

"Look at yourself...out of uniform...no shave...no tie ...no pass...no..."

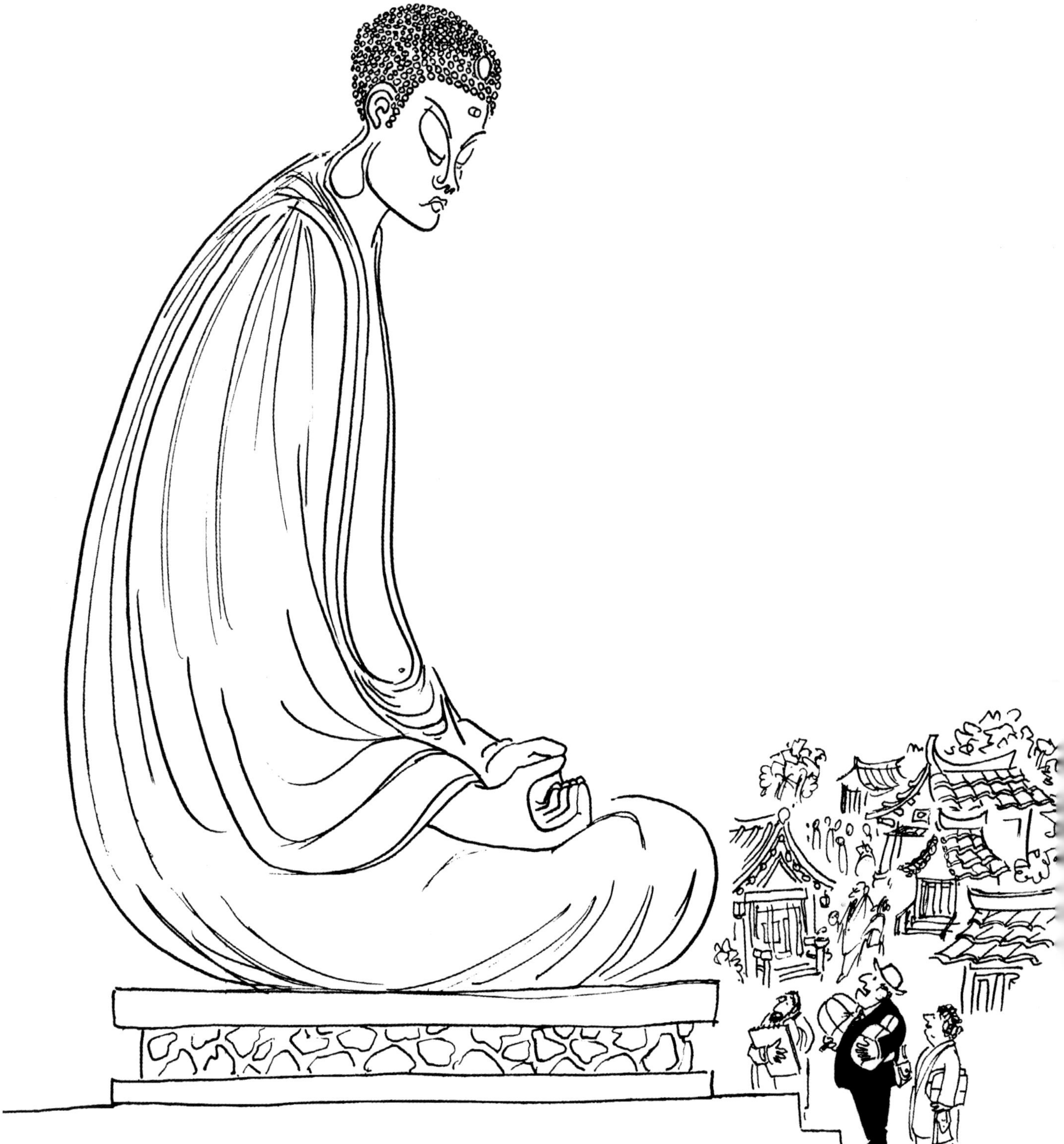

"But, Martha, where would we put it?"

SILVERSTEIN *continued*

"Tell me, Mr. Silverstein—is it true what they say about American women?"

"Contrary to popular Western beliefs, the Geisha girl confines her entertainment to singing, dancing, playing a musical instrument..."

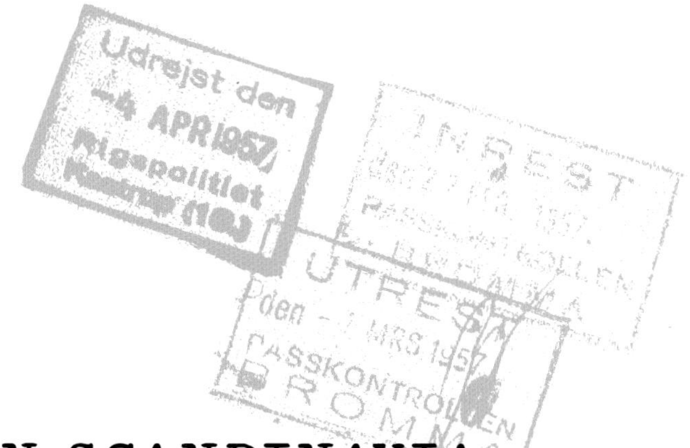
Udrejst den
-4 APR 1957
UTRESA
PASSKONTROLLEN
BROMMA

IN SCANDINAVIA

JULY 1957

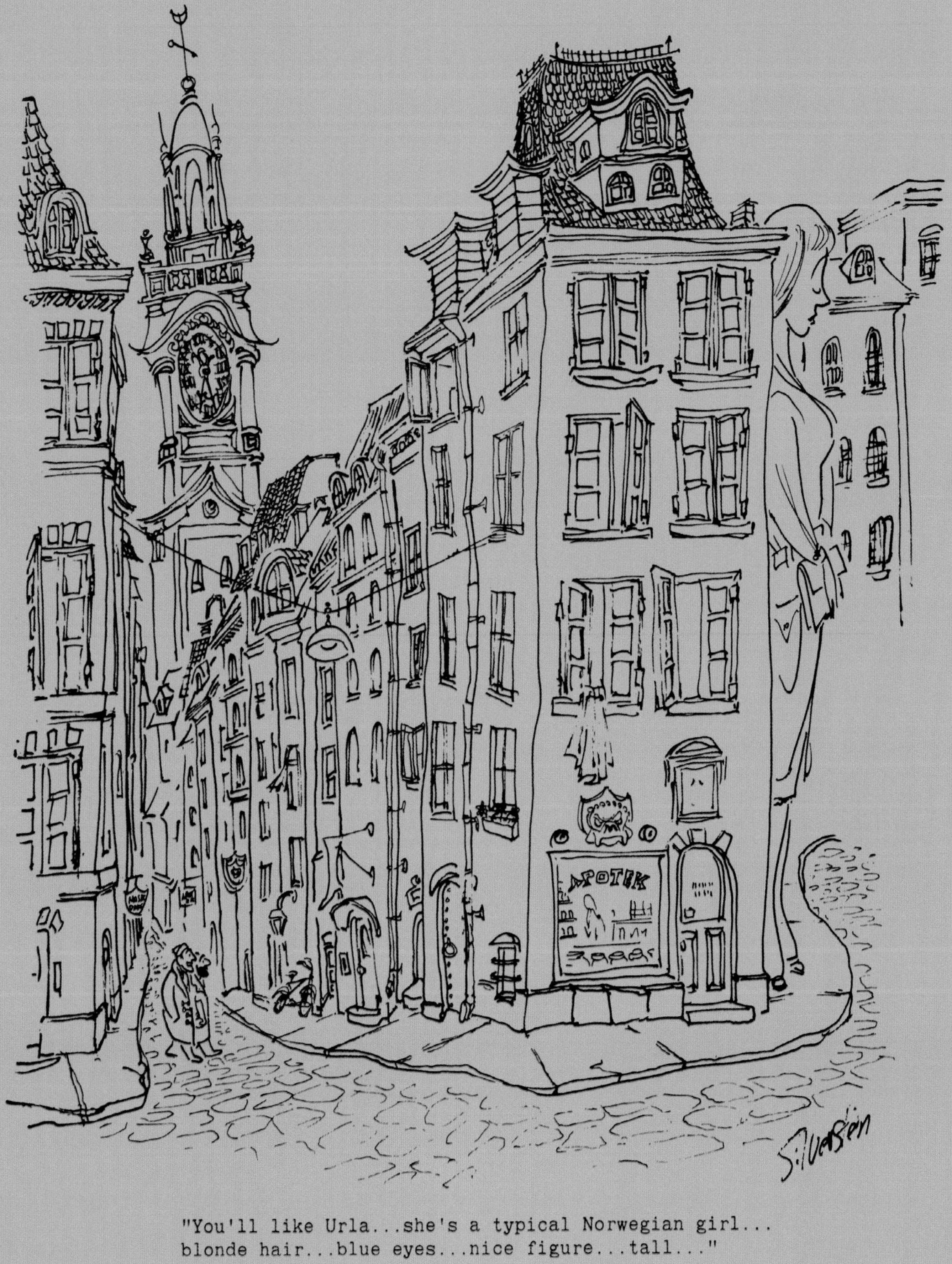
APOTEK
Silverstein

"You'll like Urla...she's a typical Norwegian girl...
blonde hair...blue eyes...nice figure...tall..."

SILVERSTEIN

IN

SCANDINAVIA

*the further wanderings of
playboy's bearded
cartoonist at large*

FROM THE LAND OF THE RISING SUN, where he sketched his impressions for our May issue, Shel Silverstein flew the great circle route, touching down briefly in Anchorage, Alaska, to the Land of the Midnight Sun — Scandinavia, the home of the Vikings, Ibsen, Grieg, Strindberg, Ekberg, Kierkegaard, smörgåsbord, sex changes and the Swedish massage. Our bearded ambassador-with-portfolio called us, collect, from Copenhagen to make certain his Scandinavian sketches had arrived safely. They had, and included with them was a brief written report on his personal adventures: "This has been one of the most hectic months of my life," he wrote. "After touring Norway and Sweden, I settled down in Copenhagen, where I thought my beard would permit me to blend quietly in with the Danes, many of whom are also bearded. I couldn't have been more wrong. Due in large part to this damned beard, I (1) became involved in a barroom brawl

"Now for heaven's sake, Harry, try to look like a <u>Viking</u>!!"

"Decisions, decisions, decisions!"

"Room for one more..."

"If you're a girl, how about having dinner with me tonight?"

Silverstein sings the blues with the Bearded Viking New Orleans Jazz Band.

(which I won) over a woman (which I lost), (2) worked as a solo washboard and featured vocalist (because I spoke the best English) of Papa Bue's Bearded Viking New Orleans Danish Jazz Band (a very popular group until I joined them), (3) suffered a slightly broken foot, acquiring a limp, a cane and a very glamorous air, (4) was under observation and investigation as a 'Russian Agent' because I was seen entering the Russian Embassy in quest of a visa, and (5) became involved in a brief but glorious romance which I'm not telling any 1,000,000 PLAYBOY readers about. As of this writing, my foot, heart and political standing are all in pretty good shape."

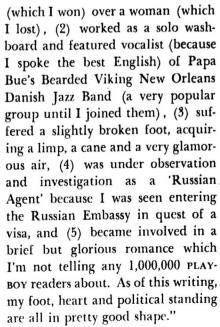

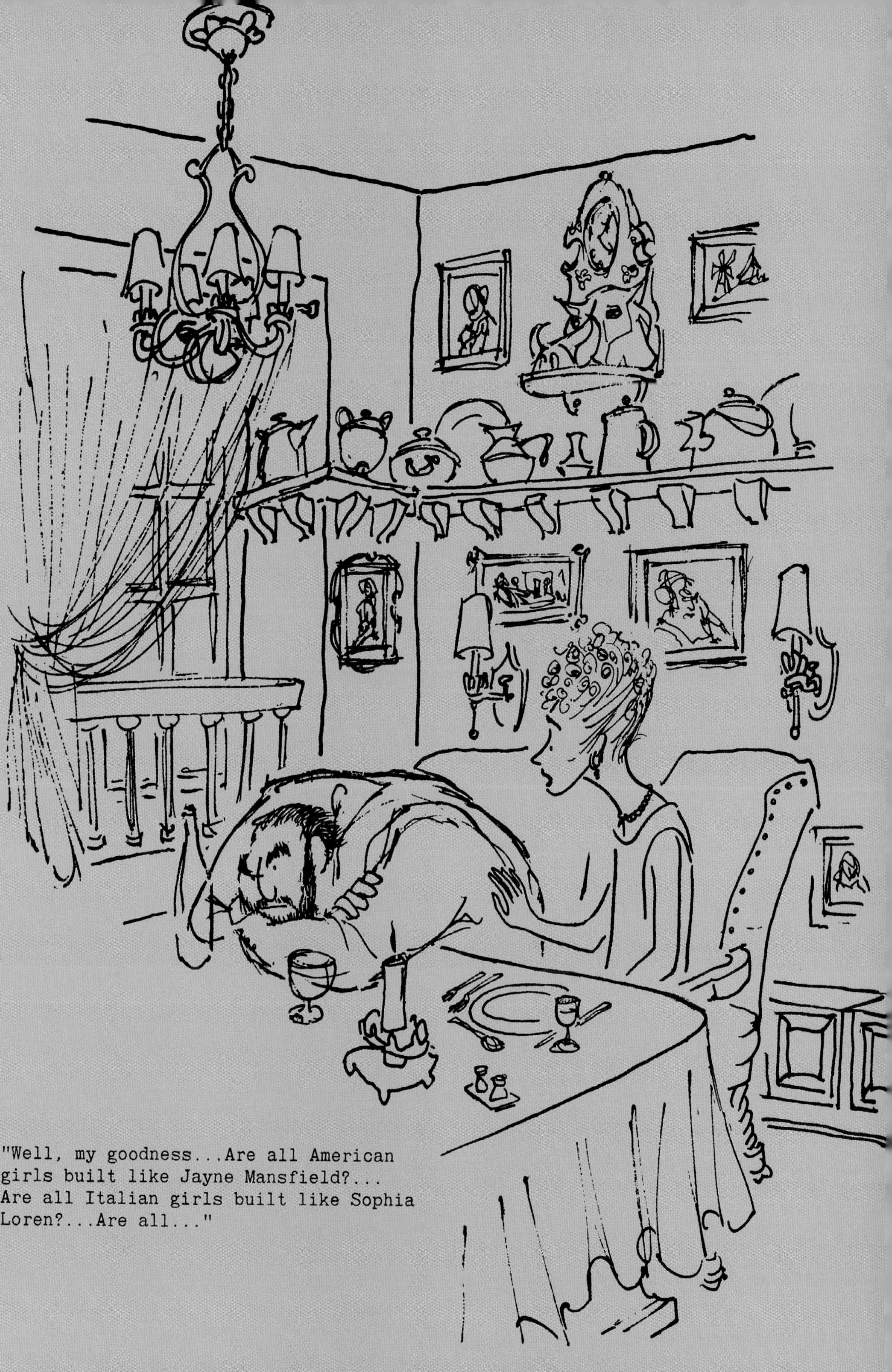

"Well, my goodness...Are all American girls built like Jayne Mansfield?... Are all Italian girls built like Sophia Loren?...Are all..."

IN LONDON

OCTOBER 1957

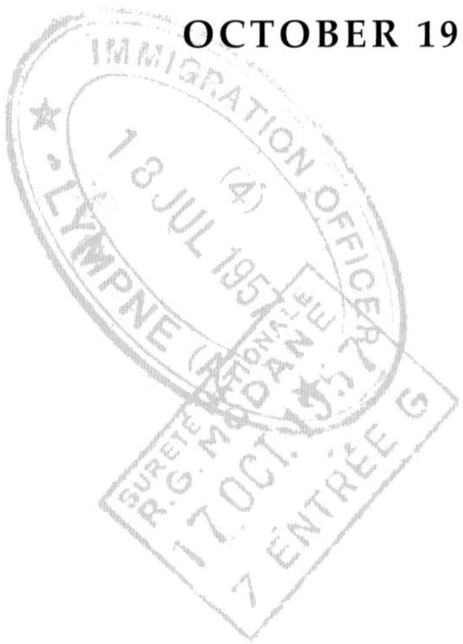
IMMIGRATION OFFICER
(4)
18 JUL 1957
LYMPNE
SURETE NATIONALE
R.G. MODANE
17 OCT. 1957
7 ENTRÉE G

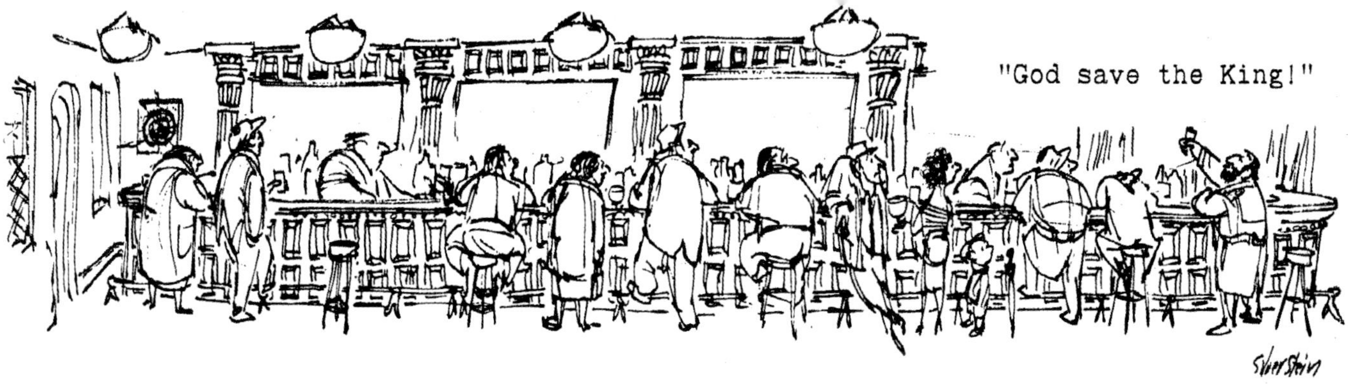

"God save the King!"

SILVERSTEIN in LONDON

pictorial

VIA THE MAY AND JULY issues of PLAYBOY, cartoonist Shel Silverstein has whisked us to Japan (where he was asked "Is it true what they say about American women?") and Scandinavia (where he was featured vocalist of Papa Bue's Bearded Viking New Orleans Danish Jazz Band). Both of these far-flung lands were lovingly limned in on-the-spot sketches bearing the saucy Silverstein stamp.

This month, his sketch pad sparkles with his impressions of the world's largest, grandest city: venerable and venerated London, the home of a teeming eight million people, the seat of mighty kings and queens, the nucleus of a once-vast empire, the city that looked upon Augustine and William Shakespeare.

Shel's view of London is not quite so lofty as all that, but it's pretty obvious he agrees wholeheartedly with Poet Laureate John Masefield's warm words about the place: "Oh London Town's a fine town, and London sights are rare./ And London ale is right ale, and brisk's the London air." Fine, rare, right and brisk as the age-old city itself are these drawings from a puckish pen.

playboy's wandering beard beards the british lion in its den

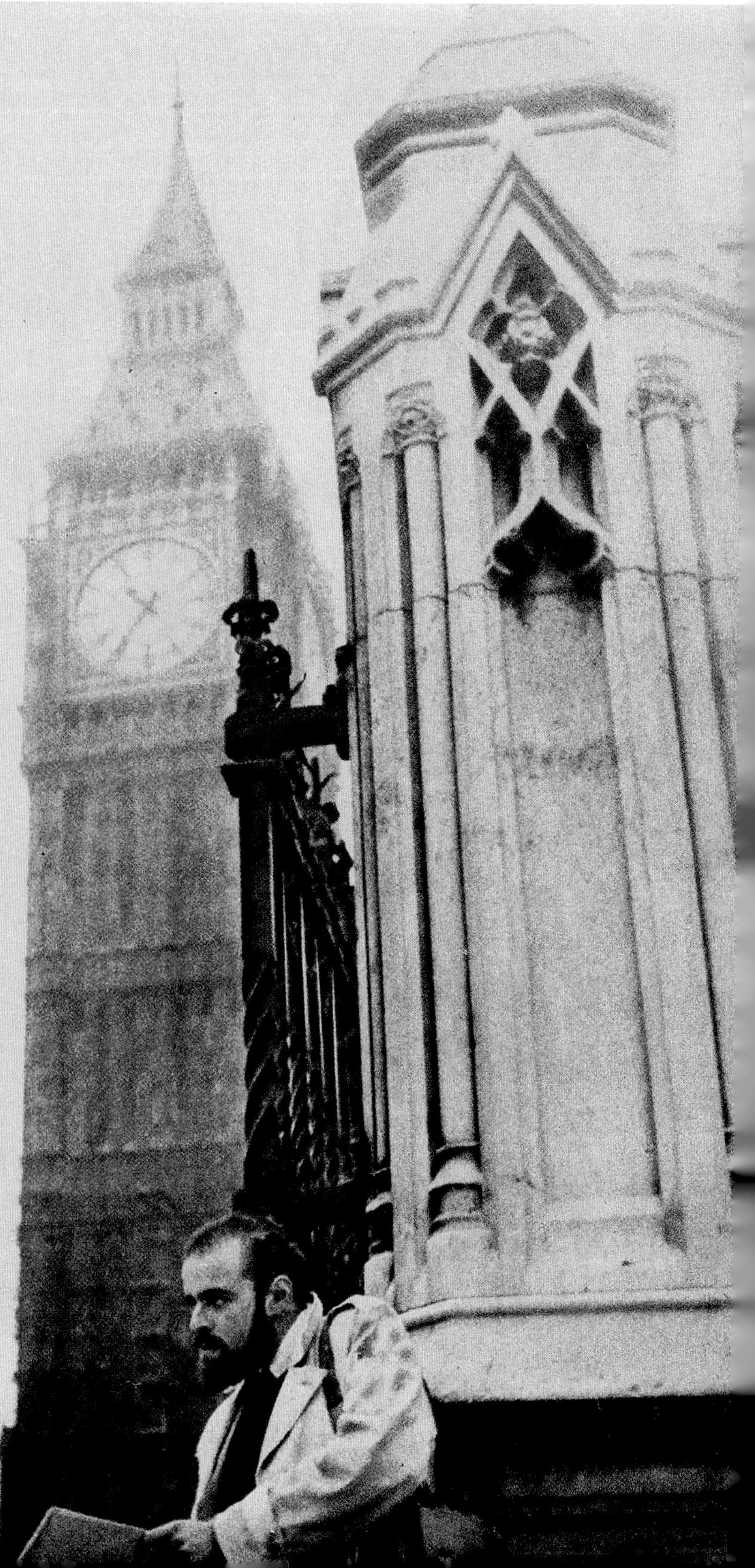

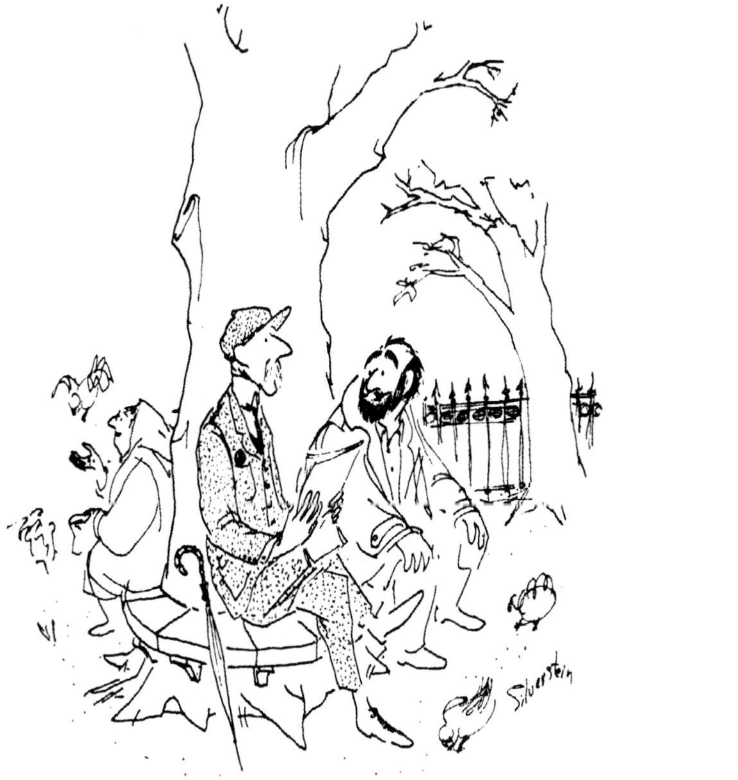
Silverstein

"Say, you fellows have really picked up on our Ivy League styles haven't you?"

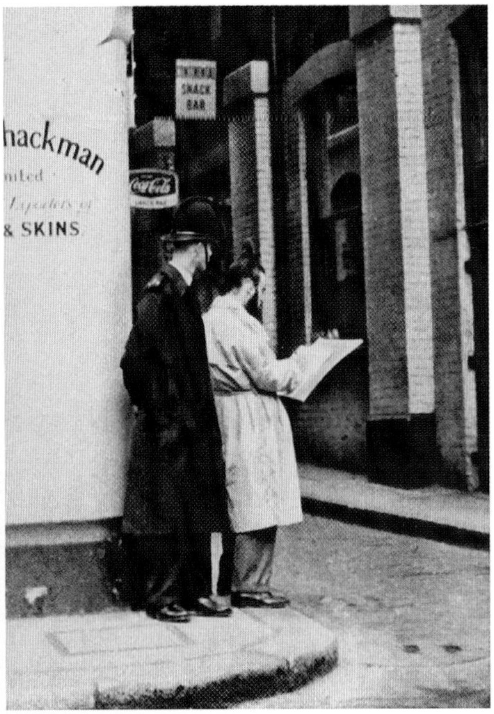
SNACK
BAR
Coca-Cola
hackman
& SKINS

The bobby and the beard: Shel and a cop collaborate in drawing a London landscape.

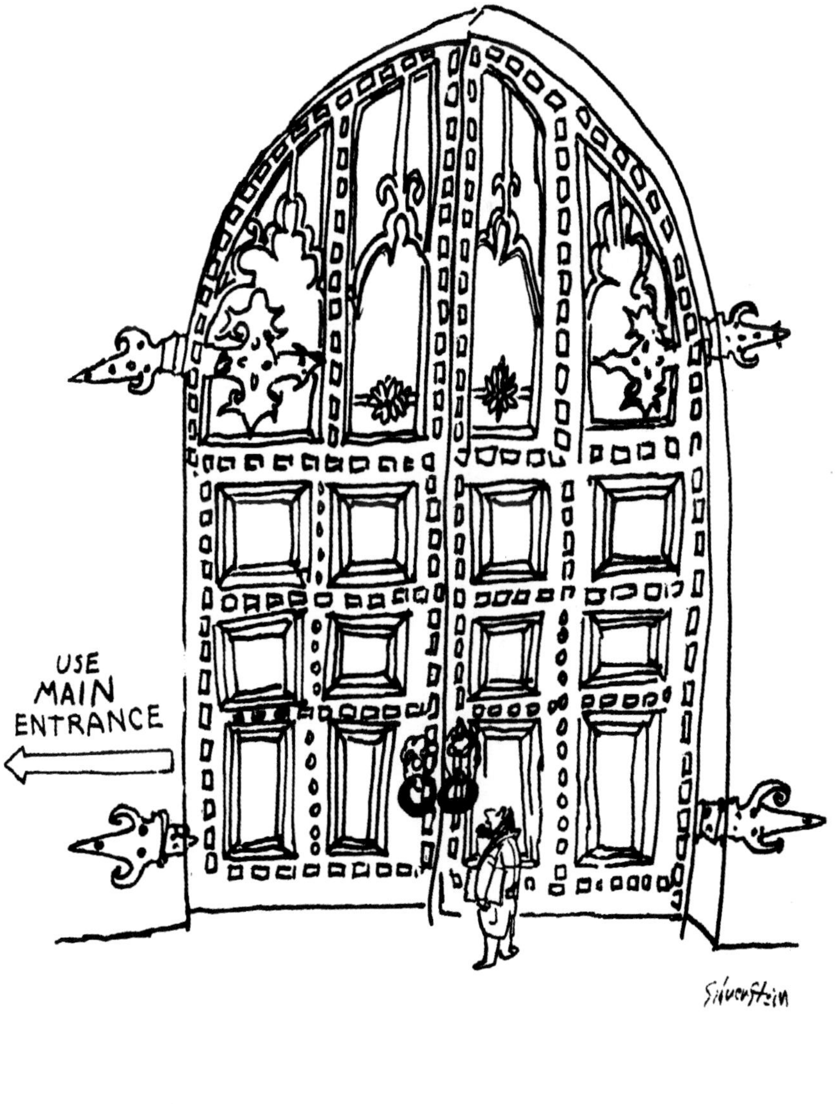
USE
MAIN
ENTRANCE
Silverstein

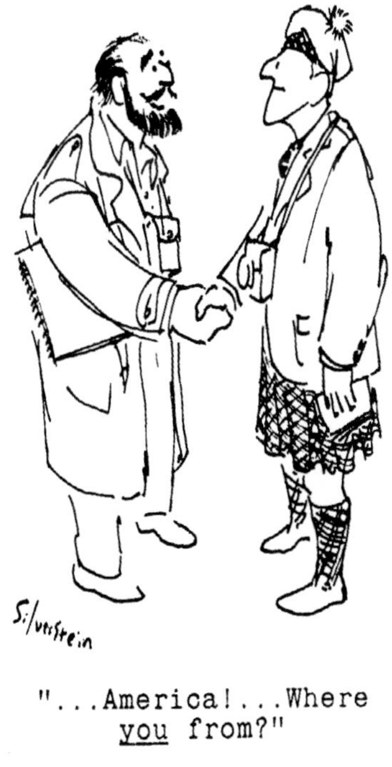
Silverstein

"...America!...Where you from?"

SILVERSTEIN in LONDON, *continued*

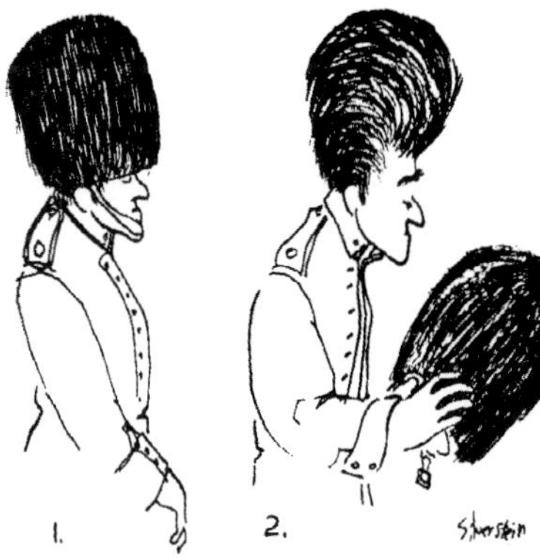

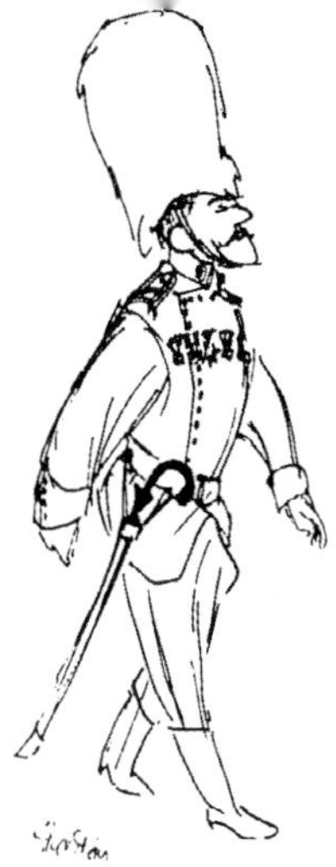

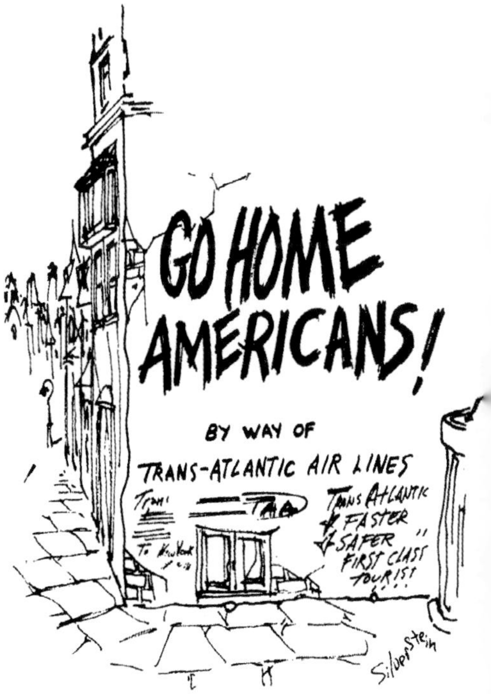
GO HOME AMERICANS!
BY WAY OF
TRANS-ATLANTIC AIR LINES

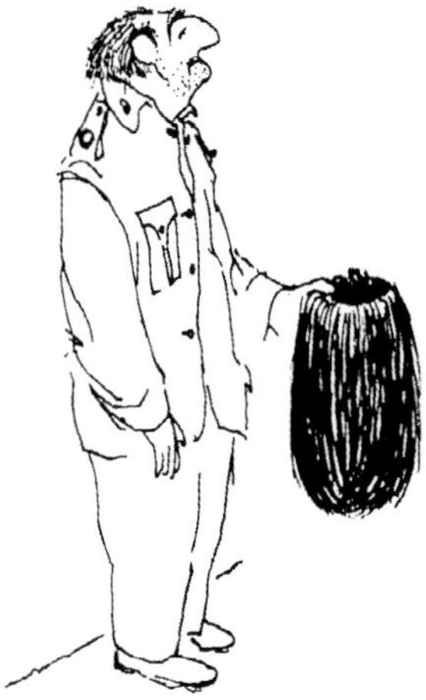

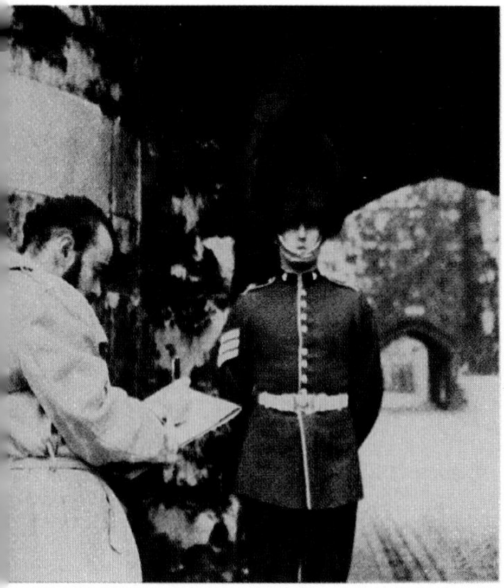

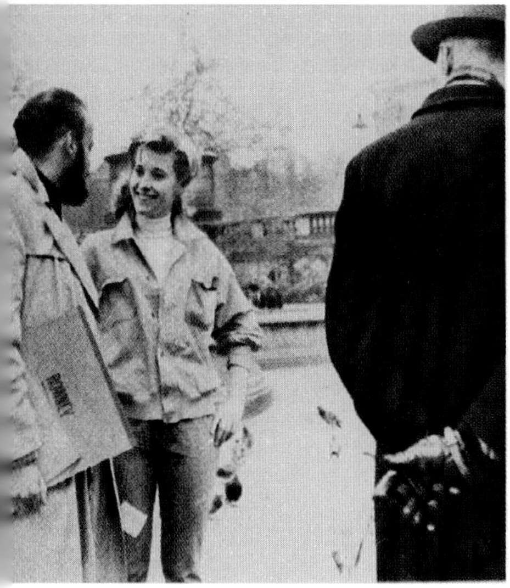

Shel makes a new friend in Trafalgar Square.

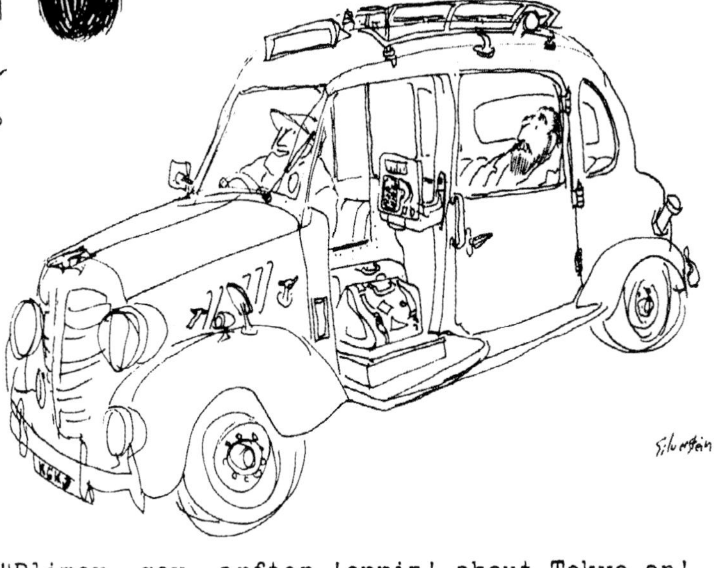

"Blimey, gov, arfter 'oppin' about Tokyo an' Scarndenyvia, hit must be a ruddy joy ter 'ear English spoke again... Lor, I recalls one noight I were 'avin' a bit o' bingo in a pub in Swyden, when I spies this 'ere chaffer 'avin' a pot o' four arf at the near an' far--regular cheese she were an' up the pole t'boot. I were a bit squiffy from the bubbly m'self an' I figured, ''ere's a bit o' Roger, sure as eggs is eggs,' when 'rarnd the Johnny Horner pops this rorty, gallows-faced cabbage gelder. Lor! Big as th' bloody tower, 'e were--25 stone at least--an' 'e were browned off proper: 'All roight, ye randy, beef-witted, hobnailer,' 'e says t'me, ''op it, afor yer gets a slosh in the gob. This 'ere's m' lawful blanket!' 'In yer 'at, 'arry,' says I. Well, sir, 'e 'its me a gooser on the bread pan an'..."

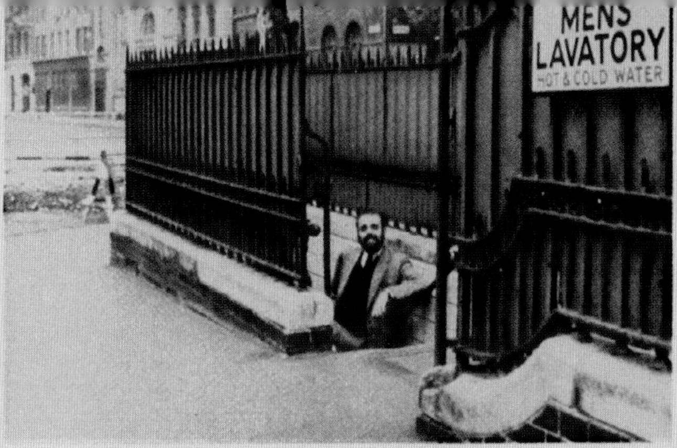
MENS
LAVATORY
HOT & COLD WATER

"London lodgings are inexpensive," says anything-for-a-gag Shel.

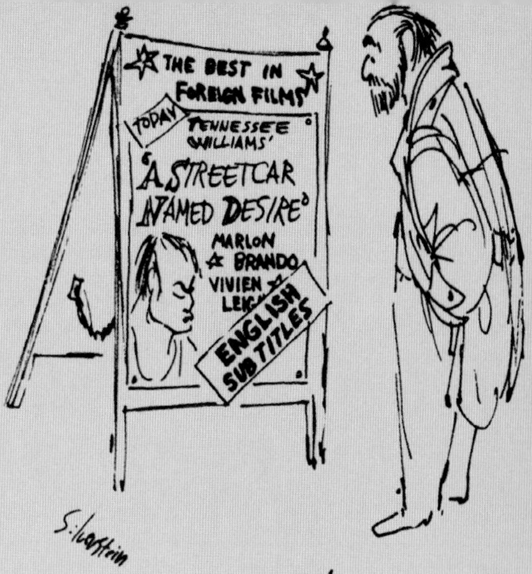
THE BEST IN
FOREIGN FILMS
TODAY
TENNESSEE
WILLIAMS'
"A STREETCAR
NAMED DESIRE"
MARLON
BRANDO
VIVIEN
LEIGH
ENGLISH
SUBTITLES
Silverstein

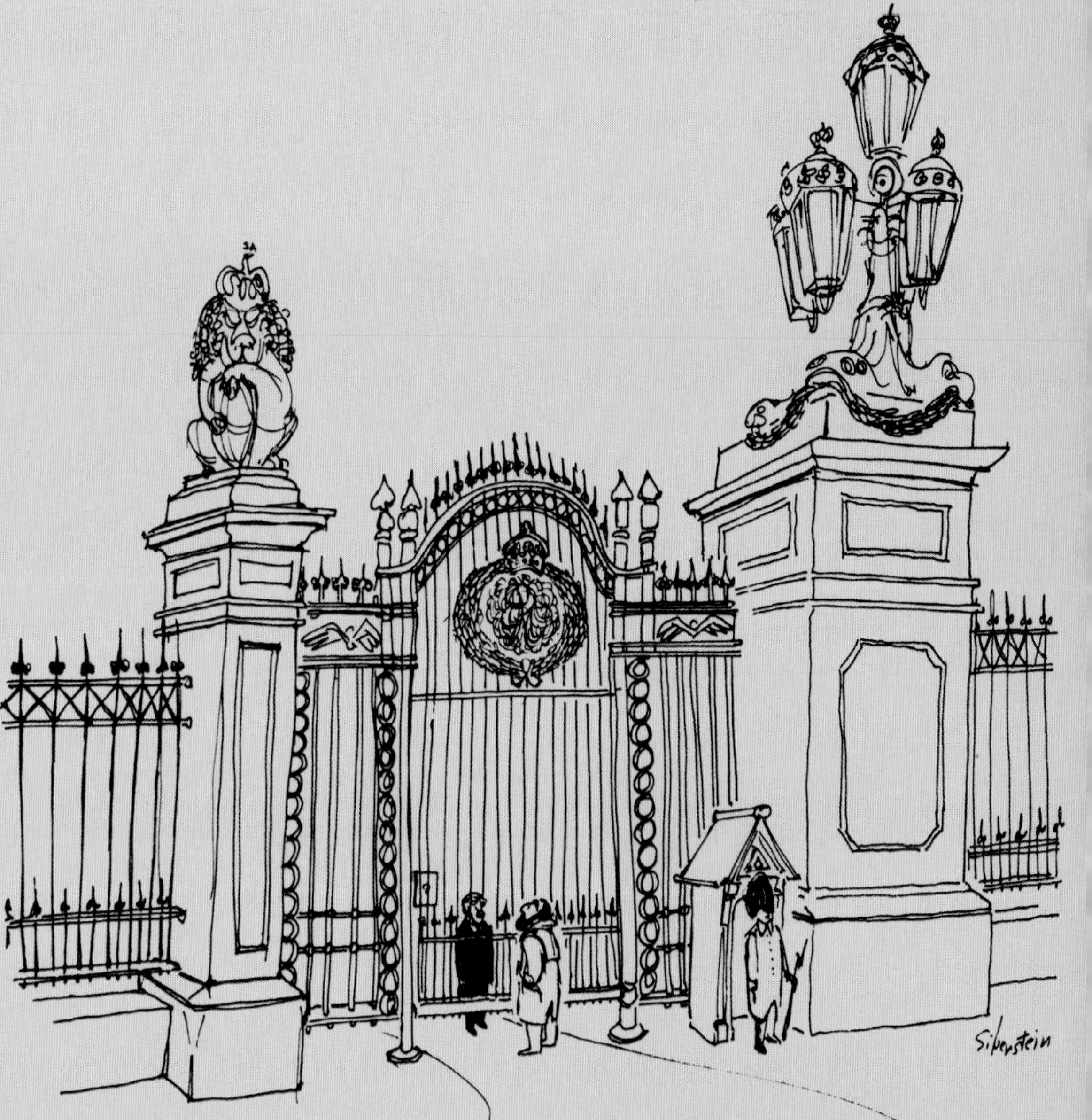
Silverstein

"I believe I can say with assurance, sir, that Princess Margaret will not be interested in appearing as January's Playmate of the Month..."

IN PARIS

JANUARY 1958

DOUANES FRANCAISES
31 OCT 1957
ST-LOUIS-BOURGFELDEN-ROUTE 1

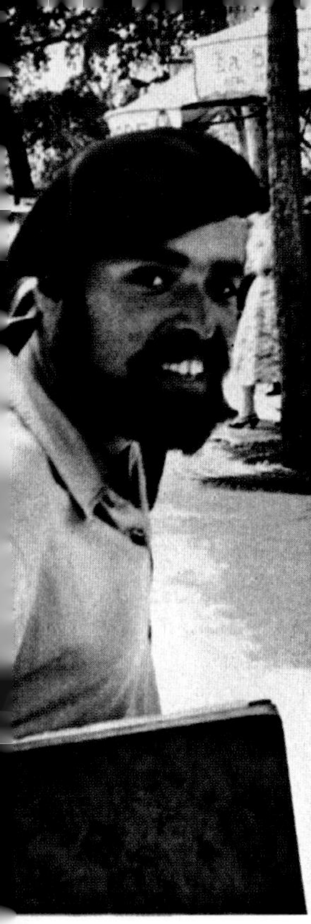
CA

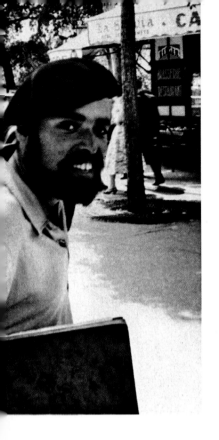

SILVERSTEIN in PARIS

the wit with the whiskers falls in love with the world's most romantic city

SHEL SILVERSTEIN has visited and sketched some lore-and-legend-haunted ports of call for these pages: Tokyo, Scandinavia and London are all atmospheric places packed with color, flavor and historic grandeur, and the antic Silverstein spirit responded to them with whimsy and warmth. But, to twist an old ballad, "no place on earth does he love more sincerely" — than Paris.

The same city that inspired Toulouse and Zola, Villon and Voltaire, Dumas, both *père* and *fils*; the city of Nostradamus and Notre Dame, Baudelaire and Brigitte Bardot, Fontaine and Fernandel — this city inspired Silverstein as well, and no wonder, for Paris (which more than one man has called the place good Americans go to when they die) is a city steeped in seductiveness, richly redolent of romance, a city few fellows of taste have been able to resist — not even sour Nietzsche who said, "As an artist, a man has no home in Europe save in Paris."

As an artist, Shel Silverstein had a wonderful time creating the labor of love that begins on this page — a pleasureful portfolio of zestful, winsome, finely funny impressions of a 2000-year-old city that captured his heart and swept him off his feet.

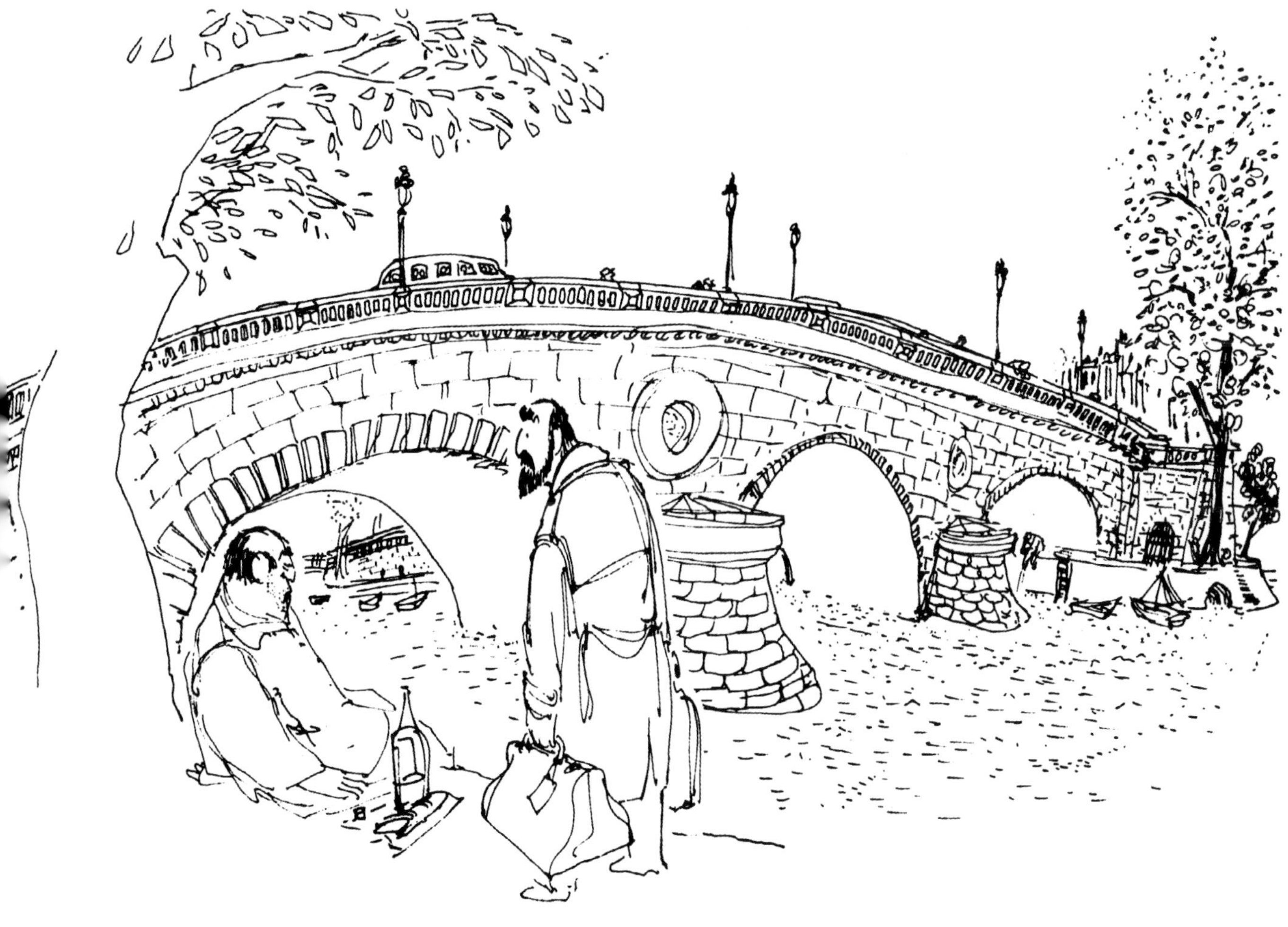

"Well, that depends, monsieur...If you face east, this is the left bank ...If you face west, that is the left bank...If you face south..."

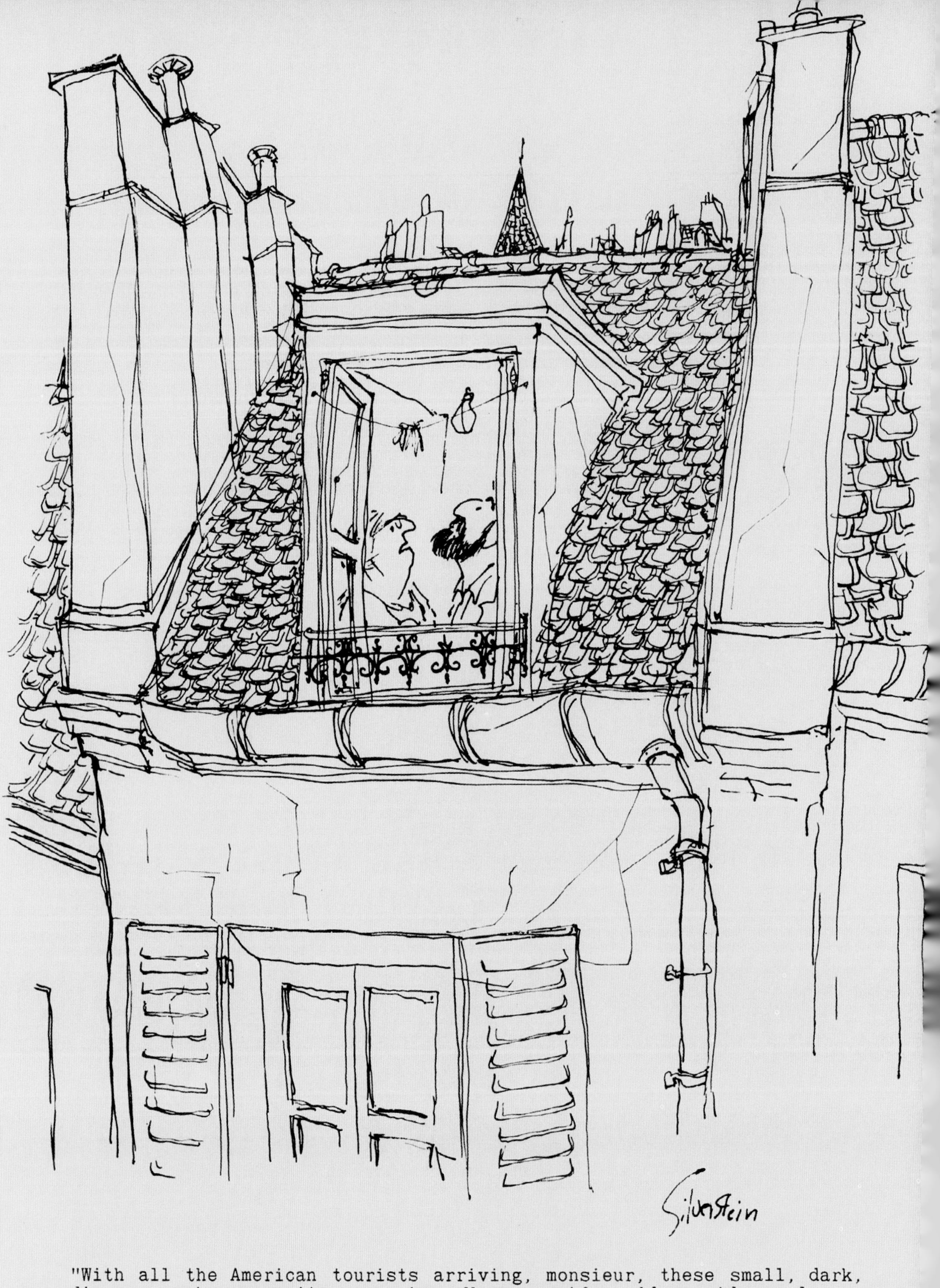
Silverstein

"With all the American tourists arriving, monsieur, these small, dark, dingy garrets are quite expensive. However, if you'd consider a large, clean, well-lit room on the first floor..."

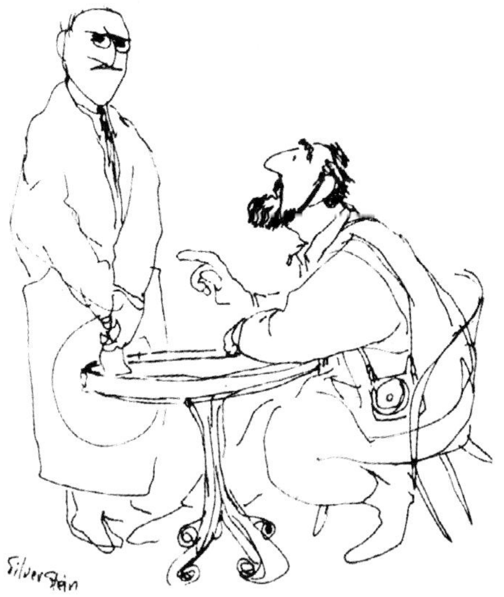
Silverstein

"A bottle of absinthe...a checkered tablecloth. . .a candle in a wine bottle..."

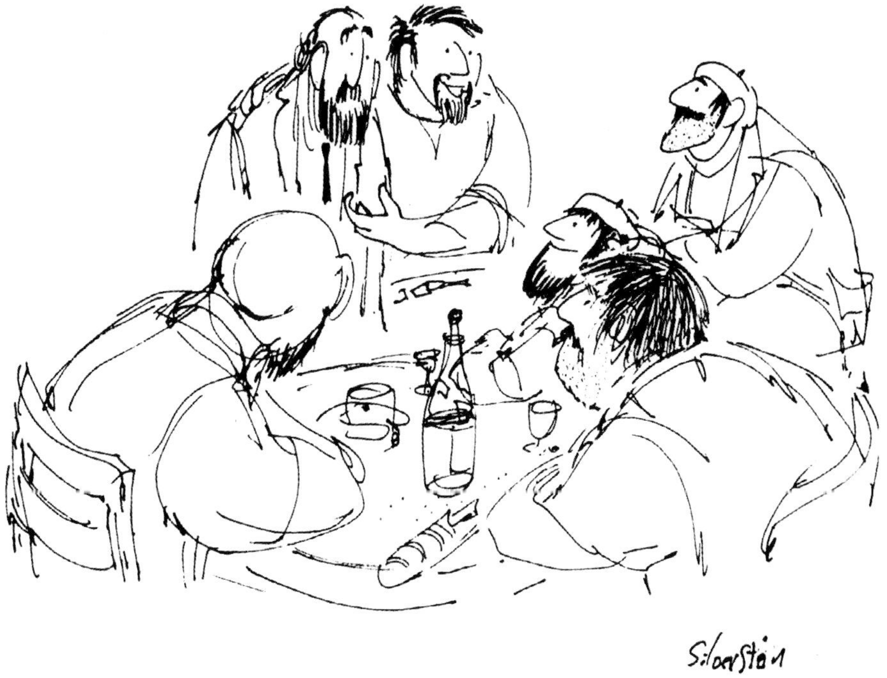
Silverstein

"Fellows, meet Shel Silverstein from Chicago. Shel, shake hands with Eddie Bell from Los Angeles, Charley Petersen from Boston, Steve Zimmerman from St. Louis and Jim Albright from New Jersey."

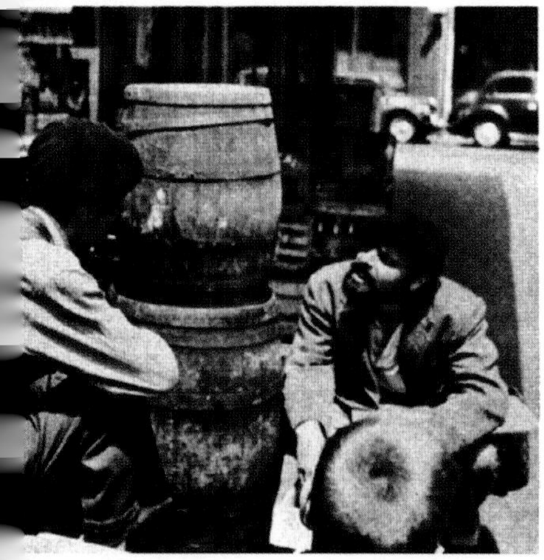

hel takes part in a spirited conversa-
on with two French wine merchants.

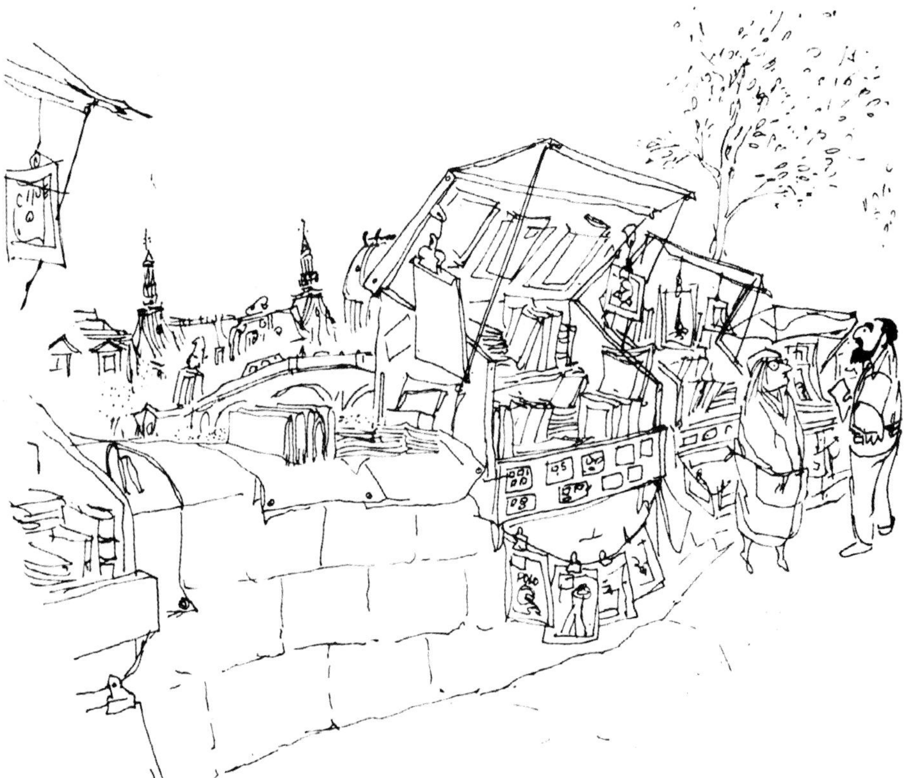

"Ten copies of 'Tropic of Cancer,' twelve copies of 'Tropic of Capricorn,' seven copies..."

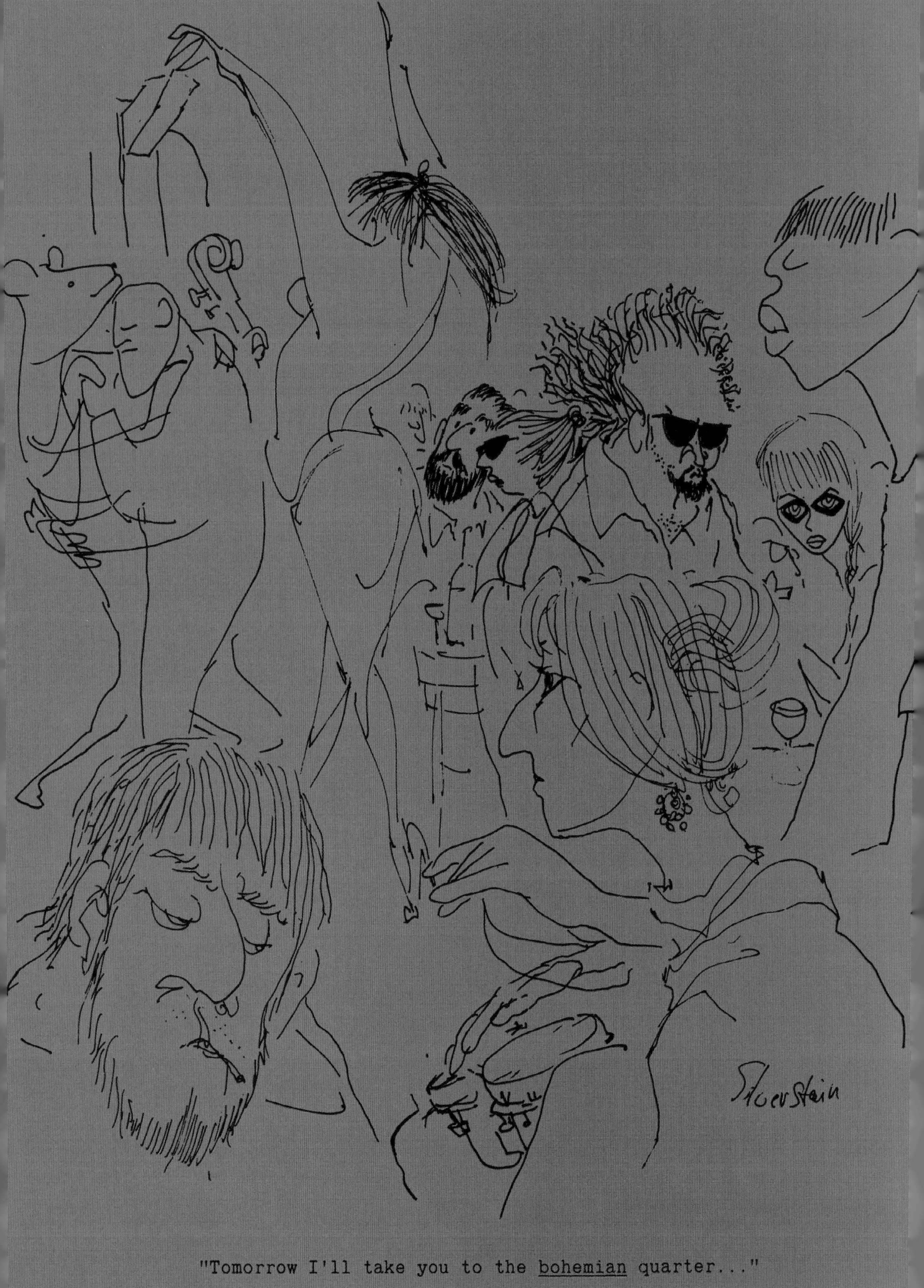
Silverstein

"Tomorrow I'll take you to the bohemian quarter..."

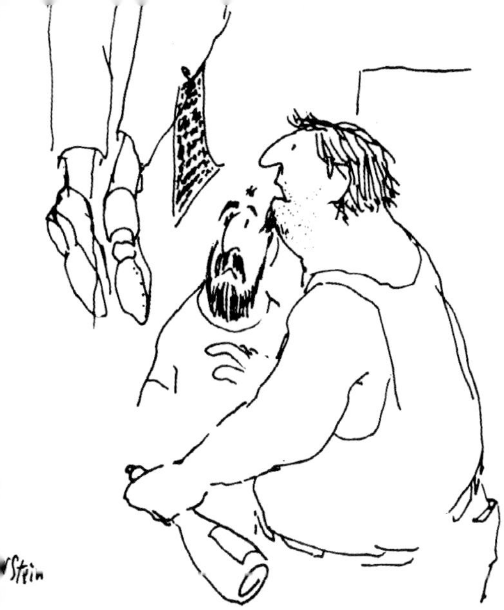

"Listen to this: 'Good-bye Paris, old friend, old comrade, old drinking companion, with your flaky green trees and your warm, playful sun and your friendly open-arm cafés, with your busy Seine and buzzing streets and bustling shops and children's laughter and lovers . . . lovers . . . lovers . . . You'll not miss me, Paris, although you were a good friend. The publishers doubted me, Paris, and the landlords and shopkeepers rejected me...and Arlette . . . Arlette . . . Arlette deserted me. But you remained loyal...you were a good friend, Paris...adieu...mon ami...adieu ...' Man, that's what I call <u>writing!</u>"

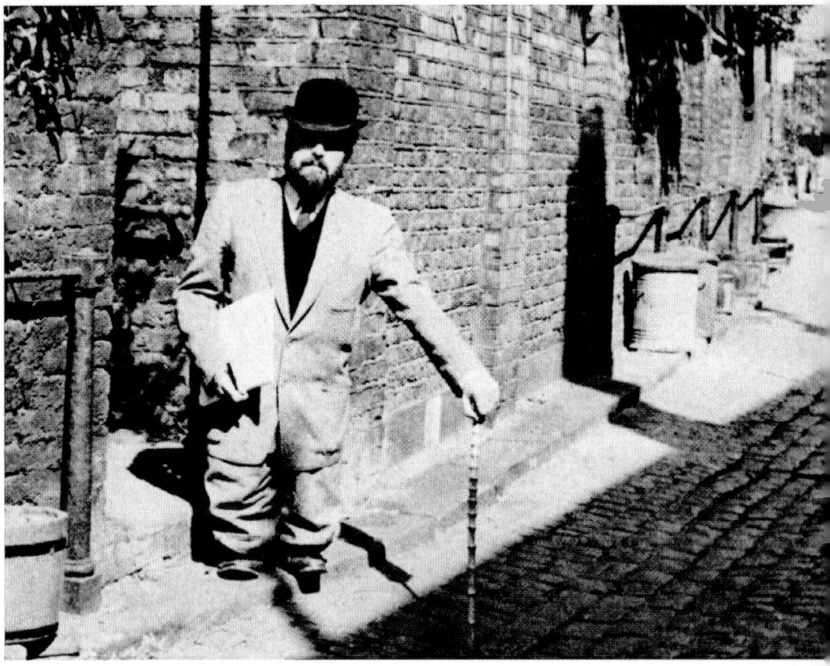

Assuming the famous hat, cane and stature (by kneeling on his shoes) of another artist inspired by Paris, Shel makes striking Toulouse-Lautrec.

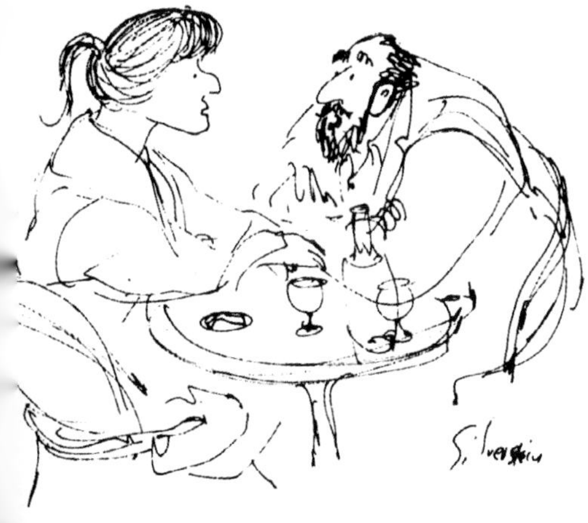

"Er...darling, je vous aime beaucoup...je ne sais pas what to do . . . morning, noon and nighttime, too...toujours wondering what to do...er... chérie..."

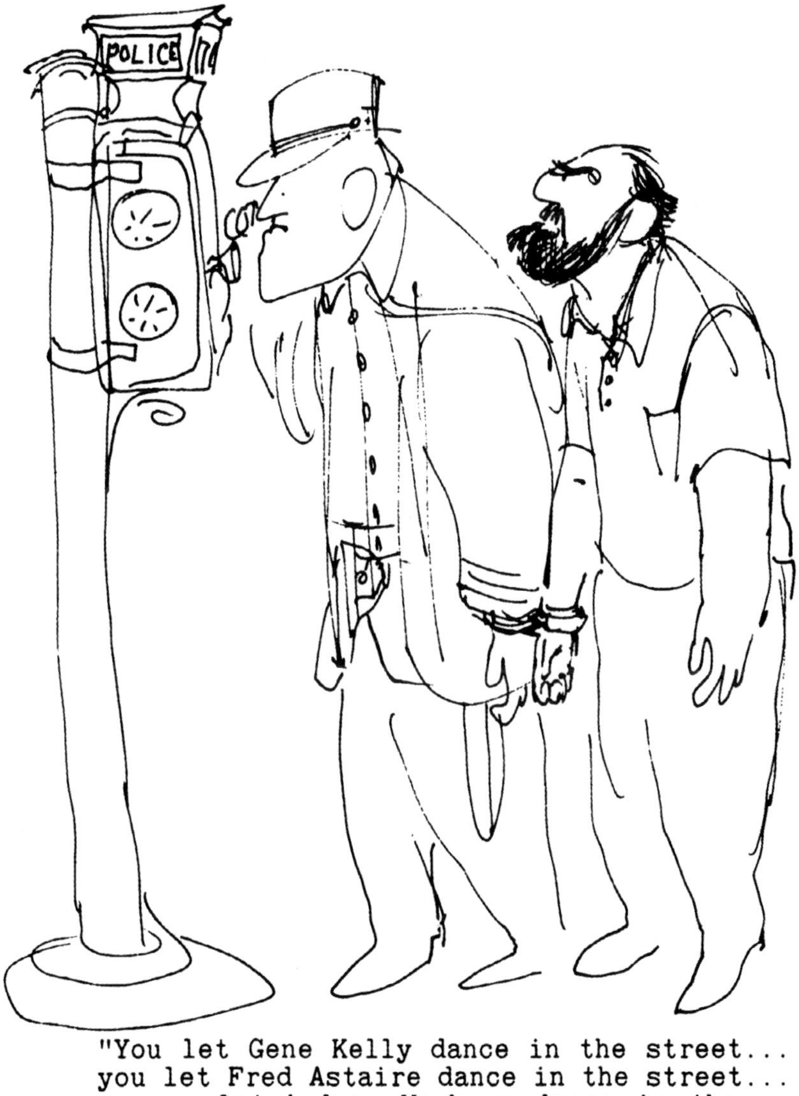
POLICE

"You let Gene Kelly dance in the street... you let Fred Astaire dance in the street... you let Audrey Hepburn dance in the street...you let..."

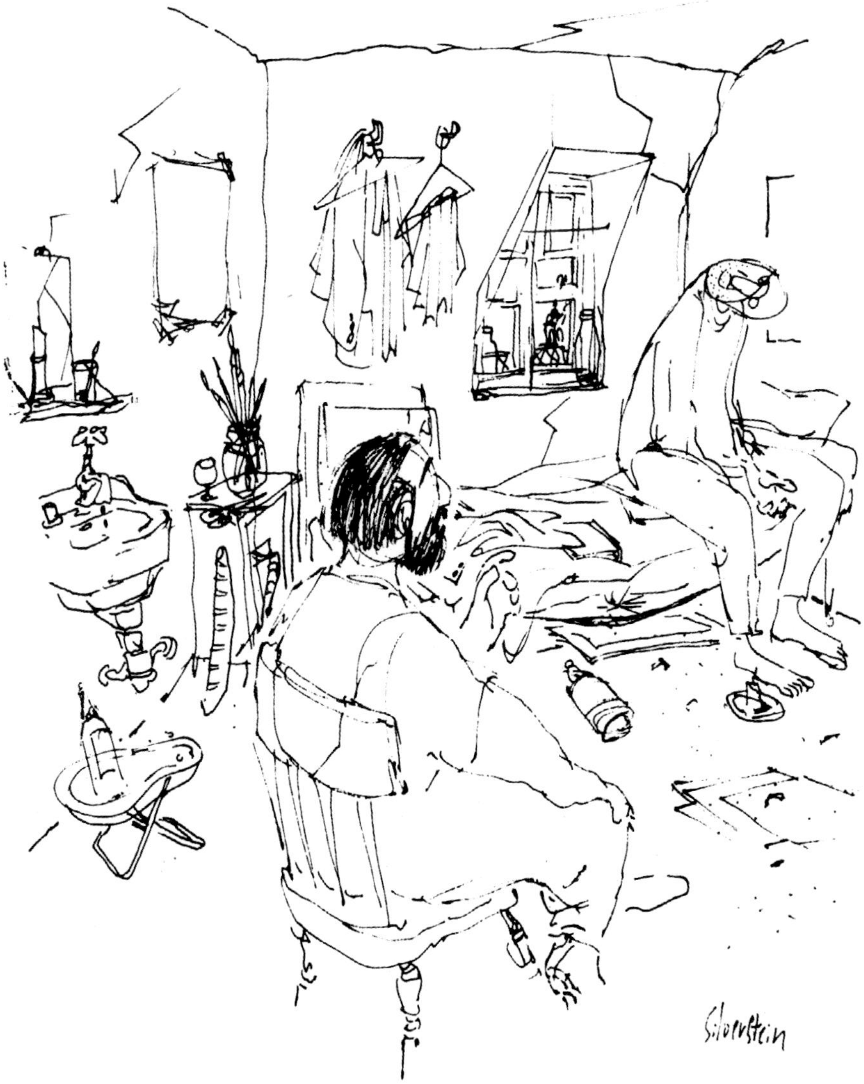
Silverstein

"Look at this place, Paul—no heat, no electricity, crawling with bugs, no icebox, no ventilation, no bathtub, no toilet, nothing to eat but a few scraps of bread and cheap wine. Frankly, I don't see how you manage to stay alive, Paul...Paul?...<u>Paul?</u>..."

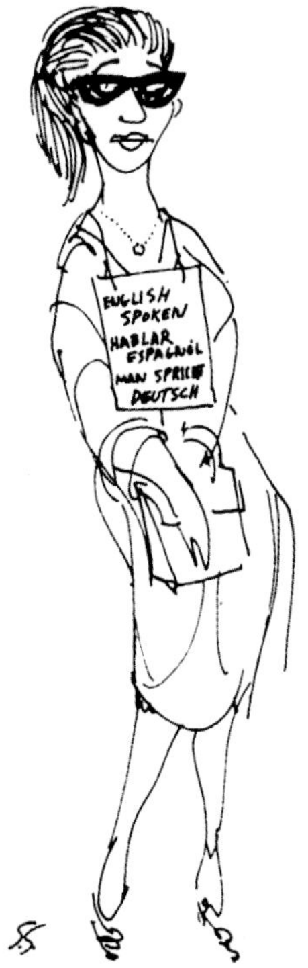
ENGLISH SPOKEN
HABLAR ESPAGNOL
MAN SPRICHT DEUTSCH

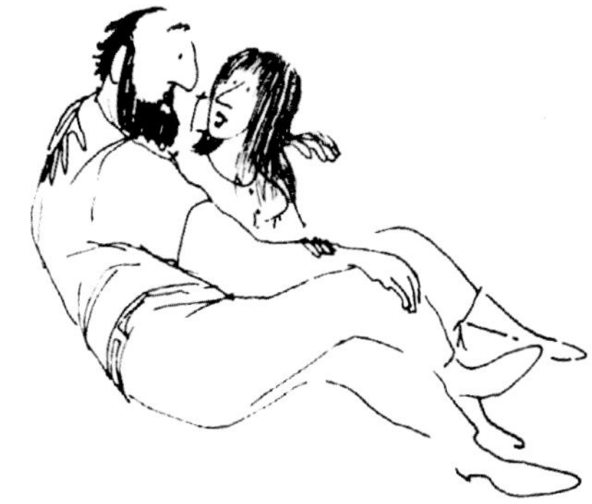

"What is this thing called an American kiss?"

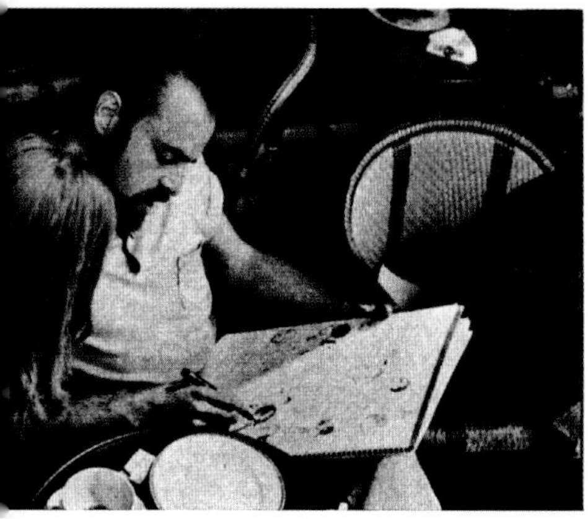

Silverstein makes friends easily. Here a long-tressed Parisienne kibitzes as he sketches in street café.

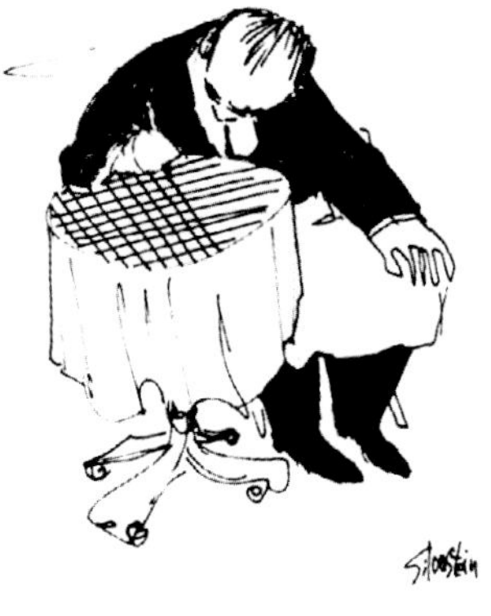

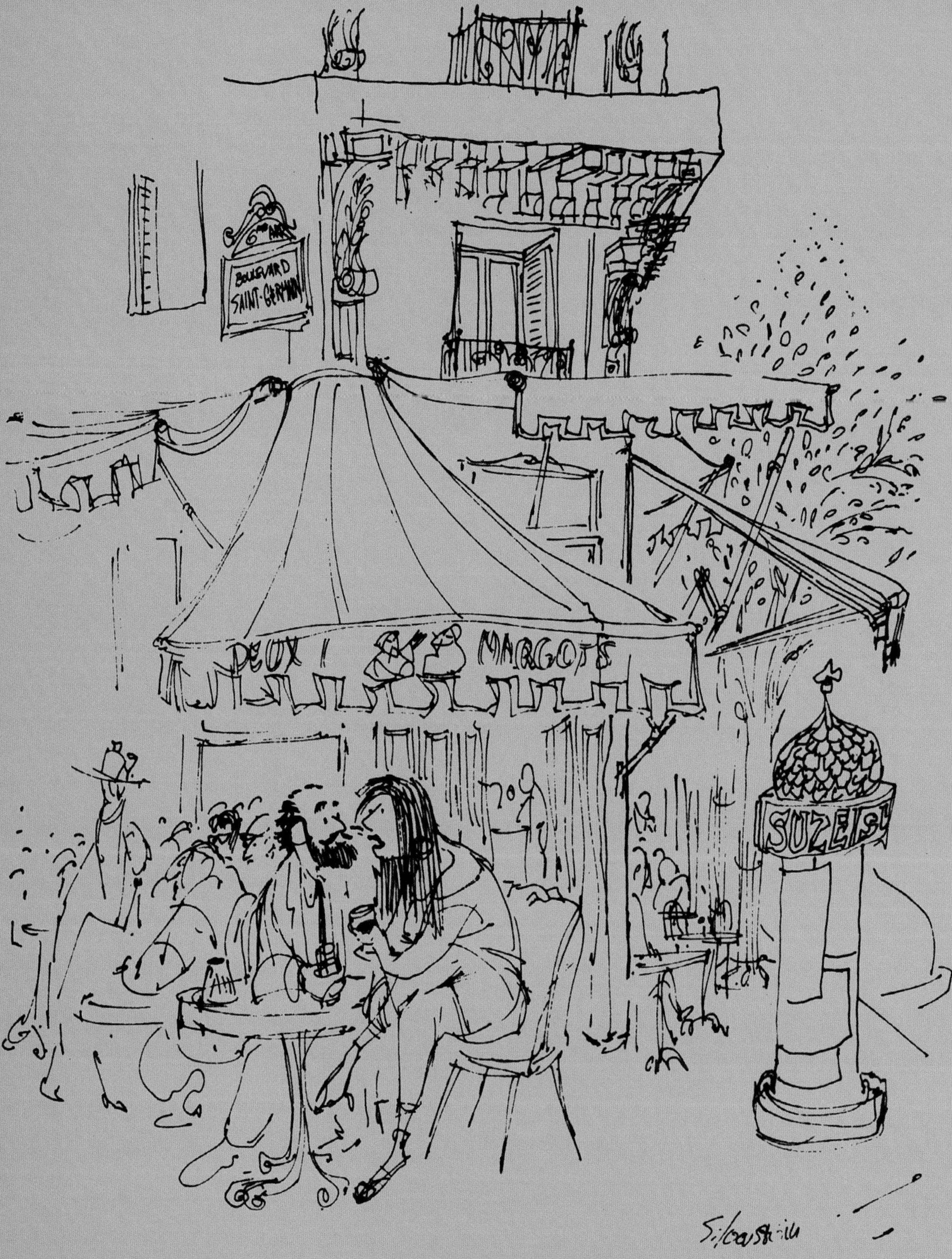
BOULEVARD
SAINT-GERMAIN
DEUX
MARGOTS
SUZE

"—Your American women — they think of sex as something dirty — something to be ashamed of — they hide their desires — they frustrate their instincts — they deny that they are human. We French— we realize that sex is good and clean and natural and beautiful — we follow our instincts. When I feel like going to bed with a man, <u>I go to bed with him!</u>"

"—Well, how about it??"

"I don't feel like it."

IN MOSCOW

MARCH 1958

pictorial

SILVERSTEIN IN MOSCOW

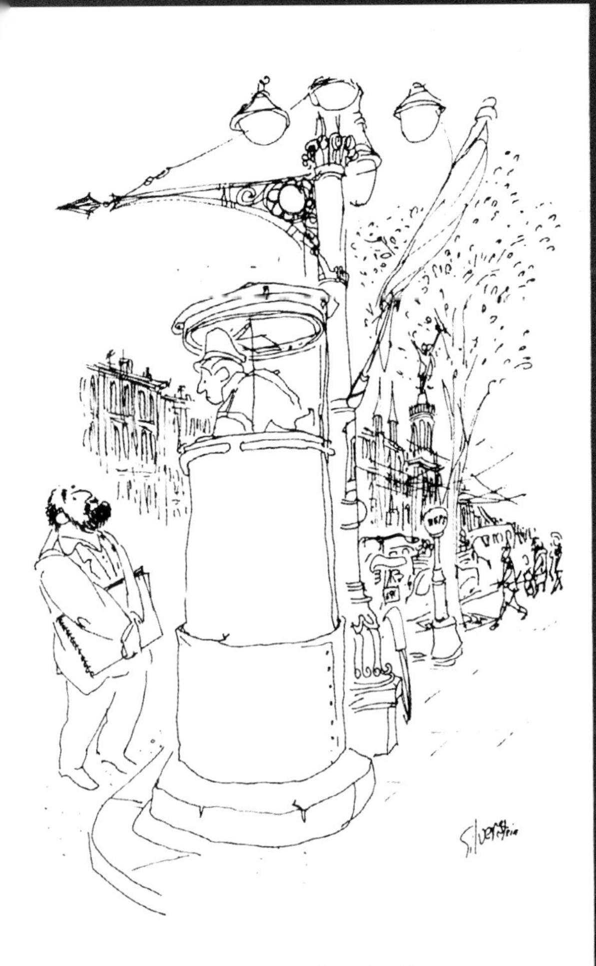

"When is the next Sputnik scheduled to take off?"

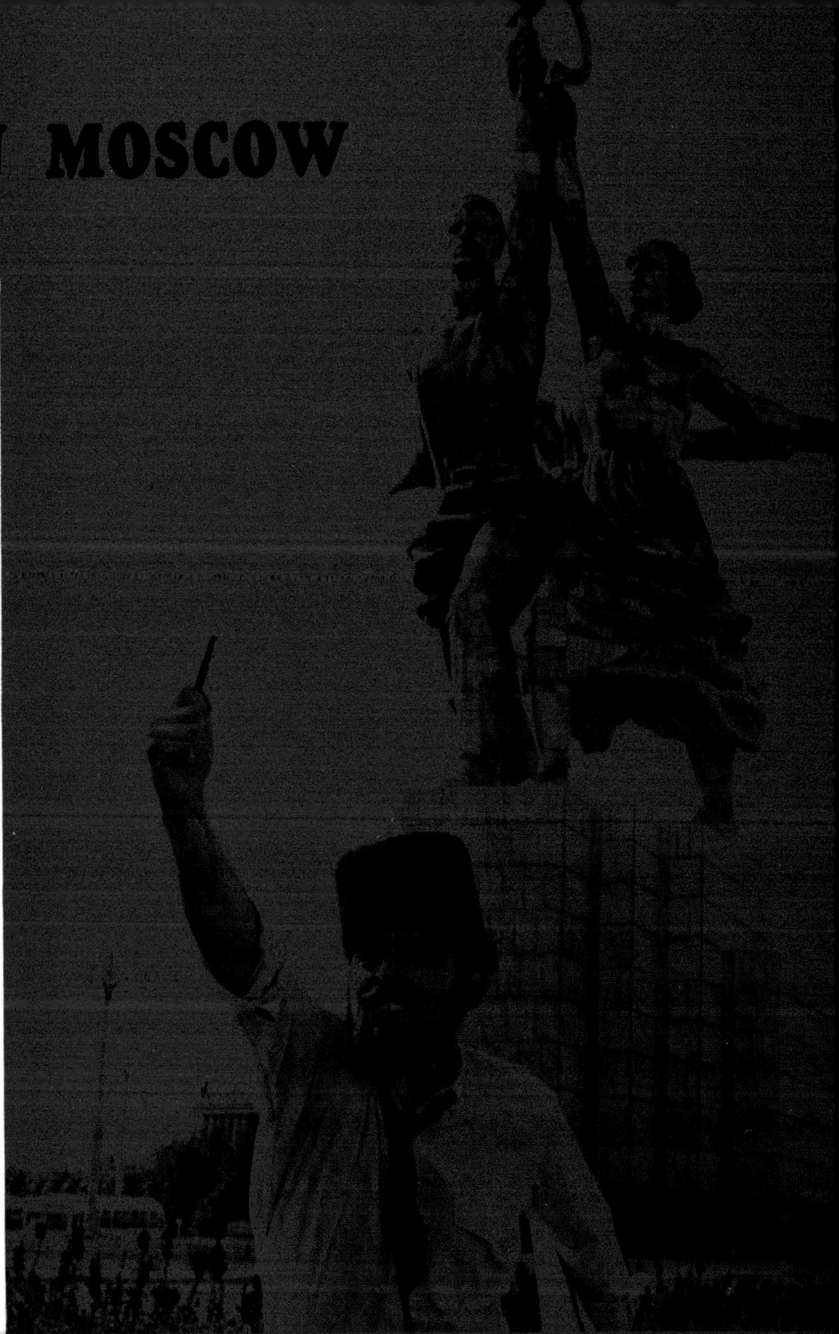

behind the iron curtain with playboy's unguided missile

Peripatetic Shel Silverstein, having amiably ambled into many a country and many a clime during his sketching tour of the world, started to amble into Moscow and stubbed his toe on a certain Curtain. Undaunted, he resorted to subterfuge and tried to get in as a tourist. No deal. He then tried again as a journalist. *Nyet.* Finally he passed himself off as a member of an American youth rally (despite his luxuriant chin-spinach), whereupon the editors of PLAYBOY received a collect phone call from a "Mr. Wilkinson" in Moscow, who told us in a suspiciously familiar voice that his mission had been accomplished and then hung up. Not too long after, we received a bulky package of Moscow cartoons and photos, accompanied by a letter from Shel, scrawled on a gigantic page of his sketch pad. It read, in part:

". . . As far as my personal adventures in Moscow are concerned, I have been bothered by no one and nothing—except amoebic dysentery, which I found to be scientifically no more advanced than American amoebic dysentery. The people on the streets of Moscow are the friendliest and warmest I've met on my travels . . . prices are tremendously high . . . the girls are lovely (photographic proof of this enclosed). I talked with the editors and cartoonists of *Krokodil*, Russia's biggest humor magazine, and had a chance to meet many young artists. Nothing very funny is happening to me here. Moscow is a pretty serious place."

Meanwhile, back at the PLAYBOY building, the staff sweated out some anxious moments when it was learned that a dozen members of the youth rally had accepted an invitation into Red China, minus State Department blessing, and were in danger of losing their passports. Might Shel be one of these reckless youths? we wondered. Assurance was forthcoming in good time: no, said Shel in another letter, the temptation had been easy to resist because he needed that passport to get him into all the other faraway places with strange-sounding names ripe for sketching by Silverstein.

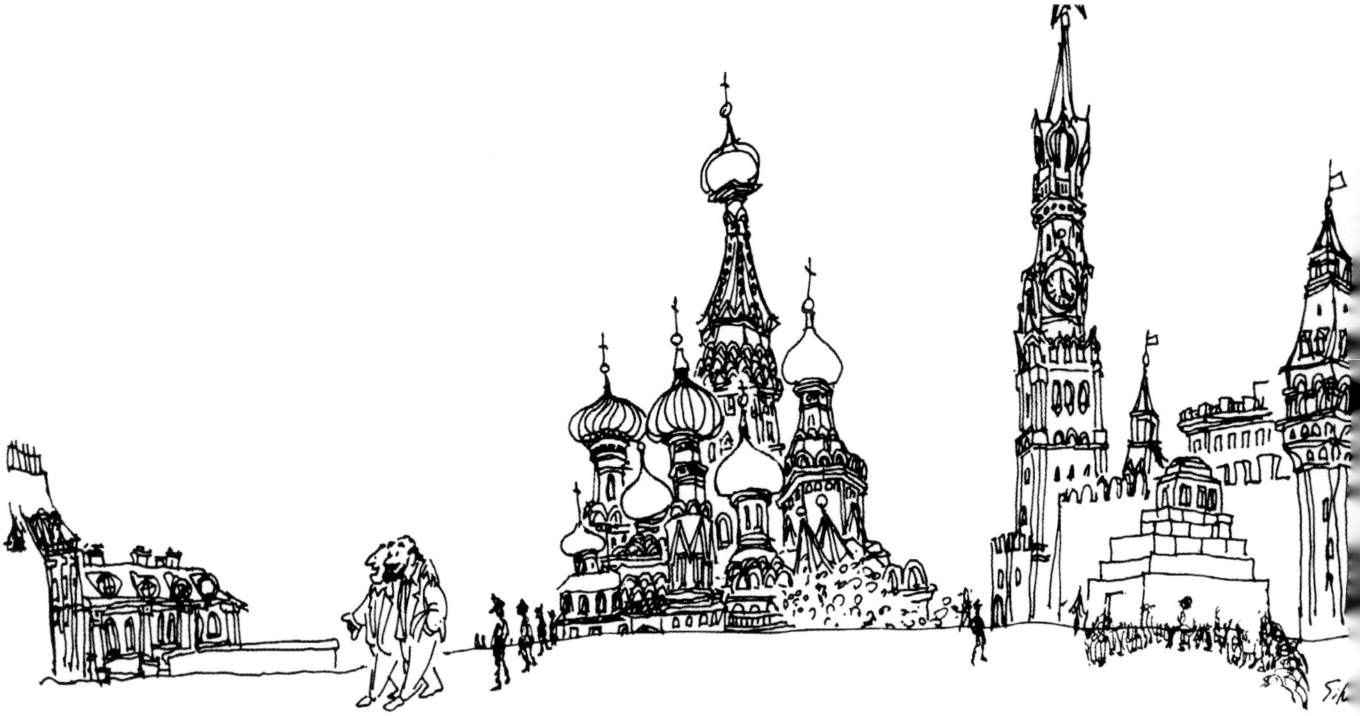

"Just think of it, comrade—under the Communist system of equal distribution, once every eight years the White Sox would win the pennant!"

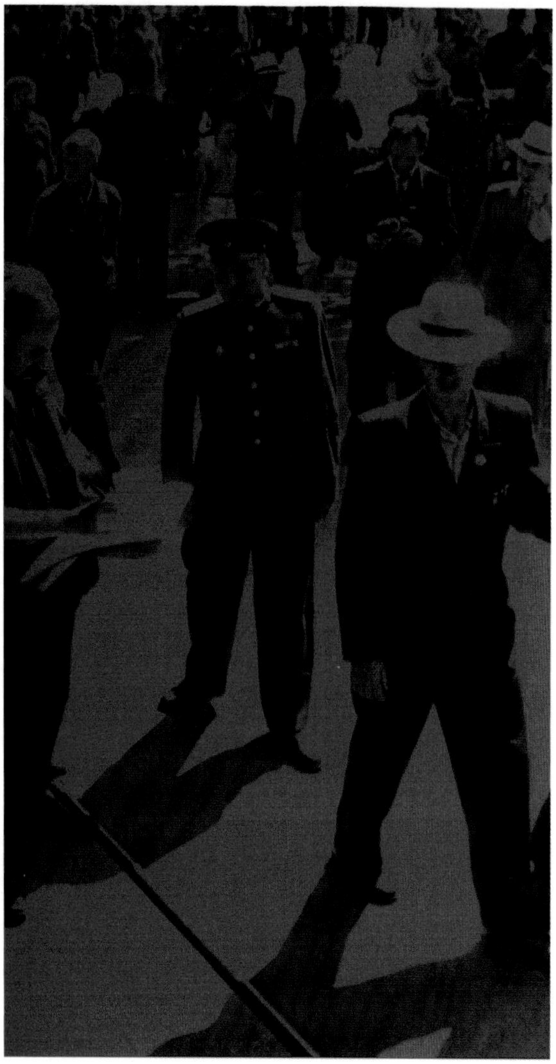

A Soviet army officer's interest is piqued. Soon after, Shel was surrounded by a curious crowd.

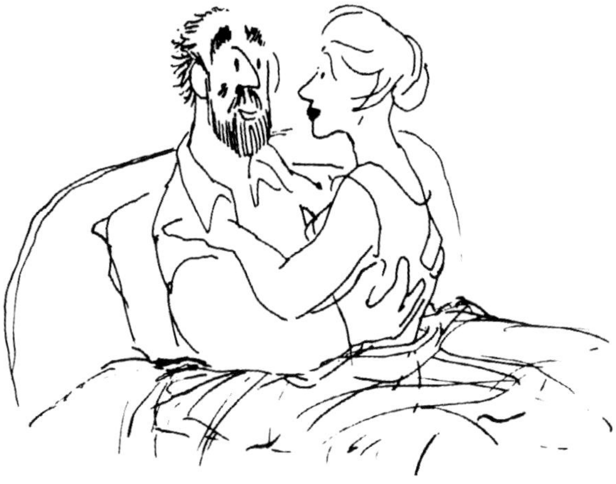

"Gee, Natasha—you mean you Russians invented this?!"

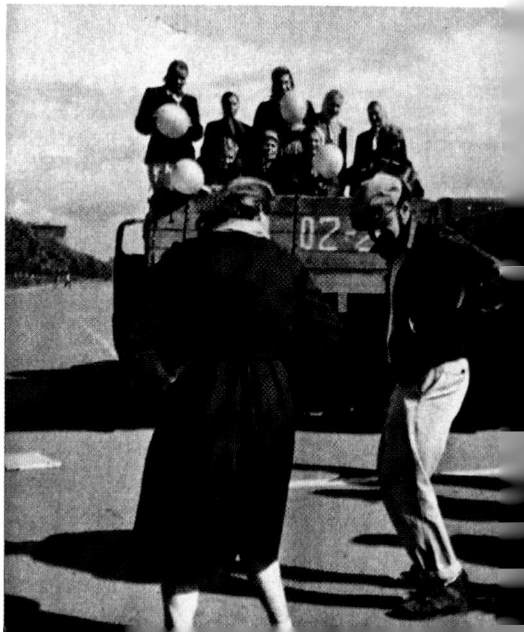

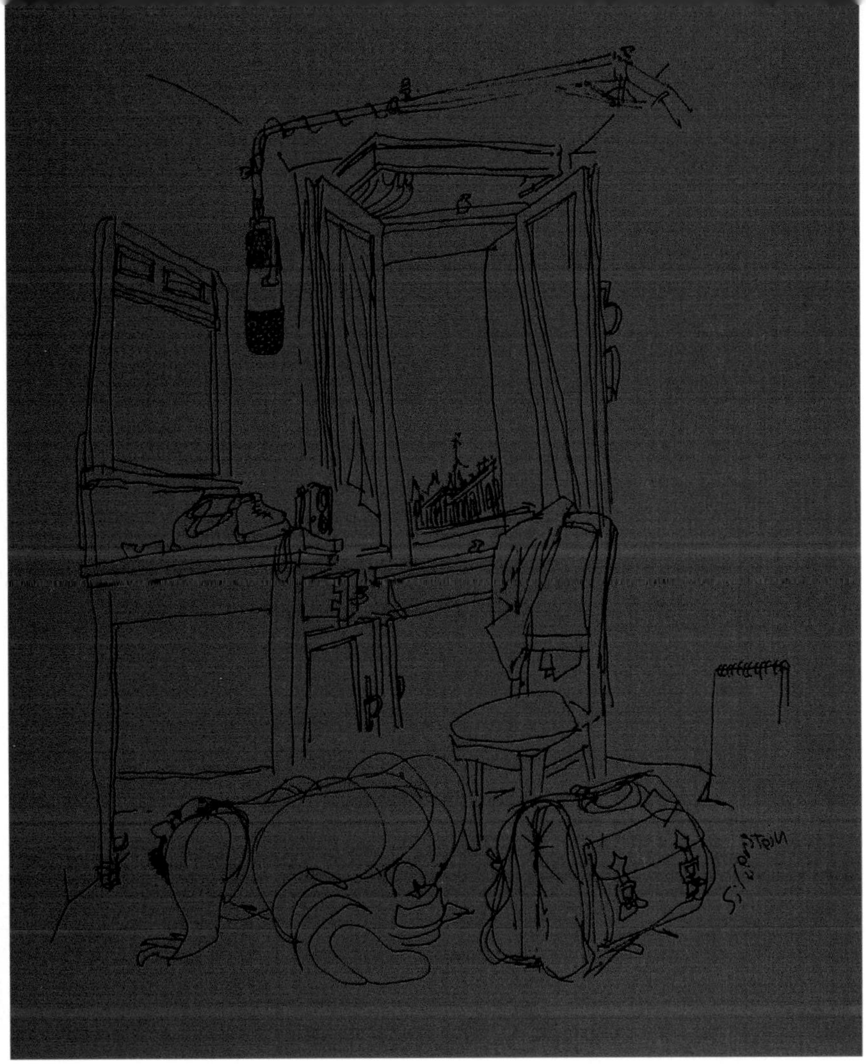

"Well anyway, there aren't any hidden microphones."

Shel sketches changing of the honor guard in front of Lenin-Stalin tomb.

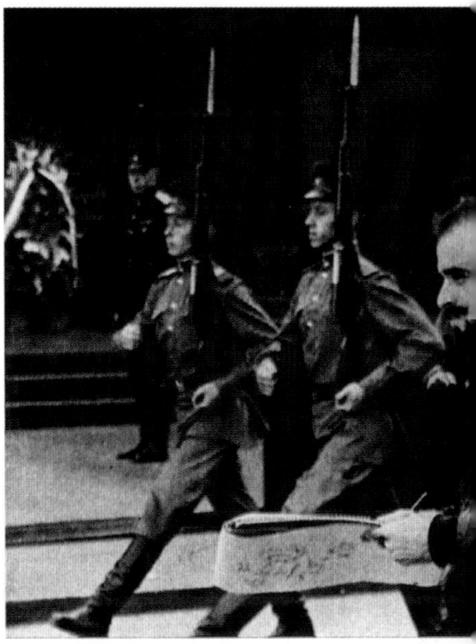

A truckload of girls from a collective farm near Moscow came to the big city on a visit and stopped long enough to dance the *gopak* with Shel right in the middle of the street.

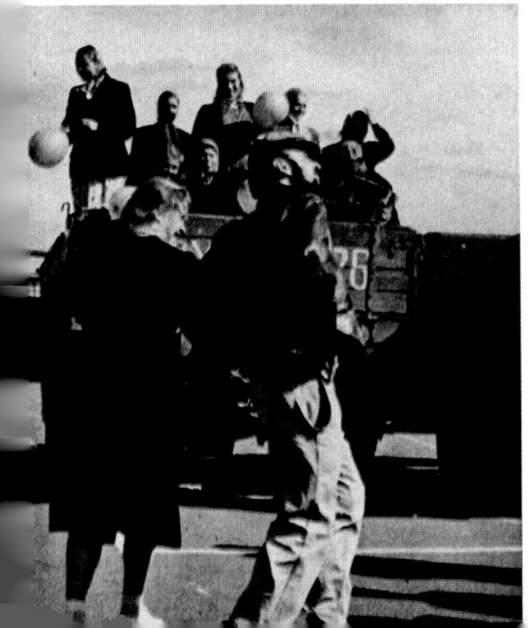

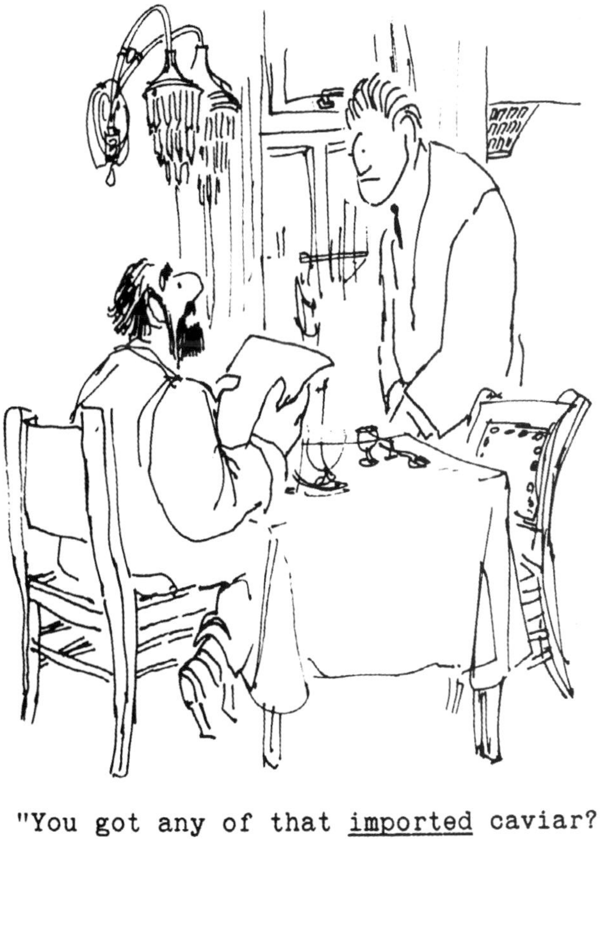

"You got any of that imported caviar?"

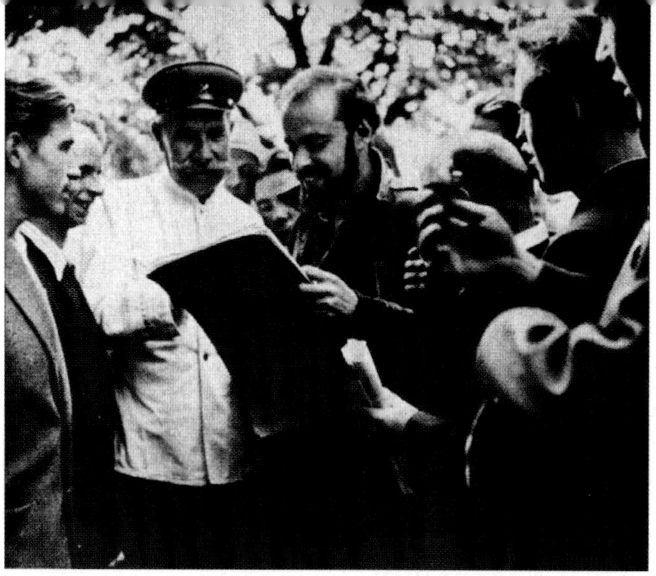

An old policeman out of a Chekhov play gets a drawing lesson.

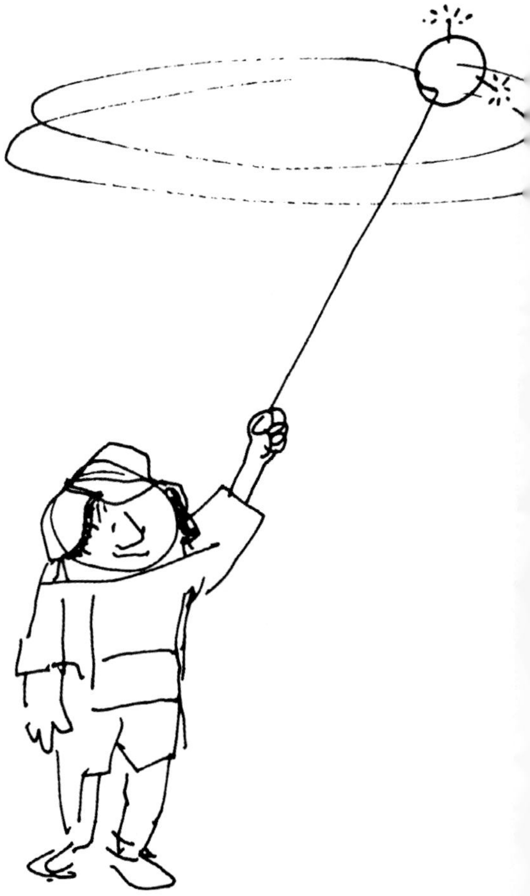

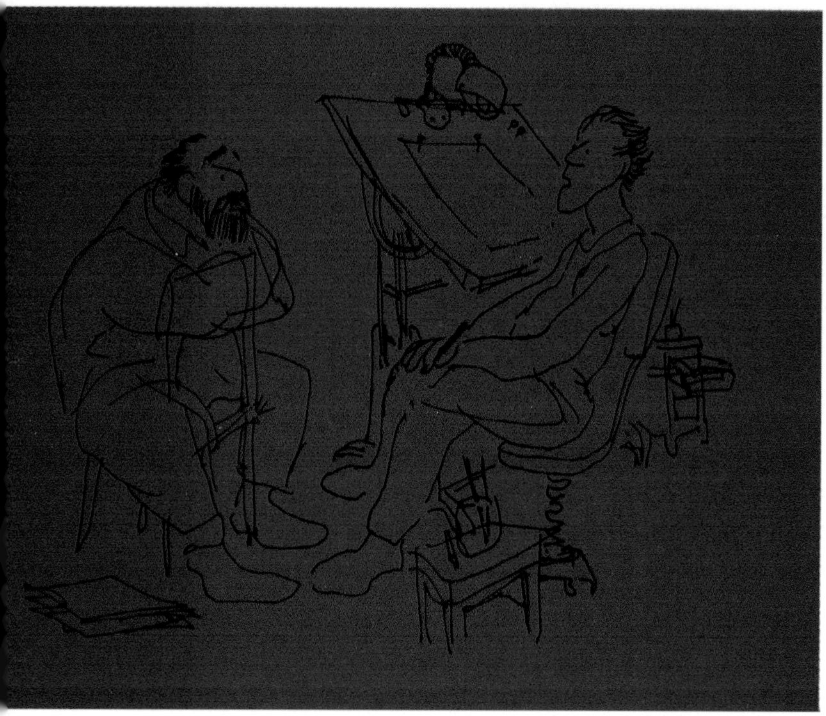

"We Russian cartoonists have the same freedom as you Americans—you're allowed to criticize America in your cartoons, and we're allowed to criticize America in ours."

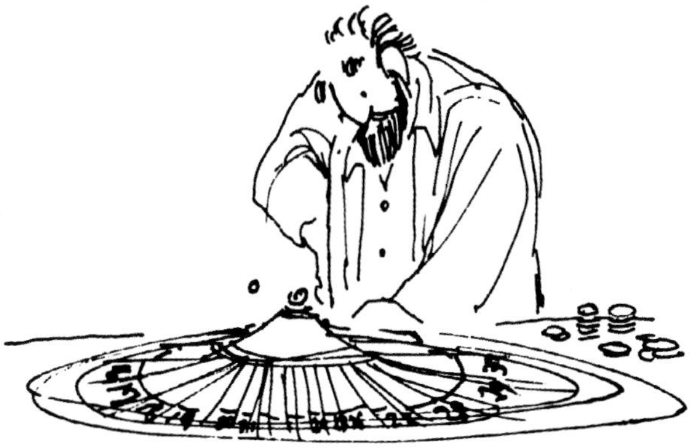

"What's so dangerous about this...?"

Wherever he goes, even to a Russian railroad station, Silverstein finds pretty girls.

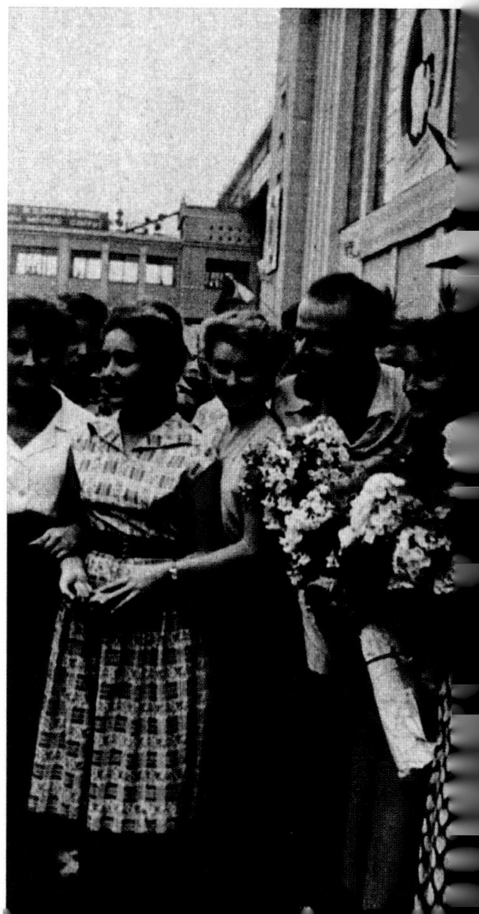

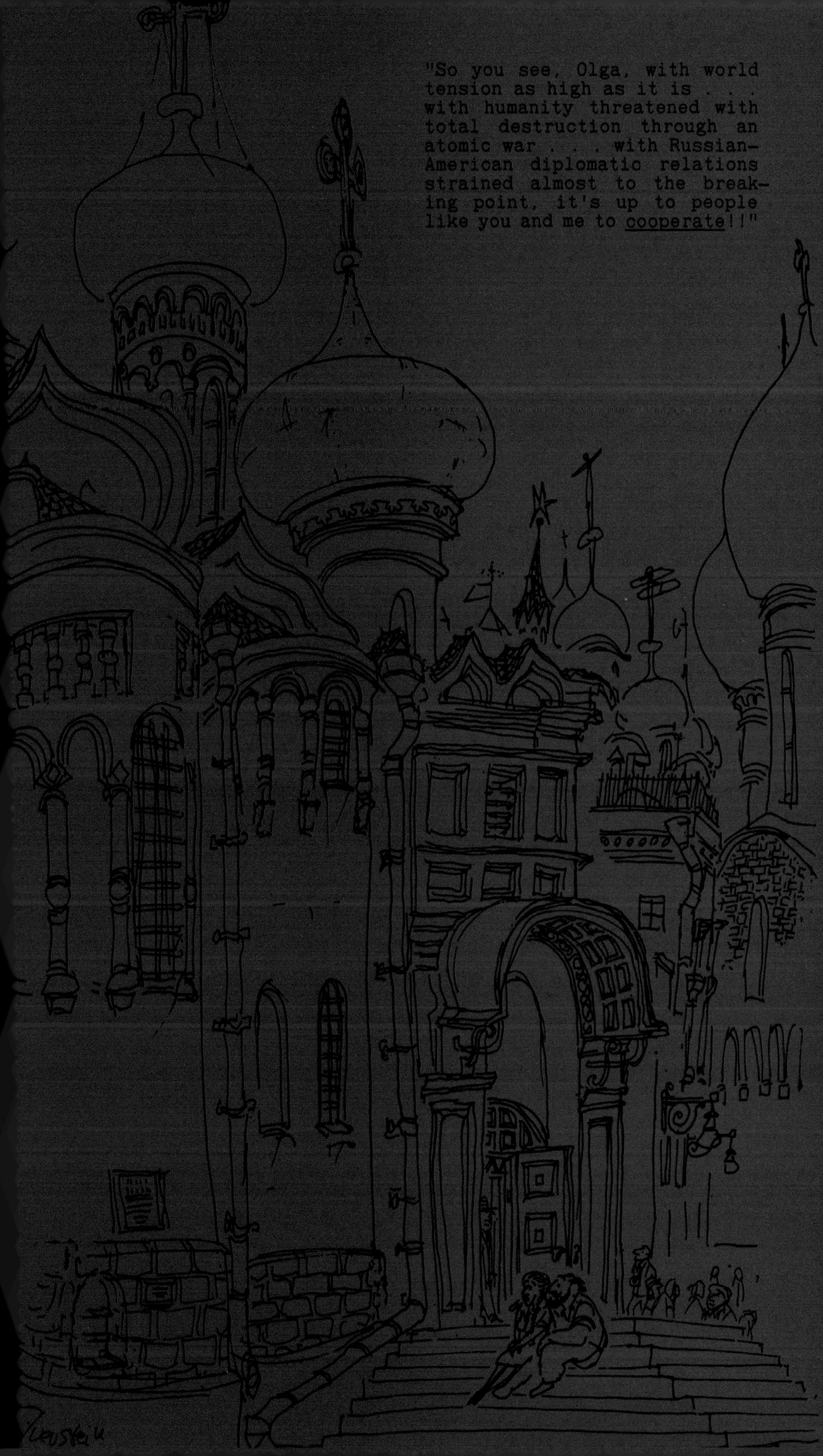

"So you see, Olga, with world tension as high as it is . . . with humanity threatened with total destruction through an atomic war . . . with Russian-American diplomatic relations strained almost to the breaking point, it's up to people like you and me to <u>cooperate</u>!!"

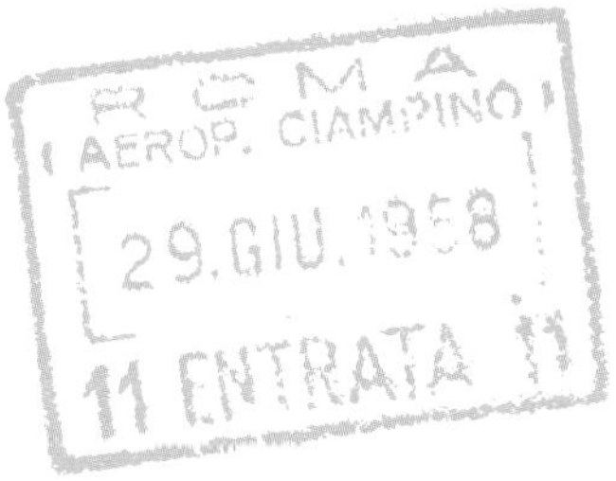
ROMA
AEROP. CIAMPINO
29.GIU.1958
11 ENTRATA 11

IN ITALY

JUNE 1958

pictorial

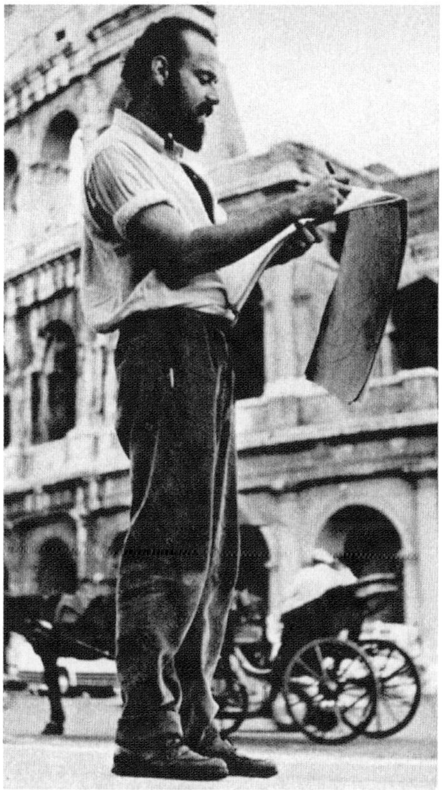

our boy capishes and finds it delicious

THE LAMBENT LAND of Italy is the home of mandolins and macaroni, olive oil and opera, gorgonzola and gondolas. Without it, there would be no Venetian glass, Florentine leather, Neapolitan ice cream or Roman fever. We of America are especially indebted to it: Cristoforo Colombo discovered us and Amerigo Vespucci lent us his name. We have a town called Italy, three called Rome, five each called Naples, Venice and Verona, and we also have an airfield called La Guardia. Our language is studded with snappy words on lend-lease from Italy: *tempo, fiasco, piano, umbrella, stucco, fresco, ditto, volcano, casino, bordello, incognito, quota, soda, stanza, vista, vendetta, manifesto, motto* and *mah-rone!* And what do we call that leaning-tower-type type in which the foregoing string of words is printed? Italic. The Boot meets The Beard this month as the fine Italian hand of Shel Silverstein — PLAYBOY's ambulating americano — sketches sunny Italy.

SILVERSTEIN IN ITALY

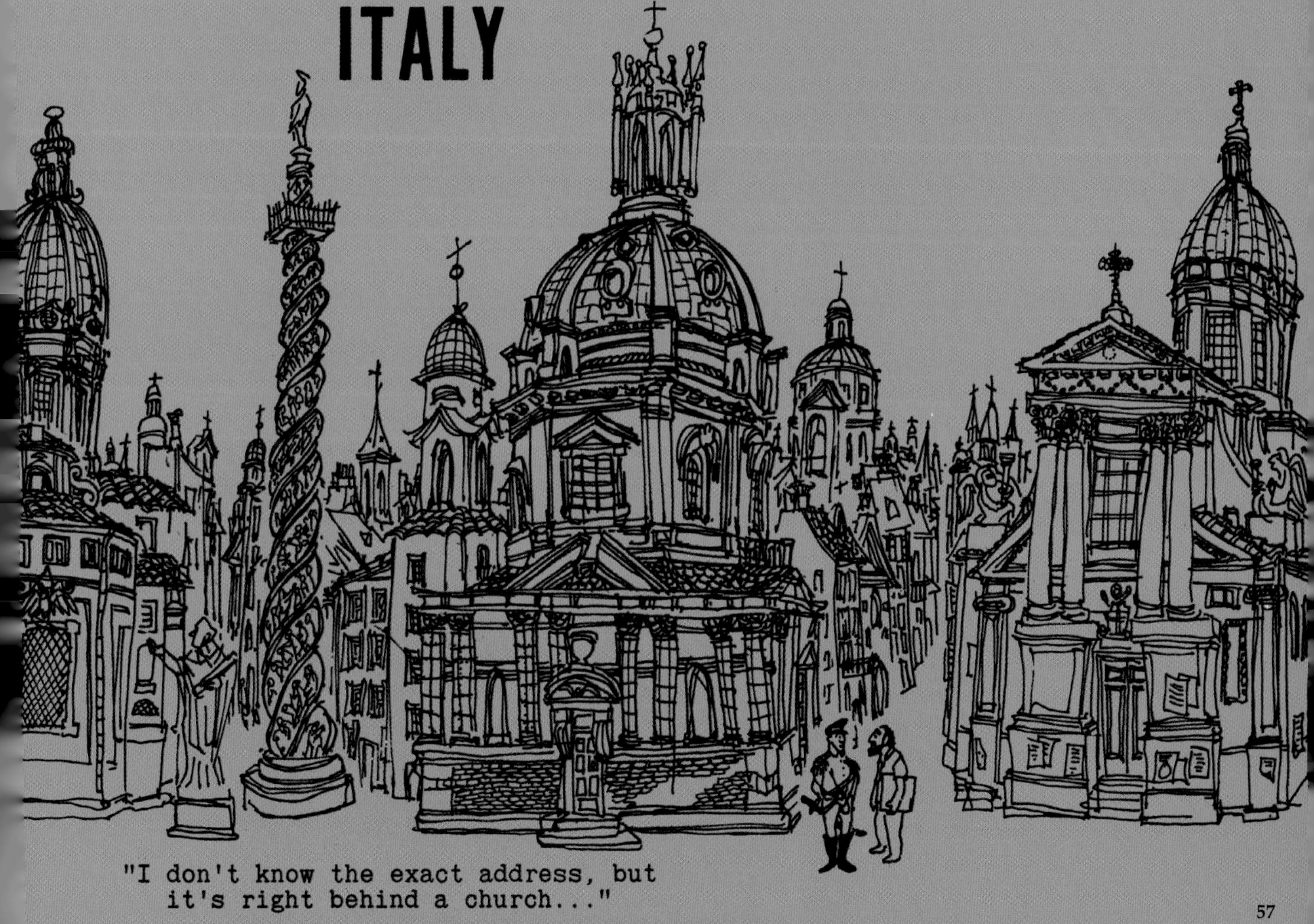

"I don't know the exact address, but it's right behind a church..."

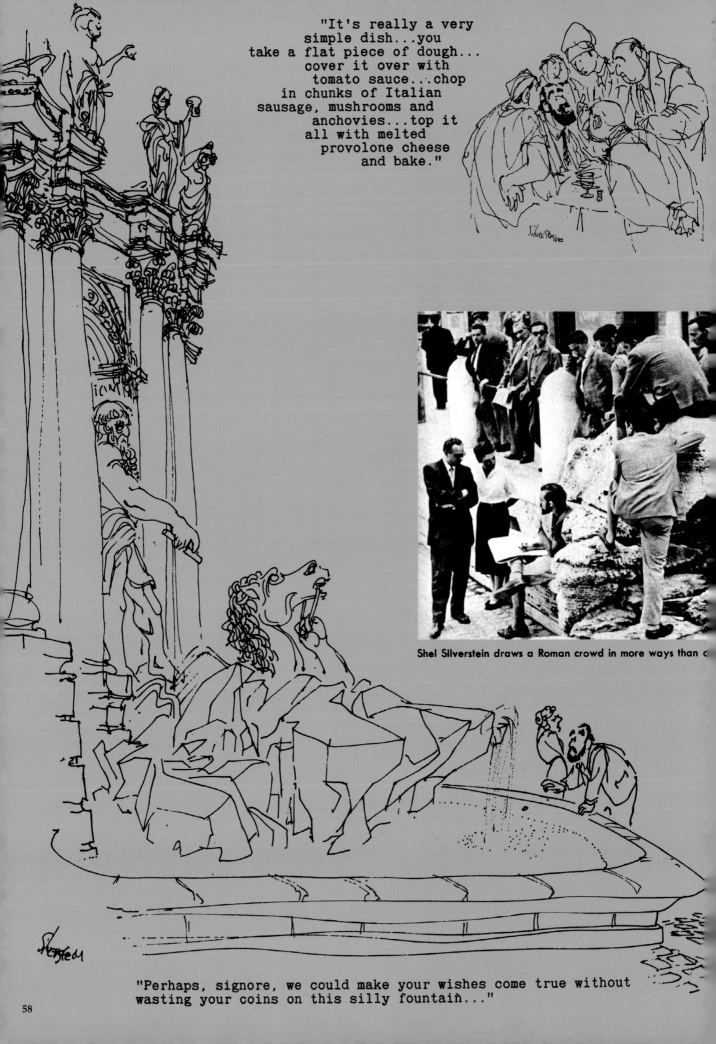

"It's really a very simple dish...you take a flat piece of dough... cover it over with tomato sauce...chop in chunks of Italian sausage, mushrooms and anchovies...top it all with melted provolone cheese and bake."

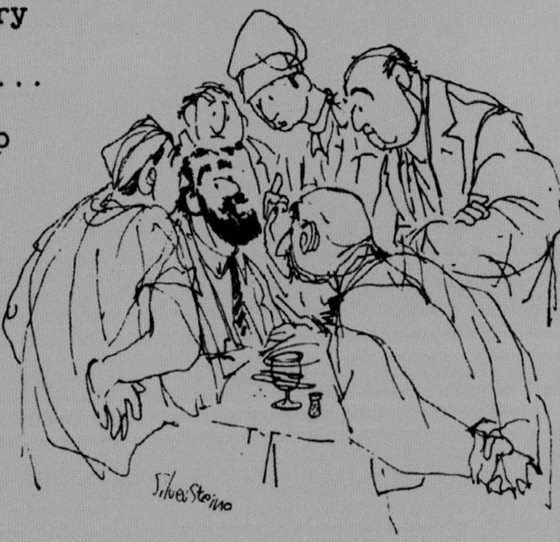

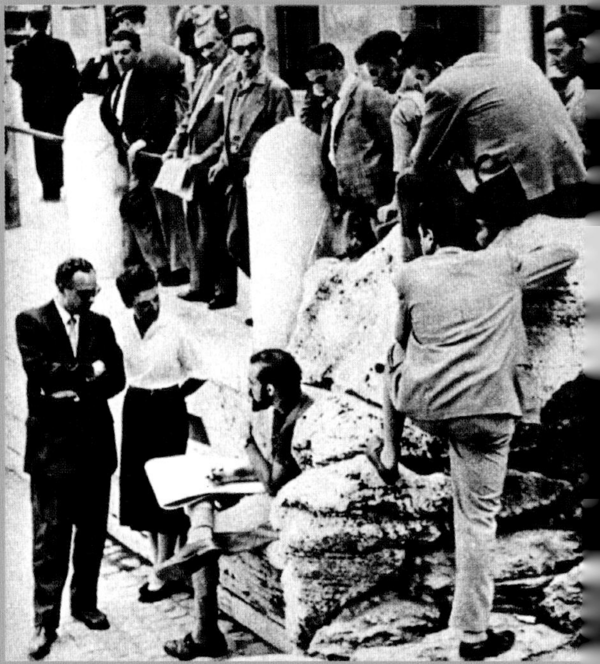

Shel Silverstein draws a Roman crowd in more ways than o

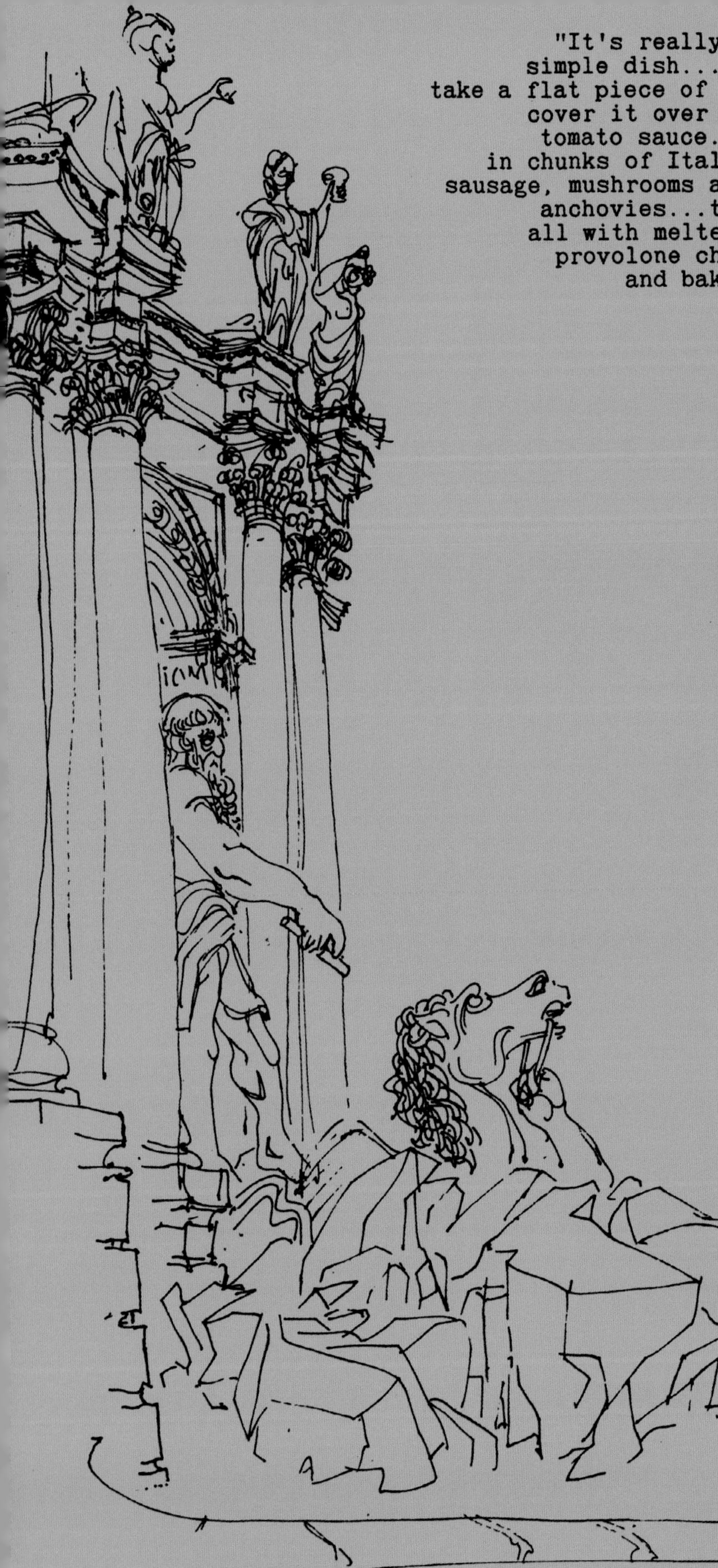

"Perhaps, signore, we could make your wishes come true without wasting your coins on this silly fountain..."

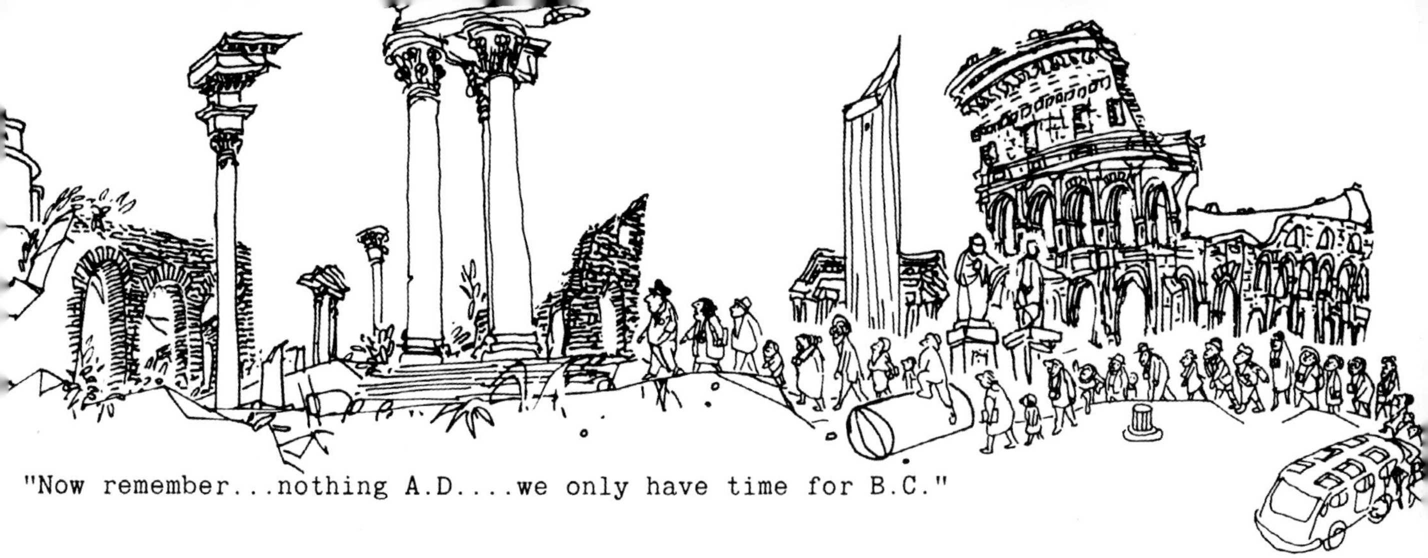

"Now remember...nothing A.D....we only have time for B.C."

"*Viva la pasta!*" says Shel as he shovels in the spaghetti.

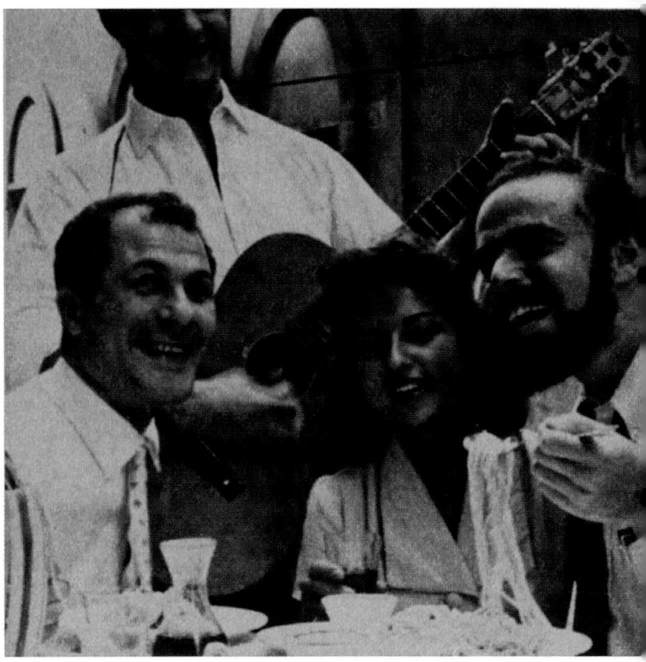

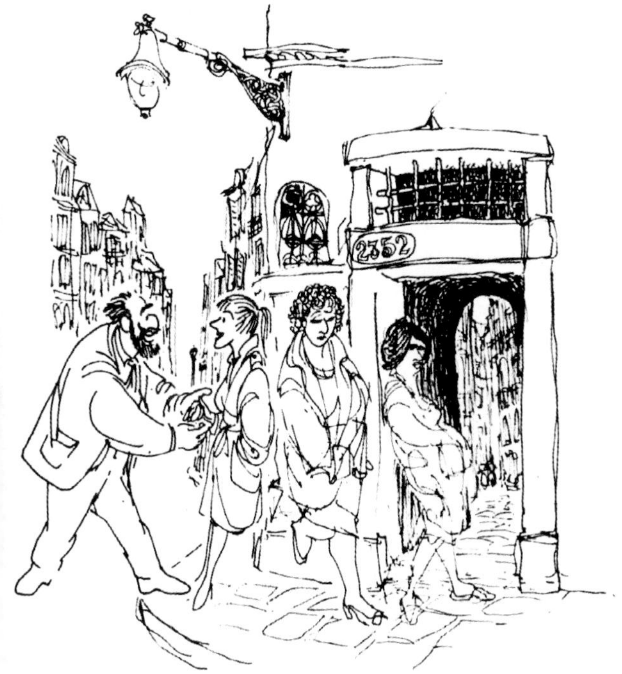

"Marge — Marge Wilson! Why, I haven't seen you since high school!"

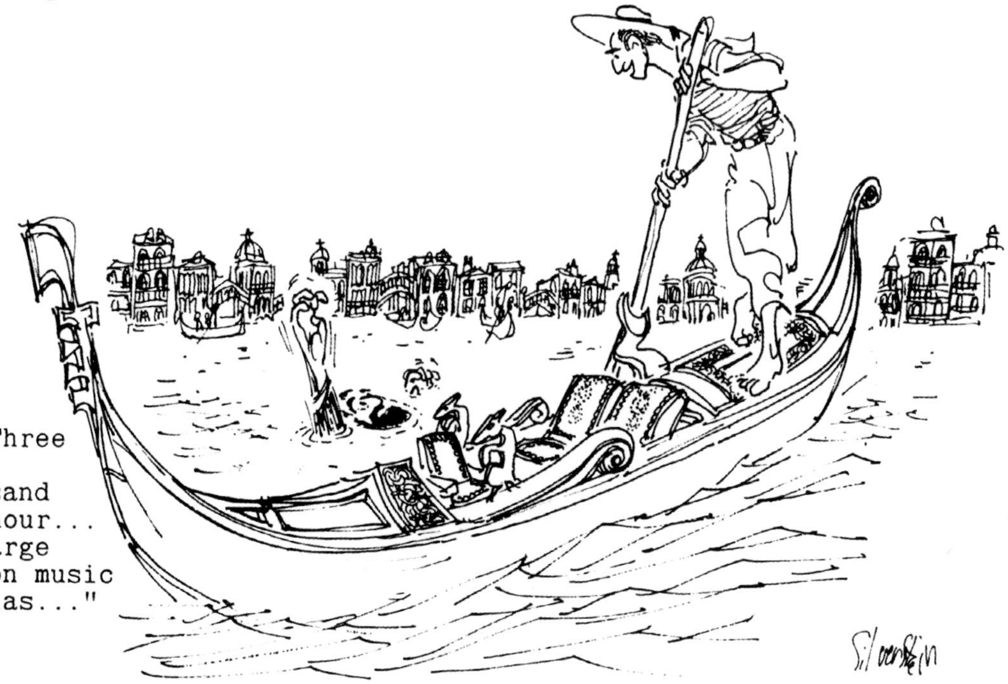

"Gondola, signore? Three
housand lire for the
first hour...two thousand
for each additional hour...
a small additional charge
if you wish accordion music
or romantic arias..."

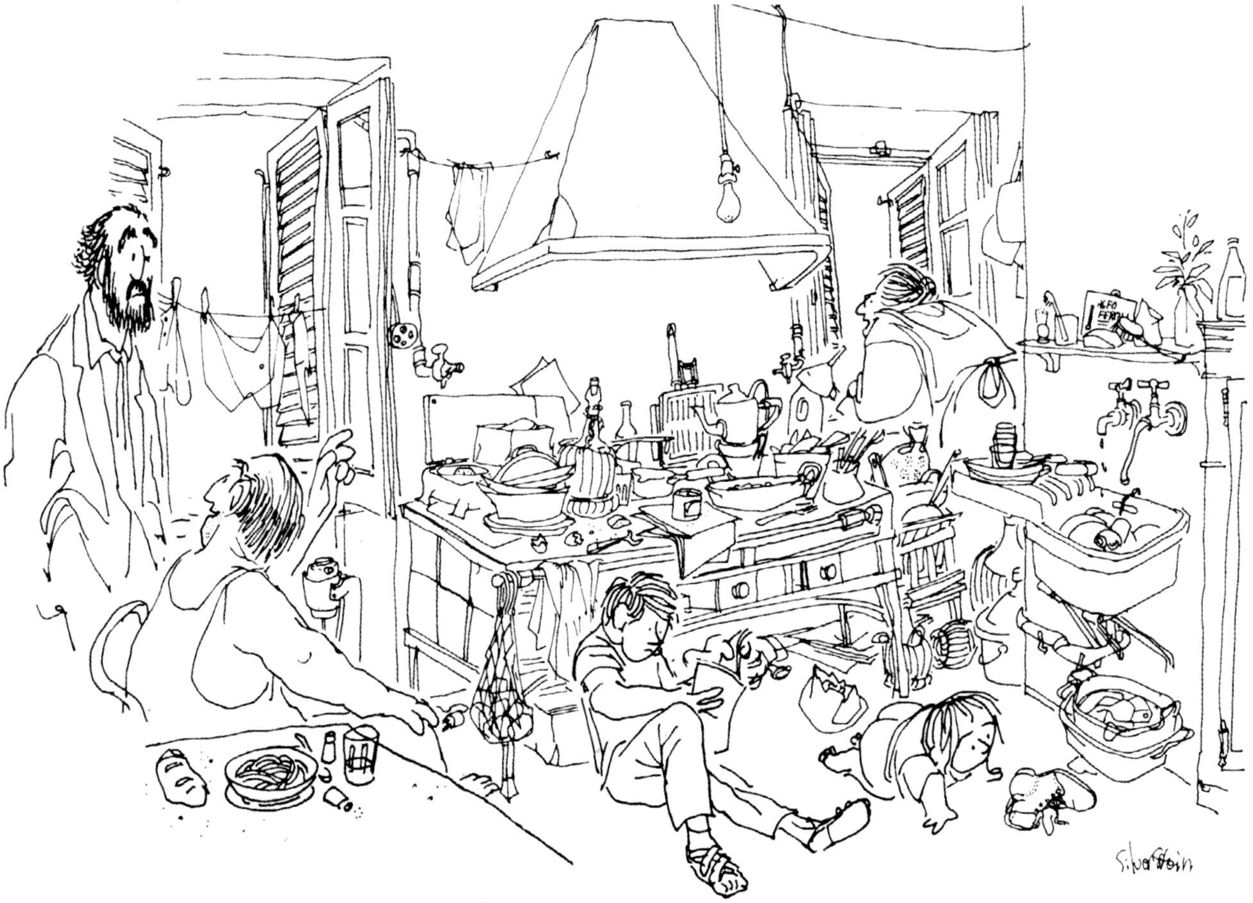

"...Most American tourists, they see nothing...they waste their time running through the ruins of the Forum, they take photographs of San Pietro, they throw coins into Trevi Fountain, they burrow into the catacombs, they whisk through the Colosseum and the Pantheon and the museums all the day and sit and drink and dance in the Via Veneto cabarets all night ...but <u>you</u>, signore, you are seeing the <u>real</u> Rome!!"

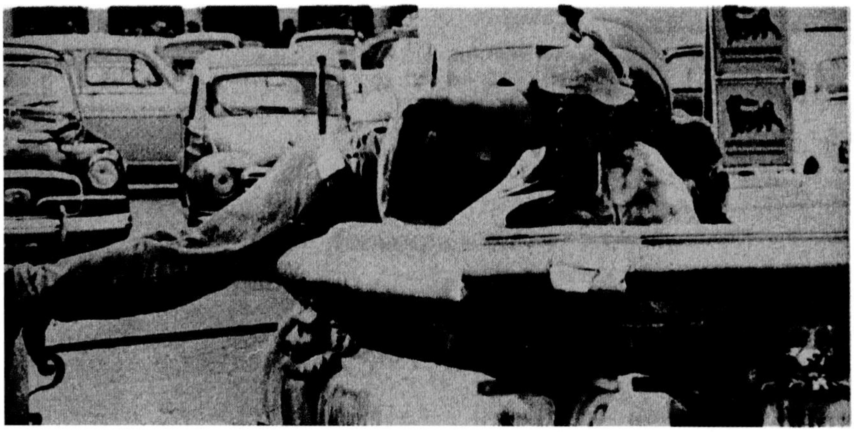

Amid the blaze of noon, Silverstein slakes the Silverstein thirst the hard way.

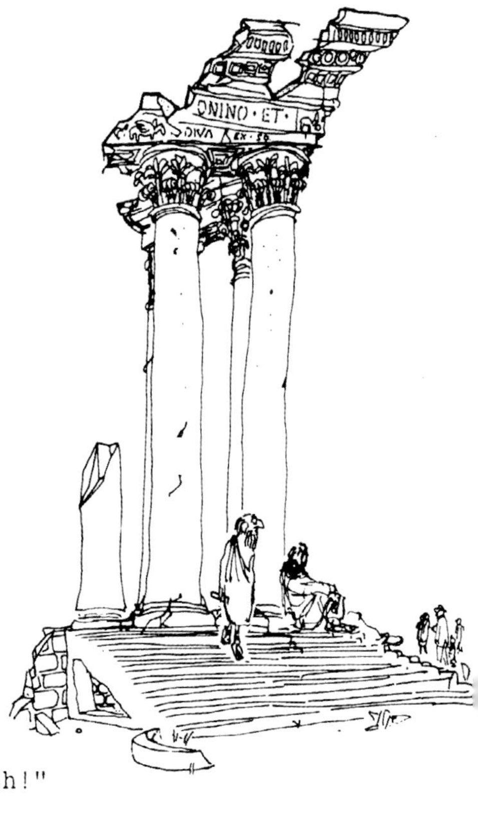

"Beware the ides of March!"

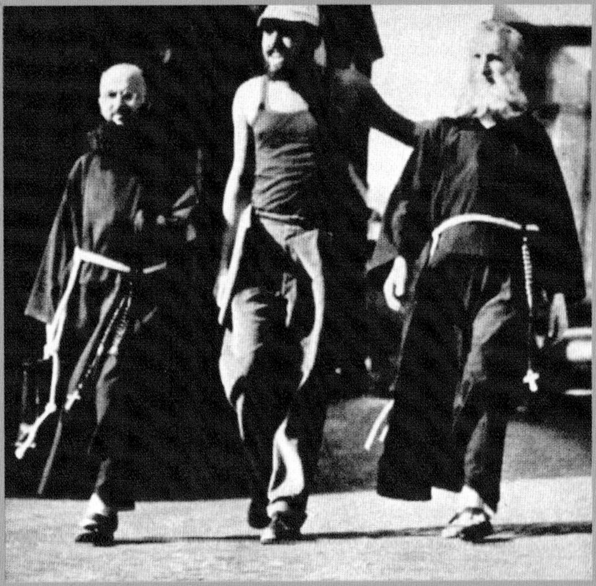

Beards billowing in the breeze, a picturesque trio takes a stroll.

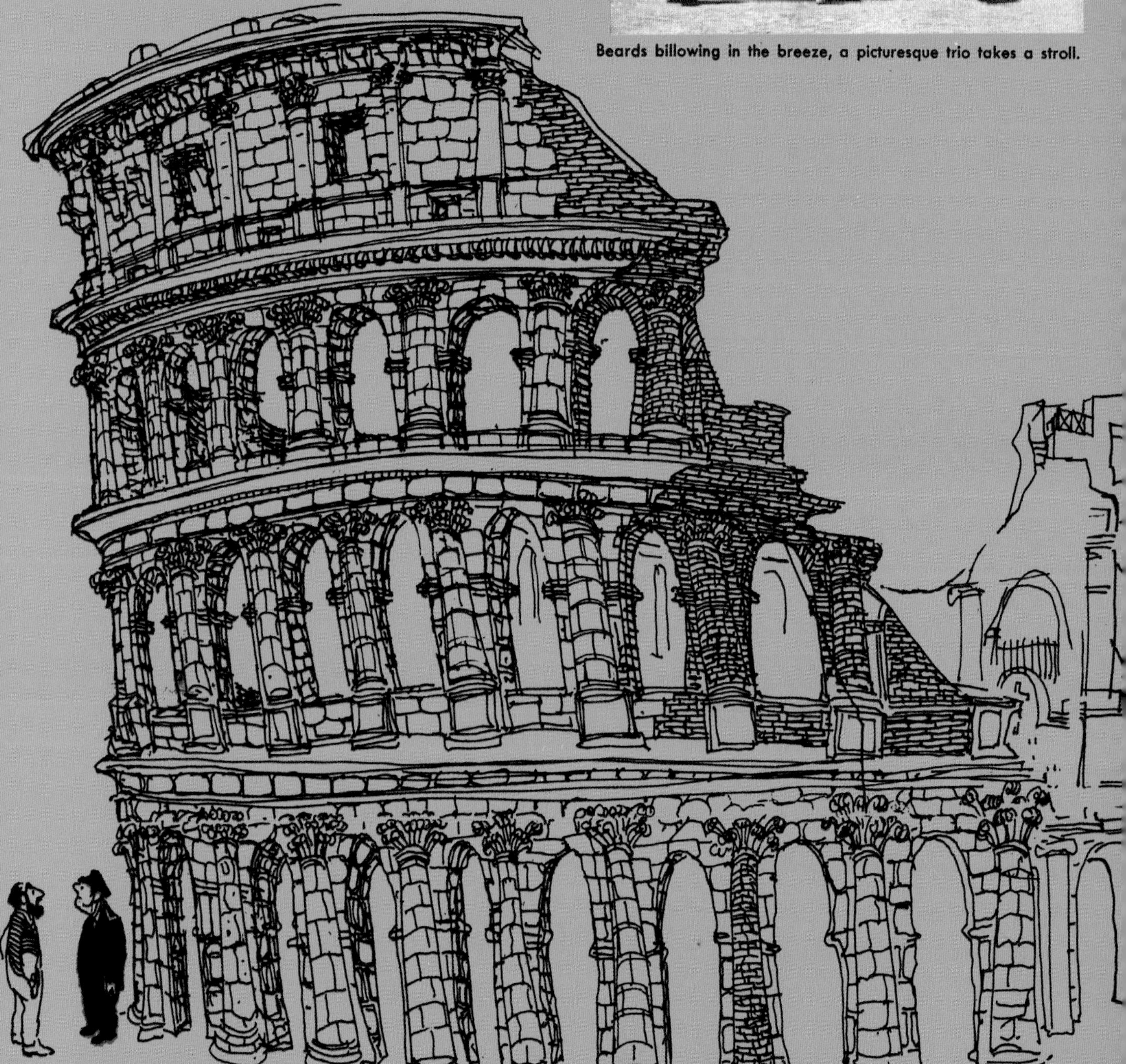

"Show over?"

IN SWITZERLAND

NOVEMBER 1958

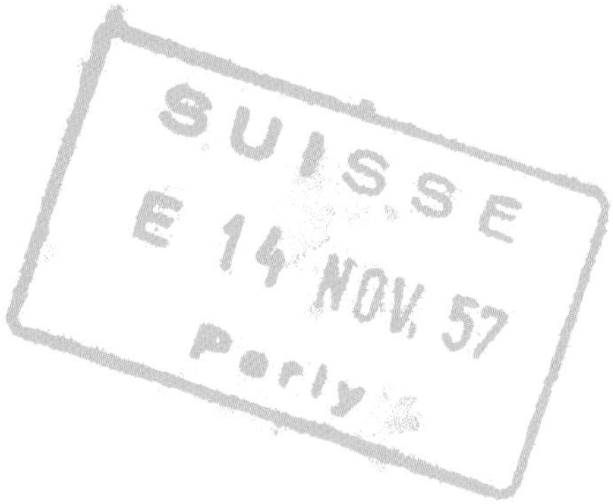
SUISSE
E 14 NOV. 57
Perly

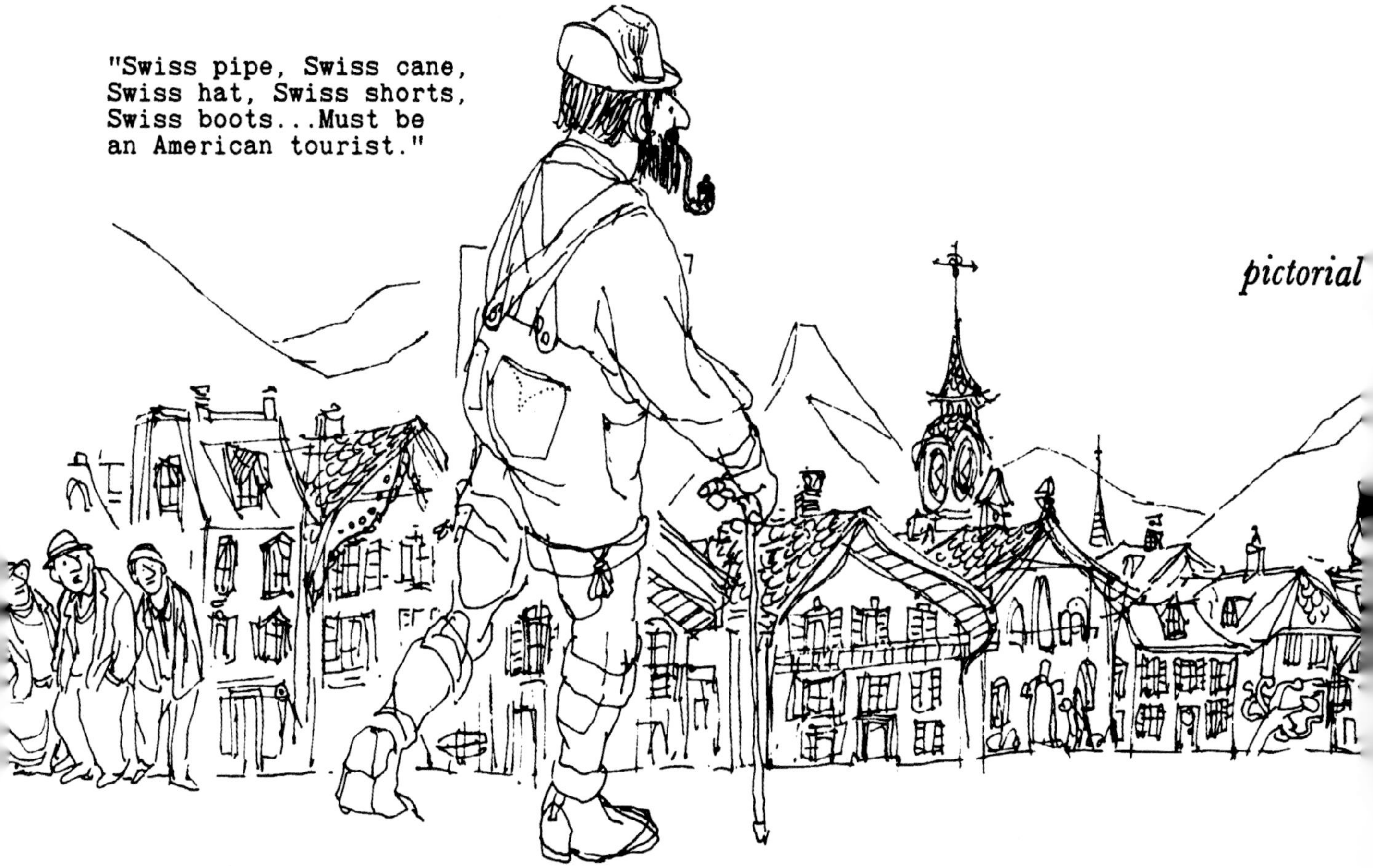
"Swiss pipe, Swiss cane, Swiss hat, Swiss shorts, Swiss boots...Must be an American tourist."

pictorial

SILVERSTEIN IN SWITZERLAND

our roistering roamer digs the land of ventilated cheese

HANNIBAL needed a whole menagerie of elephants, horses, donkeys and leopards-with-spears-attached to get him over the Alps, but Shel Silverstein needed only his sketchbook, his pencil, his beard and his lively curiosity. Entering Switzerland, Shel got right into the spirit of things (as he always does)—donning the required sweater, *Lederhosen* and pointy, shaving-brushed hat; investigating the cuckoo clock situation; checking out the native quail; venturing a scratchy yodel and blowing hot bells with a combo of Swiss bell-ringers. He also found time to sketch his own highly personal impressions of Switzerland for PLAYBOY.

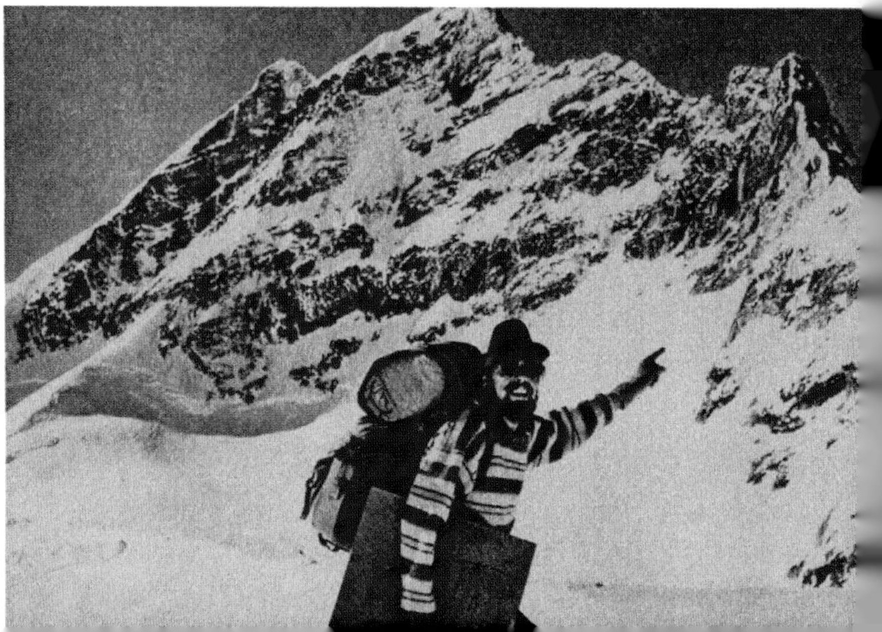

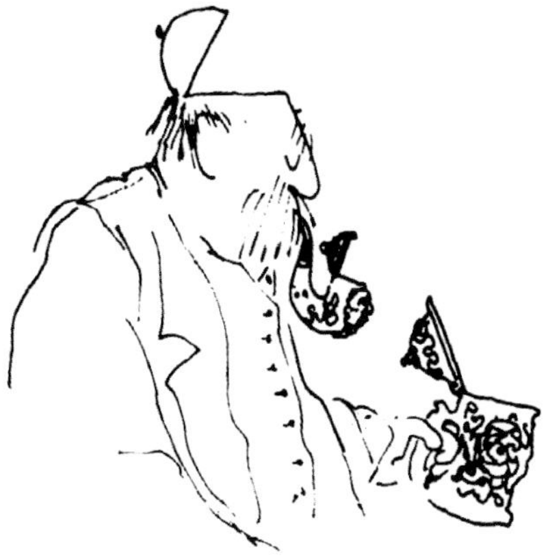

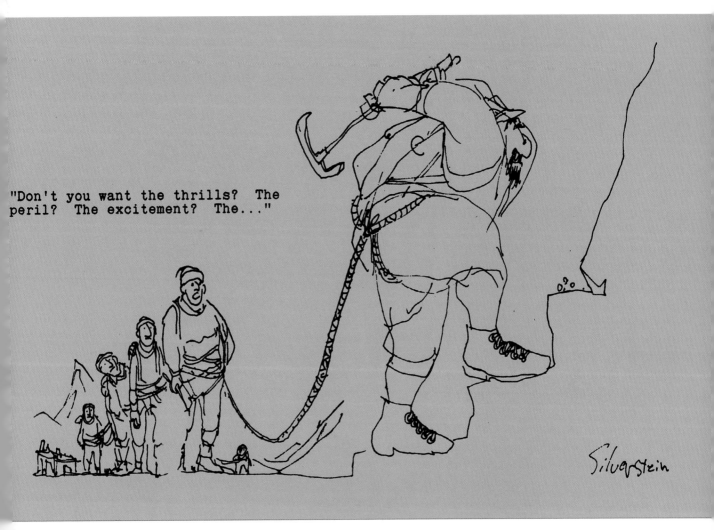

"Don't you want the thrills? The peril? The excitement? The..."

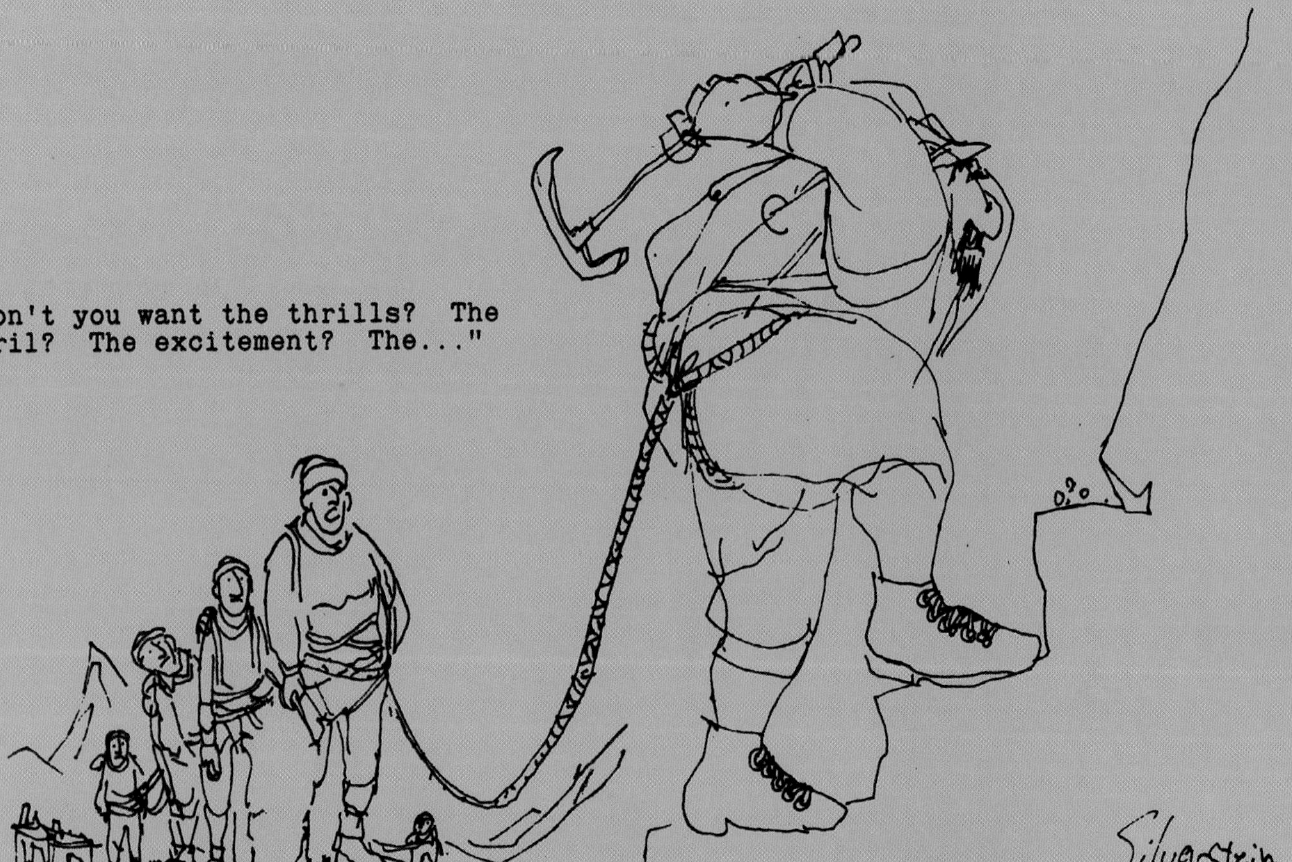
Silverstein

"Well, I've tasted better brandy..."

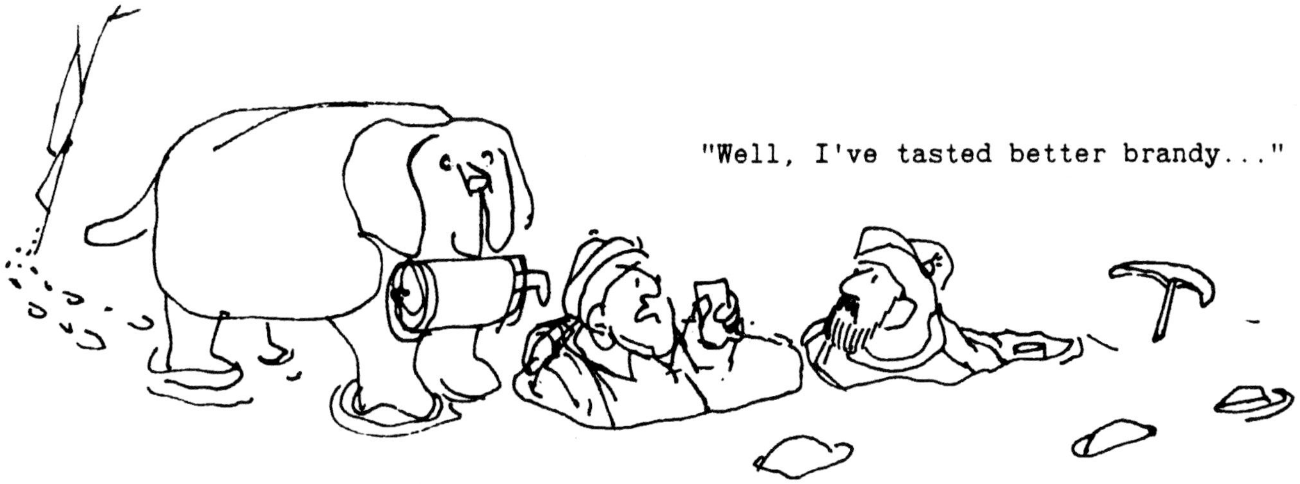

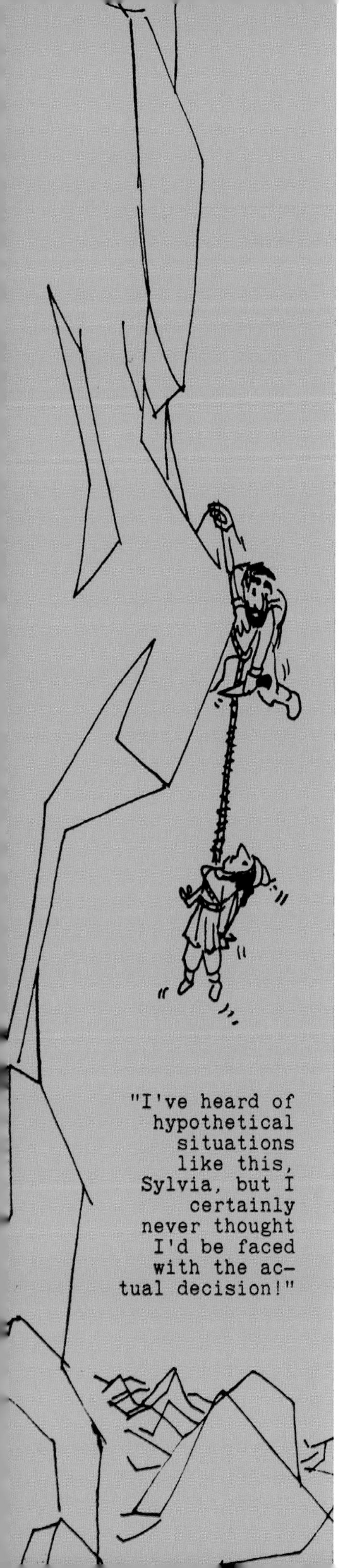

"I've heard of hypothetical situations like this, Sylvia, but I certainly never thought I'd be faced with the actual decision!"

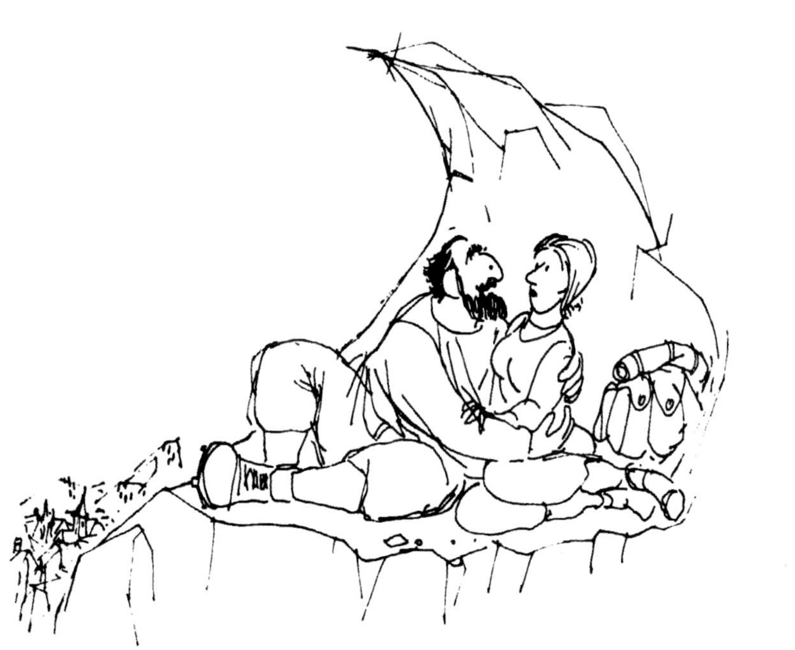

"You realize of course, Miss Gruber, that the slightest noise on your part could send thousands of tons of snow and ice avalanching down...crushing us to an agonizing, suffocating end...and bringing death and destruction to the innocent people of that picturesque village below..."

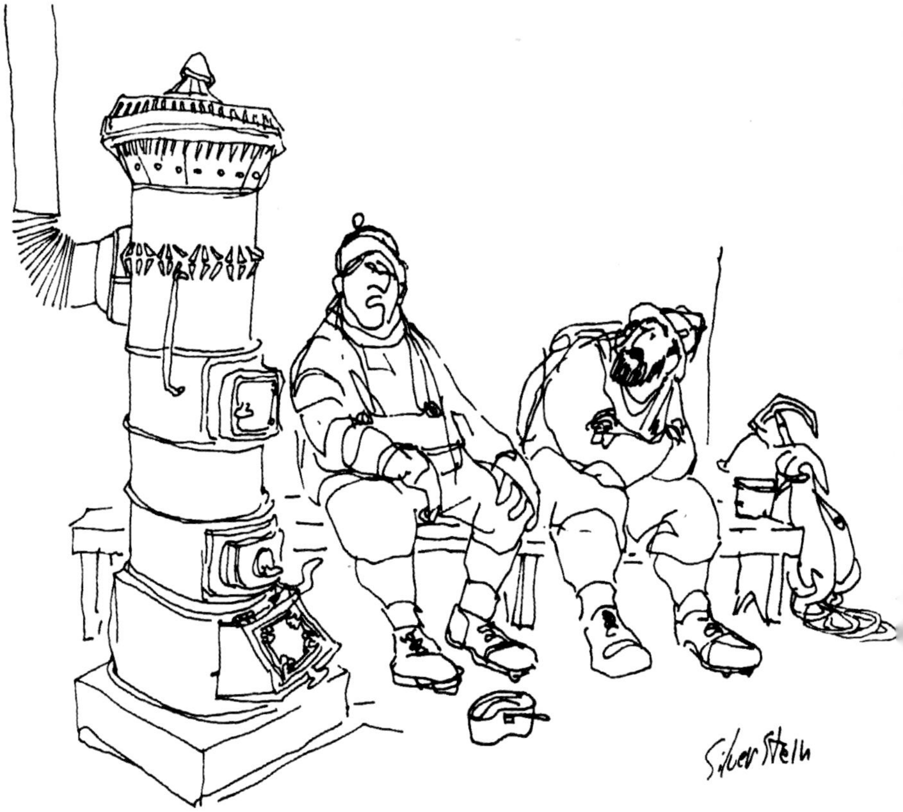

"Yes, sir, give me a mountain any time. You conquer a mountain and it <u>stays</u> conquered! Does a mountain ever keep you waiting for hours? No! Does a mountain ever lie to you or try to squeeze money out of you? No! Does a mountain ever leave a lot of dirty lingerie cluttering up the bathroom? No! Does a mountain ever go off cheating on you the minute your back is turned? Does a mountain ever run off with some shoe salesman from Detroit, Michigan? <u>Hell, no!!</u>

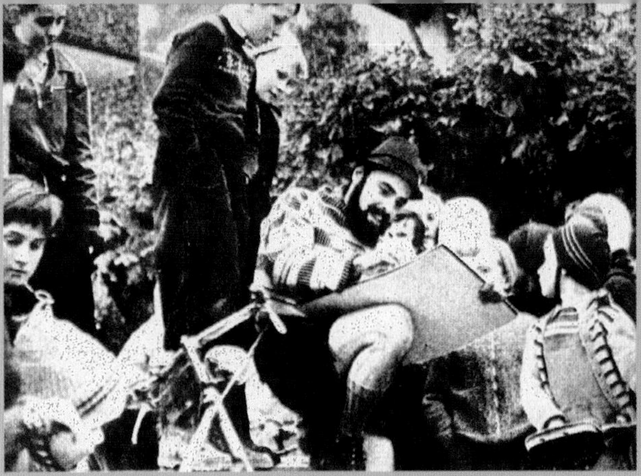

Non-shaver Shel sketches for a crowd of little shavers.

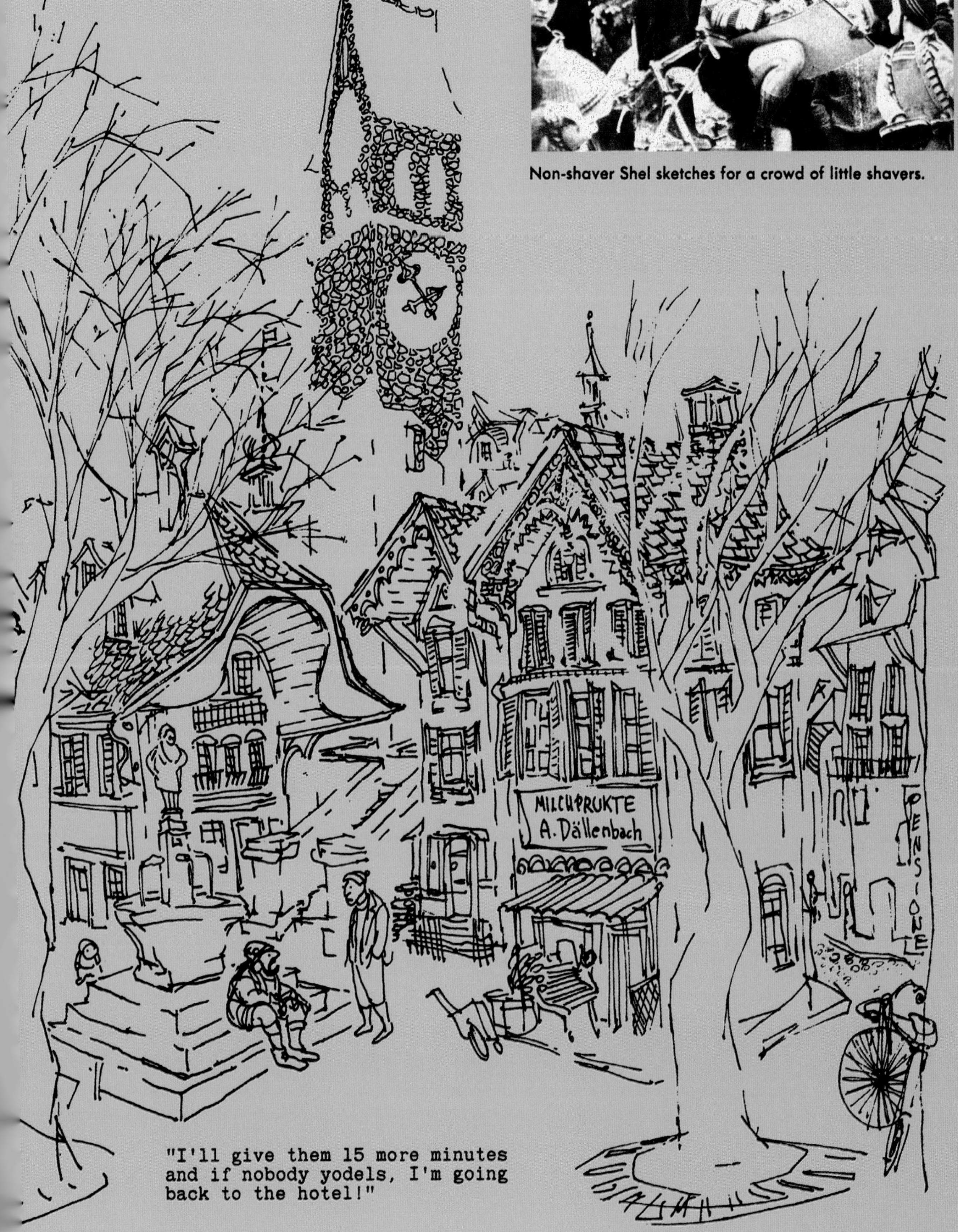
MILCHPRUKTE
A. Dällenbach
PENSIONE

"I'll give them 15 more minutes and if nobody yodels, I'm going back to the hotel!"

IN SPAIN

MARCH 1959 | APRIL 1959

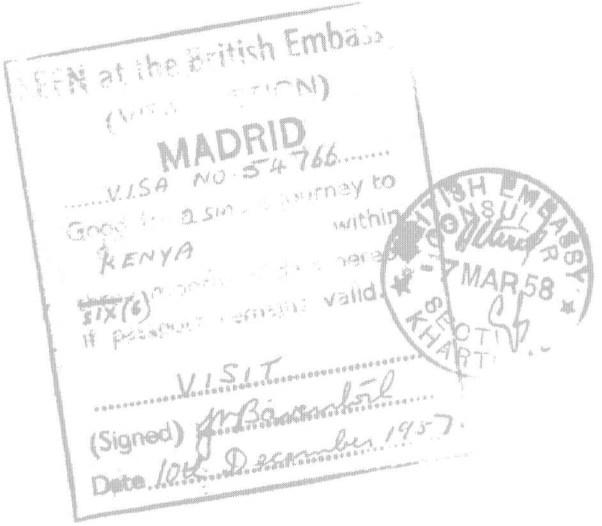
at the British Embass
MADRID
VISA NO 54766
journey to
within
KENYA
valid
VISIT
(Signed)
Date
BRITISH EMBASSY
CONSULAR
MAR 58
KHART

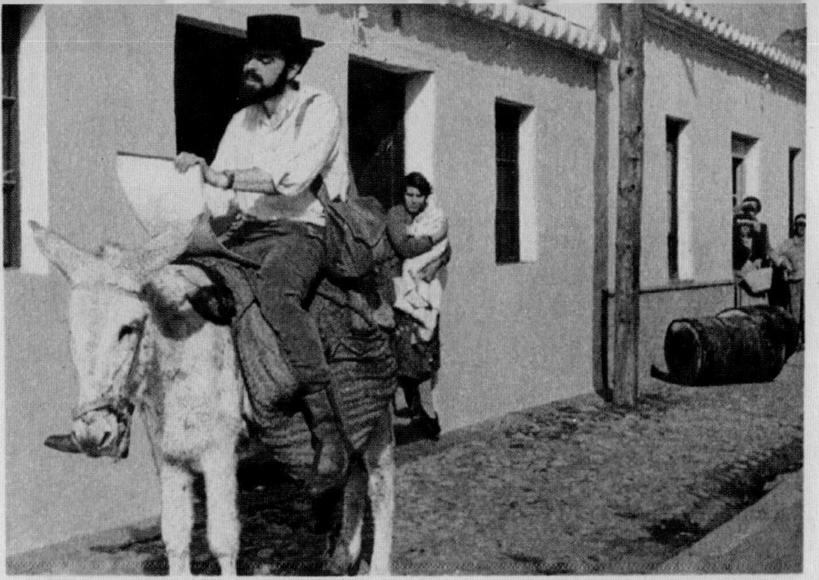

SILVERSTEIN IN SPAIN

THE RAIN IN SPAIN was mainly on the wane while Silverstein was there—for in addition to the well-known Hispanic sun, there was Shel's own private stock of sunshine which he never fails to sneak past Customs wherever he goes.

In Spain, he visited the tradition-rich towns of Madrid, Seville and Granada. In true Silverstein style, he plunged heart, soul and beard into several old Spanish customs. He donned native attire, danced the flamenco, clicked castanets, rode a burro, drank out of wineskins, ate fried bananas, garlic soup and *paella*; he even fought a bull. "Ava Gardner was there at the same time," Shel confided to us. "We never met."

shel sketches the siesta set: the first of a two-part portfolio

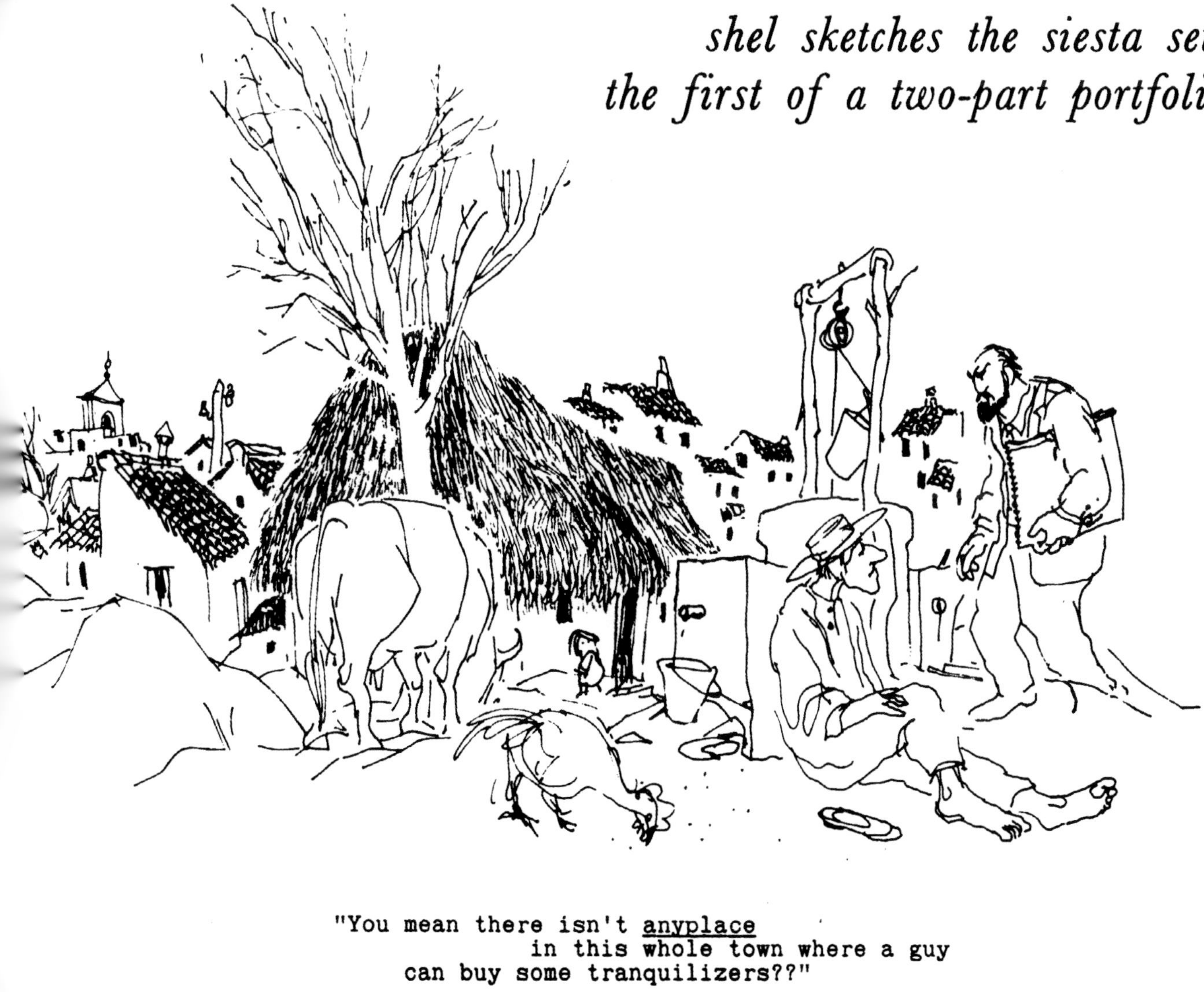

"You mean there isn't <u>anyplace</u> in this whole town where a guy can buy some tranquilizers??"

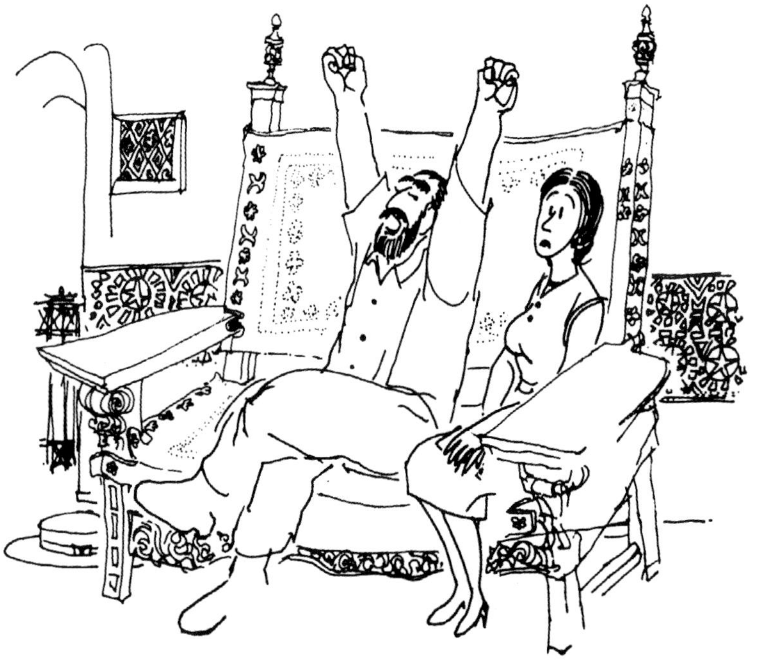

"Well ... one o'clock ... time for the old siesta ..."

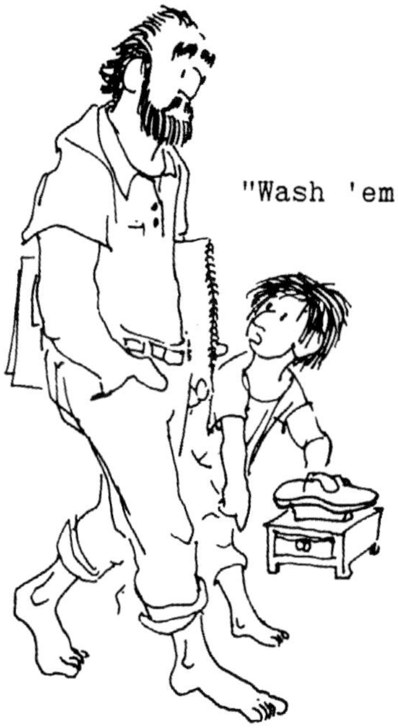

"Wash 'em up?"

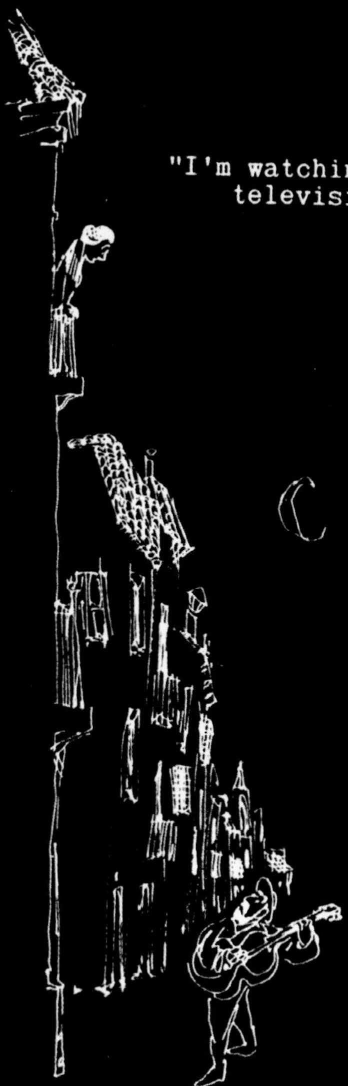

"I'm watching
television..."

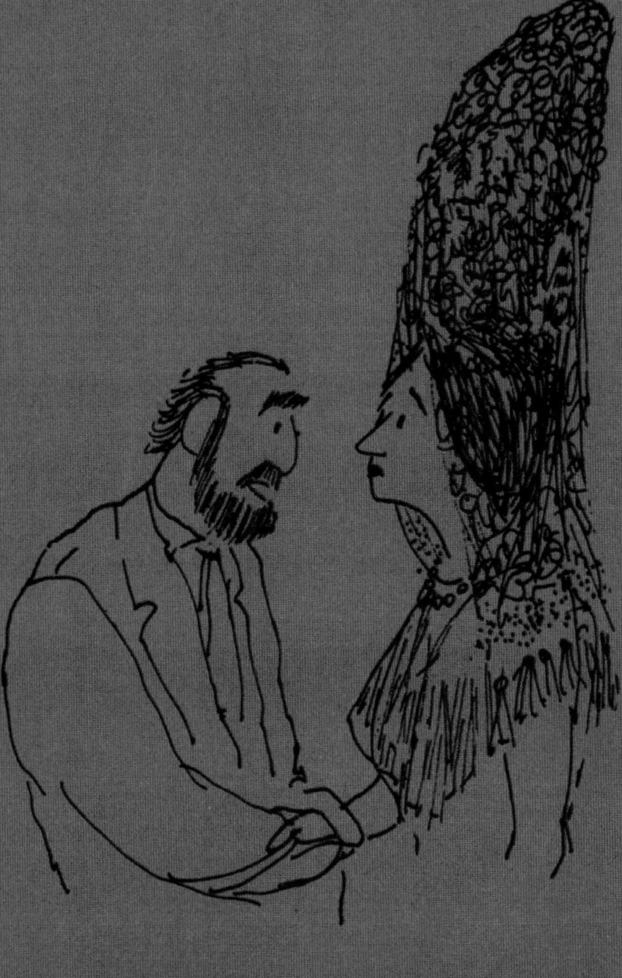

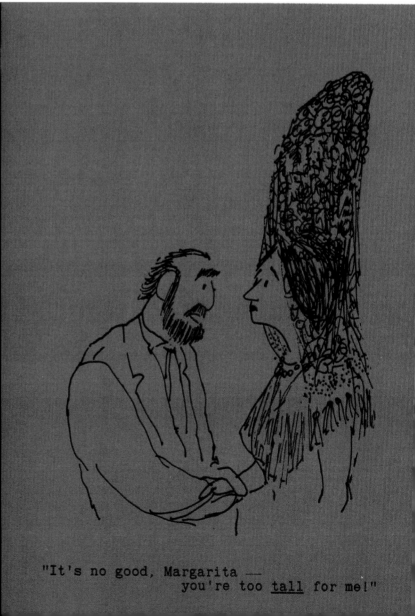

"It's no good, Margarita —
you're too <u>tall</u> for me!"

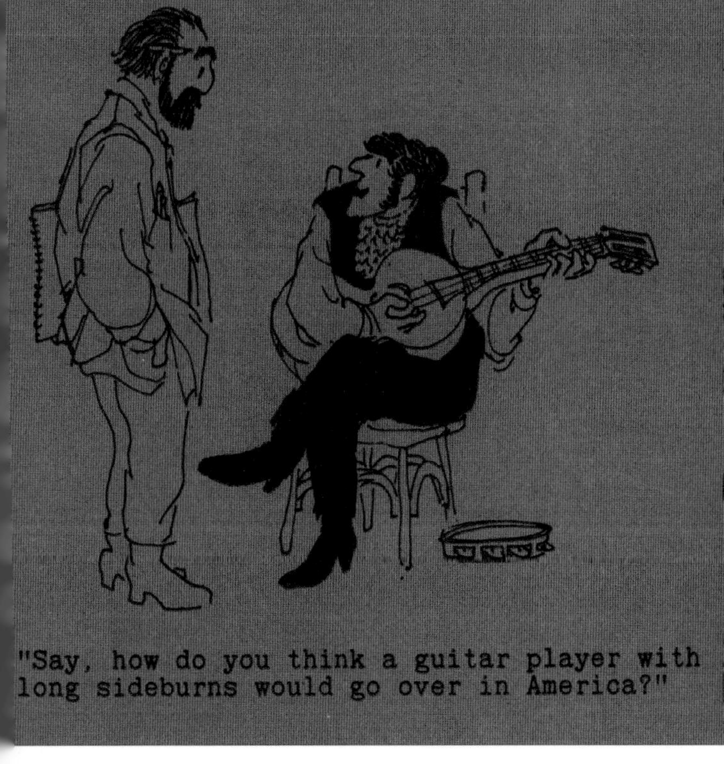

"Say, how do you think a guitar player with long sideburns would go over in America?"

In an inn of legended Granada, Shel dances the traditional flamenco with a group of high-spirited gypsies. Wherever he roams, Silverstein trips the local fantastic, sings local songs.

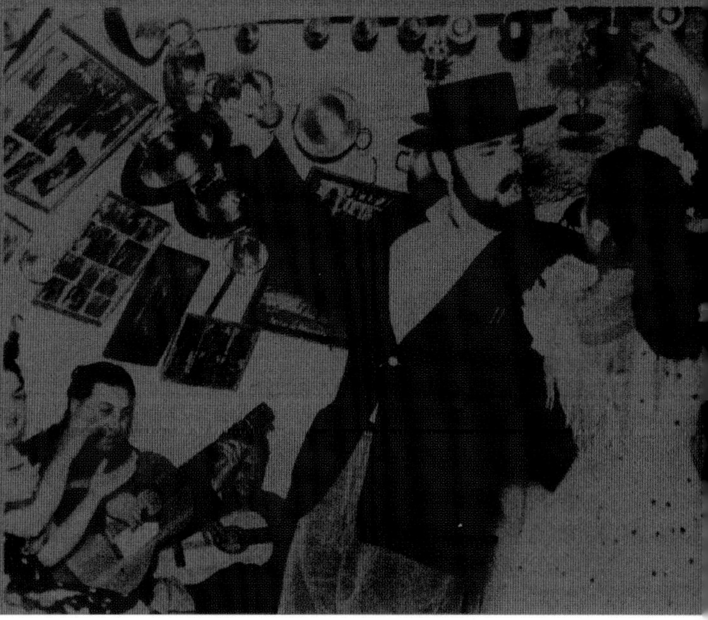

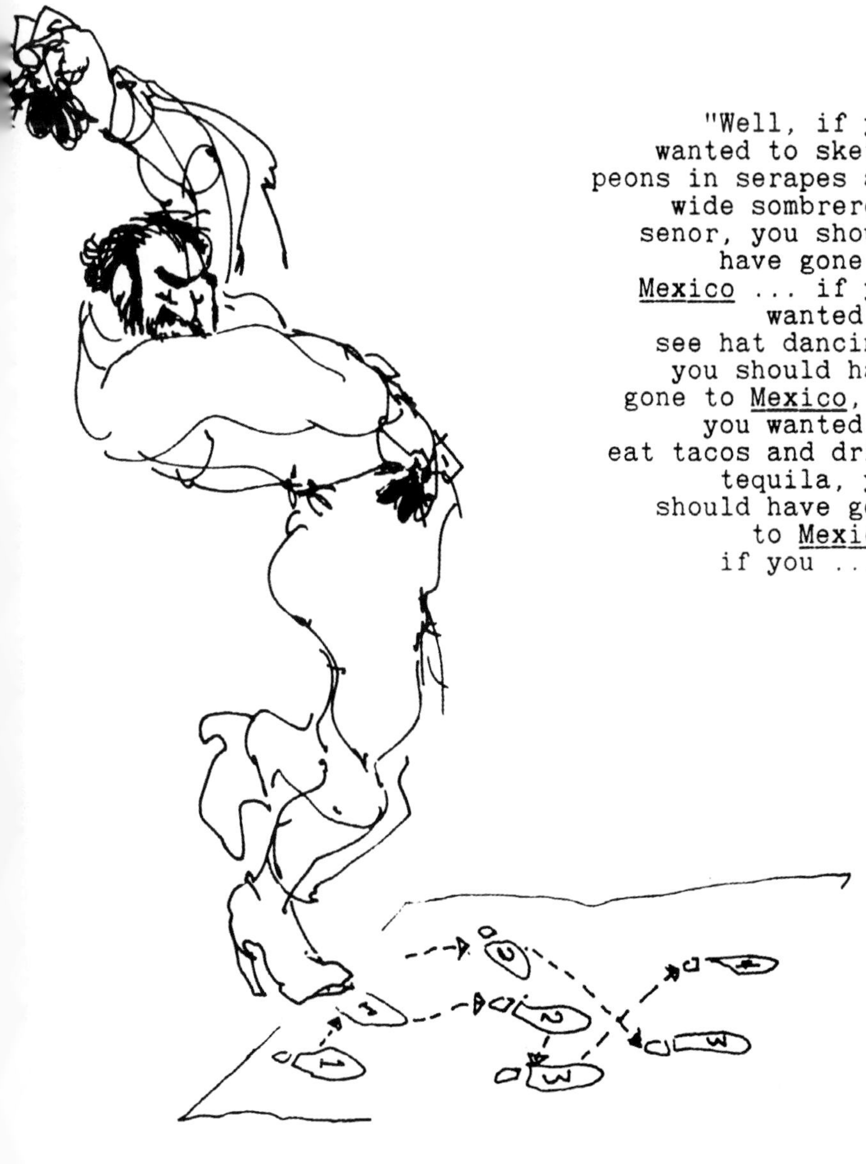

1
2
3

"Well, if you wanted to sketch peons in serapes and wide sombreros, senor, you should have gone to Mexico ... if you wanted to see hat dancing, you should have gone to Mexico, if you wanted to eat tacos and drink tequila, you should have gone to Mexico, if you ... "

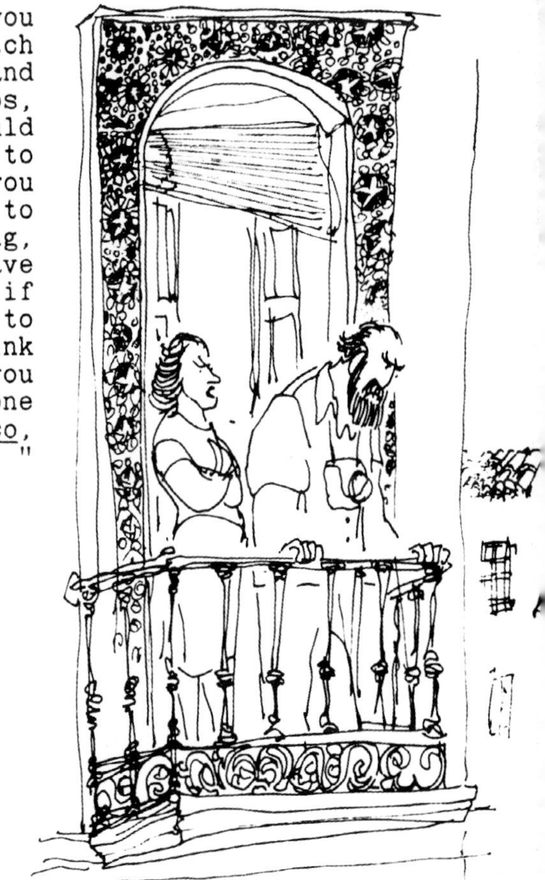

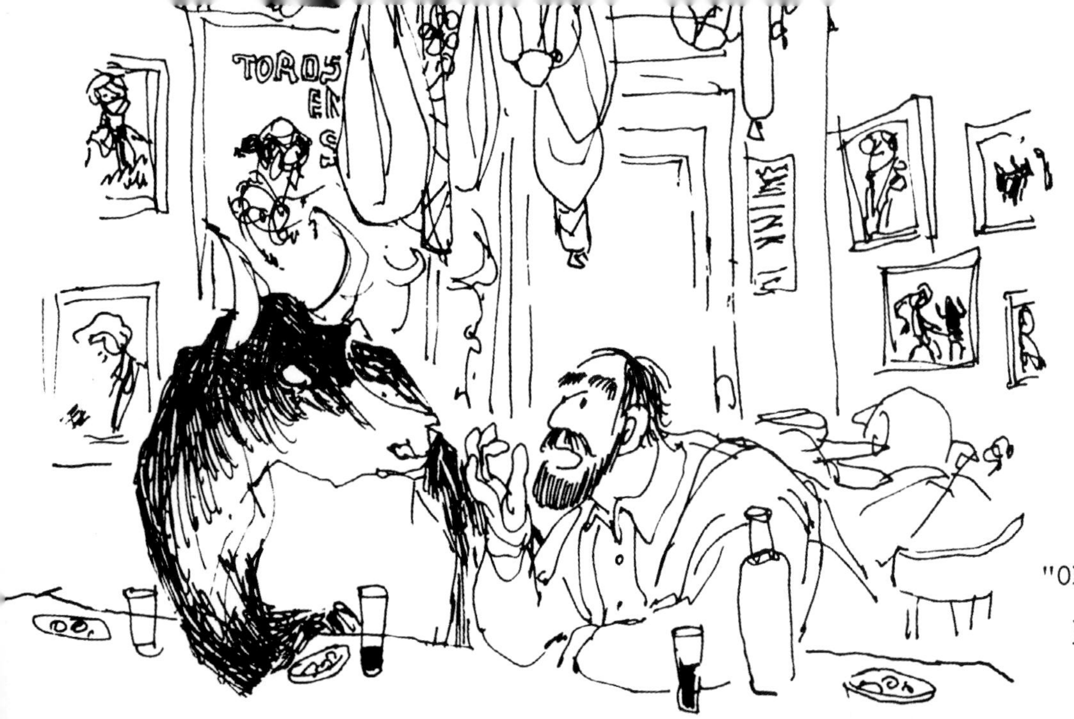
TOROS

"OK, but now let's look at it from the bullfighter's point of view! . . ."

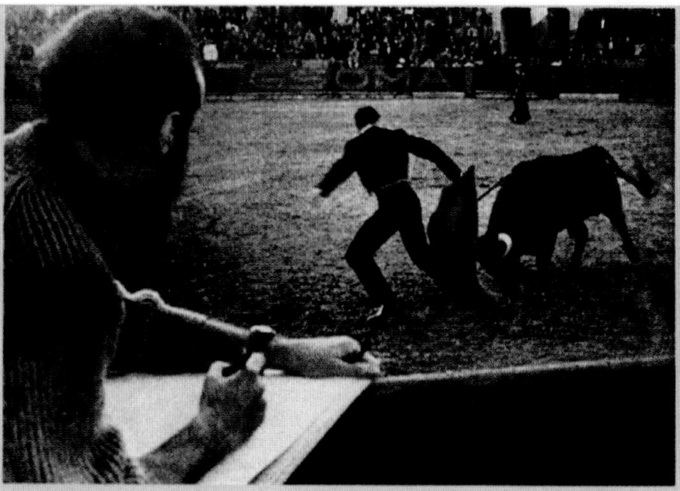

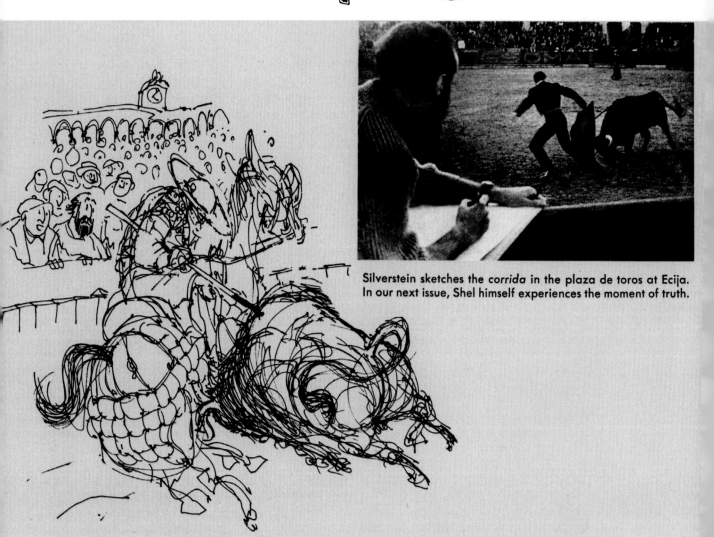

Silverstein sketches the *corrida* in the plaza de toros at Ecija. In our next issue, Shel himself experiences the moment of truth.

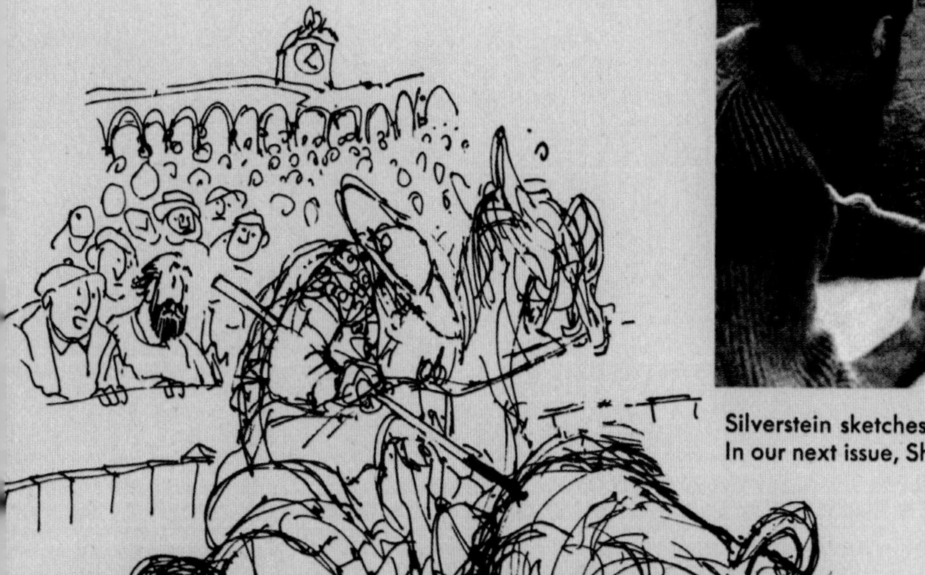

"That is the picador, senor. After the colored ribbons of the breeding ranch have been stuck into the bull, he drives his spike deep into the bull's neck — then the banderilleros plant their banderillas into his back, then the matador, after his muleta work, will drive his sword in over the horns — and the bull will fall, then the cachetero will stab the bull with his puntilla and will cut off his ears and tail ... then, senor, if you have a weak stomach I would advise you to leave at that moment, because then ... "

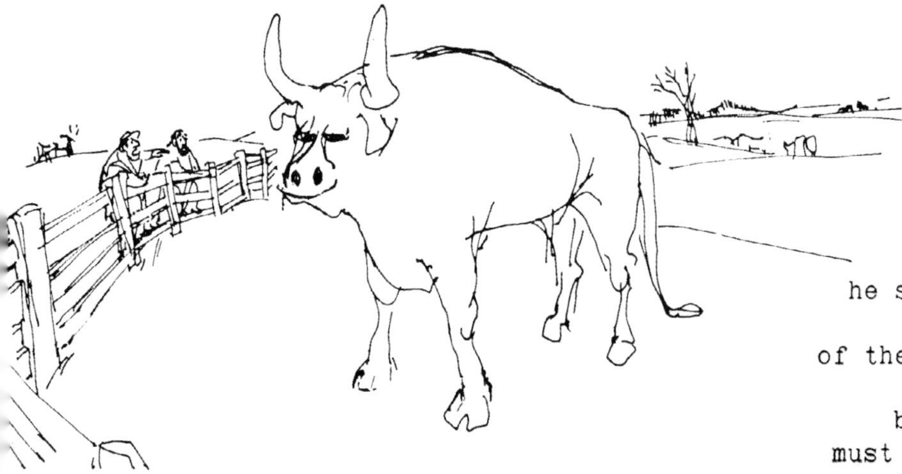

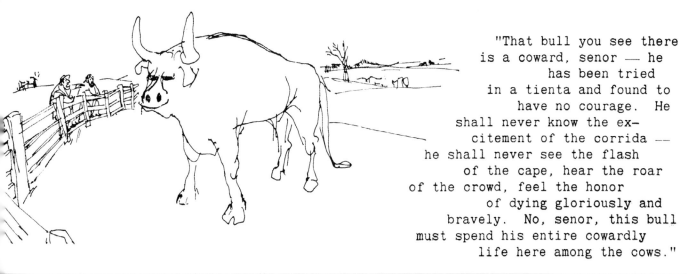

"That bull you see there is a coward, senor — he has been tried in a tienta and found to have no courage. He shall never know the excitement of the corrida — he shall never see the flash of the cape, hear the roar of the crowd, feel the honor of dying gloriously and bravely. No, senor, this bull must spend his entire cowardly life here among the cows."

SILVERSTEIN FIGHTS A BULL

shel makes the blood-and-sand scene: the second of a two-part portfolio on spain

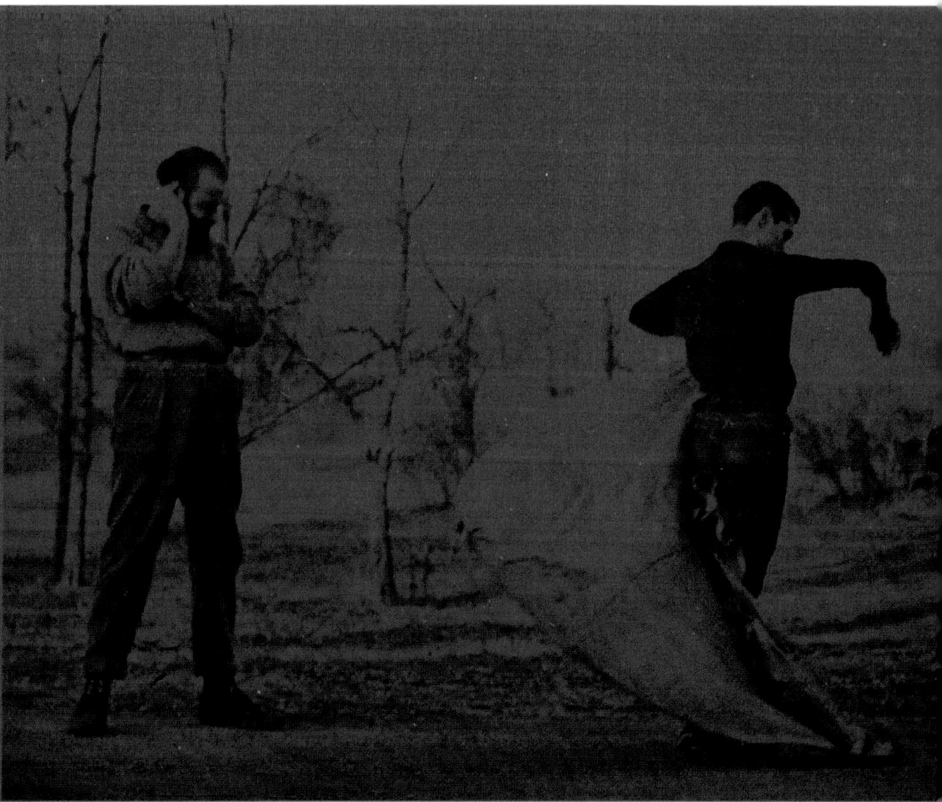

LA BARBA (THE BEARD) is what the citizens of Seville called the world's only whiskered bullfighter, Shel Silverstein. Gags about La Barba of Seville would seem in order, but these would tend to tarnish the glamor and dignity of the noble *corrida* tradition, so we will refrain. Before matching wits with *el toro,* Shel trained for a month at the ranch of Count Maza, just outside Seville. His instructors were Tito Palacios and John Short, both bullfighters of note, the latter a compatriot of Silverstein's. After mastering such intricate passes as the *veronica,* the *chicuelina* and the *goanera,* Shel donned the resplendent suit of lights, strode majestically through the gates of fear and faced the bull in the formal dance of death. "After that bout, I was known as El Corazón del Pollo," Shel says, insisting that it means The Lion-Hearted even when we opened our Spanish dictionary and showed him that *pollo* means "chicken." Did Shel kill the bull? "No," he admits, "but on the other hand, the bull didn't kill me. I still have a slight scar on the, uh, hip, though, where his horn grazed me." ¡*Olé!*

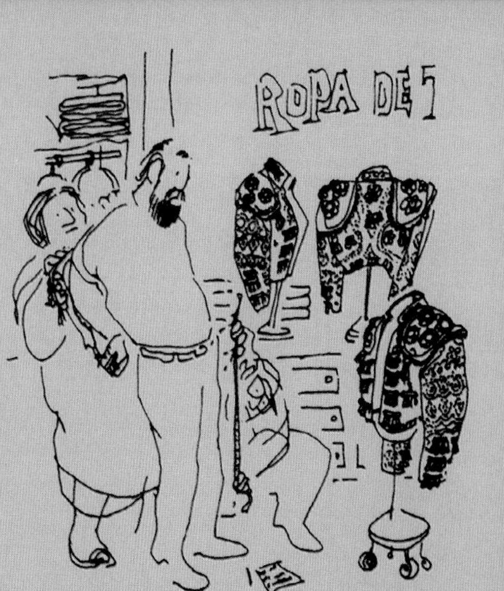
ROPA DE T

"Nothing fancy, now . . ."

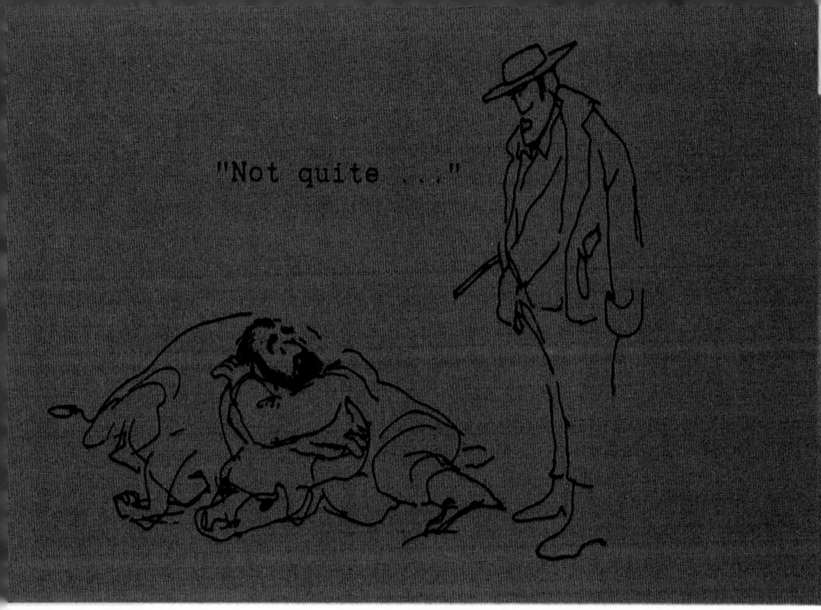
"Not quite ..."

Professional bullfighters John Short and Tito Palacios help Shel into the *traje de luces,* or suit of lights.

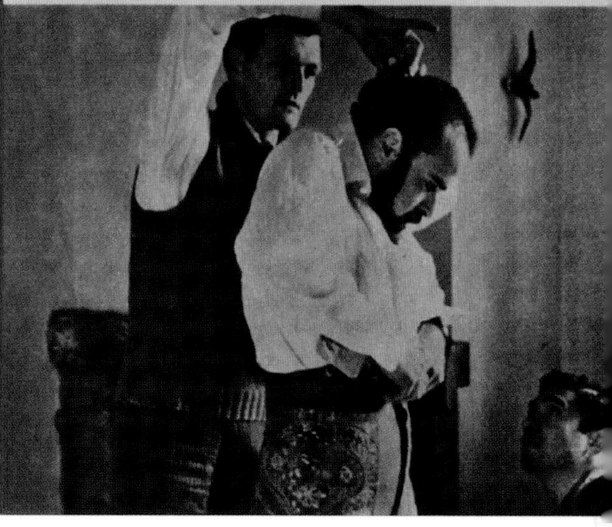

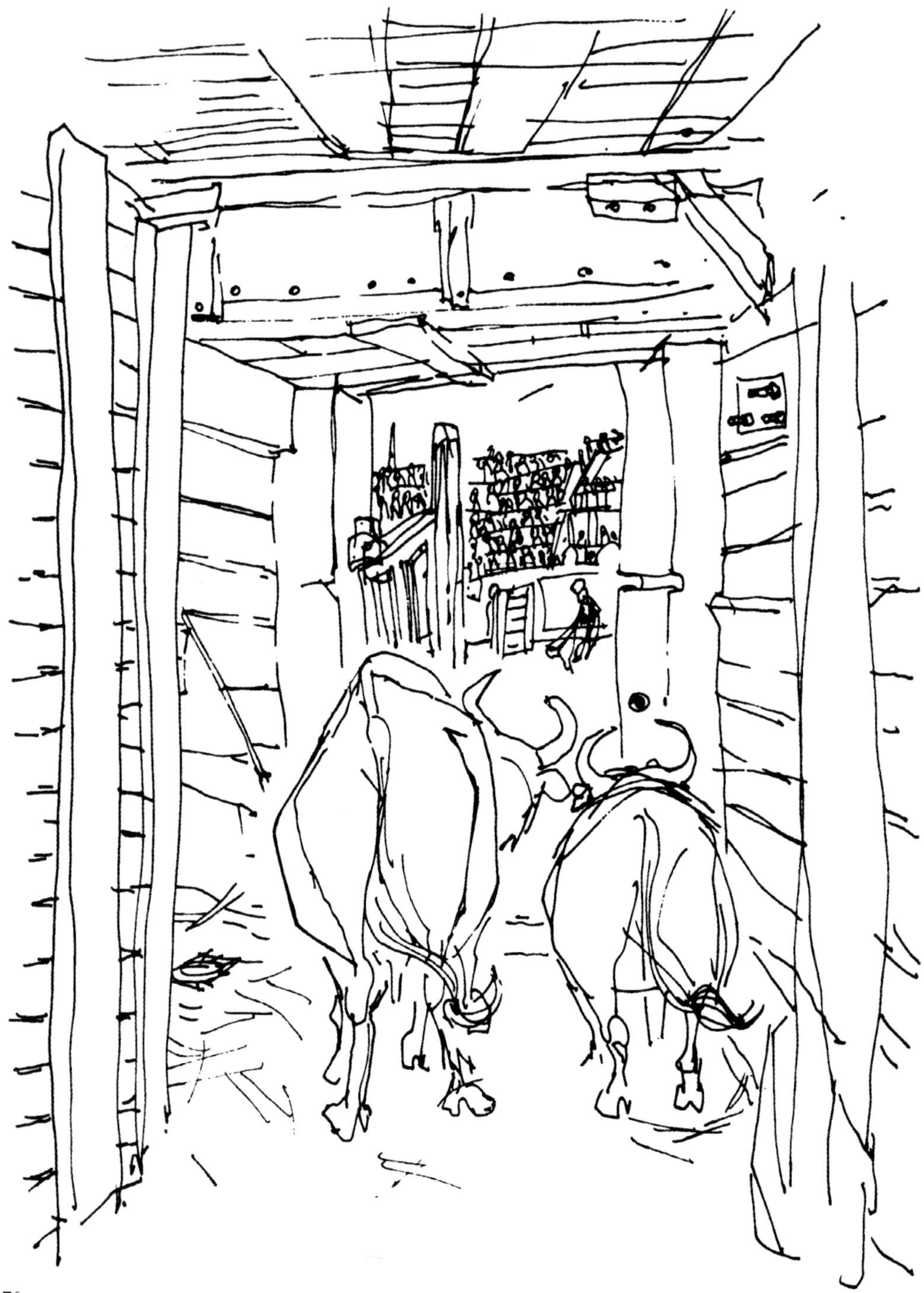

"Now watch him
closely — see how
he favors
his right hand — now
he's doing a revolera
best thing for
a revolera is to stop
short and catch him
in the middle
of his swirl — now
he's doing a right-
handed round pass.
If you can — fake hi
off to the left
and then bring your
horns up fast
and to the right and
pow! Now watch
this — he's trying
a desplante. This
is really fun.
You wait until he's
kneeling directly in
front of you
and then ..."

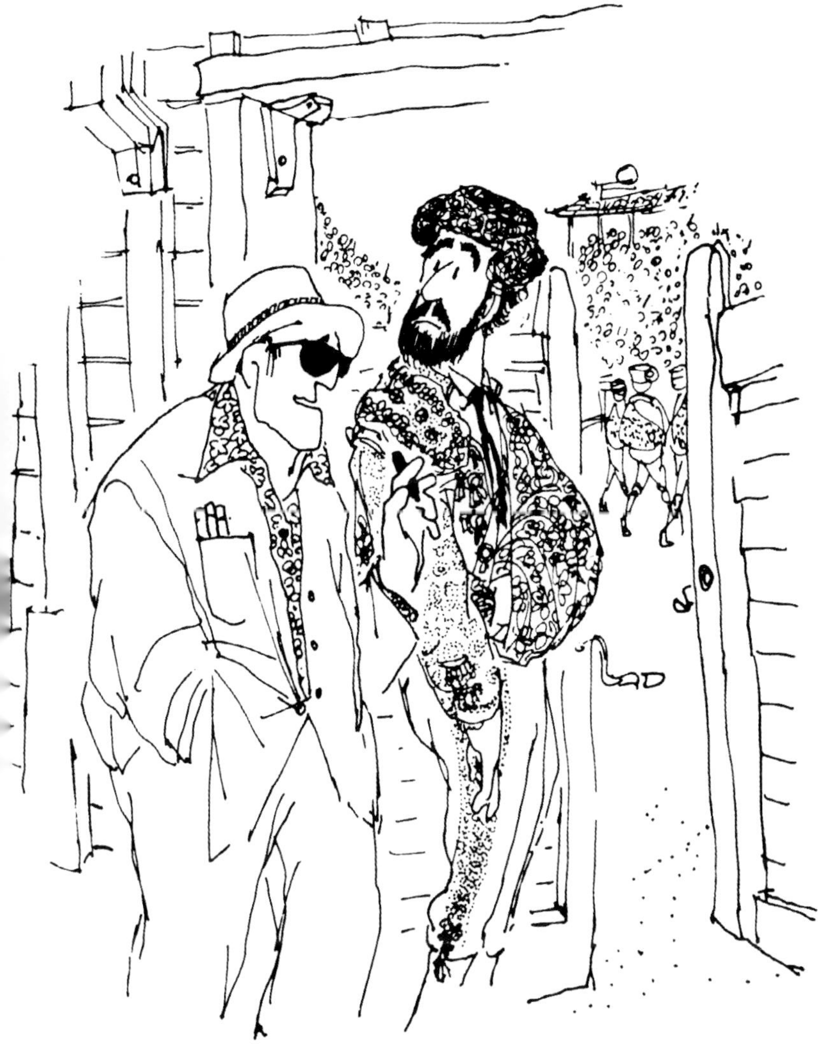

"That's my proposition, kid ...
five hundred fast bucks and all
you got to do is go out
there and take a dive ..."

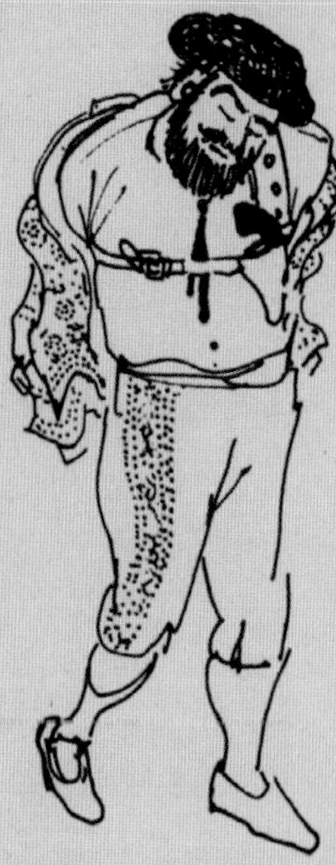

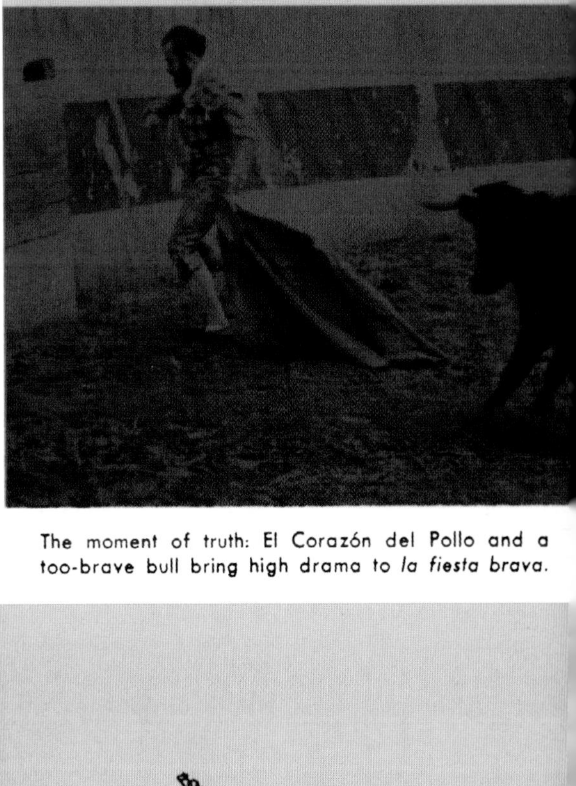

The moment of truth: El Corazón del Pollo and a too-brave bull bring high drama to *la fiesta brava*.

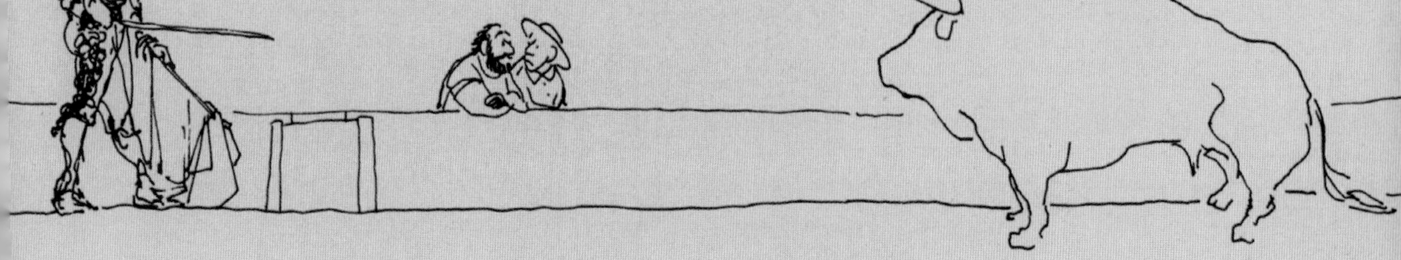

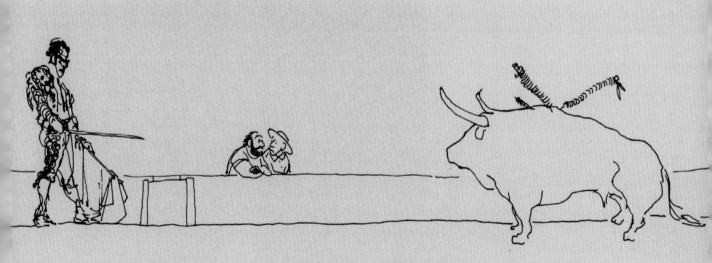

"Who you for?"

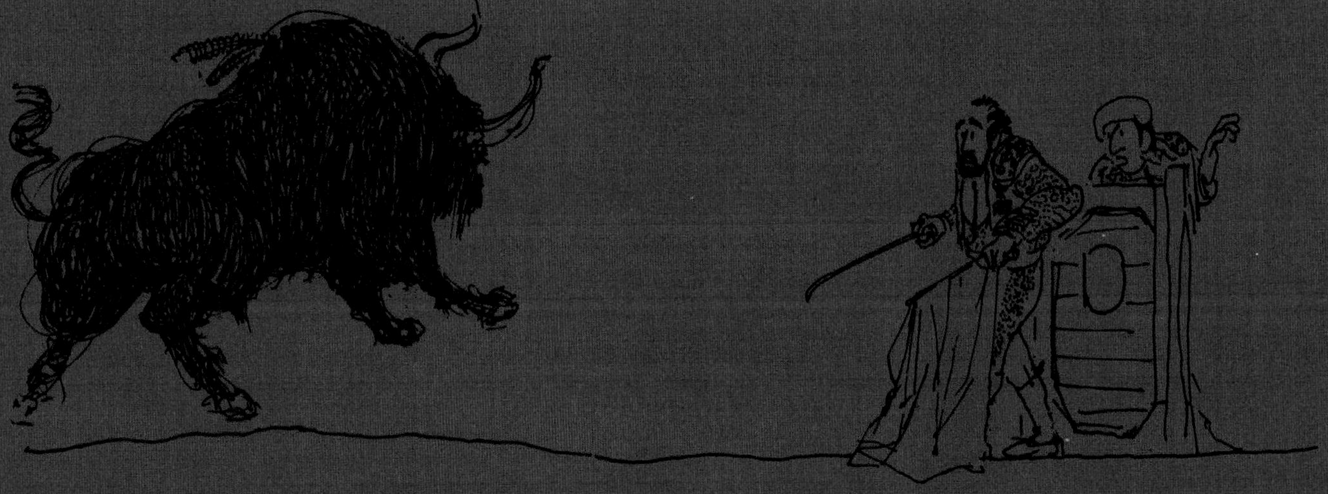

"Feel no sympathy for the bull, senor — he was born to die in this moment of truth. He was bred for this moment — it is his purpose, his tradition, his destiny to die on the sword of the torero ... Of course he doesn't realize this ..."

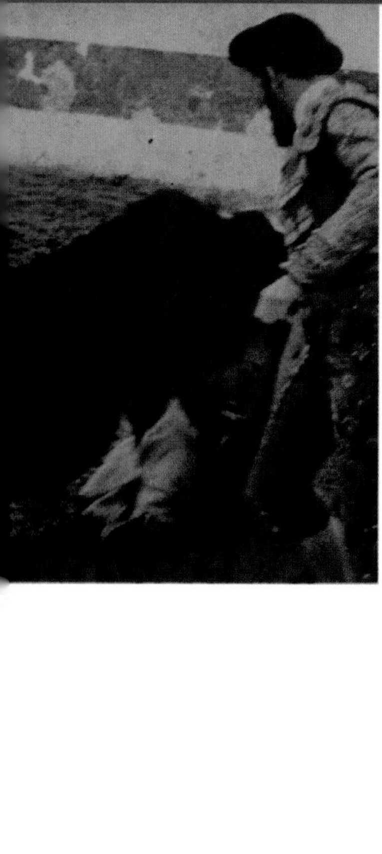

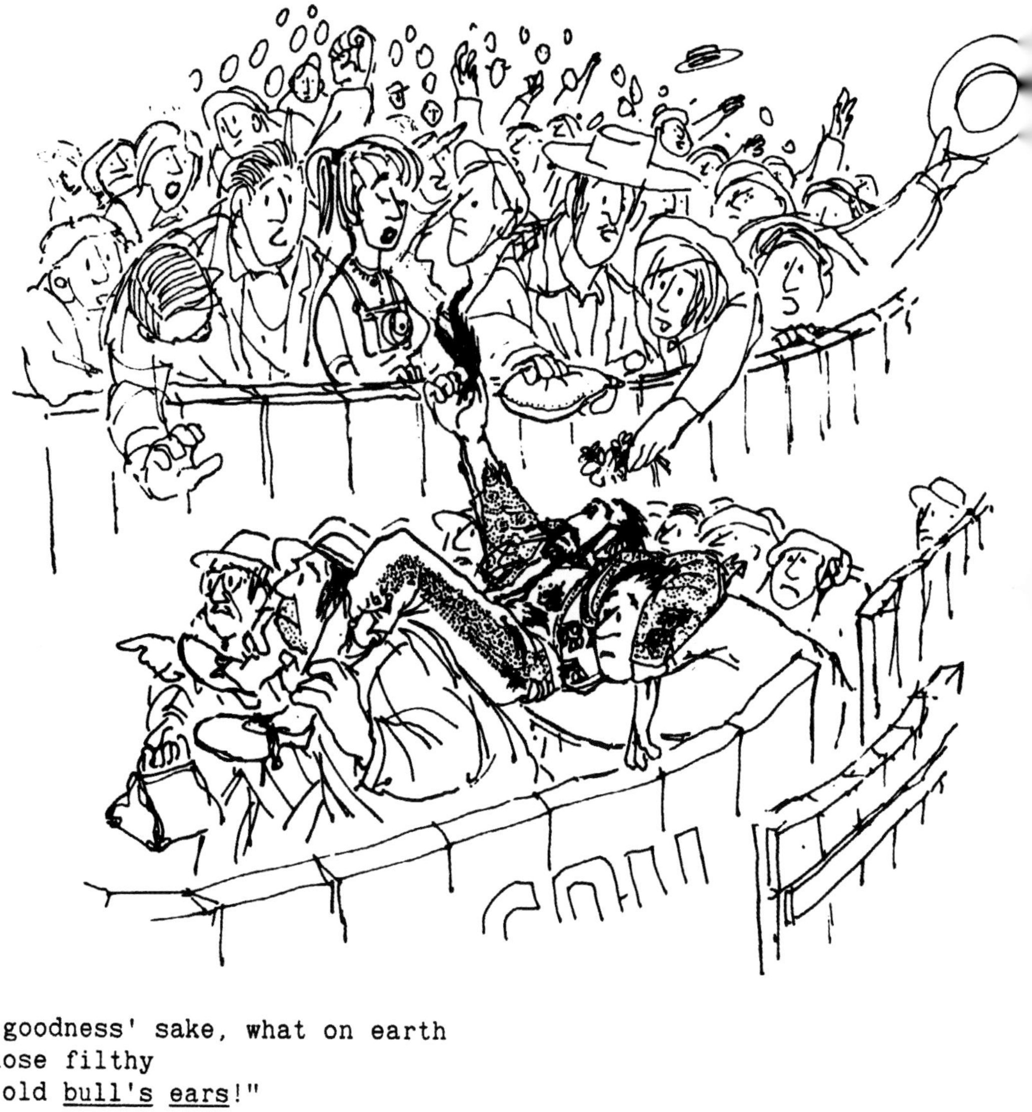

"Well for goodness' sake, what on earth do I want with those filthy old bull's ears!"

AMONG THE ARABS

AUGUST 1959

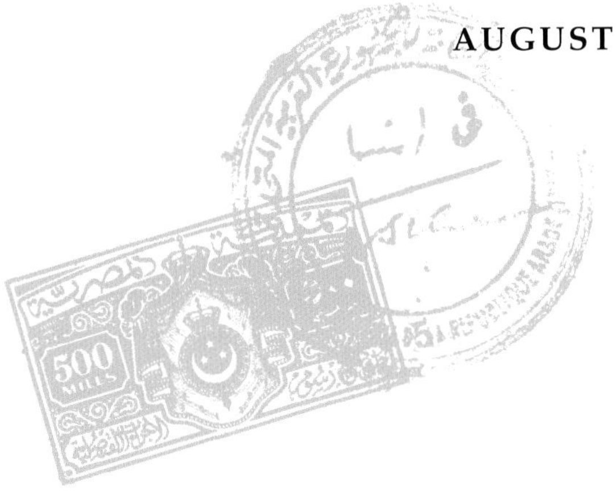
500
MILLS

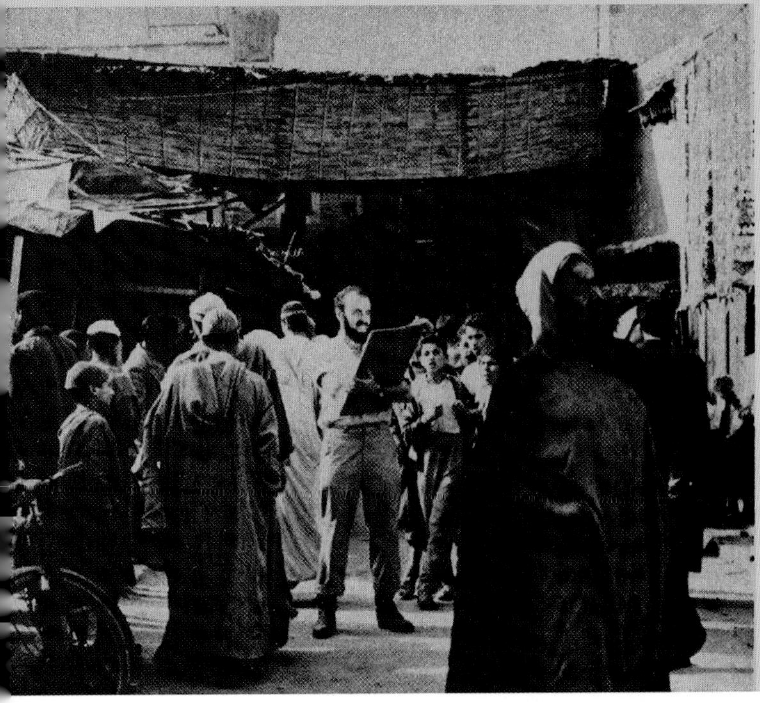

sheik shel in the land of dervishes and dromedaries

"I'LL SING THEE SONGS of Araby," said Silverstein as he departed for that locality, "and tales of fair Kashmir." Or, anyway, he said something to that effect. On foot and on camel, he roamed North Africa, visiting Tangier, Cairo, Rabat and Casablanca, where he swears he saw individuals remarkably like Claude Rains, Paul Henreid, Ingrid Bergman and other old Warner Brothers types lurking behind the mosques and minarets. "But they may have been mirages," he adds; "that desert sun . . ." Even though he was not invited to come to the casbah, Shel was enthralled by the land of the Arabs. "And I was pleased to learn that the barbaric practice of buying and selling beautiful young women has been abolished," he scowled.

SILVERSTEIN AMONG THE ARABS

"Pssst—a word of warning,
o bearded one—
beware the fatal
charms of Fatima, of
the flashing eyes,
who dances nightly
at the Casbah Club, 23 Rue
Rakir, continuous
shows from 9:30 to 1:30, no
cover, no minimum——"

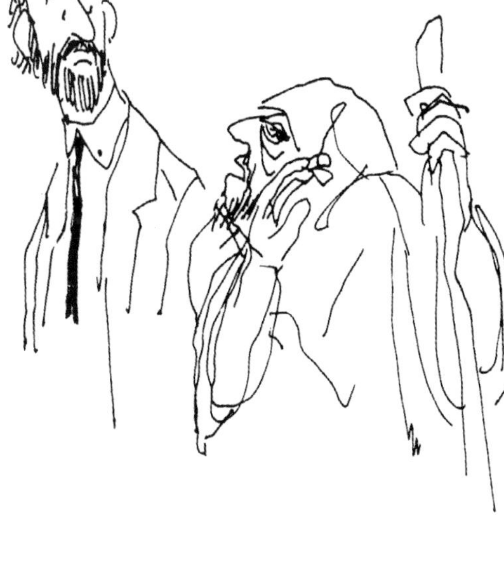

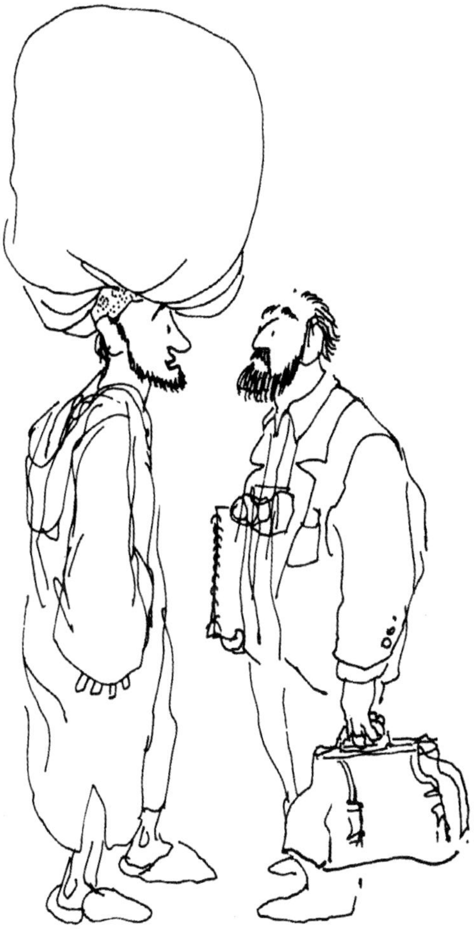

"That's funny—I
always wondered
how you of the west
could carry so many
things with your hands."

"You refuse to buy
my souvenirs,
you refuse to save
my wives and
children from starvation,
you refuse to aid
our tottering economy,
o foolish one--
you _drive_ us into
the arms of
the Communists!"

"But it _is_
form fitting."

"For heaven's sake, cut out
the 'Open Sesame' stuff
and ring the _doorbell_!"

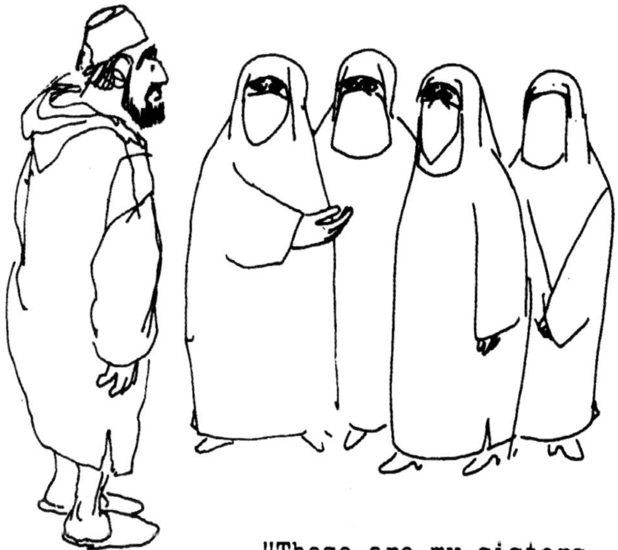

"These are my sisters—
Aicha, Zohra and Halima.
Halima is the shy one."

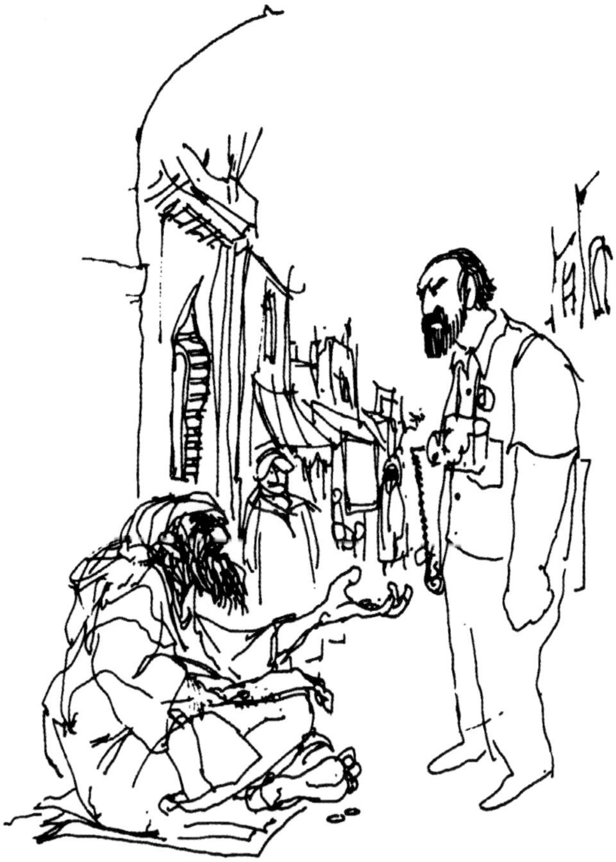

"Sure I'll say,
'Alms for the love of
Allah,' but not for
a lousy 20 francs!"

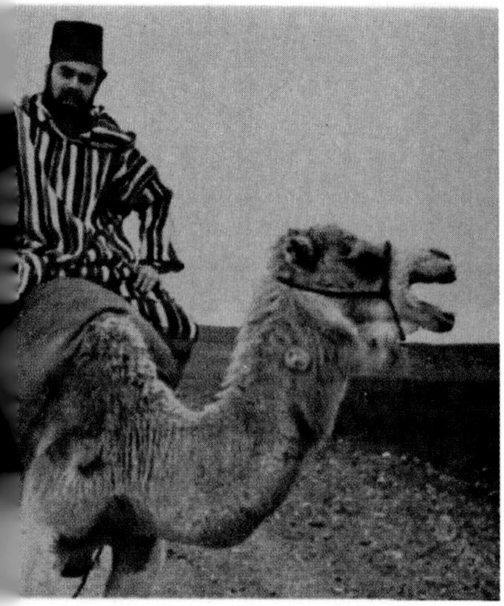

Arrayed in the fez and galabia of a desert chieftain, Shel glowers from his camel.

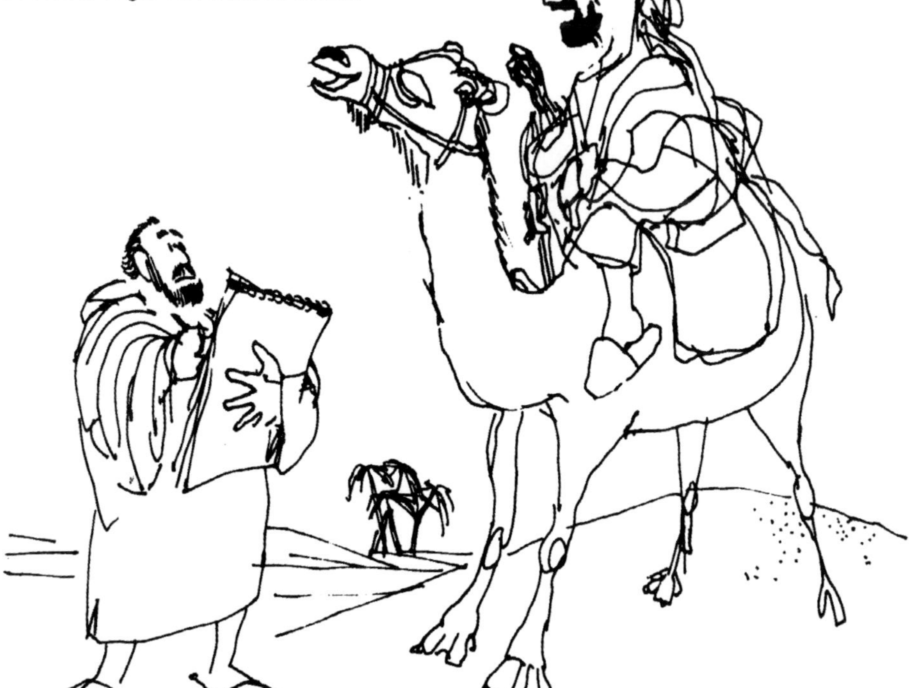

"...Or how about a camel alone on the desert saying, 'I'd walk a mile for a Camel.' Get it? Or maybe you can draw a pack of camels. Get it? A pack of Camels? Ha! Or maybe you can draw a camel trying to squeeze through the eye of a needle. Or how about a camel salesman saying, 'One lump or two?' Get it? 'One lump or two!' Or how about a..."

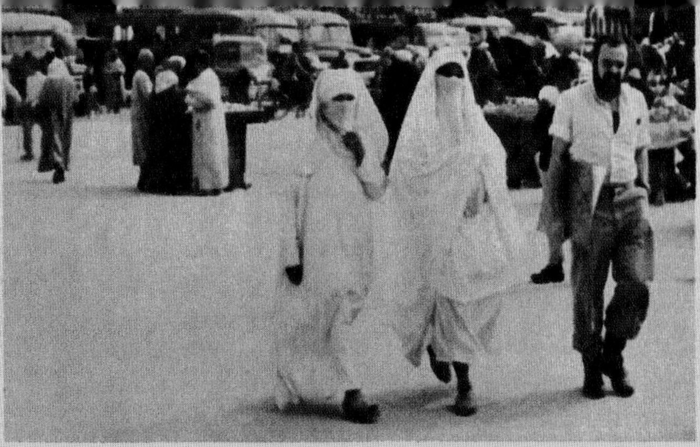

Silverstein strolls through a *suk,* or outdoor market, of Marrakech, alongside the veiled women of an exotic culture.

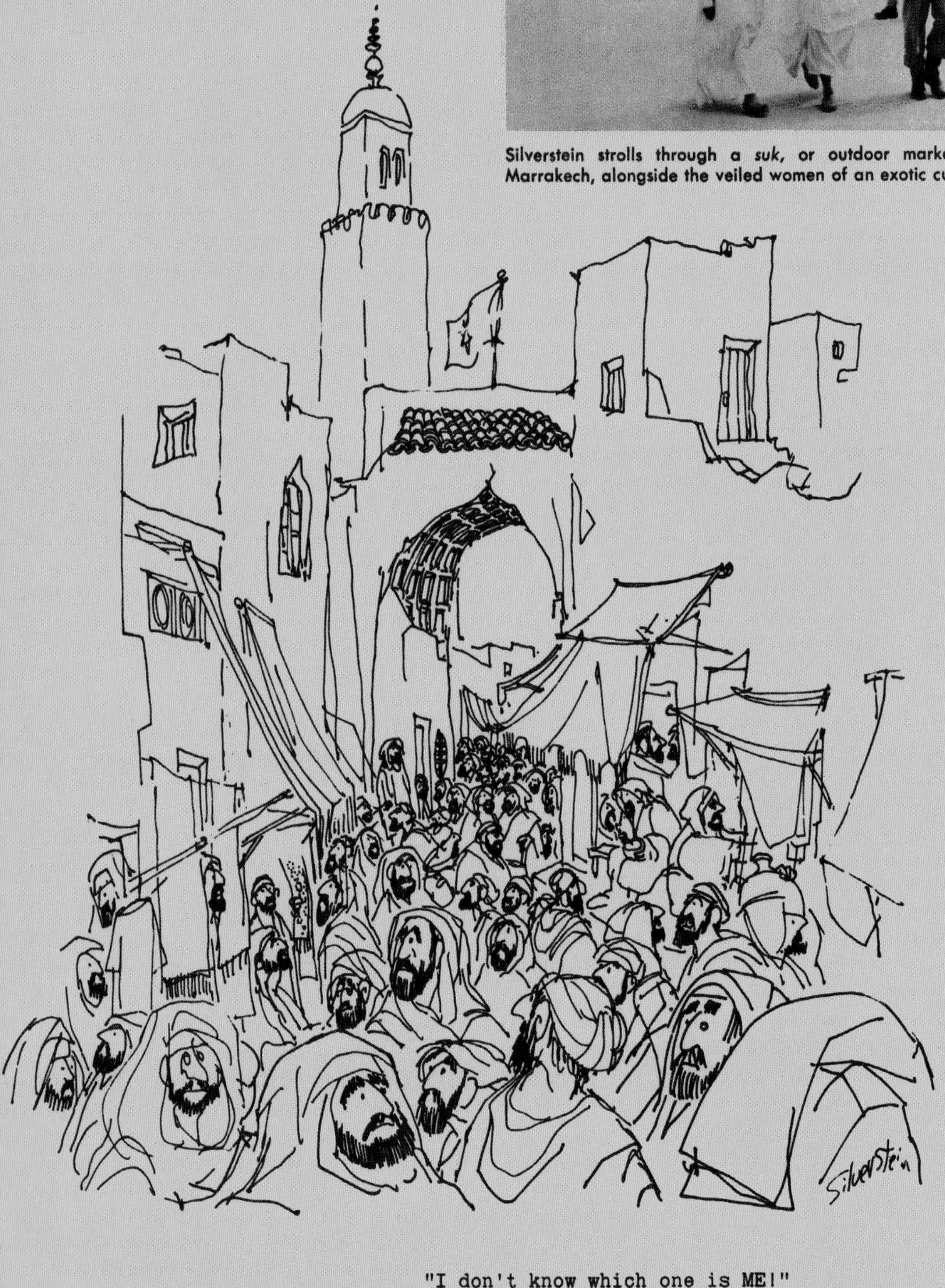
Silverstein

"I don't know which one is ME!"

IN AFRICA

OCTOBER 1959

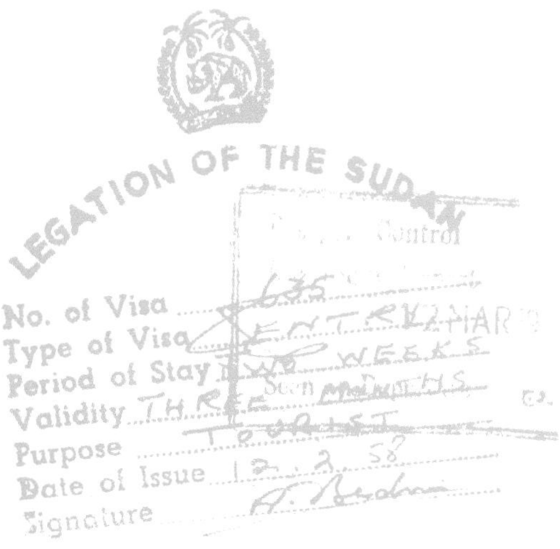
LEGATION OF THE SUDAN
No. of Visa
Type of Visa
Period of Stay
Validity
Purpose
Date of Issue
Signature

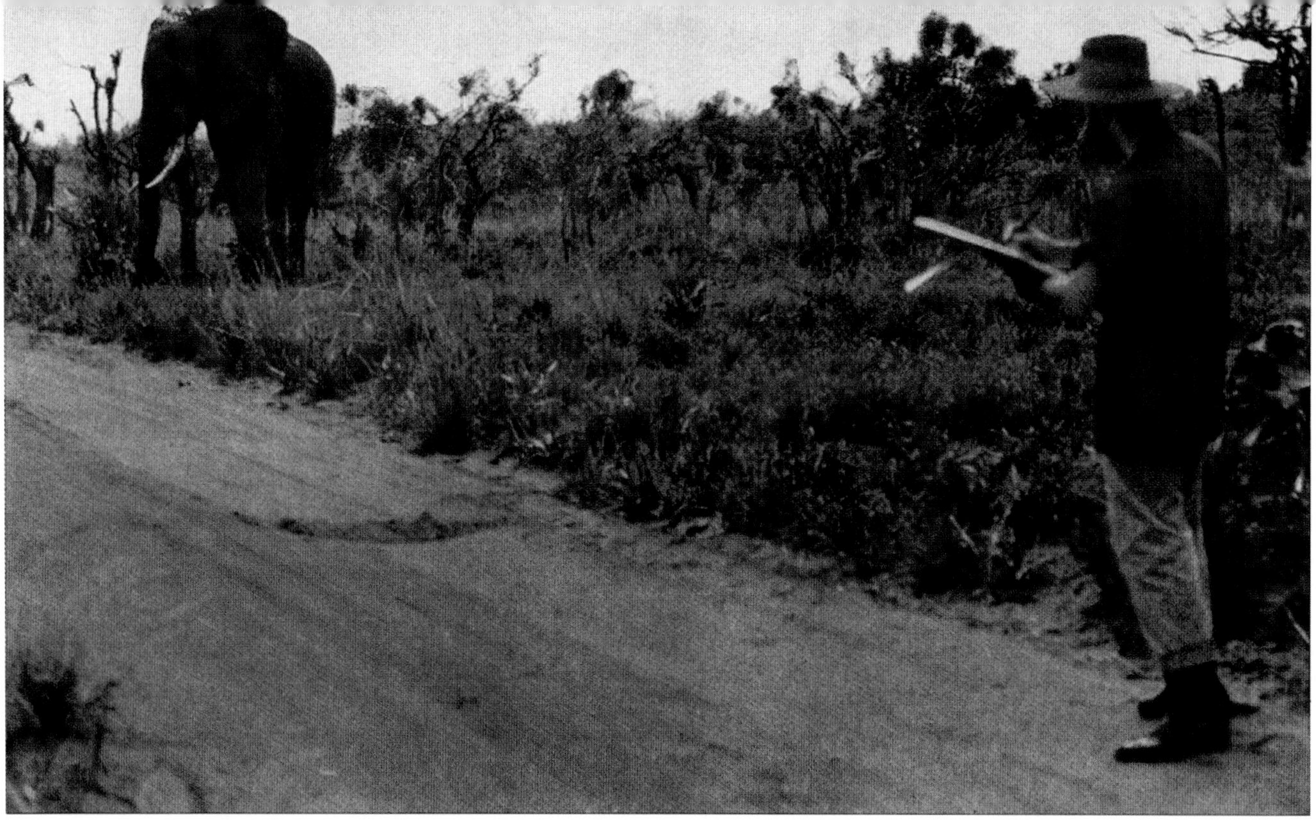

SILVERSTEIN IN AFRICA

THE FABLED THRILLS of big-game hunting in Africa are too enticing for the wandering adventurer to resist for long. Accordingly, after sketching the Arabs, Shel Silverstein went on safari. He proved hunter enough to fell a water buffalo, called the most dangerous game.

As our regular readers well know by now, Shel has traveled yon, hither and thither for PLAYBOY these past two years, enjoying adventures in Japan, Scandinavia, England, France, Russia, Italy, Switzerland, Spain and Araby with hardly a scratch on the tough Silverstein hide (he doesn't count the minor wound received in a Spanish bullring). But, returning from this safari in Central Africa, driving along the nearly deserted road to Kampala in Uganda, Shel and photographer-friend Pat Morin collided head on with a truck full of natives. Both men were badly hurt, Shel with his side caved in and left leg slashed open. They asked the natives to take them to a hospital, but the aborigines would do nothing without payment, and the minds of the two men were so fogged by shock they couldn't remember where they had put their money. The natives left them lying by the side of the road. Hours passed under the white-hot African sun and the two men, unable to move, calculated that they would almost certainly die from their wounds and exposure, if prowling lions, drawn by the scent of blood, didn't eat them first.

Near dusk, a car carrying a Scottish couple came down the road. They took the injured pair 40 miles over a rough and rocky road to a tiny four-bed hospital at Fort Portal. Shel was hospitalized for three months; he came out of the experience 50 pounds lighter, his beard eight inches longer, toting a cane for a persistent, perhaps perpetual limp. But the Silverstein spirit remained undaunted: he brought back to the U.S. a sketch pad full of his humorous personal impressions of the Dark Continent.

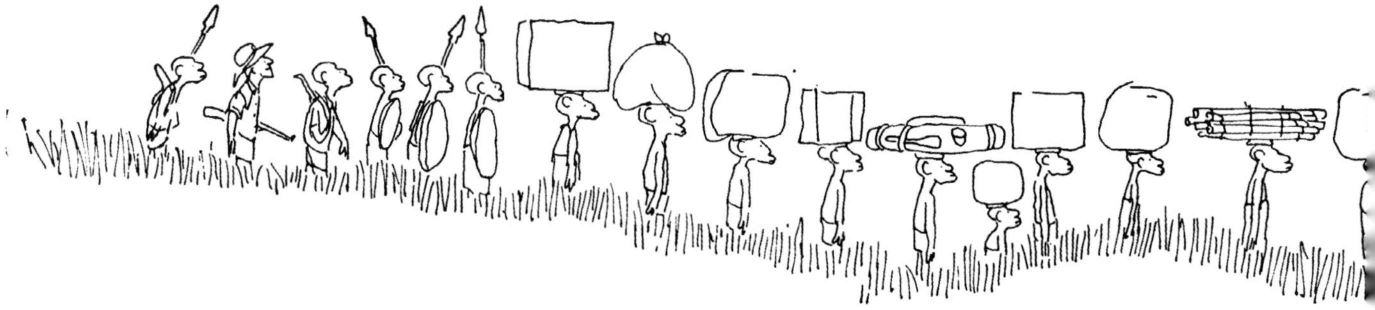

shel courts danger as a big-game hunter on safari

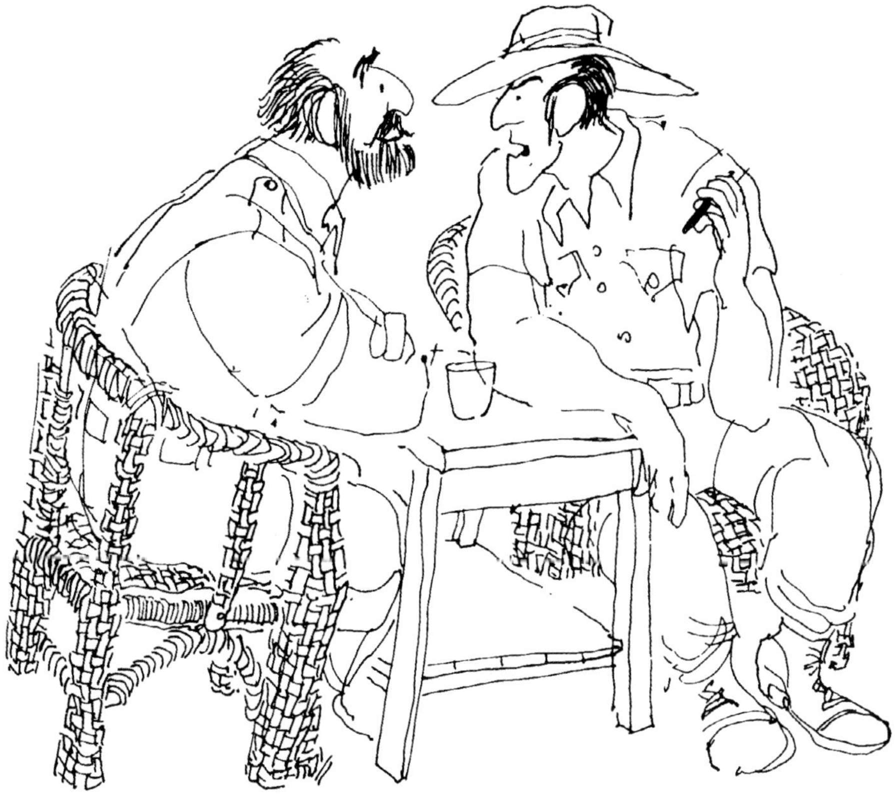

"To be honest with you, Silverstein,
you've given me the greatest challenge
in my 23 years as a white hunter.
I've found lions for Hemingway...
I've found white rhino for Gunther...
I've found Mau Mau for Ruark...
But 18-year-old blue-eyed blondes—
that's really going to take some doing."

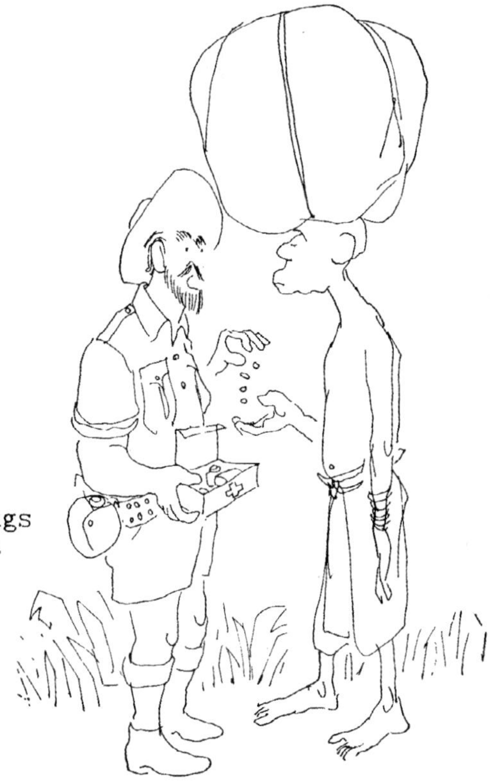

"Now these little white things
called aspirins. You take two with a
glass of water and in
10 minutes...headache gone!"

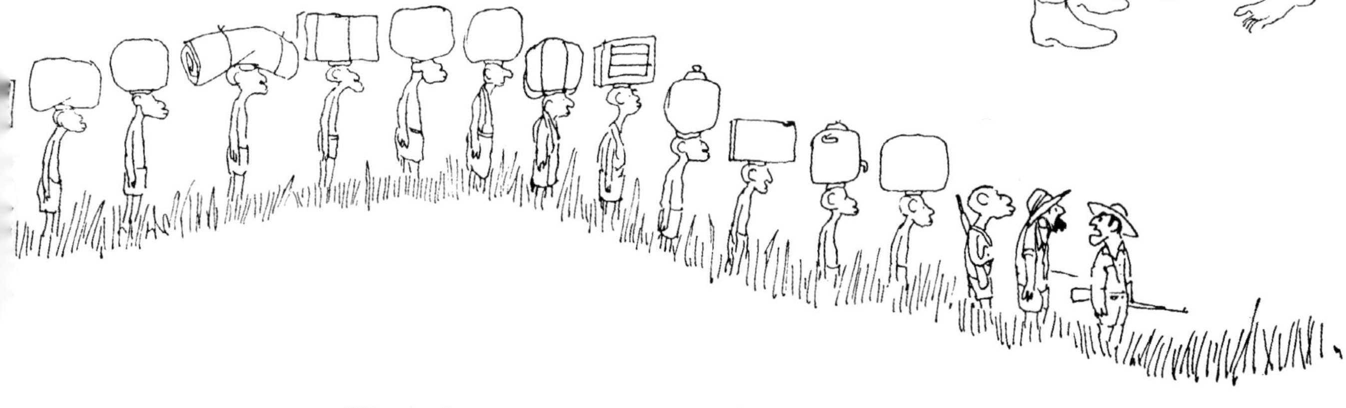

"What do you mean -- you just remembered
you can't stand the sight of blood?!"

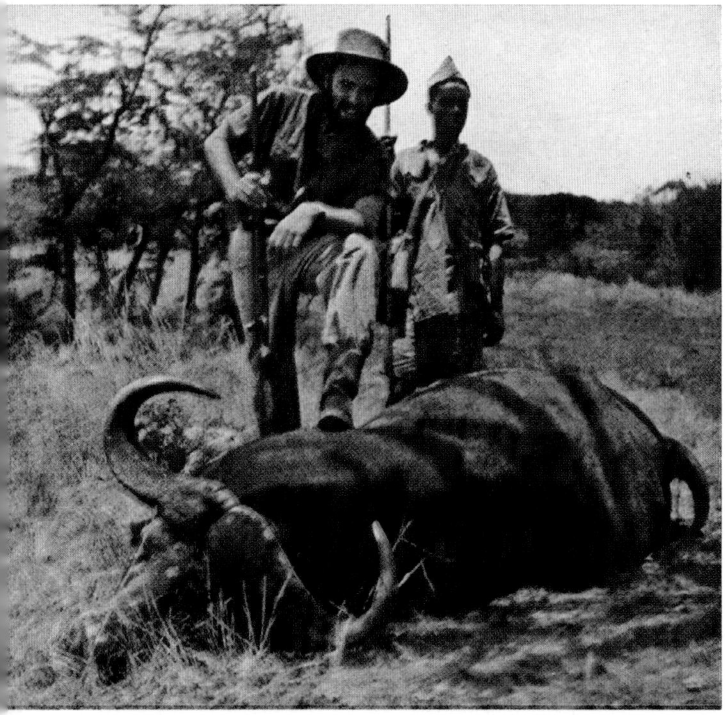

Having just felled a water buffalo, Silverstein strikes the classic pose of the triumphant hunter. The feat was accomplished in Ubangi country, where Shel hoped to see the fabled saucer-lipped women. He saw none. "Progress!" he snorted.

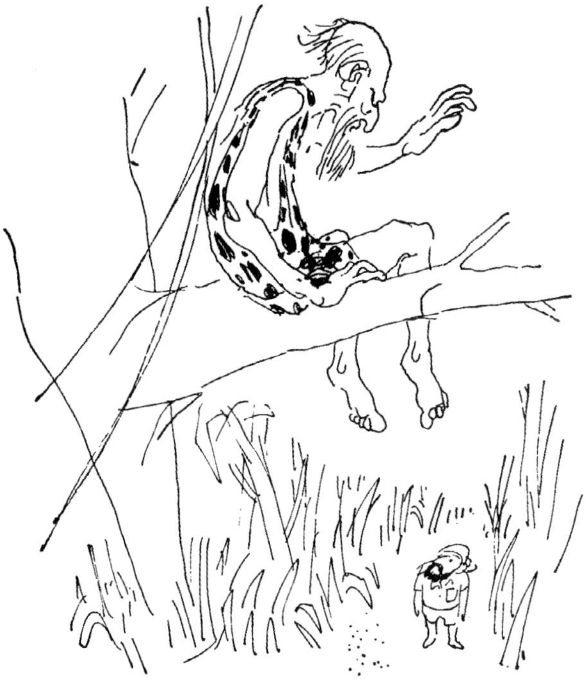

"...And if you see
Edgar Rice Burroughs,
tell him for me
he's an ungrateful, cheap,
plagiarizing, thieving...."

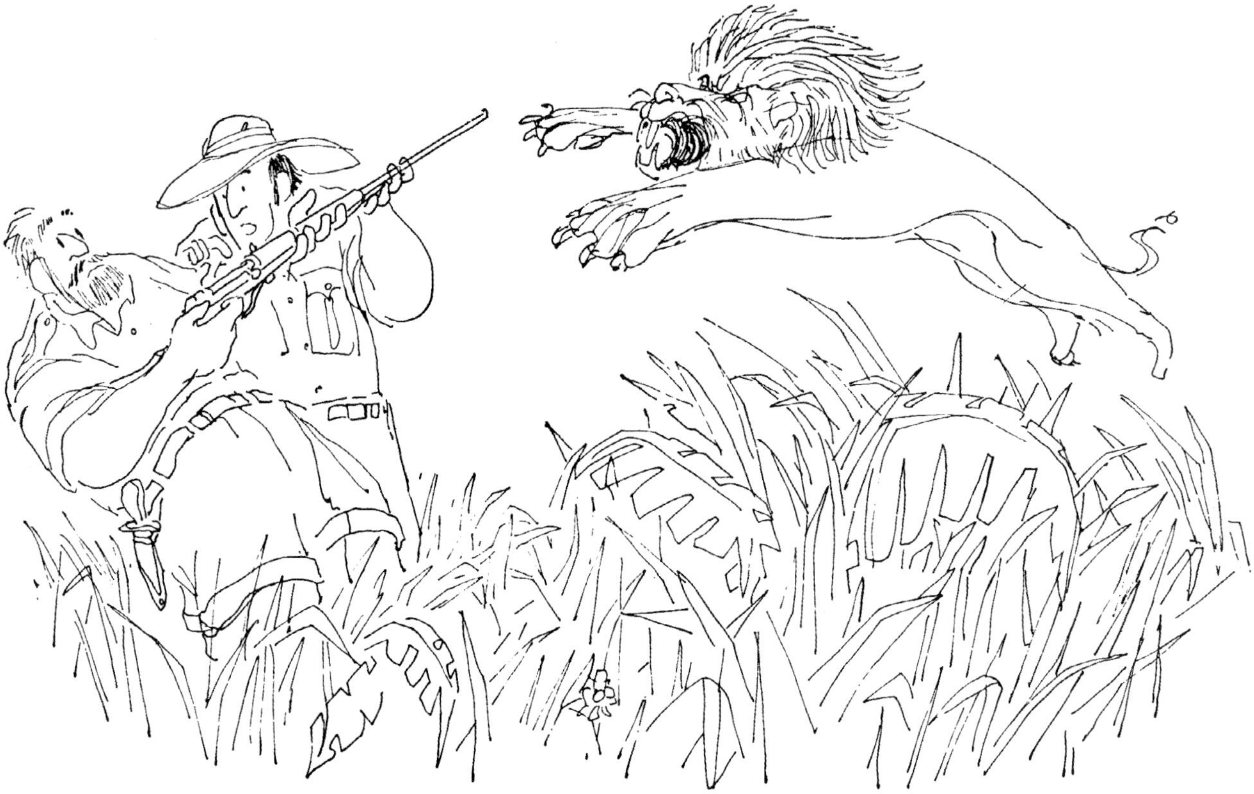

"I guess I'd better explain this in a hurry.
This is the bolt...after each round you pull it back
and the shell ejects. This is your rear sight...
you line this up with your front sight,
allowing for windage and...."

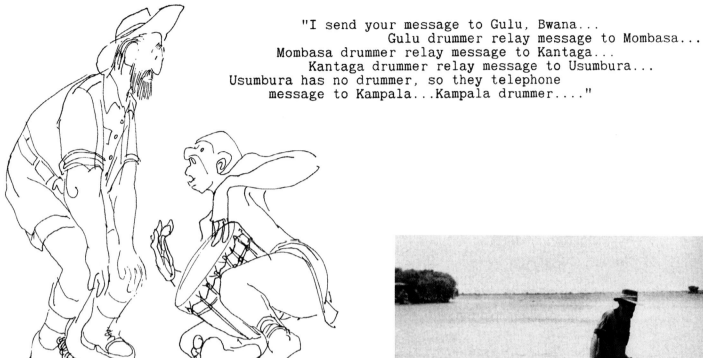

"I send your message to Gulu, Bwana...
Gulu drummer relay message to Mombasa...
Mombasa drummer relay message to Kantaga...
Kantaga drummer relay message to Usumbura...
Usumbura has no drummer, so they telephone
message to Kampala...Kampala drummer...."

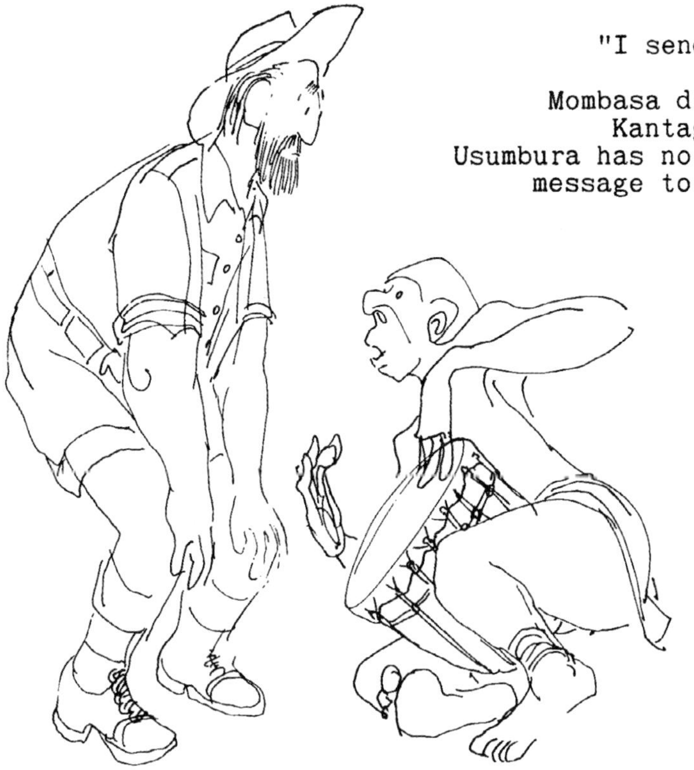

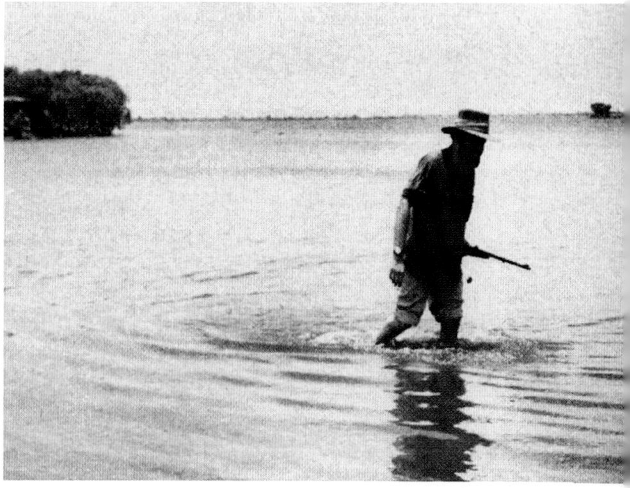

Rifle in hand, cartoonist Silverstein wades in the hippo-infested waters of Lake George in Uganda.

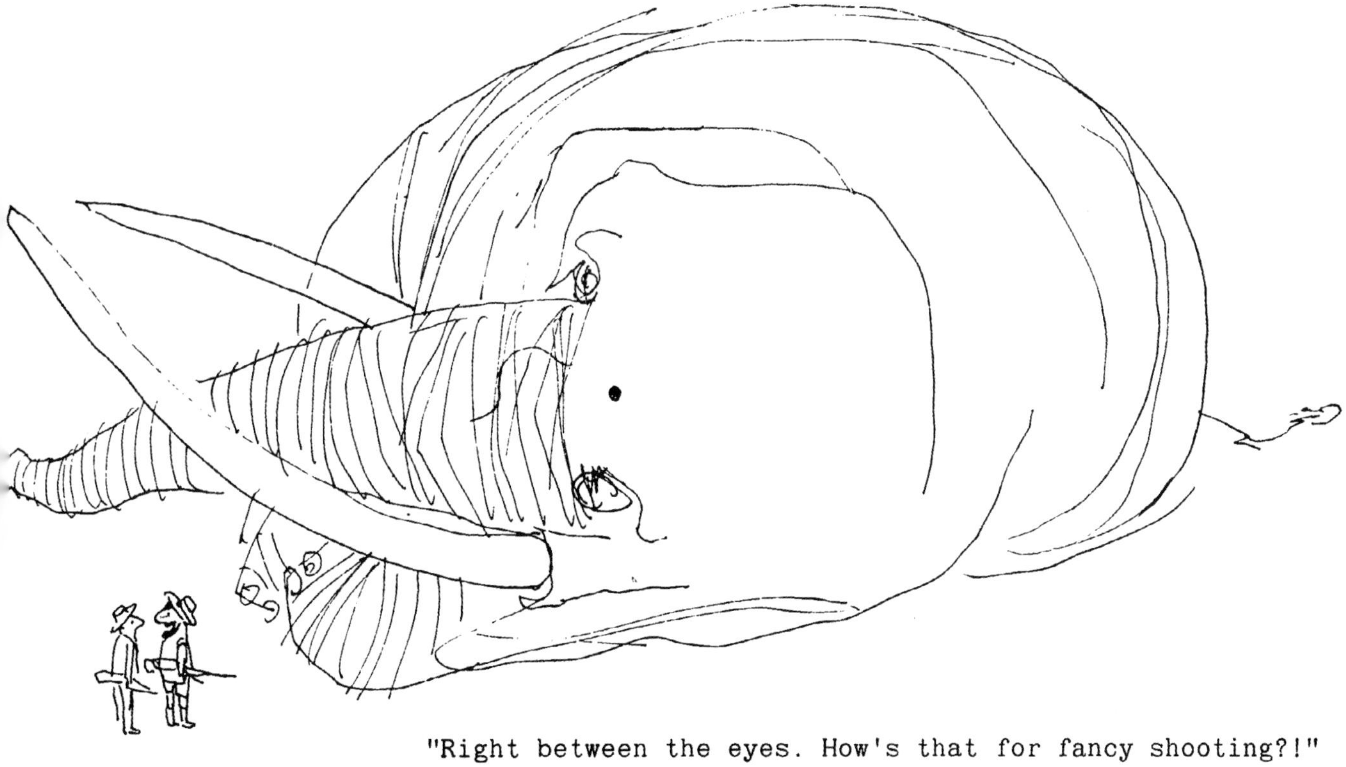

"Right between the eyes. How's that for fancy shooting?!"

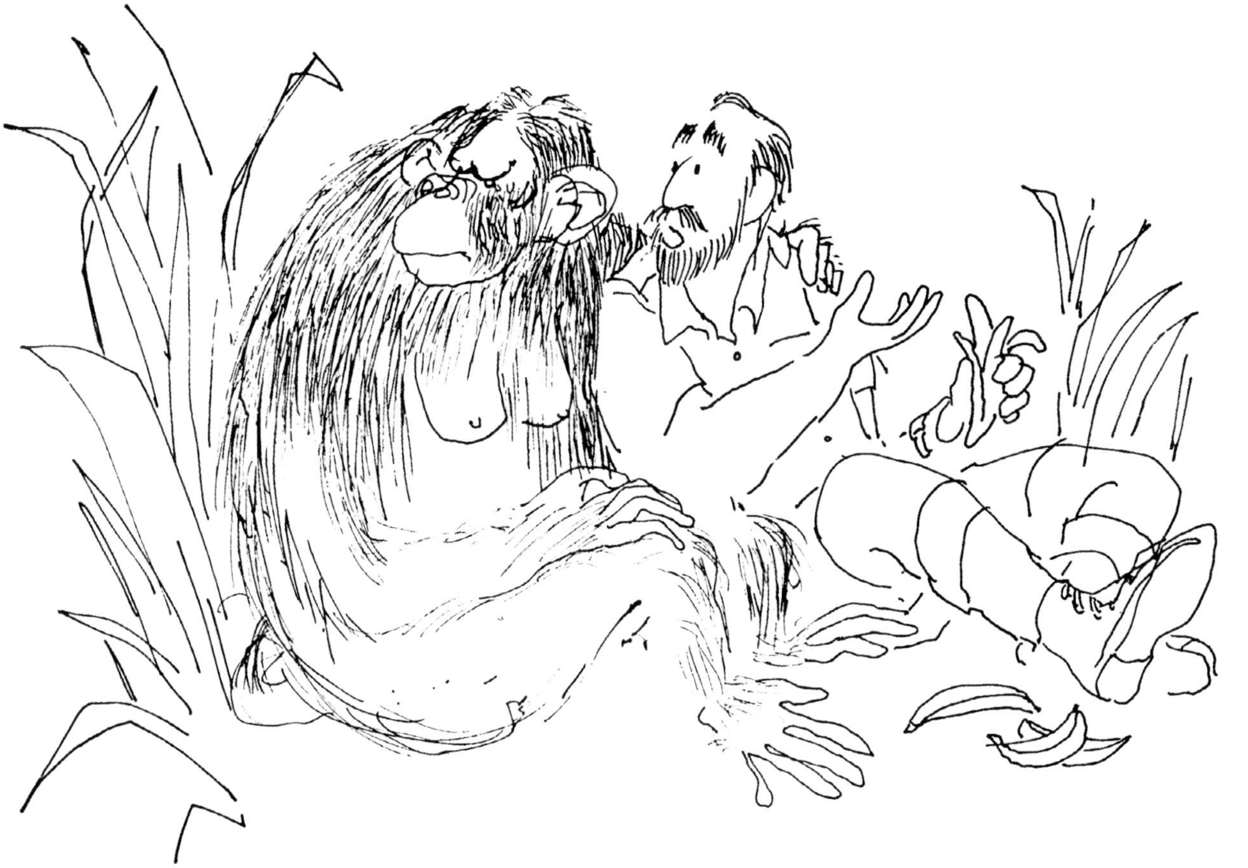

"It just wouldn't work out, Mzaba--
you have <u>your</u> world and I have <u>mine</u>!"

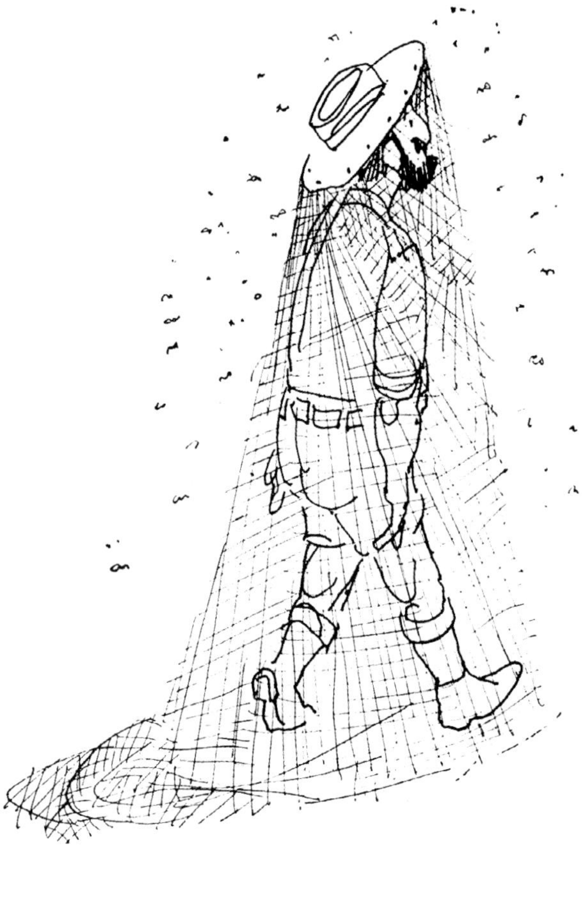

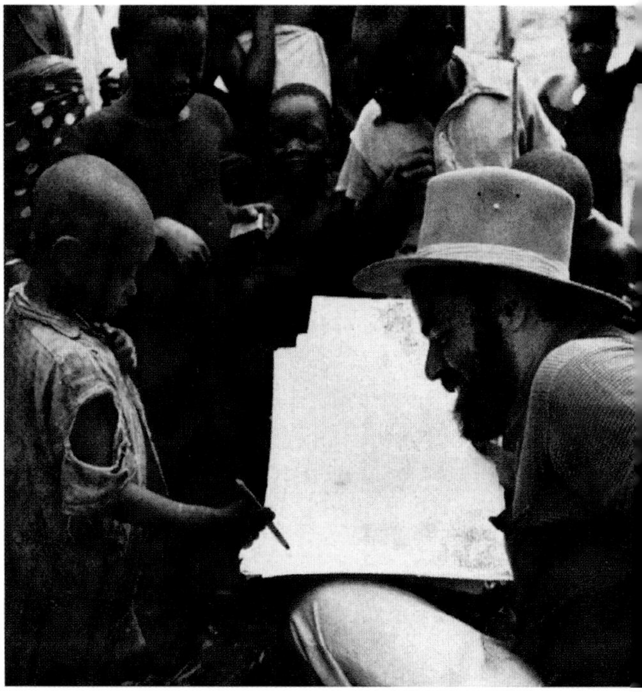

Watusi children contribute to Shel's sketch pad. Shel claim[s] the adult Watusi "aren't as tall as they were in *King So[l]omon's Mines.*" He also claims "the pygmies aren't as short.

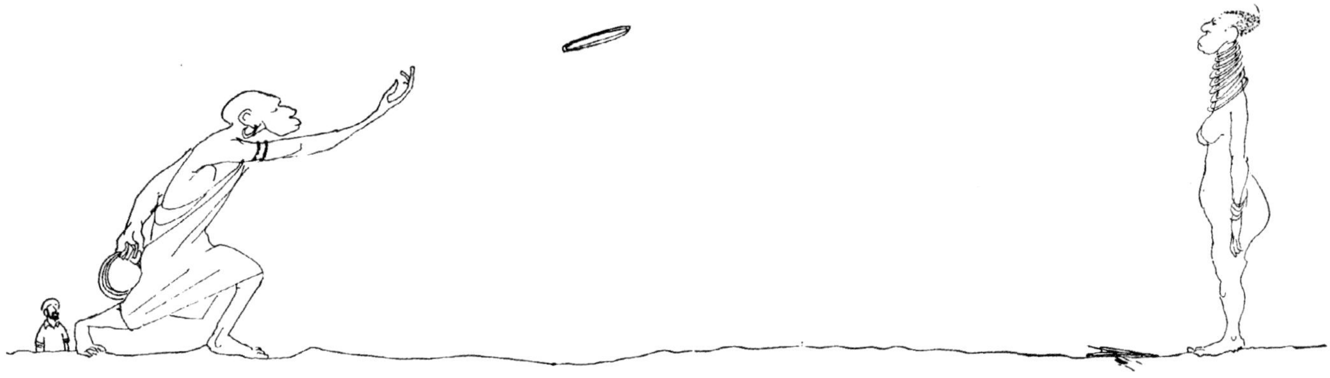

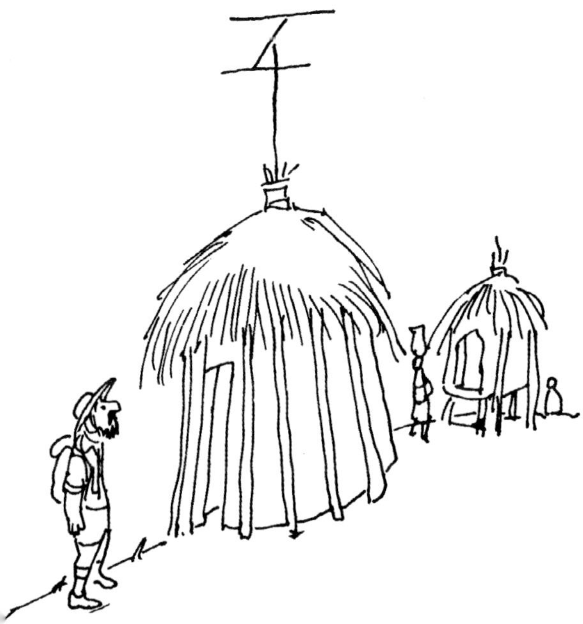

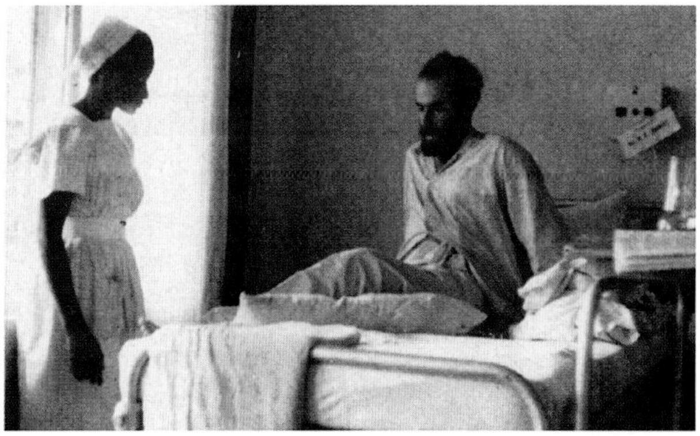

A shattered Silverstein was nursed back to health in this miniature four-bed hospital, manned by one English doctor, one German nurse, and natives. He passed the time sketching.

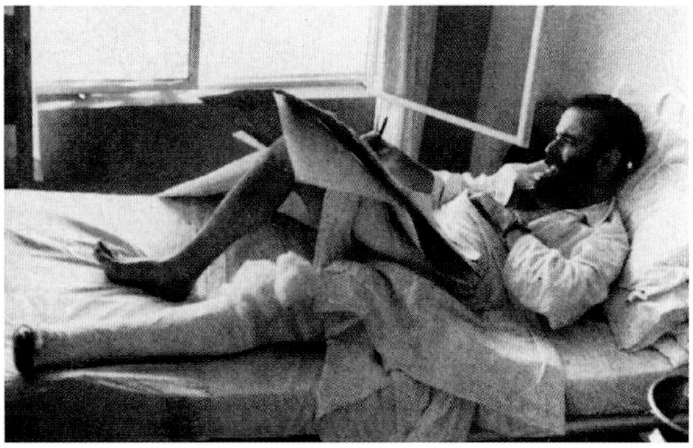

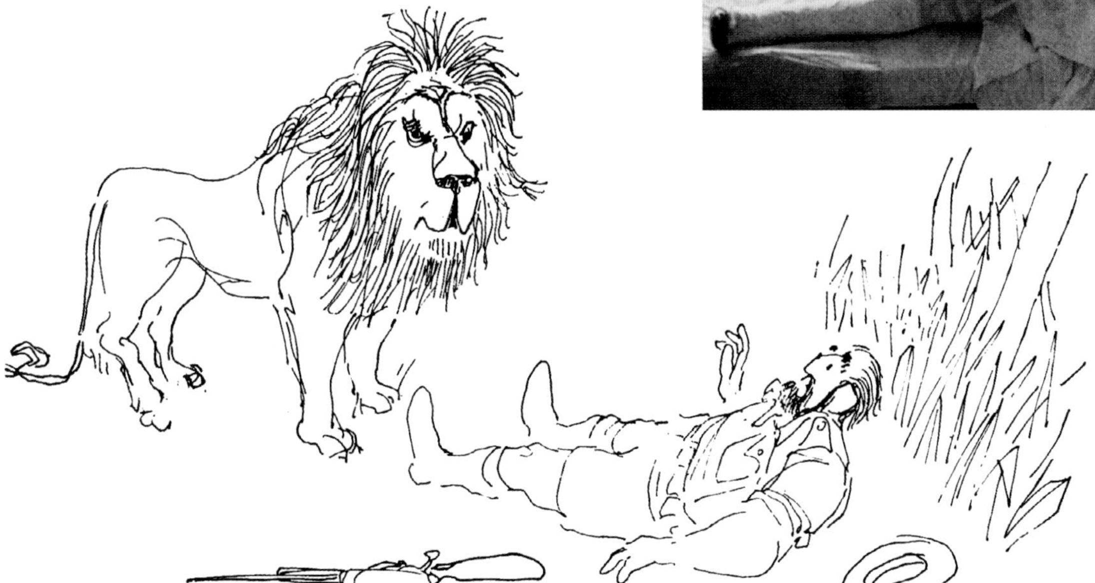

"...And so the good kind lion let the little mousey go free
and later when the lion was trapped in a big net
and couldn't get loose, the grateful mousey came to his aid
and gnawed through the net and saved his life and...."

IN GREENWICH VILLAGE

SEPTEMBER 1960

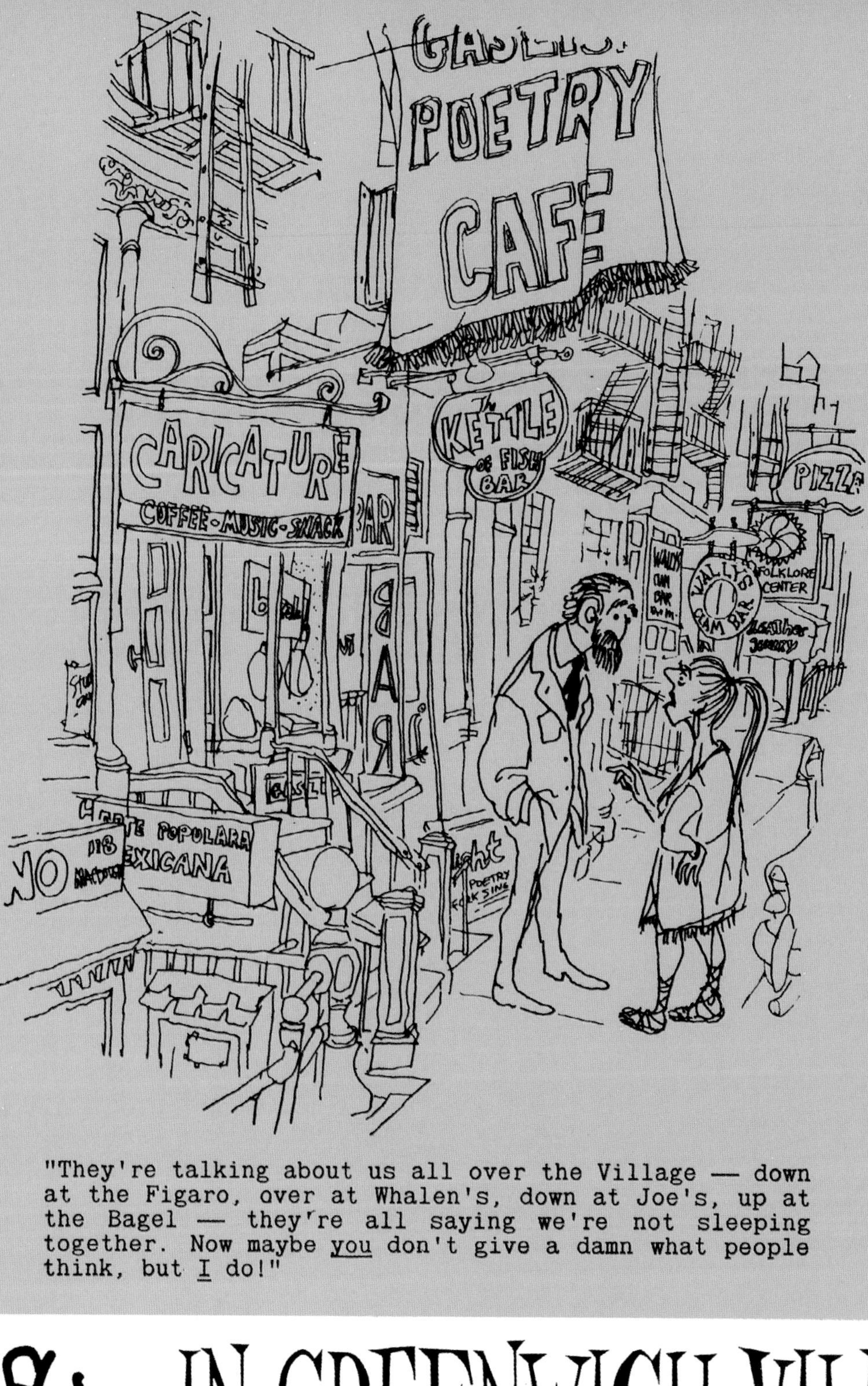
POETRY
CAFE
CARICATURE
COFFEE-MUSIC-SNACK
KETTLE OF FISH BAR
BAR
FOLKLORE CENTER
CLAM BAR
MEXICANA

"They're talking about us all over the Village — down at the Figaro, over at Whalen's, down at Joe's, up at the Bagel — they're all saying we're not sleeping together. Now maybe you don't give a damn what people think, but I do!"

Silverstein IN GREENWICH VILLAG

our globetrotting cartoonist reports on a beat and bizarre segment of the american scene

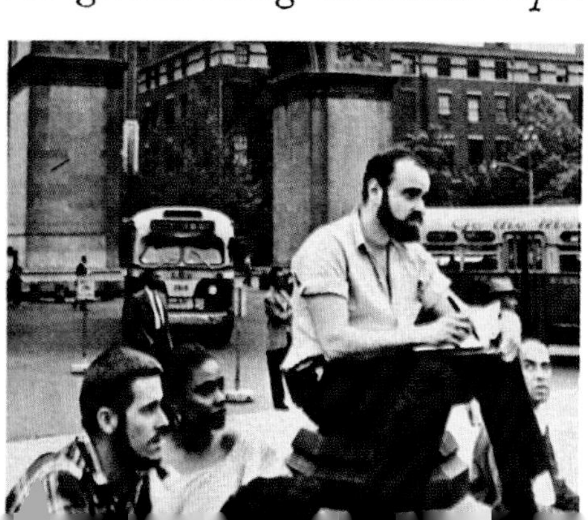

SHEL SILVERSTEIN, the free-wheeling humorist who has sketched many of the world's most exotic lands for PLAYBOY, has been living in Greenwich Village for the past year, recuperating from wounds incurred on safari (*Silverstein in Africa*, PLAYBOY, October 1959), working at drawing board and recording studio (his disc, *Hairy Jazz*, was reviewed in February's *Playboy After Hours*), and just generally absorbing. Before long, he will journey forth again to far-flung places, but in the meantime he has set down his impressions of a locale in many ways as exotic as any he visited across the great waters. A whole new philosophy, called Beat, blossomed forth in America while he was away, and it took root in the Village. On these pages, Shel depicts this town-within-a-town in all its beat and bawdy glory.

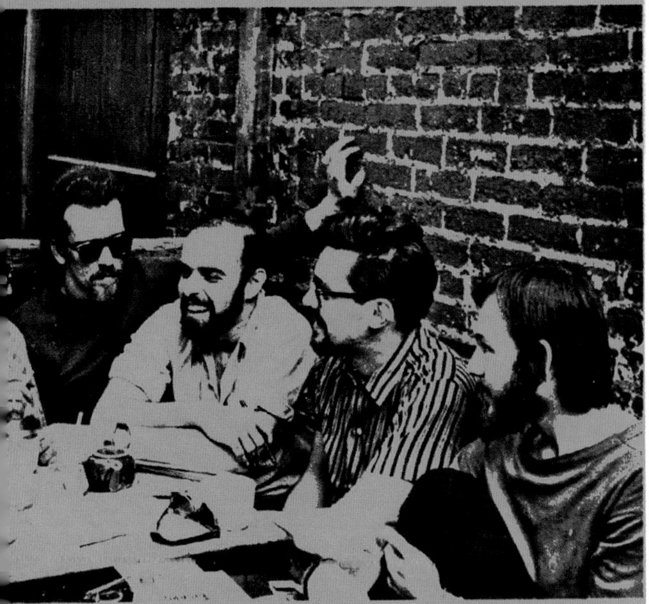

n the garden of Greenwich Village's Figaro coffee house, Shel ives it up with several other bearded artists and artisans.

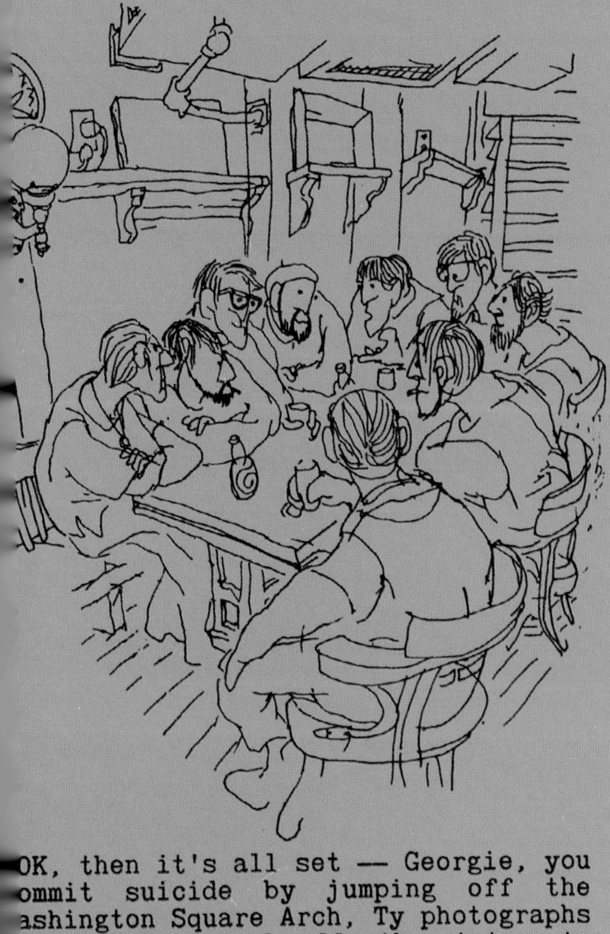

OK, then it's all set — Georgie, you ommit suicide by jumping off the ashington Square Arch, Ty photographs im in mid-air and sells the picture to he Daily News, Ted writes a short story bout him and sells it to The ew Yorker, Herb writes a play about im and sells it to the Phoenix Theatre, ou writes a folk song about him and ecords it for Decca, John writes a oem about him and sells it to Harper's, do a movie scenario starring Gene and ois and sell it to Hollywood, Vern aints a..."

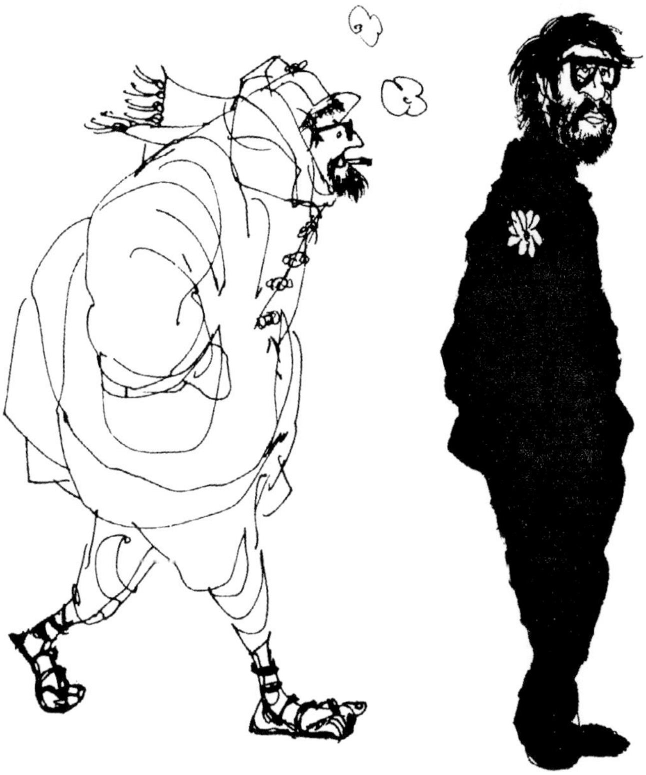

Winter in the Village   Spring in the Village

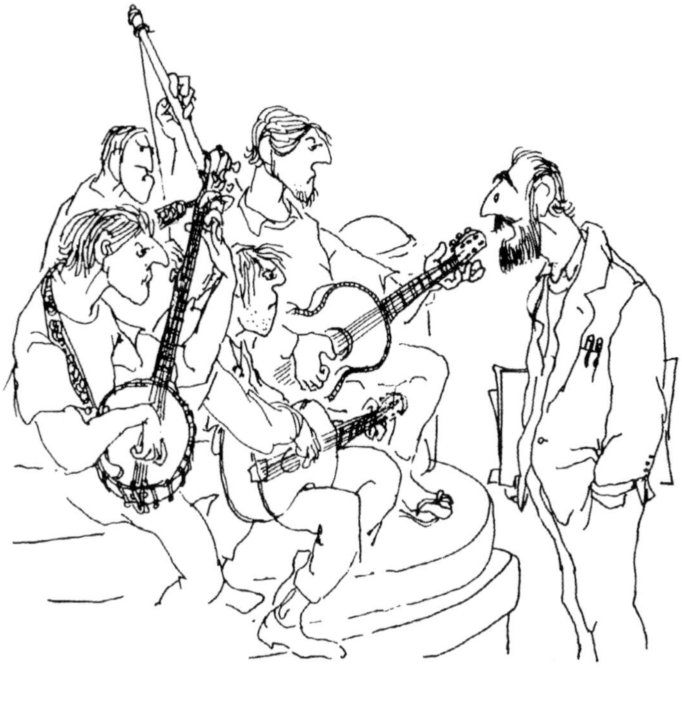

"Well how do you <u>know</u> you can't play 'Stardust' if you've never <u>tried</u> playing 'Stardust'?"

"What do you mean,
you'd sooner have a Marlboro?!!..."

"First of all,
you're not _thinking_ like a swan..."

"Boy, you should hear the lines of bull these guys give me. Some come on like lost little boys — they need me to mother them — what a laugh! Then the hippies, they come on cool — they will 'let me make it if I dig to!' Ha!! Then the college boys from the Bronx — they want something sincere — an 'intellectual relationship.' Some try to overwhelm me — they say, 'I don't know you, but I want your body!!' Some come on gay and want me to help them be men again. Brother! How corny can you get? And yet they keep giving me these same square stories to get me to go to bed with them. Bull! Pure bull! I don't know why I always go."

"Marie?"

"What, baby?"

"Why don't you like me, Marie?"

"Baby, I dig you the end."

"You dig me? Does that mean you
like me?"

"You're too much, baby, too much!"

"Too much what, Marie?"

"Tooooo much...you're something
else!"

"What else, Marie — I don't
understand???"

"You are the end. Uncool, man, but
like I groove behind you!!"

"Marie, I..."

"Let's split, baby."

"You want to split up? You want
me to go away?"

"No, baby, but this scene drags
me...I am bugged..."

"You mean the mosquitoes, Marie?
I think the light attracts —— "

"Let's cut out to your pad, baby.
I dig to wail..."

"You mean, to cry, Marie? Did I
say anything...?"

"To ball, baby...I dig to ball...."

"Whatever I said, I'm sorry, Marie.
Here, use my handkerchief..."

"Man, later!"

"Later what, Marie? Do you want
my handkerchief later? I don't
under —— "

"No, man, like forget it!"

"Marie..."

"What?"

"May I hold your hand?"

"And every night at twelve-fifteen there she
was at the stage door — waiting, so I
figured, well, it won't do any harm to say
hello. So I did, and the next thing I knew we
were having coffee, and then I found myself
taking her to dinner that Saturday, and I told
her we could only be friends, and I explained
all about Harvey and me, but the next thing I
knew I was seeing her every night and sending
her flowers and writing her poems, and I can't
sleep and I keep thinking about her, and I think
I'm falling in love with her!...I'm going to see
a psychiatrist."

"OK, baby, now let me lay the ground rules on
you. First of all, if you hit a fair ball to a
fielder who is stoned, it's an automatic double.
If you lose a sandle running to first, you're
out. No smoking when you're on base and no
hiding the ball in your beard. No fooling with
the chicks except between innings. Now their
butch right fielder has power, so keep the ball
low to her. Their shortstop is great, but he
should be busted by the fuzz by the third
inning. Now the ump is a Method actor, so..."

Top: the less-than-silver Silverstein voice is raised in ethnic song, to the delight of professional folksinger Jo March. Bottom: Shel evaluates the work of a fair artist at an artists' fair on the Village sidewalks.

"Ernie... seeing as how I'm new in the Village...and seeing as how this is our first date...a blind date... and since we don't really know each other very well yet...would it be all right if...would it be all right if we went to bed after the movie?"

"Gosh, Louise — the last time I saw you, you were voted Miss Ohio State of 1956...now you'll have to fill me in from there..."

IN ALASKA

MAY 1961

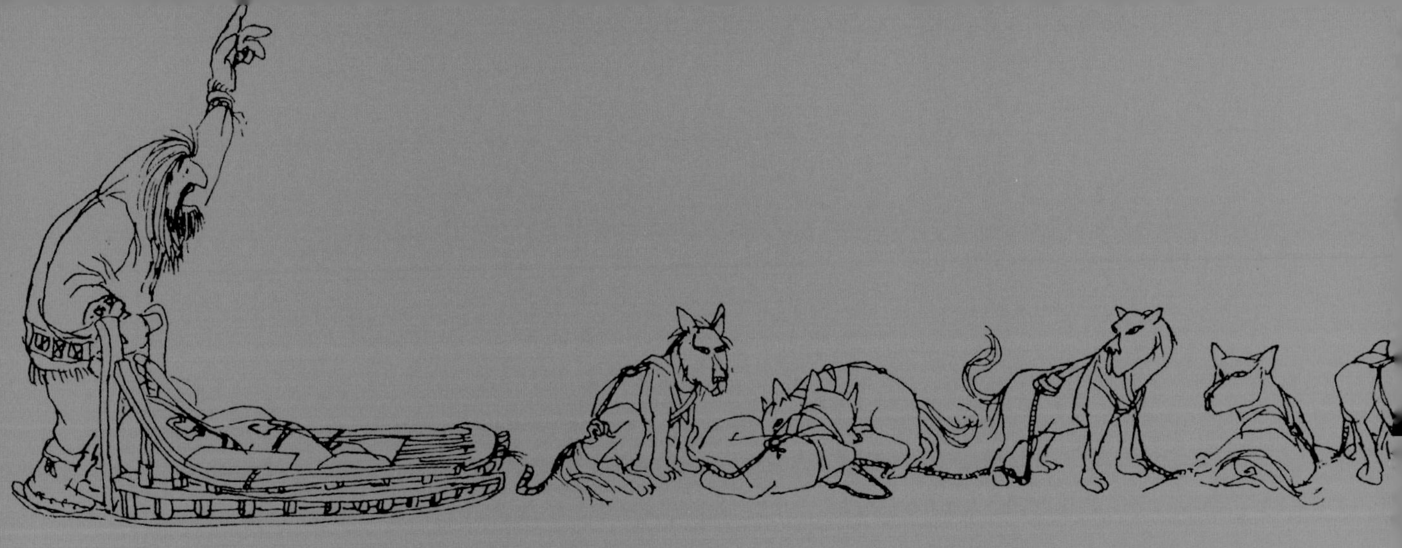

"GIDDYAP...er...LET'S GO...uh...what the hell is that word?!! GET ALONG, LITTLE DOGI

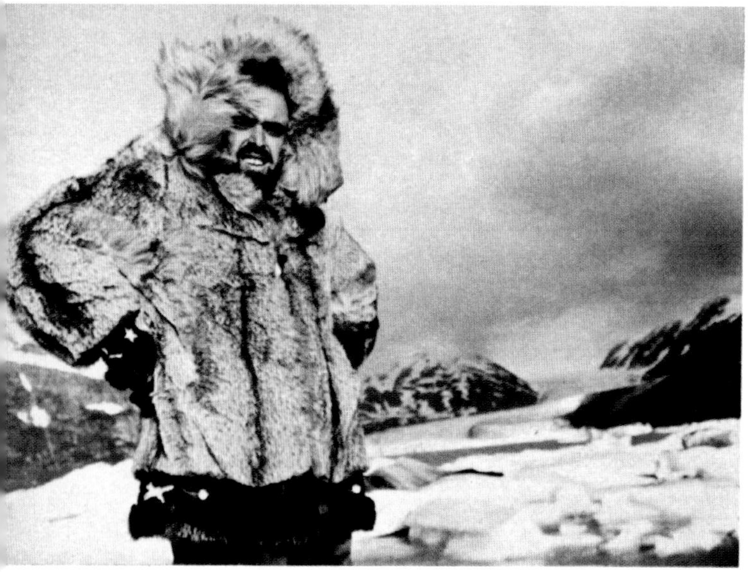

Silverstein IN ALASKA

our own abominable snowman sketches the 49th state

PACKED IN A PARKA and humming *Midnight Sun,* our bebristled cartoonist Shel Silverstein recently stomped through the snows of Alaska and found the last frontier to be a magnificent land of warm-hearted Eskimos and hard-drinking settlers. Snowshoeing and dogsledding his way, Shel mushed on to Anchorage, Fairbanks, Kotzebue, Nome and Point Barrow on the frosty Arctic Ocean. There's still gold in them thar hills, he discovered, but more panning is done by north country film critics than by adventuresome treasure seekers. Putting the lie to a crop of Hollywood fictions, Shel found nary an igloo, but did find an array of Eskimos weary of flicks about intrigue in the ice domes. Another myth exploded by Shel was the one about the accommodating Eskimo husband and the itinerant tourist. "It simply isn't so," moaned Shel. What impressed him the most? The stunning scenery and the innate good sense of the people. "Shooting a moose out of season," Shel says, "is considered a worse offense than shooting your wife."

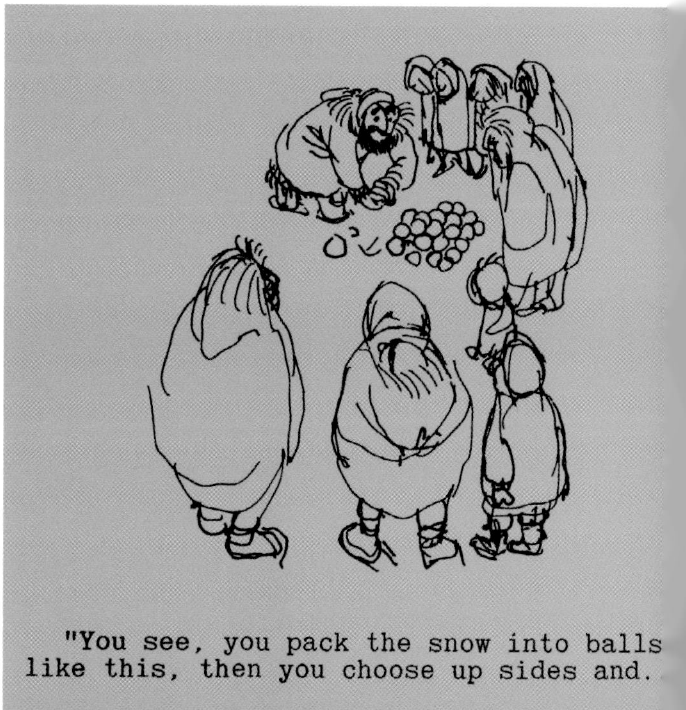

"You see, you pack the snow into balls like this, then you choose up sides and.

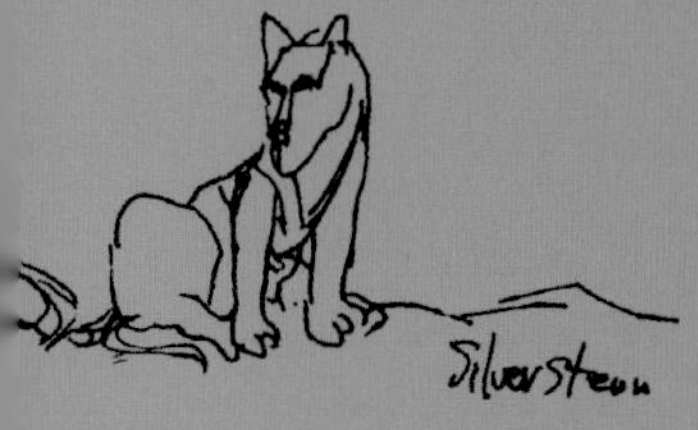

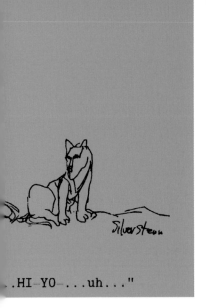

"..HI YO...uh..."

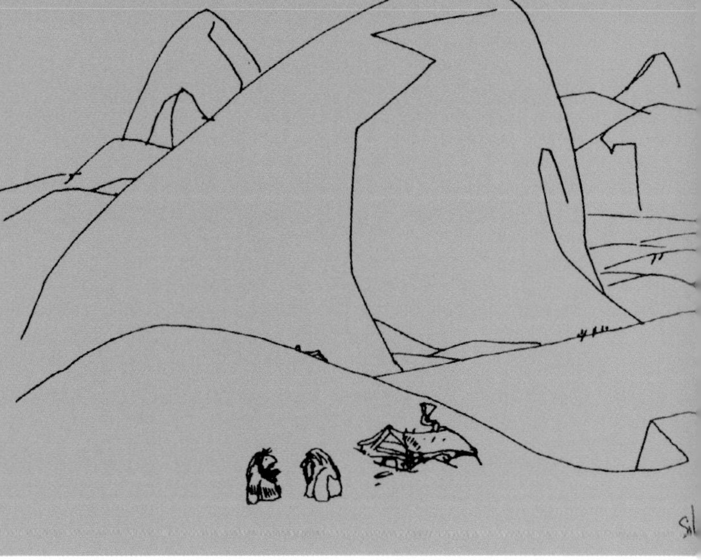

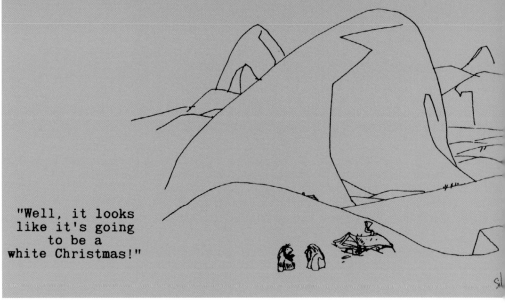

"Well, it looks
like it's going
to be a
white Christmas!"

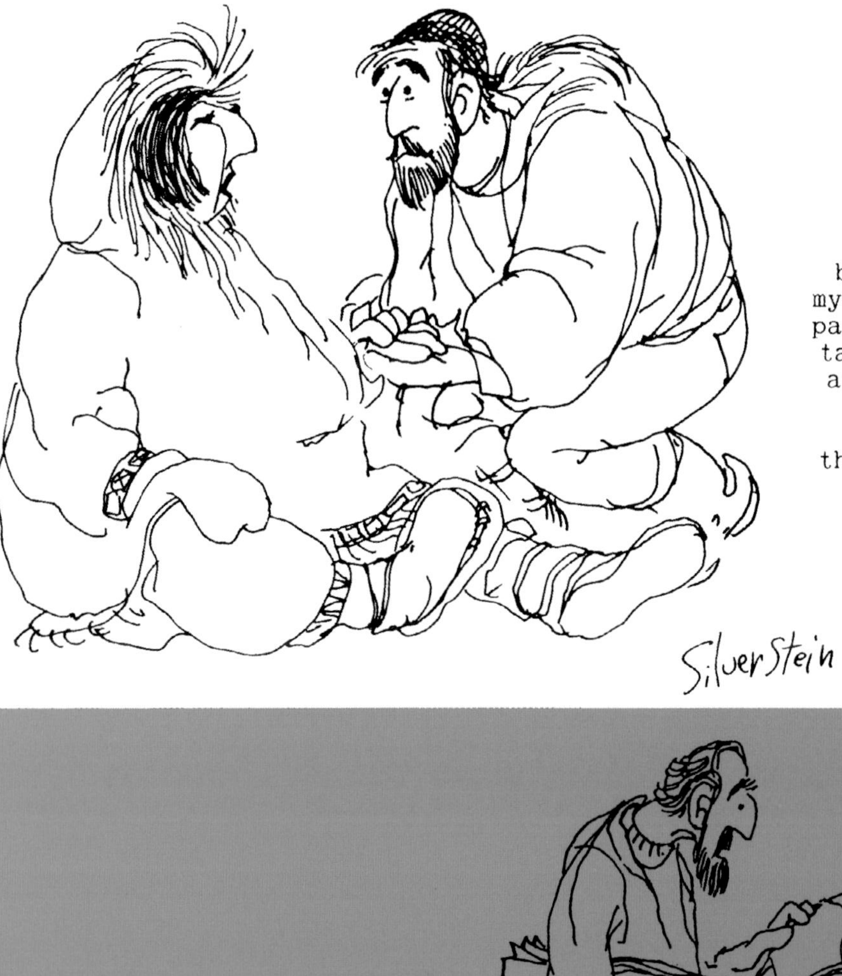

"Sure, it would be fun,
but I'd have to take off
my outer parka, then my fur
parka, and then I'd have to
take off my sealskin vest,
and then my sweaters, and
then I'd have to take
off my flannels, and by
that time I'd be too tired."

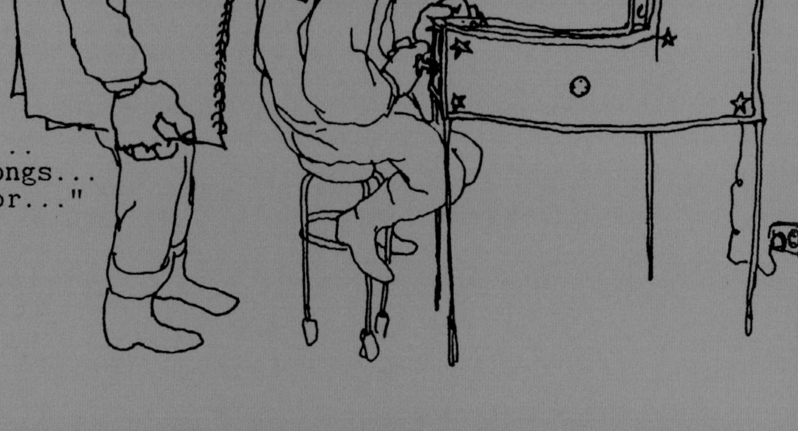

"Don't you ever go whale hunting...
or paddle a kayak...or sing Eskimo songs...
or eat blubber...or build igloos...or..."

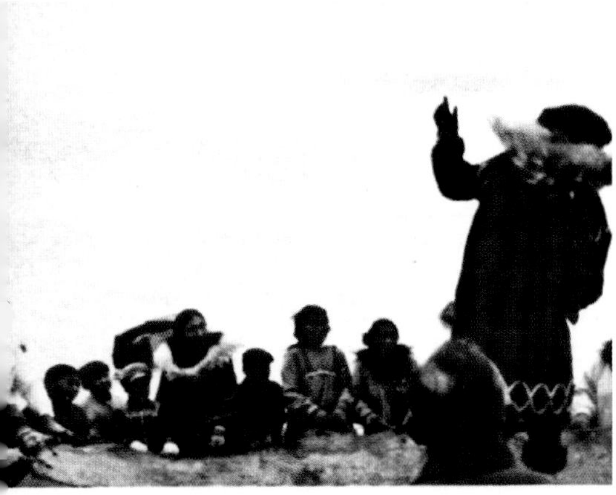

Above: shaggy Shel joins in a local bounce-the-Eskimo rite. Foraging hunters devised this stunt to sight the next meal over the next hill. Below: Shel and a crusty gold-rush vet compare pans in reconfirming the adage about all that glitters.

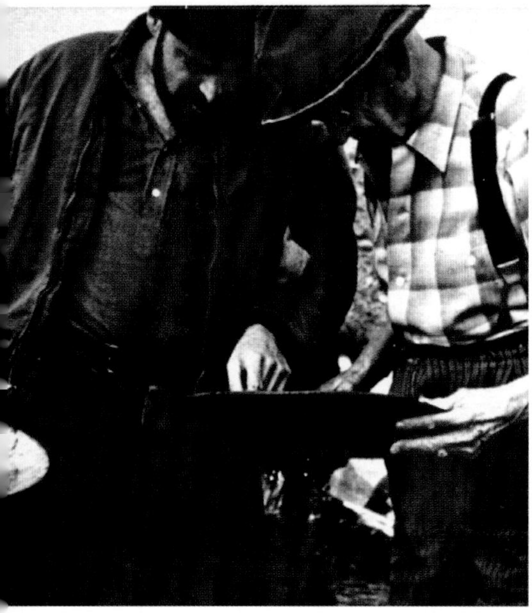

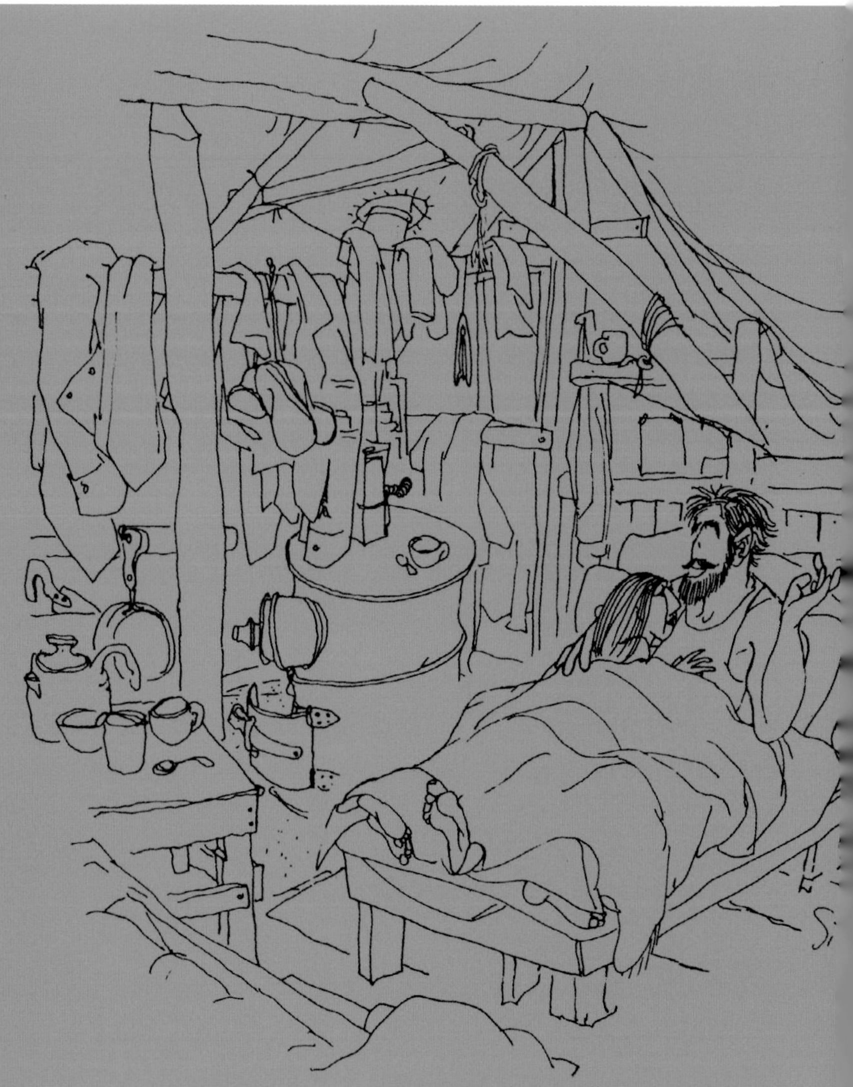

"Tell me, Ara, how did that silly nose-rubbing story get started, anyway?"

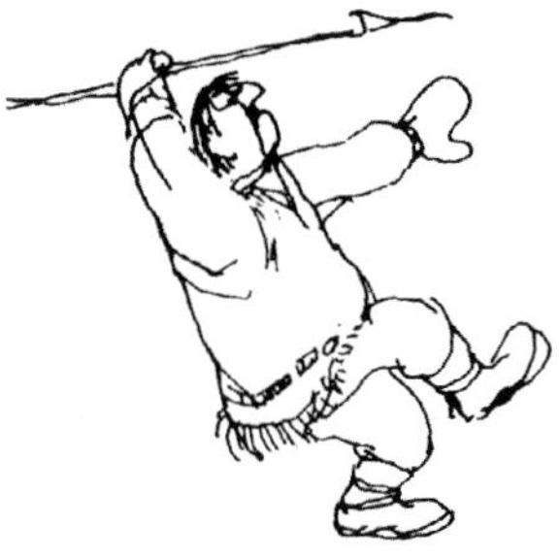

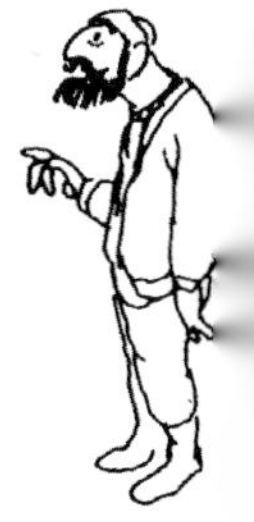

"You see, back home we always believed the stories that you guys *wanted* a visitor to sleep with your wives...that you'd be *insulted* if he *didn't* sleep with your wives...tha

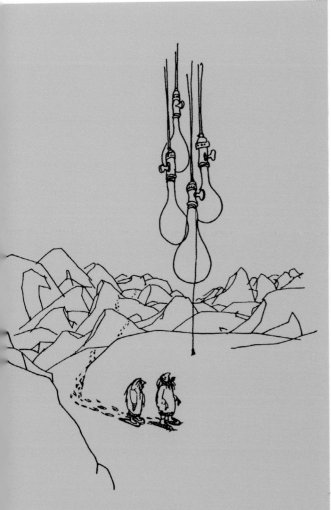

"Why, those are
the Northern Lights,
what did you think?"

'Now that Alaska has become the forty-ninth
state, do you feel that the influence
exerted politically by the state will
affect national and international
policies to such an extent that our
economic horizons will eventually..."

OK, OK, so the hamburger was tough. What
o you expect for a lousy $3.75, anyway?!"

"Let's see now — interesting characters
that I knew during the gold rush...well,
there was Suicide Laura, and Diamond
Tooth Lou, and Dolly the Virgin, and
the Never Eat Sisters...there was the
Gimme Kid, and the Baroness, and Black
Jim Wilson, and the Ham and Egg Twins,
and Fugemall Jack, and Bullcow Nelson,
and the Scurvy Kid, and the Crooked Kid,
and Inandout, and Queen Bess...but they
weren't really very interesting..."

IN HAWAII

JUNE 1961

Approved for departure from Japan
Date of departure
HANEDA
Port of departure
Immigration Inspector

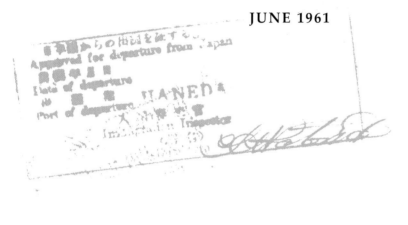

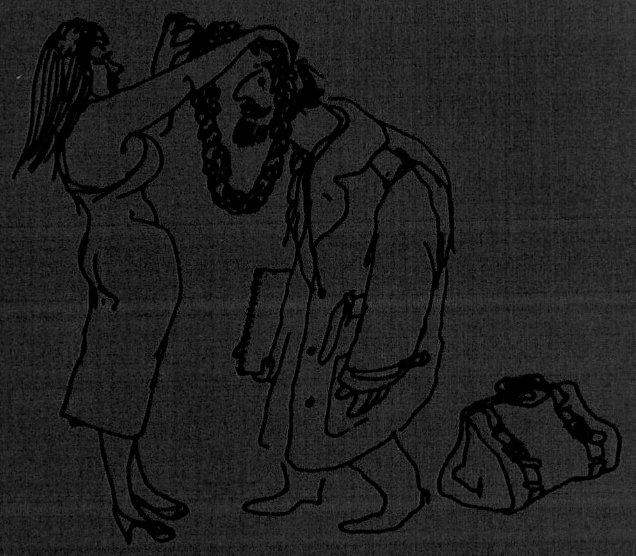

"Aloha, sir...and I hope you enjoy Hawaii, sir...
and it's spelled l-e-i, sir...
and I've heard that joke 3,227 times, sir..."

Silverstein IN Hawaii

humor

our bearded beachcomber says aloha to the fiftieth state

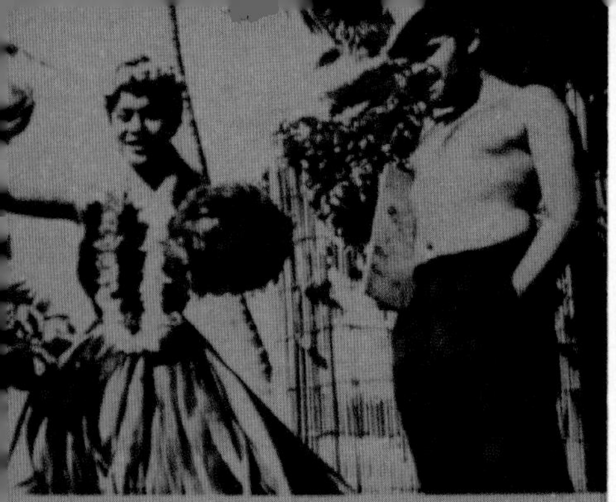

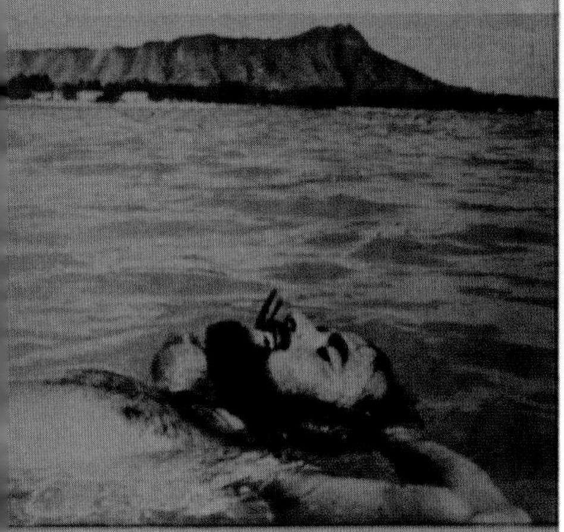

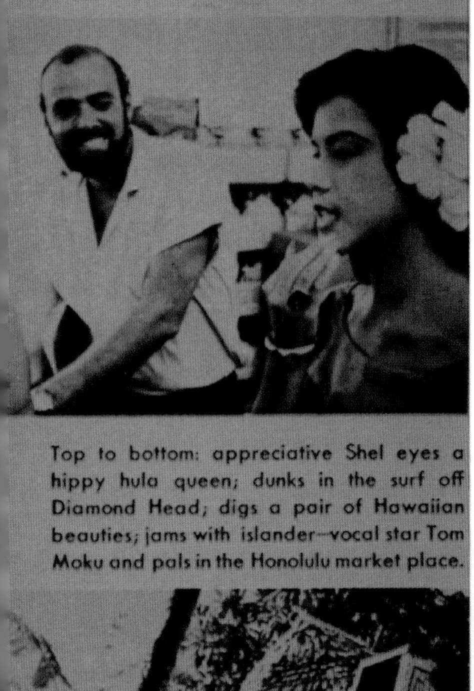

Top to bottom: appreciative Shel eyes a hippy hula queen; dunks in the surf off Diamond Head; digs a pair of Hawaiian beauties; jams with islander—vocal star Tom Moku and pals in the Honolulu market place.

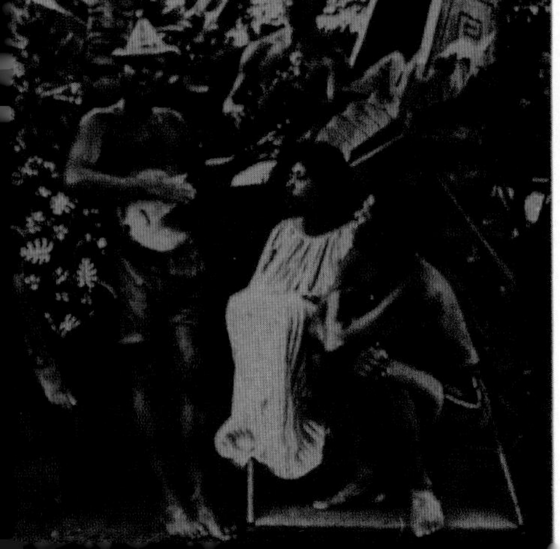

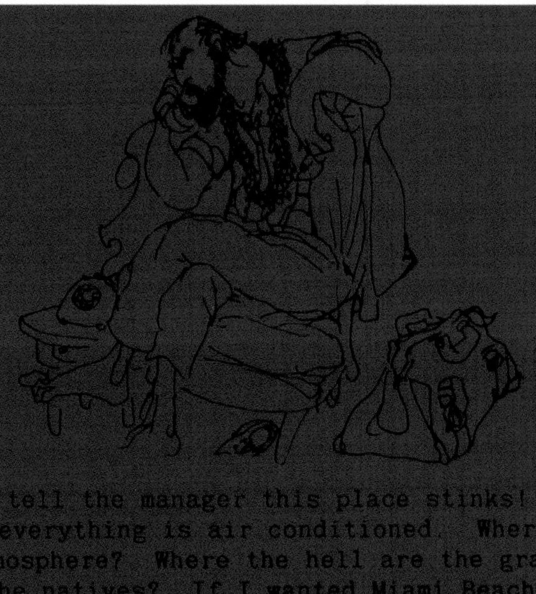

"Listen, you tell the manager this place stinks! Everything is modern...everything is air conditioned. Where the hell is the atmosphere? Where the hell are the grass huts, where are the natives? If I wanted Miami Beach, I'd have gone to Miami Beach. Where is your 'tropical paradise'? Where is the simplicity...where is the serenity? And also, where the hell is that damn bellboy with my drink?!!"

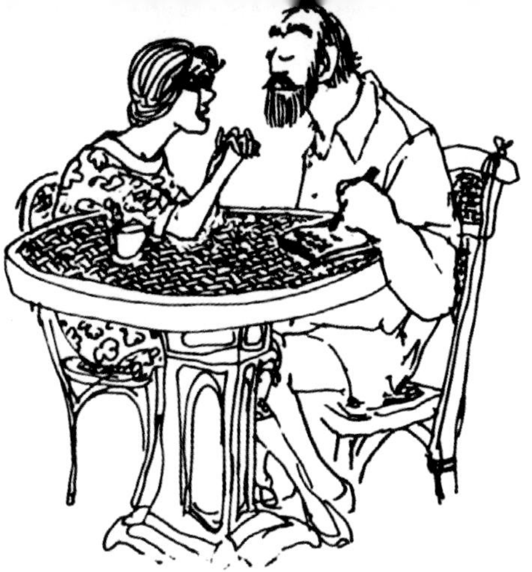

"And that's the story of King Kalakaua and how he conquered the islands. You know, it's really wonderful to find someone from the mainland who is interested in our history and culture. Most tourists who come here just seem to be looking for — excuse me, ›ut would you mind taking your hand off my leg."

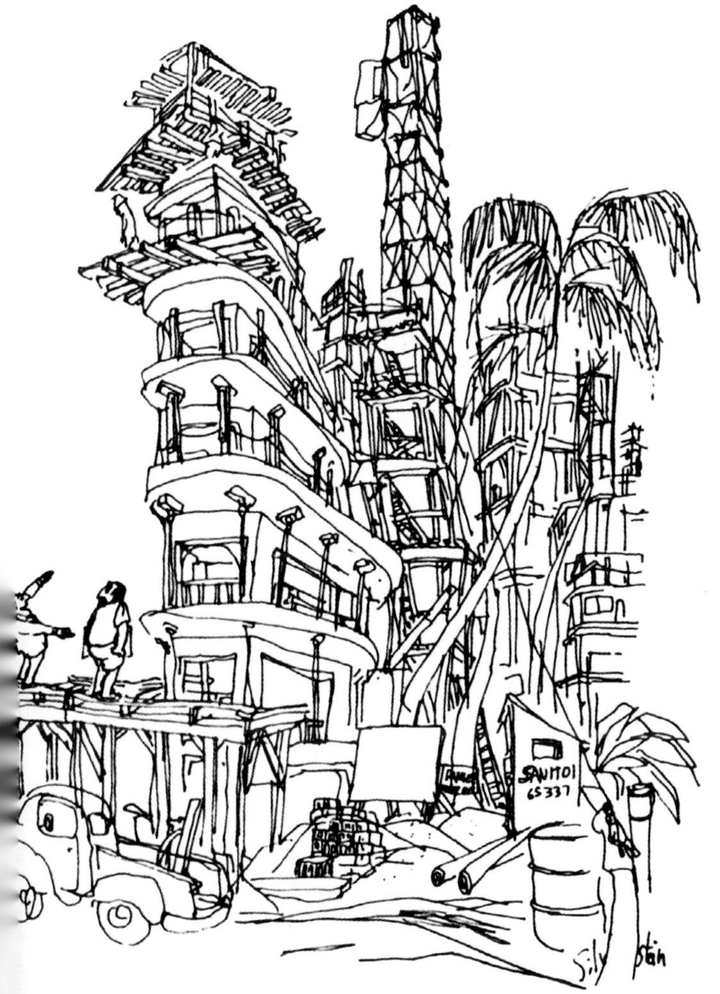

nd we're going to build more hotels and bigger hotels and better hotels, and we're going .o get rid of all those damned palm trees and build still more hotels, and get rid of that each and build greater hotels...and then when ie tourists arrive, we'll be <u>ready</u> for them!!"

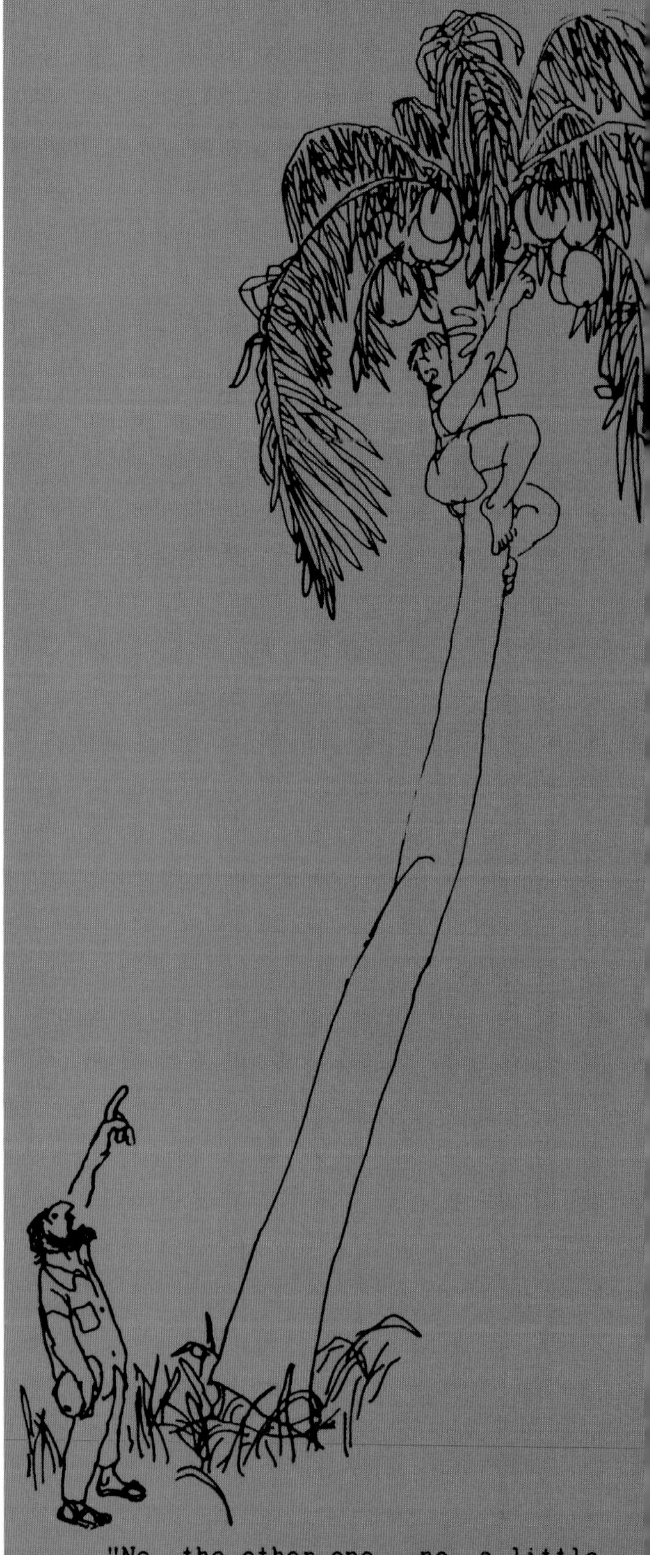

"No, the other one...no, a little to the left...now straight down...no, a little above that one...no, no... a little to your right...now just above...that's it...no, that one just next...you almost had it... just a little to your left...no..."

"No use, Shel — I can't fake it. If I show the surfboard, the sand shows, too. If I don't show the sand, then I can't show the surfboard. I think we're going to have to go into the water."

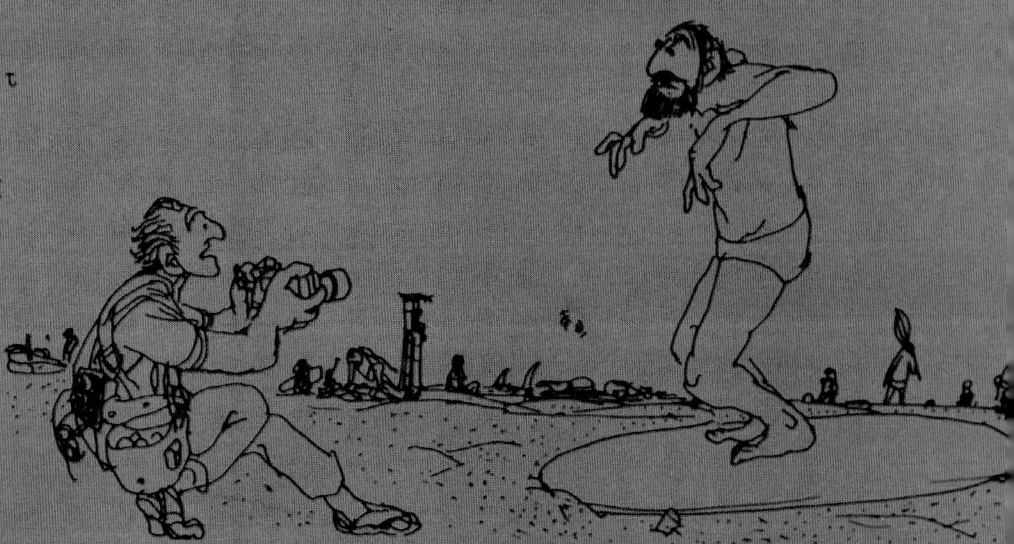

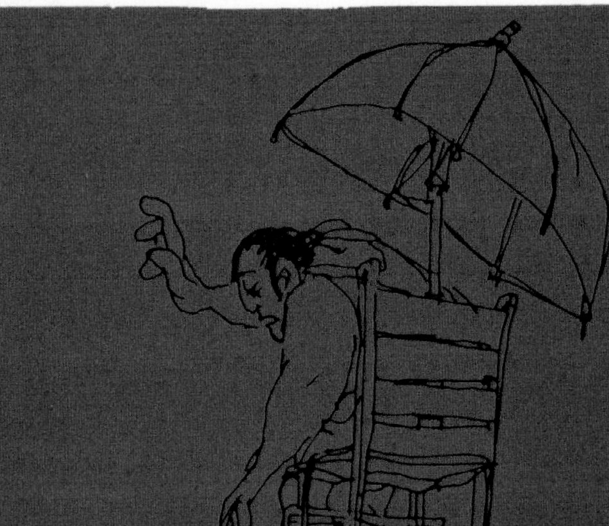

"Man, these rich American girls — they too bossy — they want to take me to nightclub...I say OK — I go to nightclub...they say let's go to bed— OK, I go to bed. They say they want to buy me present — I say OK, buy me present. Then they say, 'You come to store, pick out present' and I say, 'Just a minute, enough is enough!'"

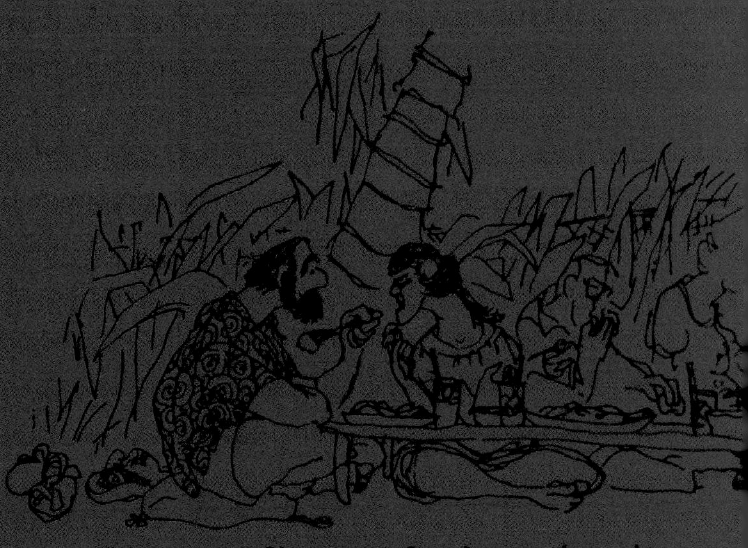

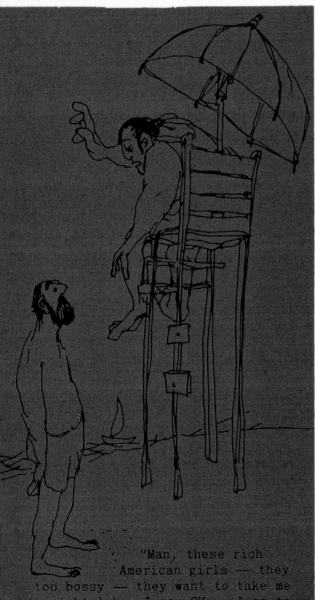

"Use your fingers, for heaven's sake — were you brought up in a barn?!"

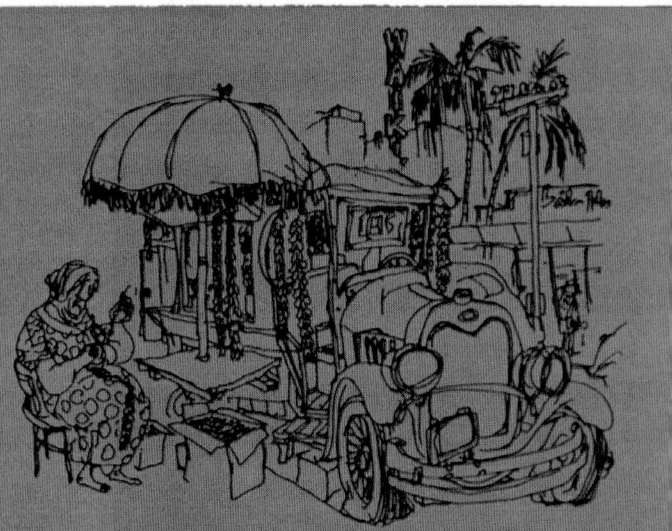

"...A few carnations...some rose petals. an orchid...And then the missionaries come.. and they take away our land and make us wear muumuu...and by'm'bye many Hawaiia die and Big Five own everything...but Hawaiians not mad at white people... Hawaiians make leis for white people tourists A few carnations...some rose petals... a little poison ivy..."

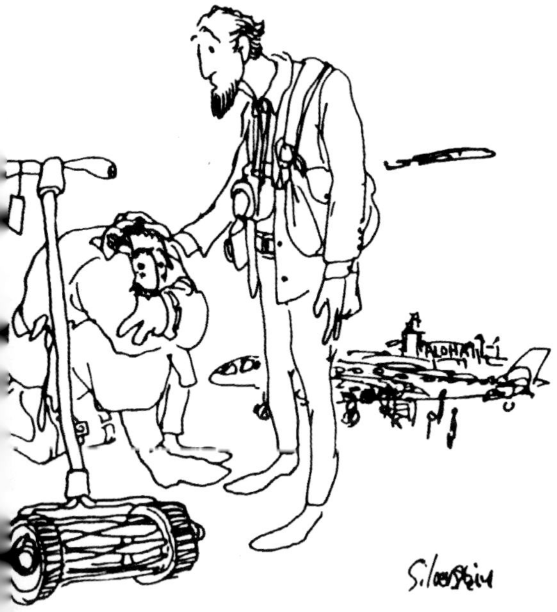

"But even if they were still wearing grass skirts, you've got to admit it would have been a pretty corny gag!"

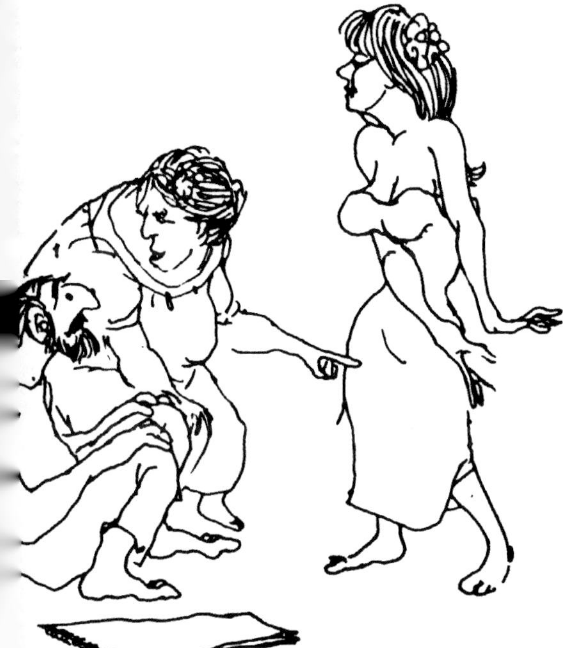

"You see, Mr. Silverstein — in the hula, the story is told with the hands...the hands, Mr. Silverstein...you have to watch the hands. The story is...uh, Mr. Silverstein... Mr. Silverstein..."

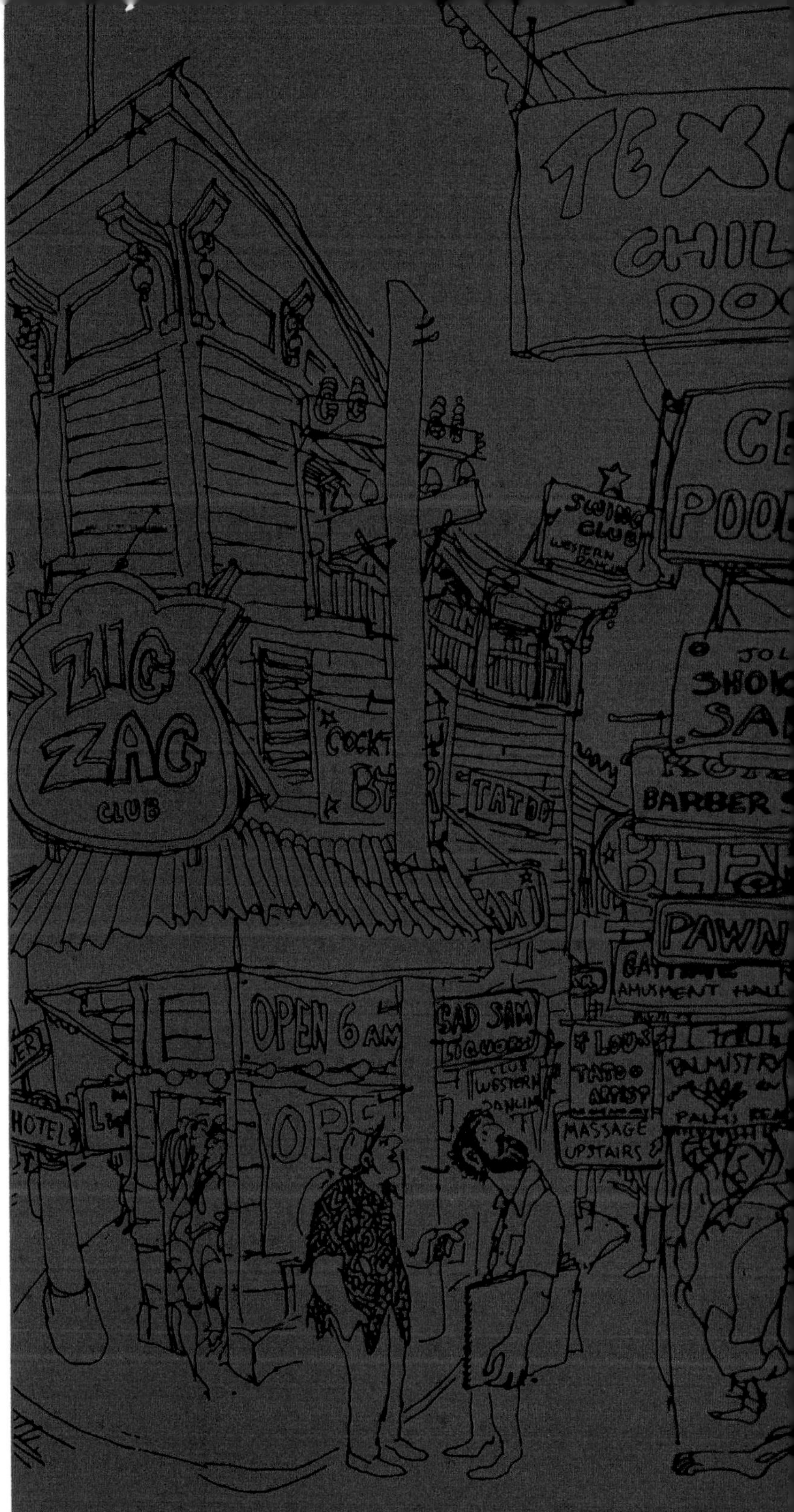
ZIG ZAG
CLUB
OPEN 6 AM
SAD SAM
LIQUORS
HOTEL
MASSAGE UPSTAIRS
PAWN

"Back on the mainland everybody thinks that this island is just a primitive, backward place with ukuleles and dancing girls in grass skirts and half-naked savages swimming in the surf. When you go back, please let them know we're just as civilized here as they are."

PLAYS BALL

JUNE 1962

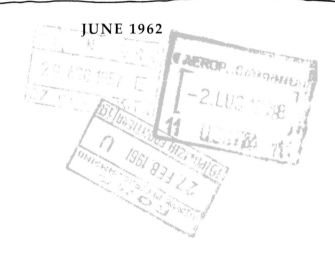

"Let's see now...Getting hit in the beard by a pitched ball...No. Getting hit by a pitched ball in the beard... No. Getting hit by..."

Silverstein PLAYS BALL

our bushy bush leaguer joins the white sox for spring training

Dressed to the nines in pinstripe baseball flannels and toting a well-padded mitt, cartoonist Shel Silverstein recently trekked to Sarasota, Florida, for a five-week spring-training fling with the Chicago White Sox. This trial introduction to the innings and outs of big-league ball was for Shel a boyhood dream of glory come true: while still a beardless Chicago youth he earned his daily bread vending beer and hot dogs at Comiskey Park, the White Sox balliwick. According to our hirsute hero, he came within a whisker of making the opening-day squad: "It was Luis Aparicio or me," he admits modestly, "and I just didn't want to hurt Luis' feelings. As of now, I'm a free agent, available to any ball club that might be a contender."

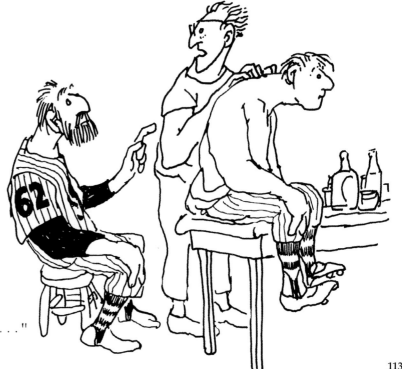

"Look, if you were a pitcher, I'd rub down your arm for you. If you were an outfielder, I'd massage your legs. But all you do is sit on the bench, and I'll be damned if I'll..."

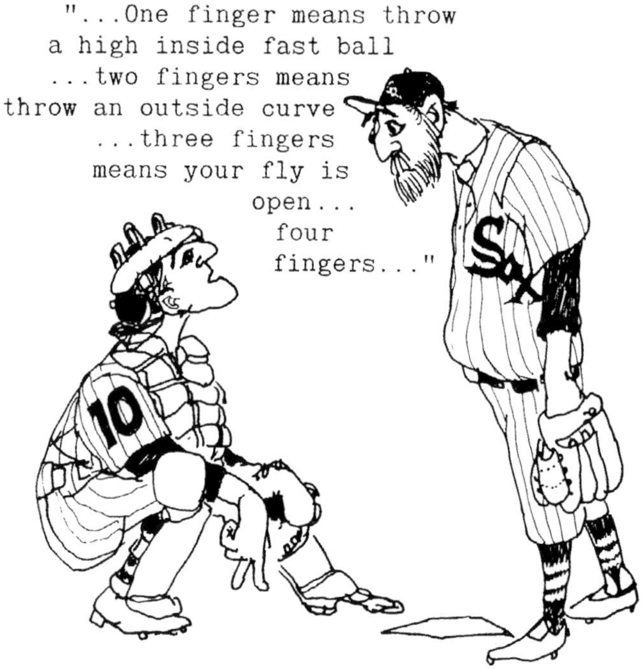
"...One finger means throw
a high inside fast ball
...two fingers means
throw an outside curve
...three fingers
means your fly is
open...
four
fingers..."

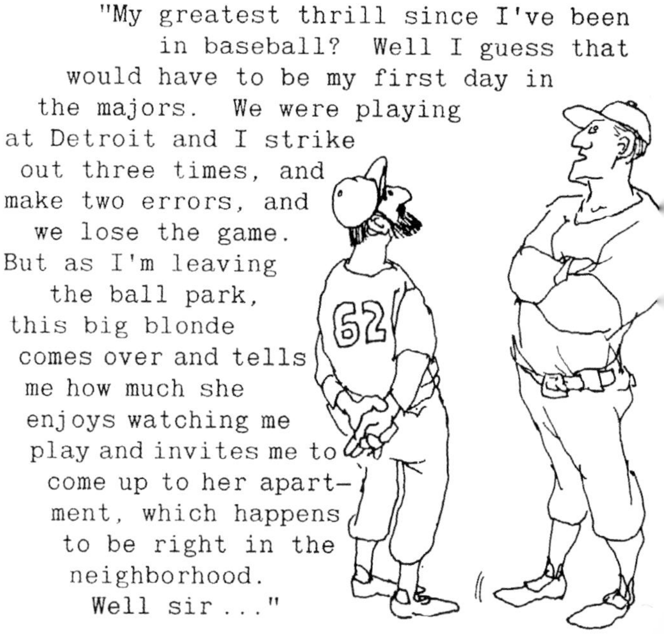
"My greatest thrill since I've been
in baseball? Well I guess that
would have to be my first day in
the majors. We were playing
at Detroit and I strike
out three times, and
make two errors, and
we lose the game.
But as I'm leaving
the ball park,
this big blonde
comes over and tells
me how much she
enjoys watching me
play and invites me to
come up to her apart-
ment, which happens
to be right in the
neighborhood.
Well sir..."

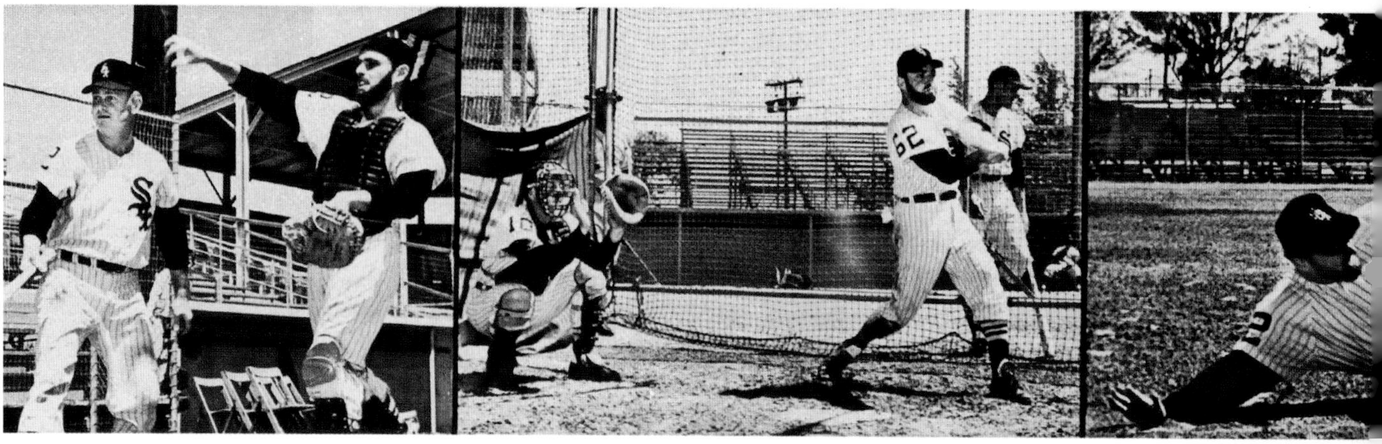

Playing the Shel game, our catcher in the wry makes a flip return, poles one to the far reaches of the pitcher's mound, and

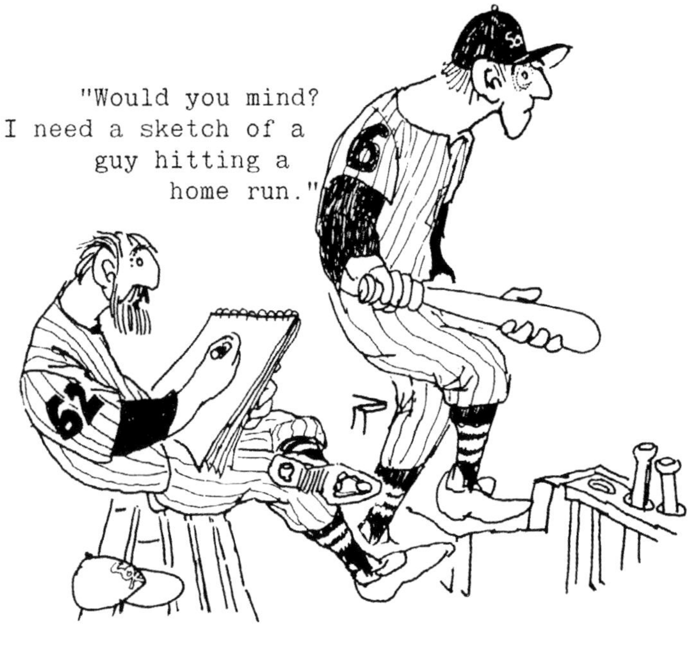
"Would you mind?
I need a sketch of a
guy hitting a
home run."

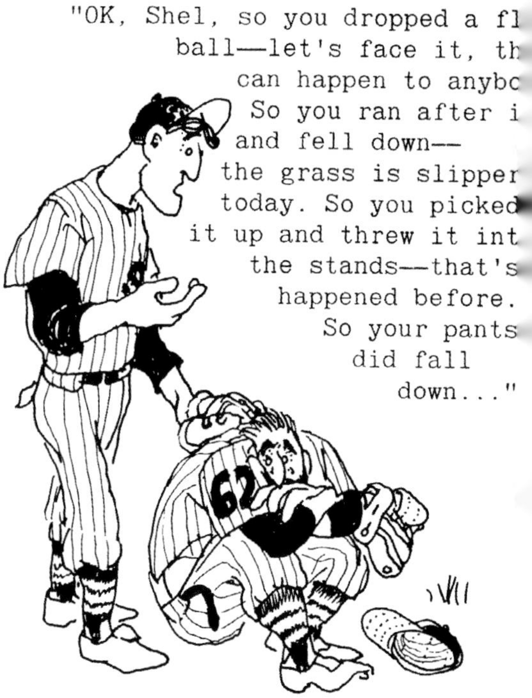
"OK, Shel, so you dropped a fl
ball—let's face it, th
can happen to anybo
So you ran after i
and fell down—
the grass is slipper
today. So you picked
it up and threw it int
the stands—that's
happened before.
So your pants
did fall
down..."

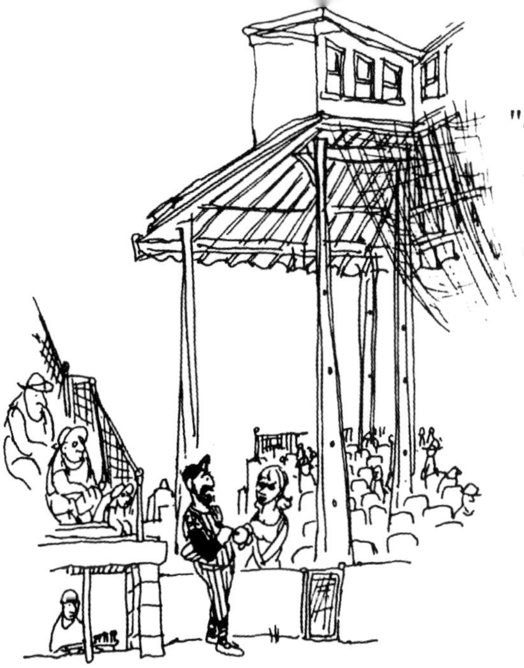

"So Al Lopez says to me, 'Mantle,' he says, 'If the Yankees ever find out that you're playing for us in your spare time, they'll be plenty mad, so how about growing a beard so that nobody will recognize you...?'"

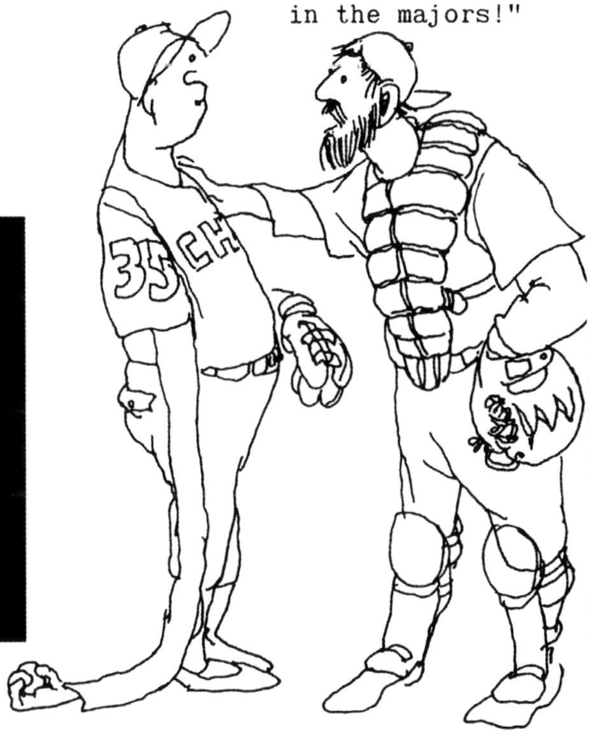

"Gee, imagine— 18 years of pitching in the majors!"

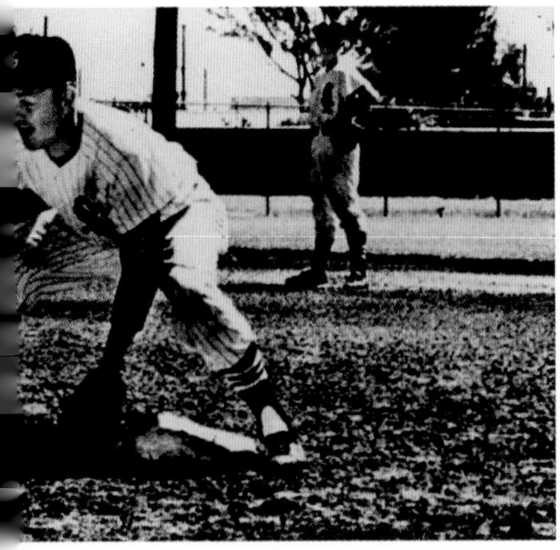

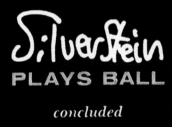

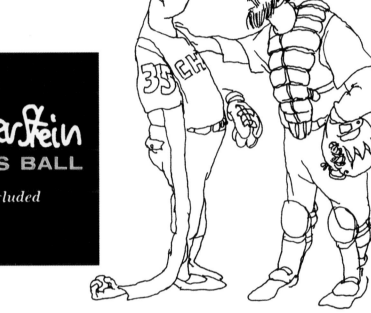

tempting to swipe second from Nellie Fox

Silverstein PLAYS BALL

concluded

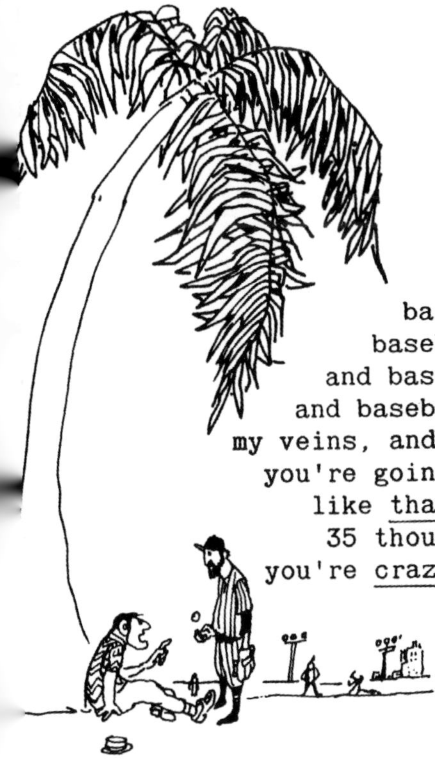

"So I says, 'Look, I'm a ball player who <u>loves</u> to play baseball. I eat, sleep and dream baseball. I got baseball in my mind, and baseball in my heart, and baseball running through my veins, and if you think you're going to get a guy like <u>that</u> for a lousy 35 thousand a year, you're <u>crazy</u>!'"

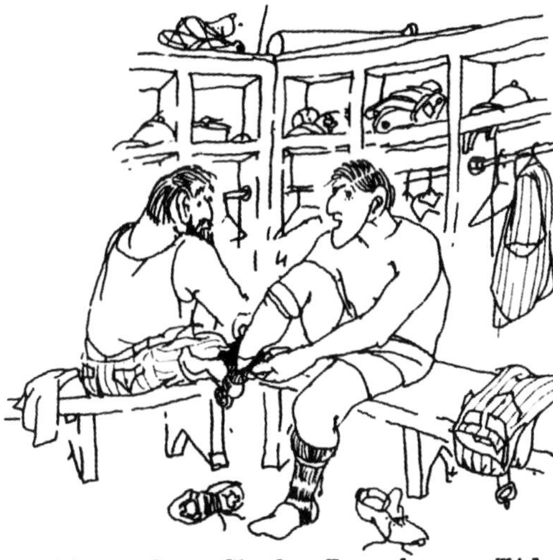

"Here's how it works, Shel: I endorse Wilson baseball shoes and they give me free shoes... I endorse Gillette razors and they give me free razors and razor blades... I endorse Wheaties and they give me free Wheaties... So maybe you'd like me to endorse those Bunnies down at that key club and..."

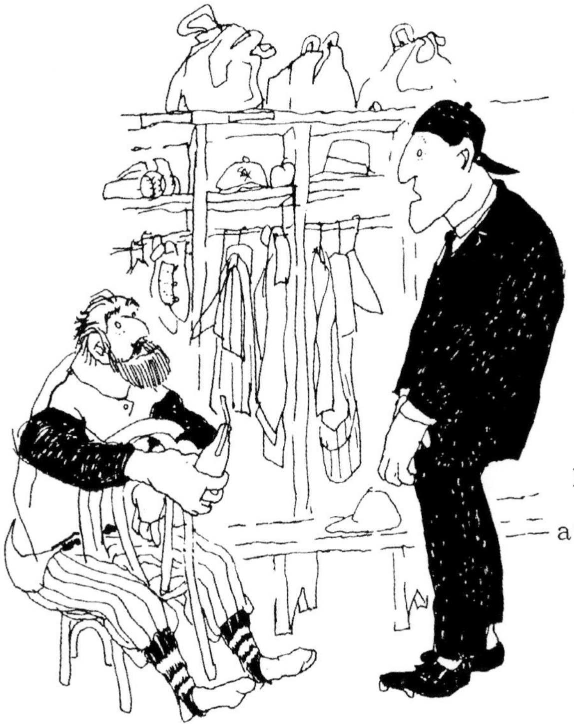

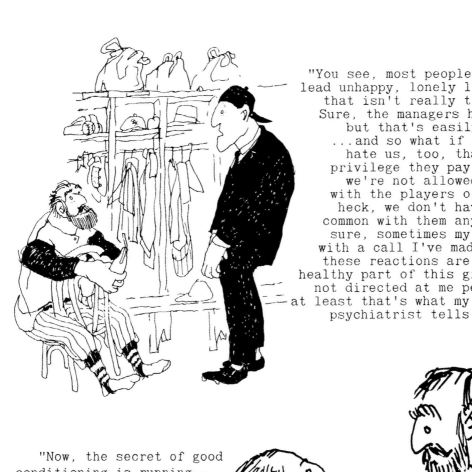

"You see, most people think umpires lead unhappy, lonely lives, but that isn't really true. Sure, the managers hate us, but that's easily understood ...and so what if the fans hate us, too, that's the privilege they pay for...and so we're not allowed to fraternize with the players off the field— heck, we don't have much in common with them anyway...and sure, sometimes my family disagrees with a call I've made, but all of these reactions are a good, healthy part of this great game and not directed at me personally... at least that's what my psychiatrist tells me..."

"Now, the secret of good conditioning is running— I want you to run out on that field...I want you to do 20 laps around the infield, and I want you to keep running, and do 10 laps around the outfield, and I want you to keep running all the way back to the hotel, and pack your bag, and keep running all the way back to Chicago, so we can get some work done here!"

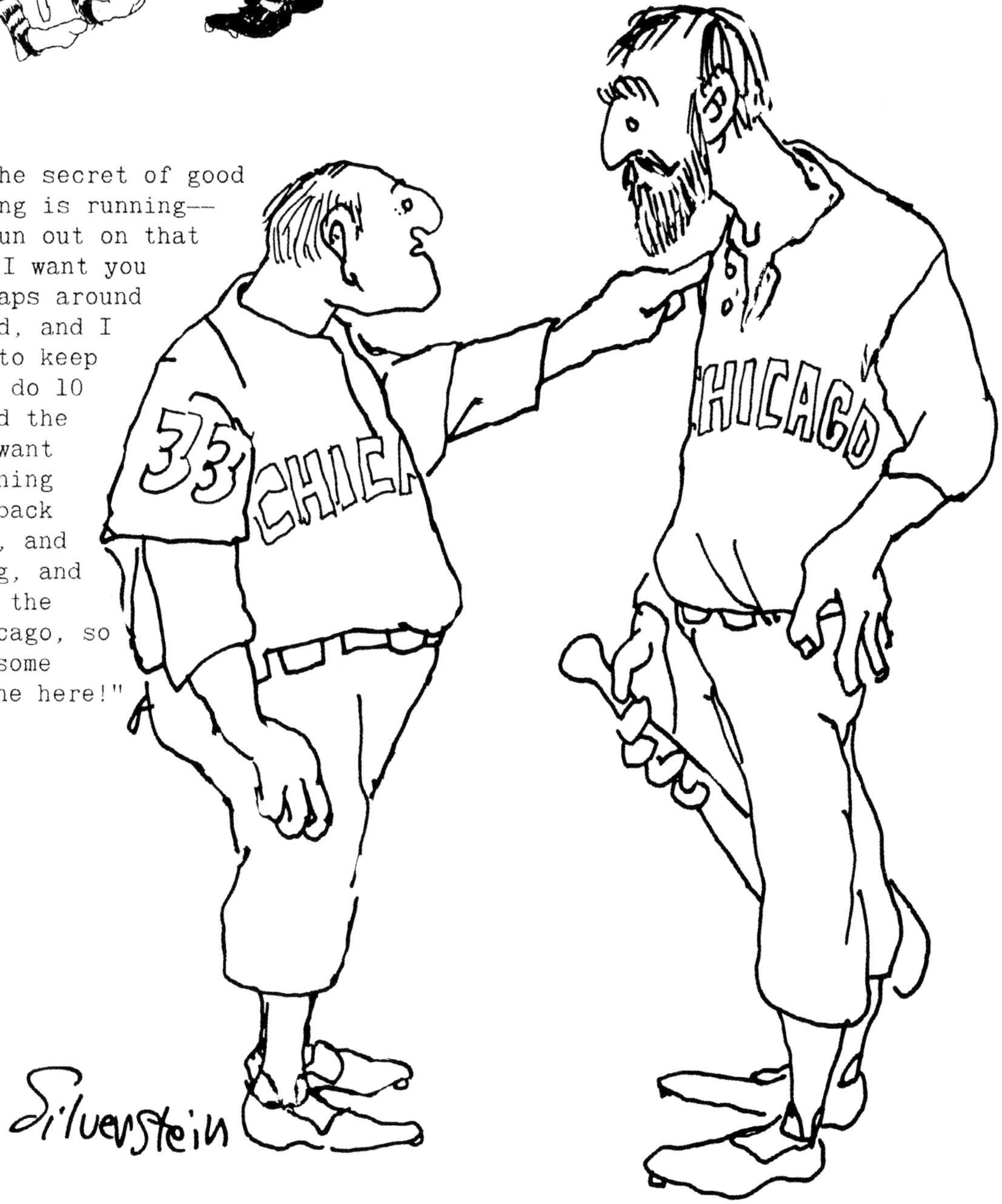
33
CHIC
CHICAGO
Silverstein

IN MIAMI

MARCH 1963

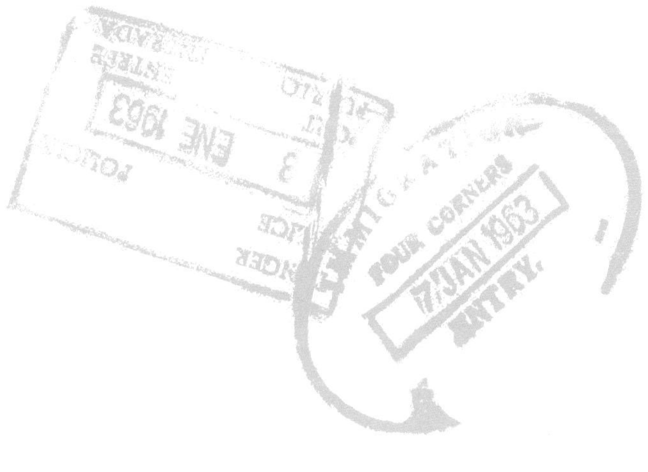
3 ENE 1963
FOUR CORNERS
7 JAN 1963
ENTRY.

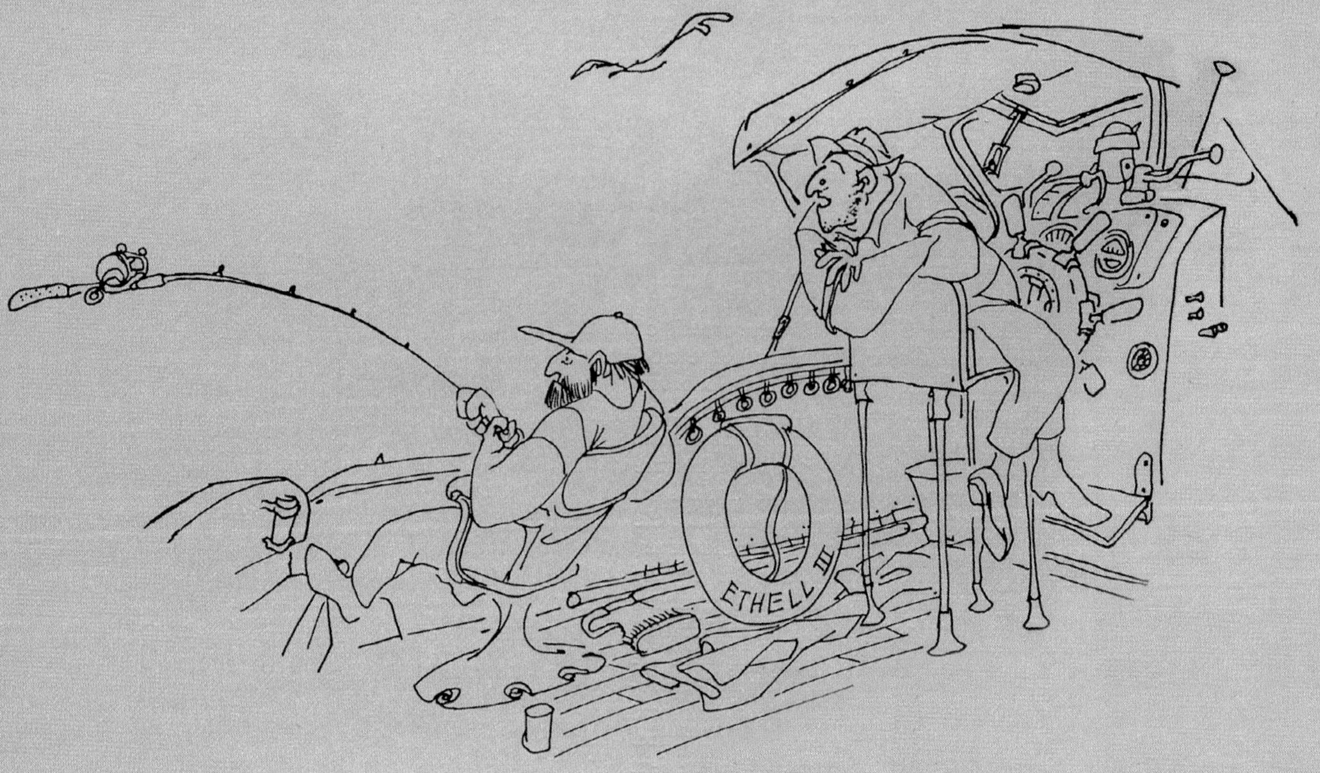
ETHELL III

"Y'know, it's a funny thing...y'all look more like a fisherman than any man I've ever seen. When I first laid eyes on you, I said to myself, 'Now there's a fisherman!' I says..."

"In March those damn college girls flock down here... in April those office girls come down here...in January the rich wives show up...in June it's the schoolteachers. A real prostitute doesn't stand a chance anymore!"

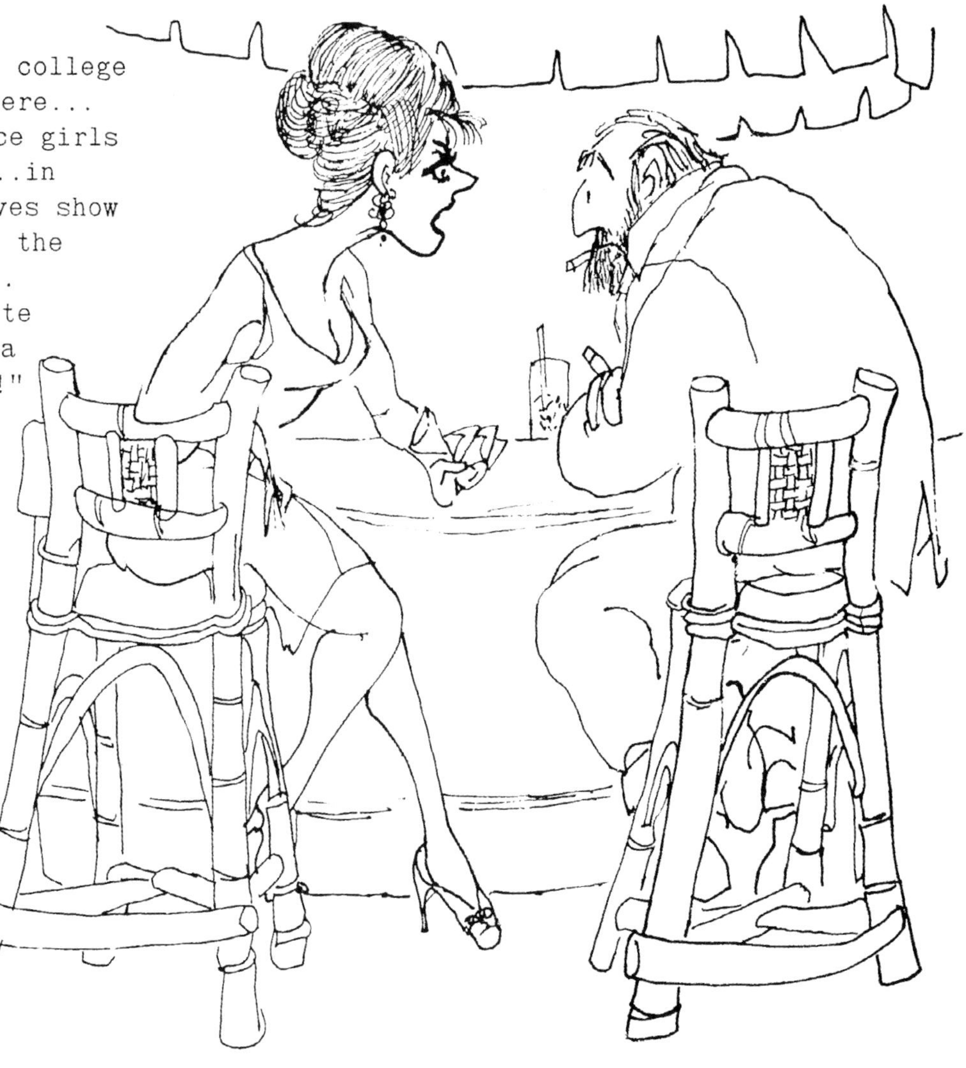

silverstein in miami

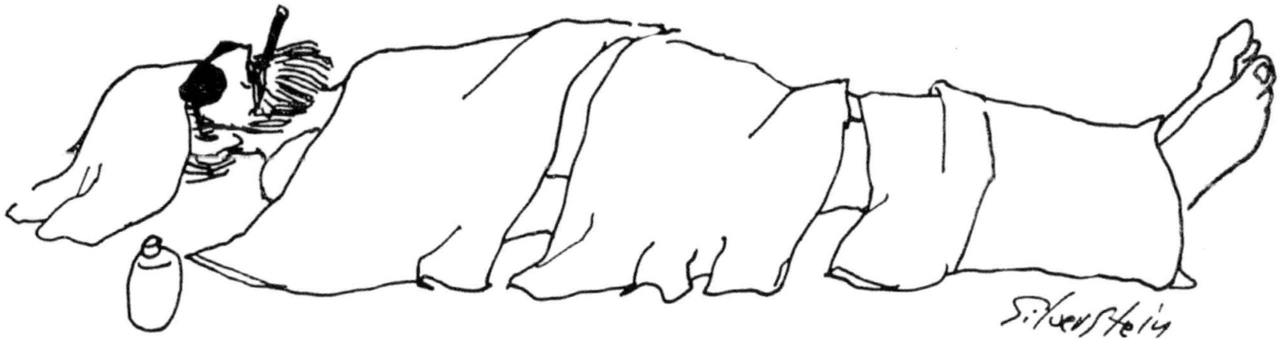

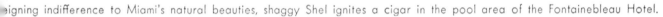

playboy's peripatetic beard beards florida's florid playground

eigning indifference to Miami's natural beauties, shaggy Shel ignites a cigar in the pool area of the Fontainebleau Hotel.

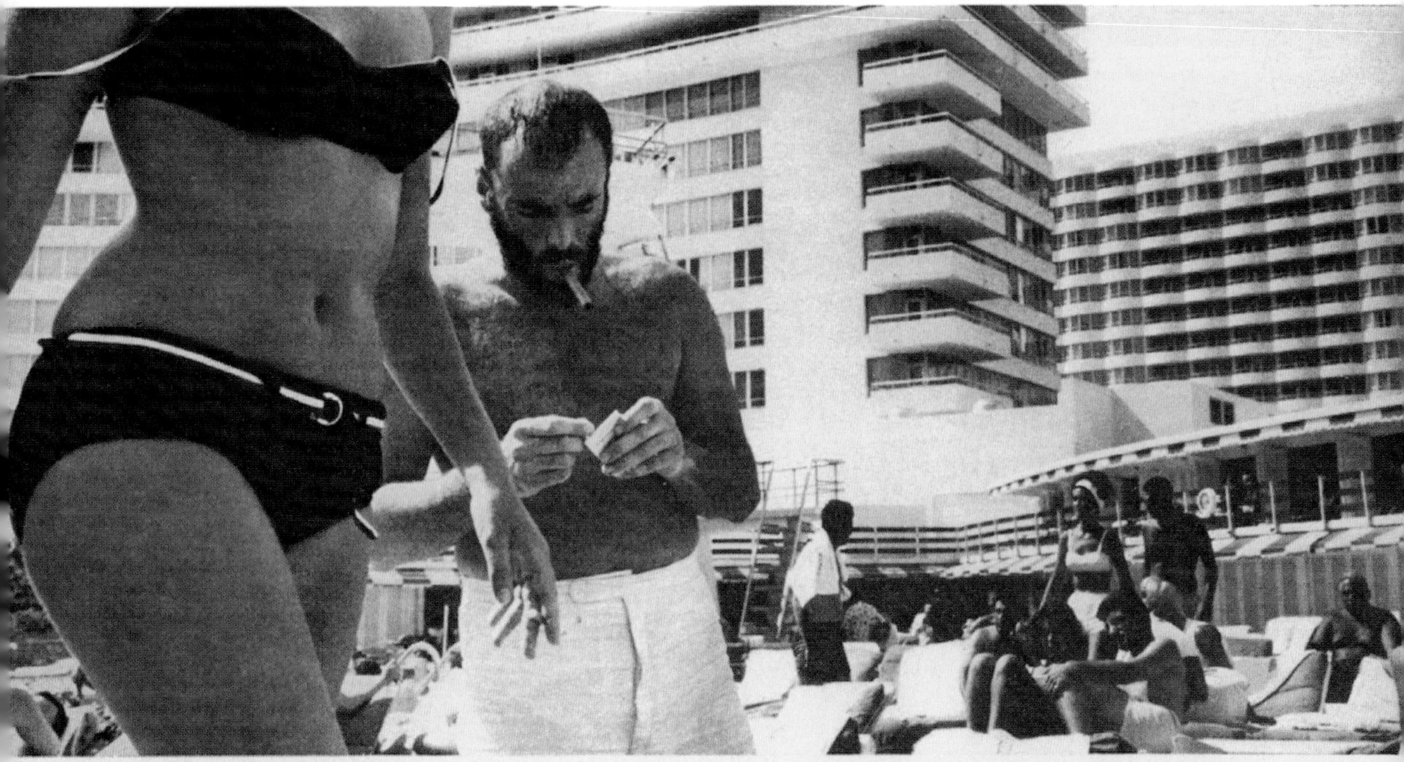

Clutching a jug of sun-tan lotion and whistling *Moon Over* you-know-what, Shel Silverstein, PLAYBOY's wandering minstrel of the sketch board, recently trekked to Miami Beach to research and relish the palm-fringed benefits of that land flowing with mink and honeys. Venturing forth from his Fontainebleau Hotel base, Shel first observed at close hand the storied playground and its sun and sand, bars and boites, fur-bearing females and go-for-baroque architecture. Then, having soaked up sufficient local color and Planter's Punch, our bushy chronicler set up his unjaded palette and recorded these wry impressions of Florida's phantasmagorial gold coast.

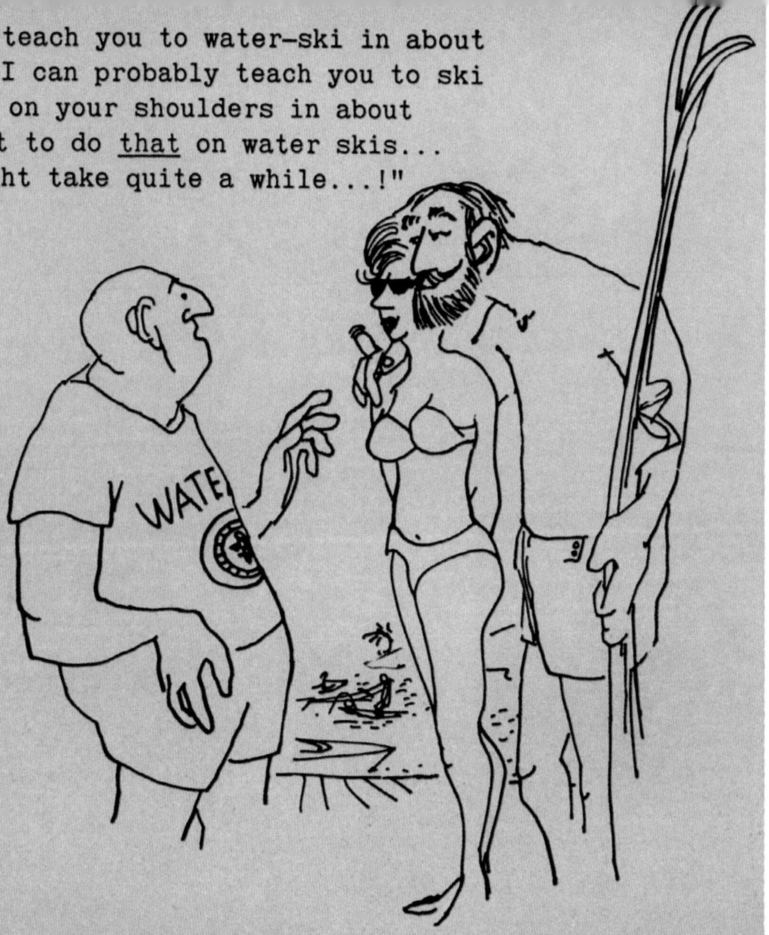
WATE

"Well, I can teach you to water-ski in about two days and I can probably teach you to ski with her on your shoulders in about a week, but to do <u>that</u> on water skis... that might take quite a while...!"

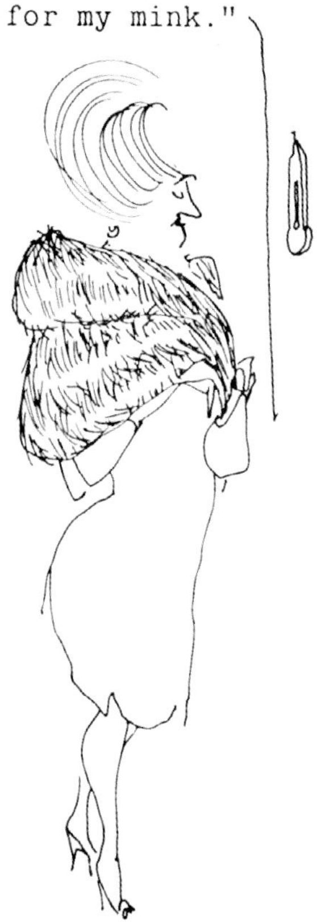

"H'mm, 103 degrees... almost too warm for my mink."

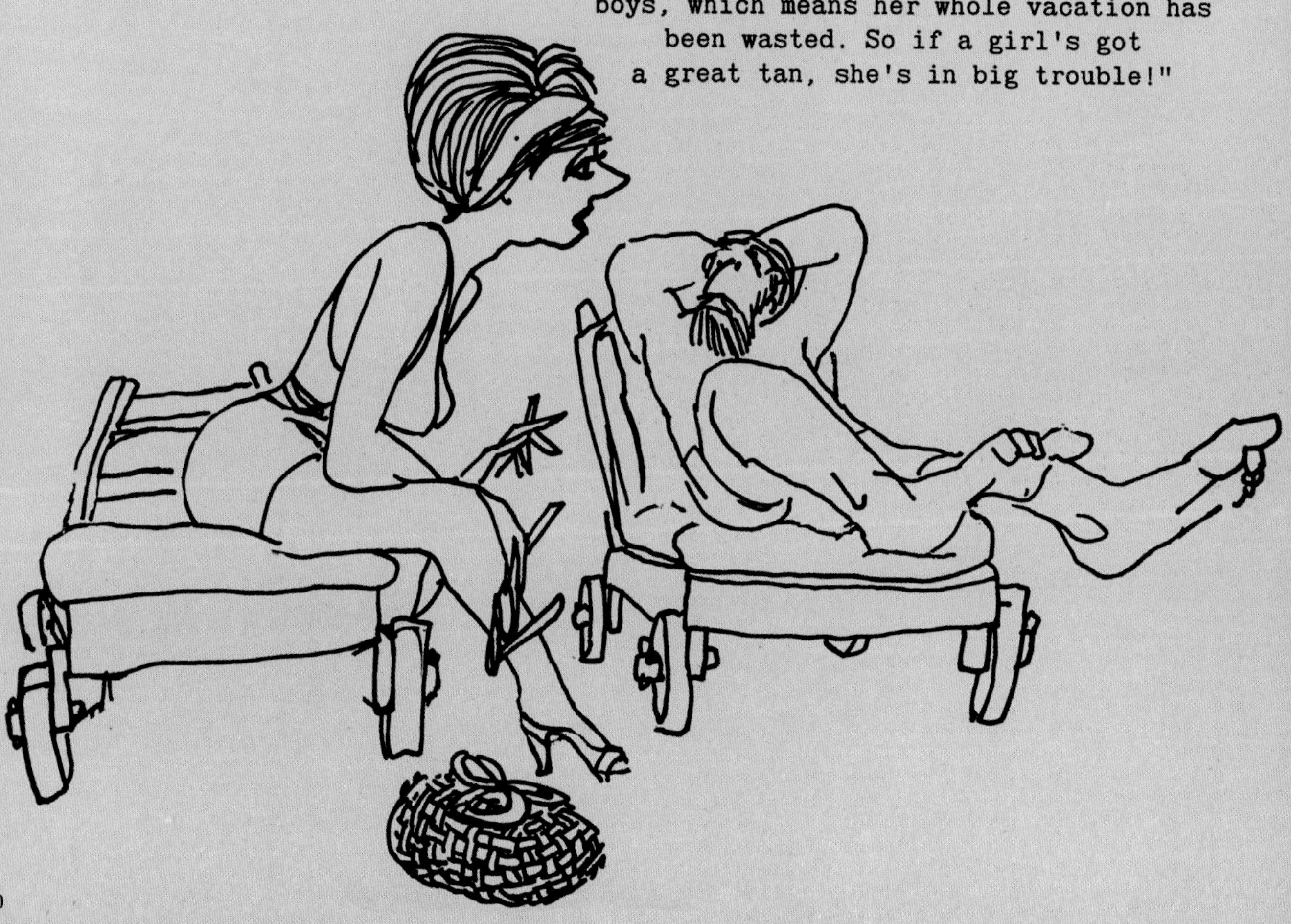

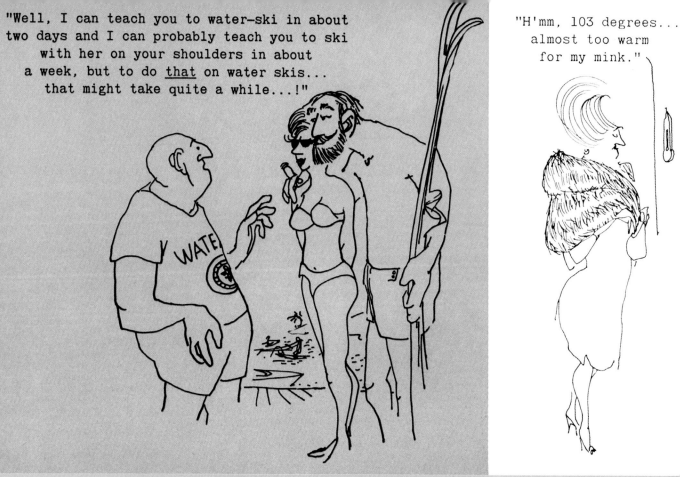

"You see, if a girl has a nice tan, that means she gets out t
the pool early in the morning, which means she wasn't out late th
night before, which means she hasn't met any boys, which means her whole vacation has been wasted. So if a girl's got a great tan, she's in big trouble!"

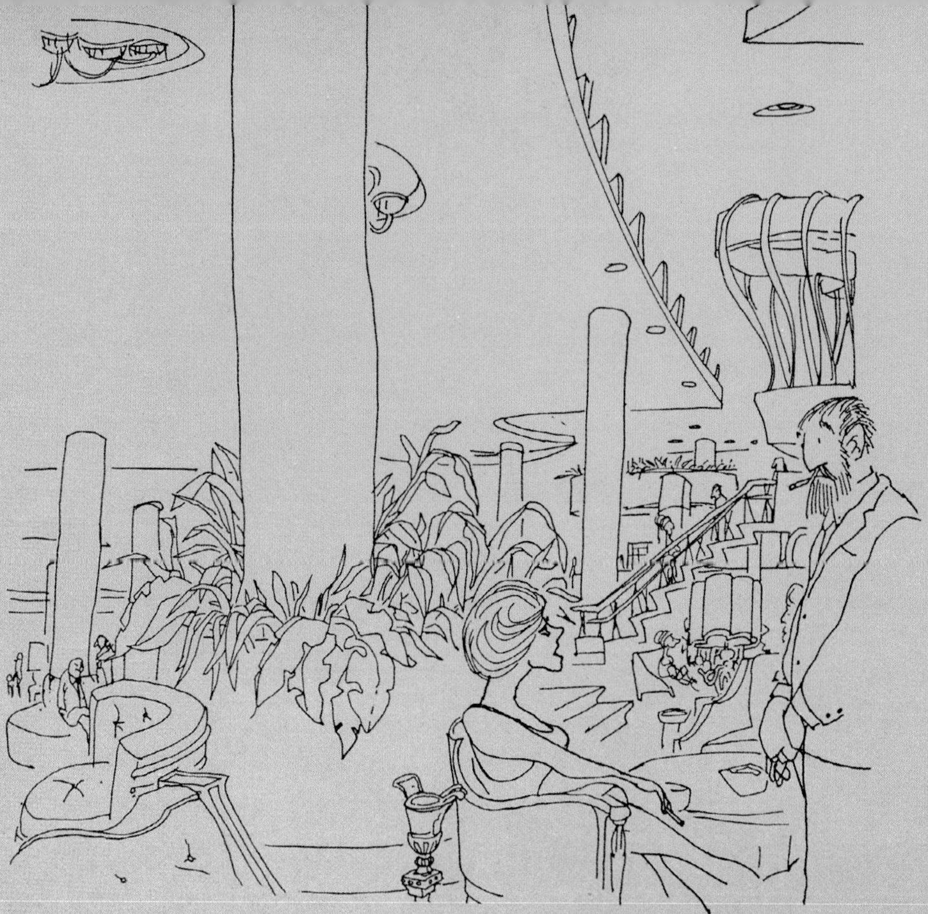

"So I decided that instead of wasting my money on a week in a dumpy hotel, I'd invest it all on one day in the best hotel—so I have till four o'clock to find a husband—that's check-out time."

appreciative clutch of Bunnies is all ears our hirsute cartoonist explains his manly art thin the confines of the Miami Playboy Club.

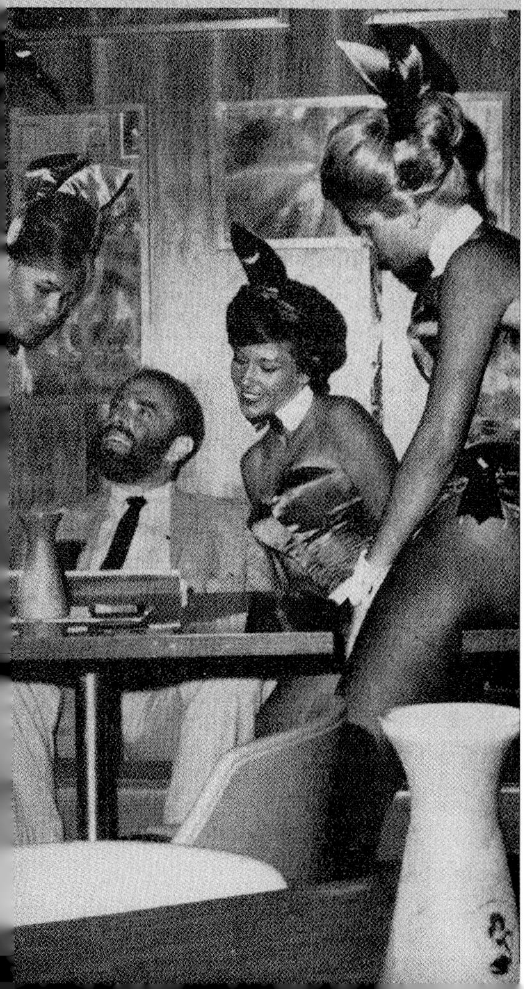

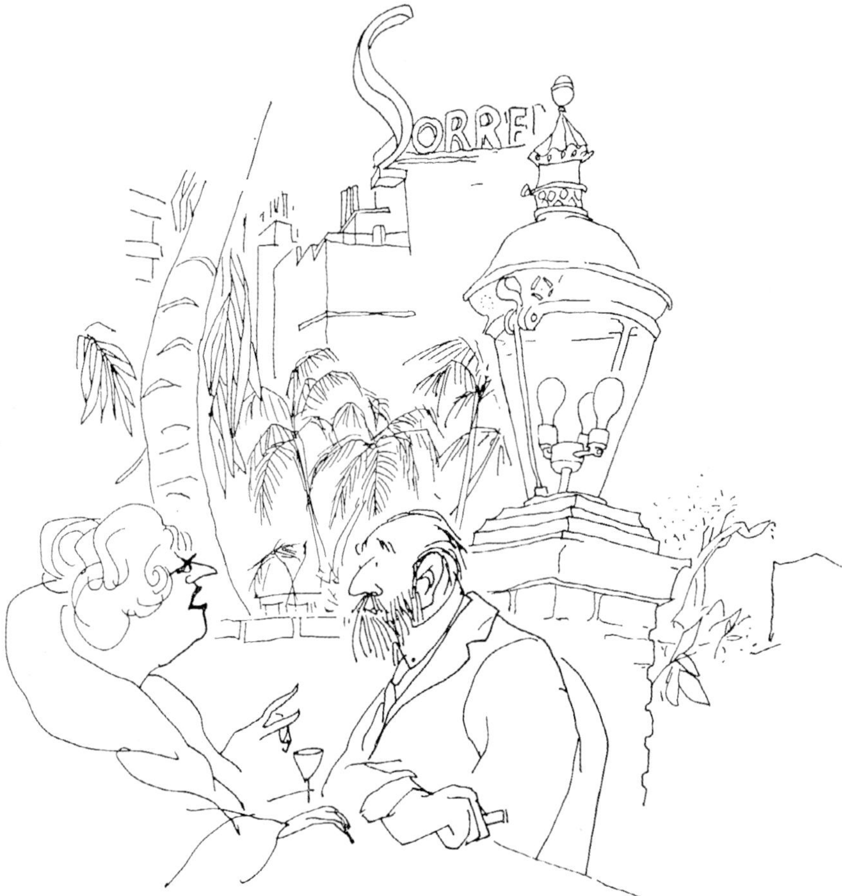

"Well, if the Cubans did shoot rockets over here, don't you think they'd wait until the off season?"

"First I heard he was single, so I wanted to meet him...then someone said he was a Cuban, so I <u>didn't</u> want to meet him... then somebody else said he was Jewish, so I wanted to meet him...then somebody said he was a rabbi, so I <u>really</u> wanted to meet him...but then I found out he's a cartoonist, so to <u>hell</u> with him!"

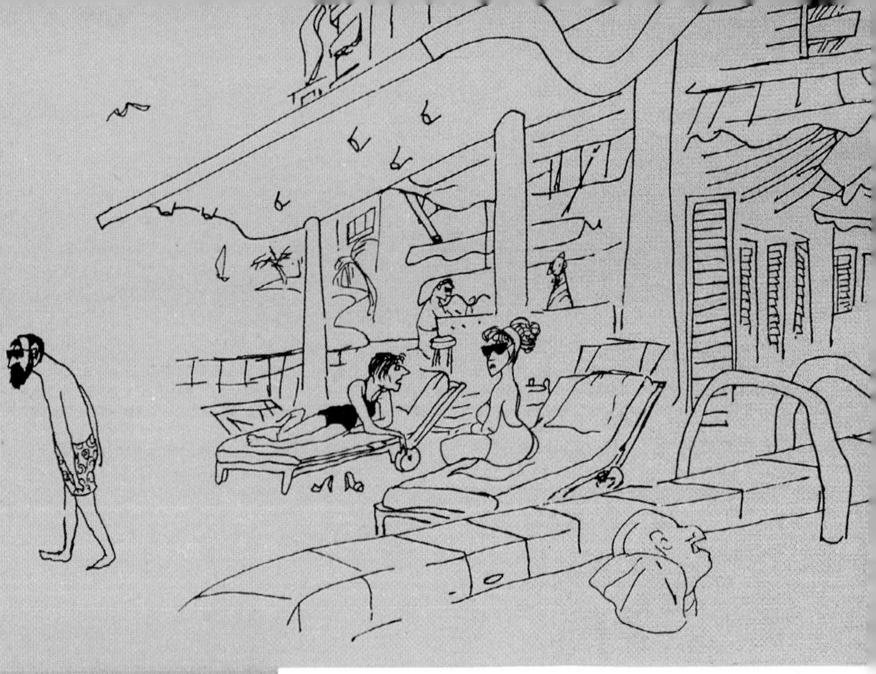

"Look—why should we give you a complimentary room? You've already drawn our hotel into one of your cartoons. We've already got our publicity—absolutely <u>free</u>!"

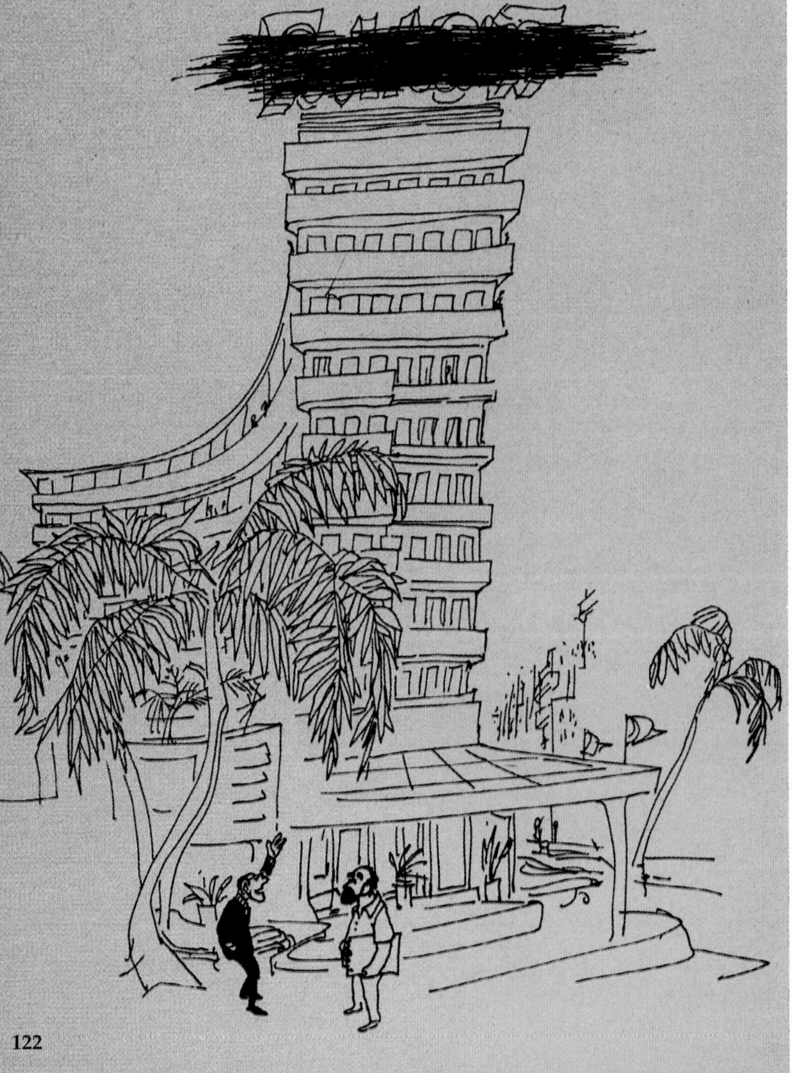

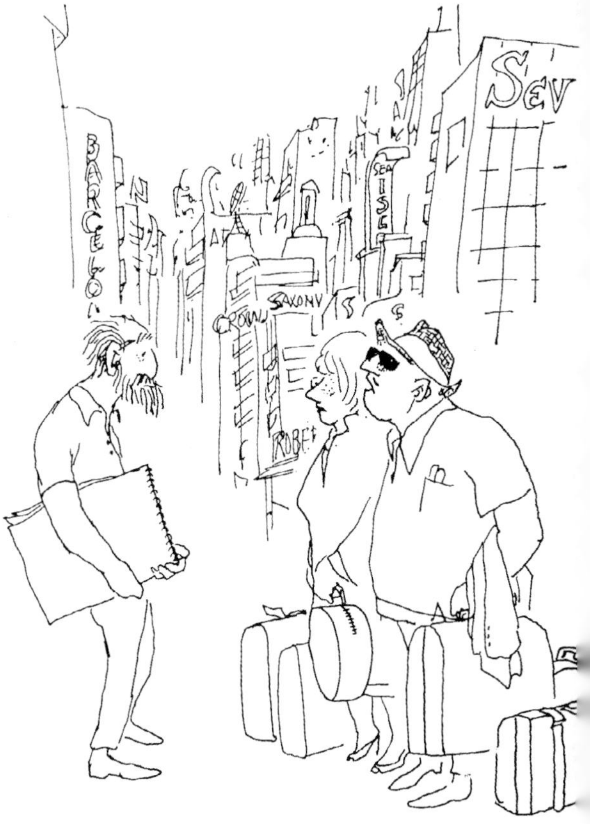

"So we arrive at our hotel, but as soon as we get unpacked, we hear there's a <u>newer</u> hotel over on Collins Avenue. So we move over there, but before we're unpacked, we hear that there a <u>newer</u> hotel right up the street. So we move over there, but before we even get our luggage up to the room..."

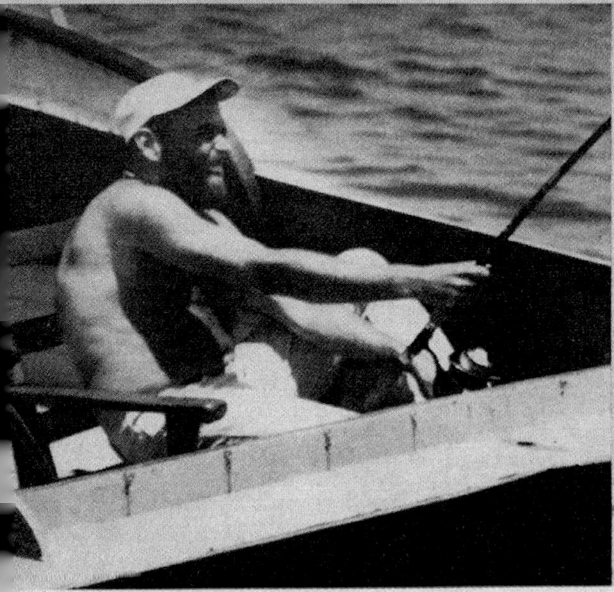

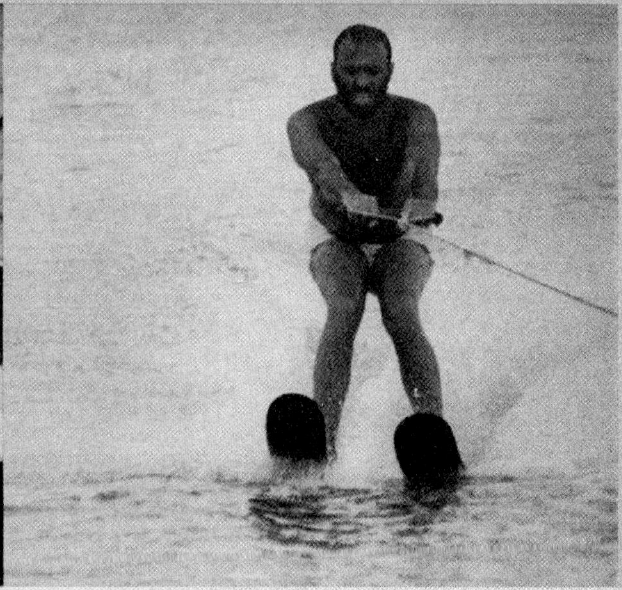

iking a pose à la Hemingway, Shel occupies a sport fisherman's fighting chair while pitting his brawn against
90-lb. sailfish, then treads the boards on a water-skiing jaunt up and down the blue waters of Biscayne Bay.

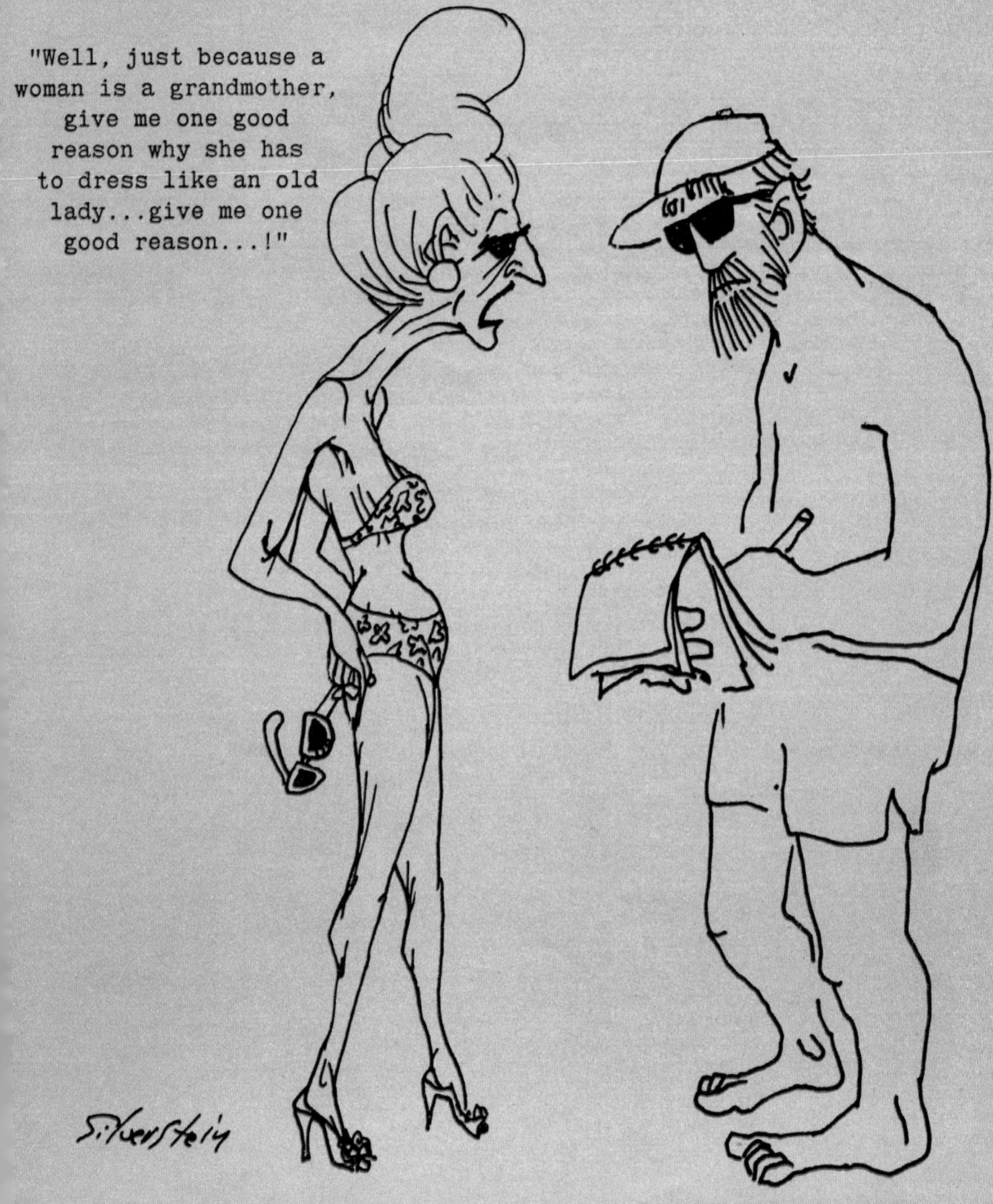
"Well, just because a woman is a grandmother, give me one good reason why she has to dress like an old lady...give me one good reason...!"
Silverstein

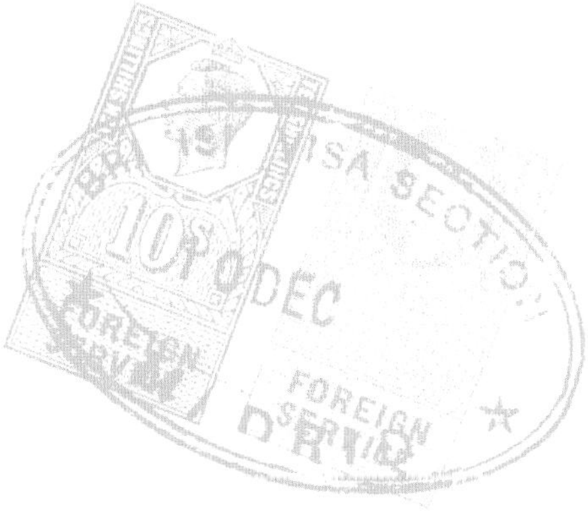
10s
DEC
FOREIGN

IN A NUDIST CAMP

AUGUST 1963

Silverstein IN A NUDIST CAMP

playboy's roving cartoonist doffs his duds and uncovers a new facet of his art

IN THE SIX YEARS that cartoonist Shel Silverstein has been roaming the globe for PLAYBOY, drawing funny conclusions from Madrid to Moscow to Miami Beach, no assignment has proven more challenging – or more off the beaten track – than his most recent: to depict the unabashed life of a typical U. S. nudist camp. The site selected was Sunny Rest Lodge of Palmerton, Pennsylvania, a well-regarded buffer zone which graciously allowed Shel carte blanche for a fortnight's stay. When he arrived, with drawing pen loaded for bare, embarrassment was his first reaction – but inhibitions soon faded as our quick-change artist, now birthday-suited, relaxed in his new environs. "These were the most pleasant, relaxed two weeks of my life," he recalls. "There was a great sense of freedom, of naturalness in the camp. Pretensions just vanished. Nobody, you might say, had anything to hide." His advice to the amateur nudist on getting past the first awkward confrontation scene: "Look straight ahead. Don't look sideways, don't look up and don't look down." Reflecting on what it is like to live amidst a platoon of unclad females, he notes, "They lose their sense of mystery. There's no question about that. On the other hand, relationships between the sexes seem much more honest." Here is the epidermal essence of Shel's excursion into a brave nude world.

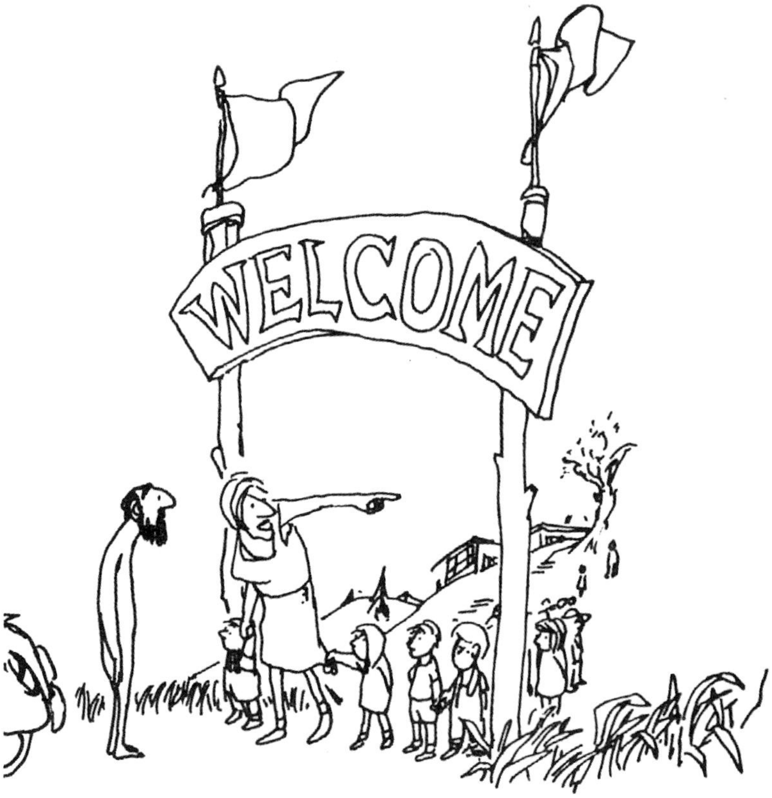
WELCOME

"No...this is Sunny Hill Day Camp. You want the Sunny Rest Nudist Camp. That's about two miles up the road and turn right at the..."

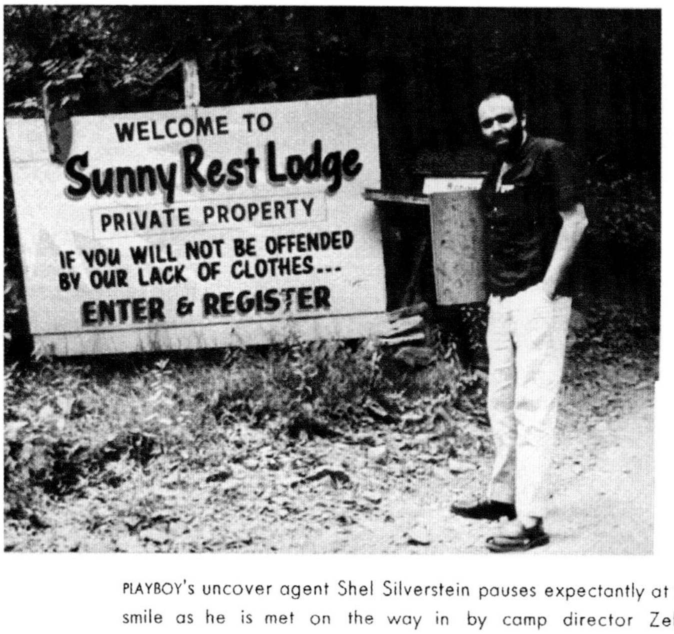
WELCOME TO
Sunny Rest Lodge
PRIVATE PROPERTY
IF YOU WILL NOT BE OFFENDED
BY OUR LACK OF CLOTHES...
ENTER & REGISTER

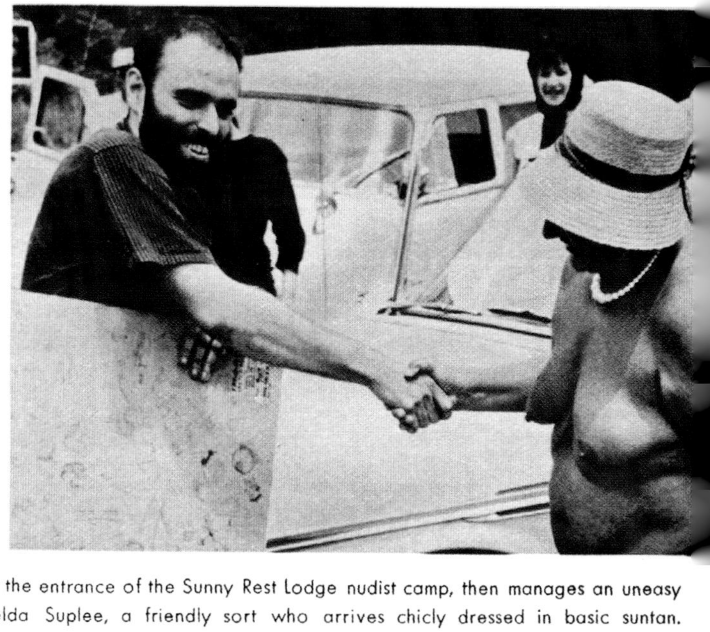

PLAYBOY's uncover agent Shel Silverstein pauses expectantly at the entrance of the Sunny Rest Lodge nudist camp, then manages an uneasy smile as he is met on the way in by camp director Zelda Suplee, a friendly sort who arrives chicly dressed in basic suntan.

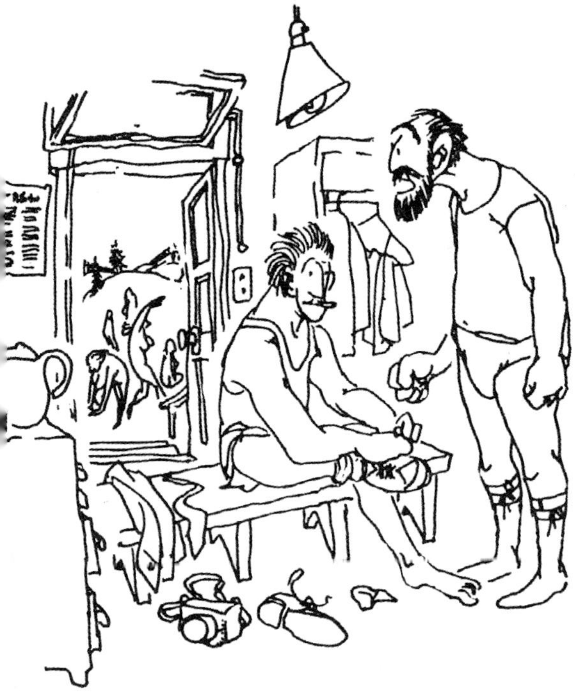

"I know nobody ever gets one...
but what do you do
if you do get one?!!"

"Hi, folks...What's nude?...
Ha-ha...Here I am, in the flesh!...
Ha-ha...Barely made it!...
Ha-ha...Gimme some skin!...
Ha-ha-ha..."

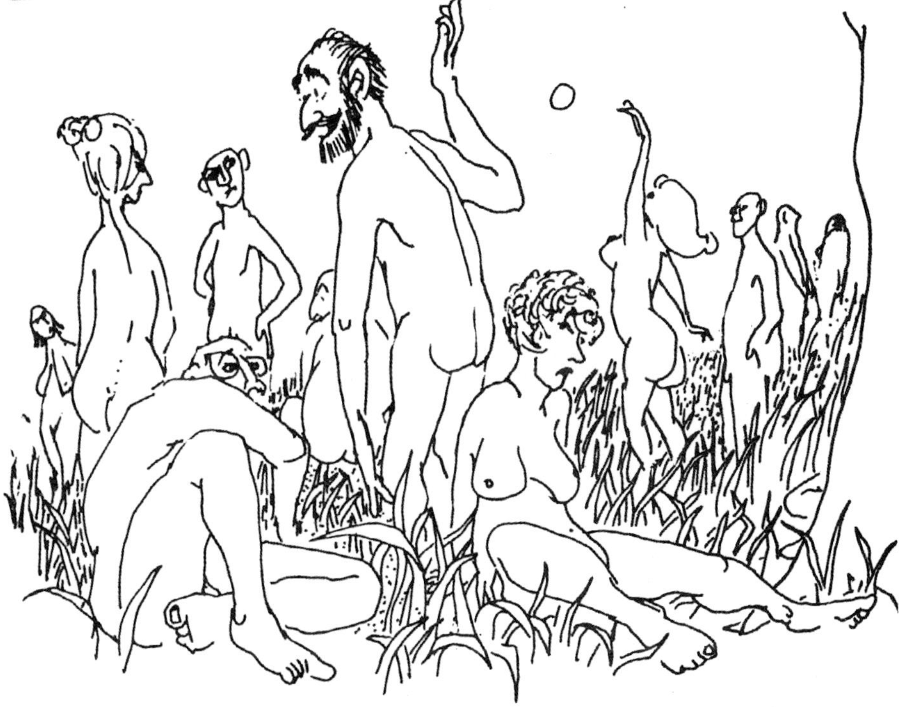

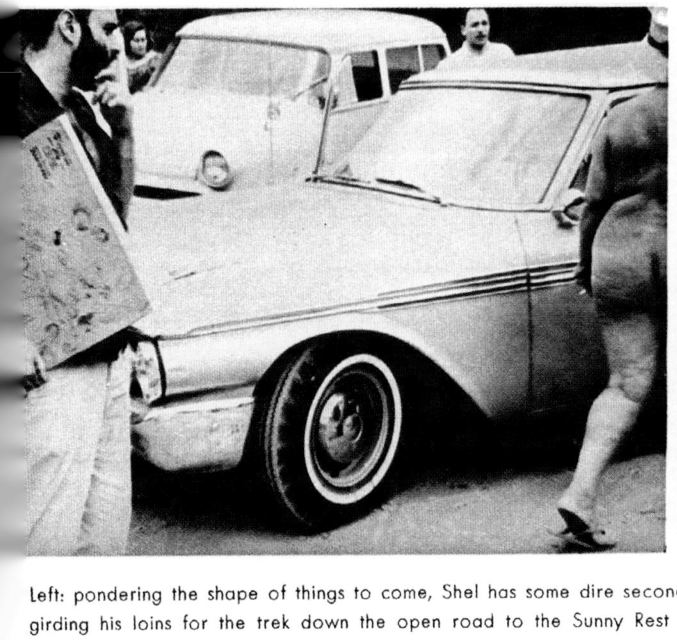

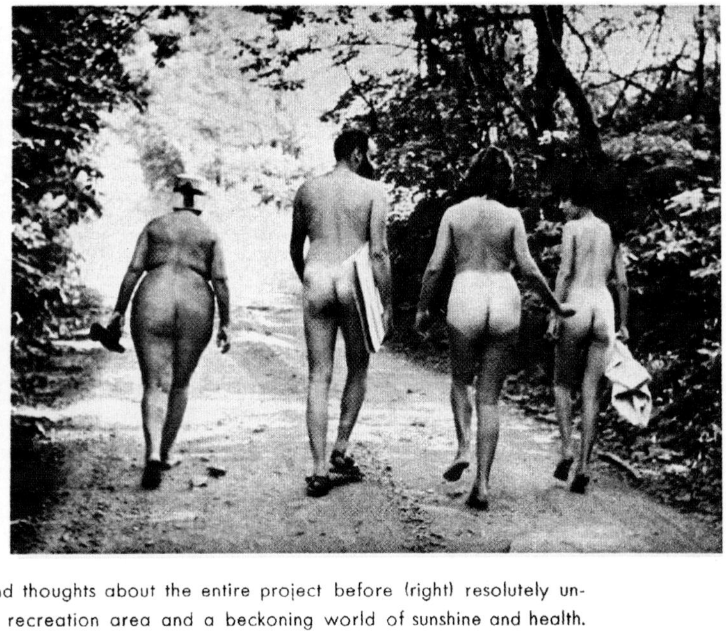

Left: pondering the shape of things to come, Shel has some dire second thoughts about the entire project before (right) resolutely ungirding his loins for the trek down the open road to the Sunny Rest recreation area and a beckoning world of sunshine and health.

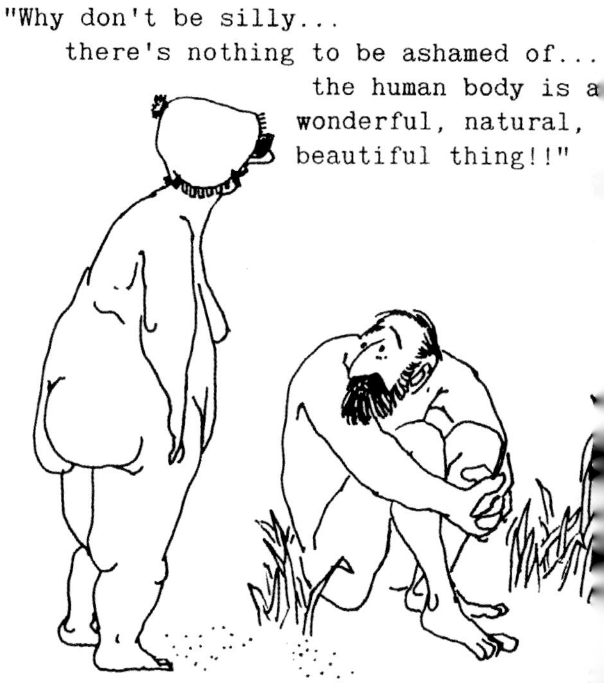
"Why don't be silly...
there's nothing to be ashamed of...
the human body is a
wonderful, natural,
beautiful thing!!"

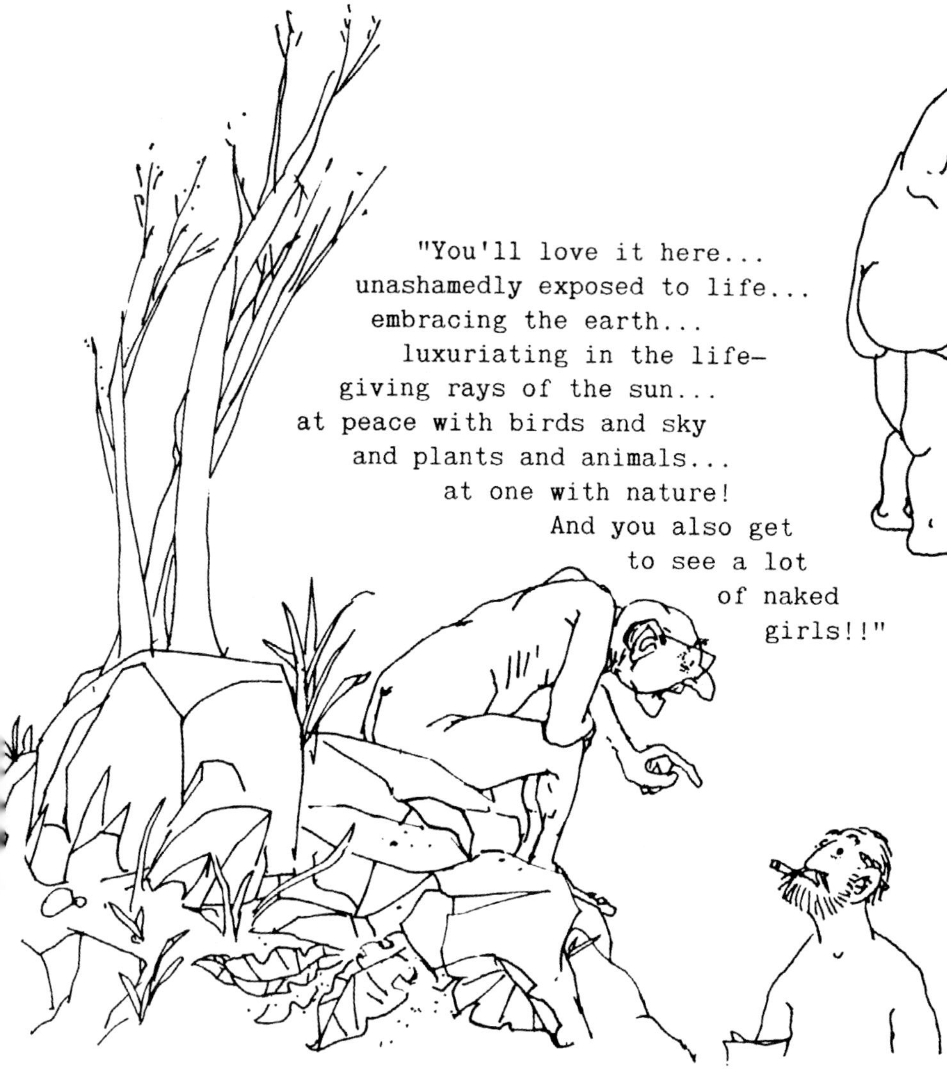
"You'll love it here...
unashamedly exposed to life...
embracing the earth...
luxuriating in the life-
giving rays of the sun...
at peace with birds and sky
and plants and animals...
at one with nature!
And you also get
to see a lot
of naked
girls!!"

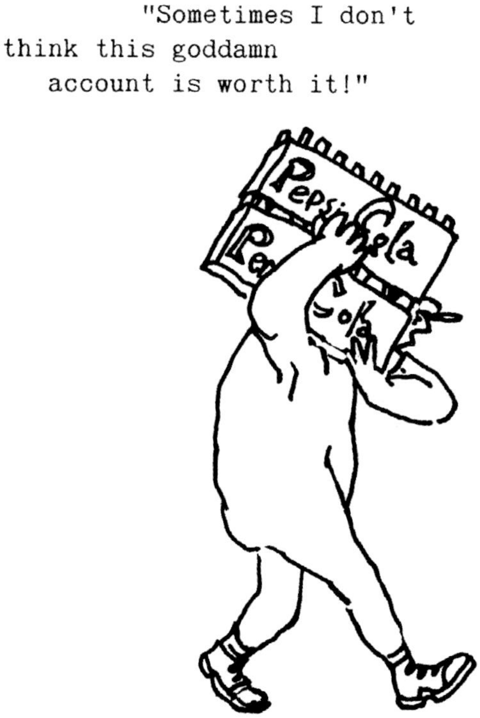
"Sometimes I don't
think this goddamn
account is worth it!"

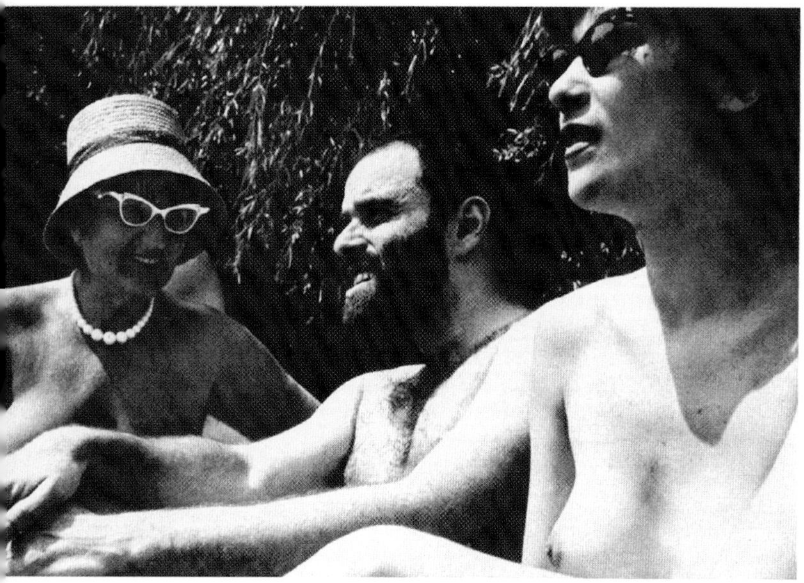

Getting his barings in the unfamiliar informality of the Sunny Rest camping grounds, Shel chats with the directress and another companionable buff buff.

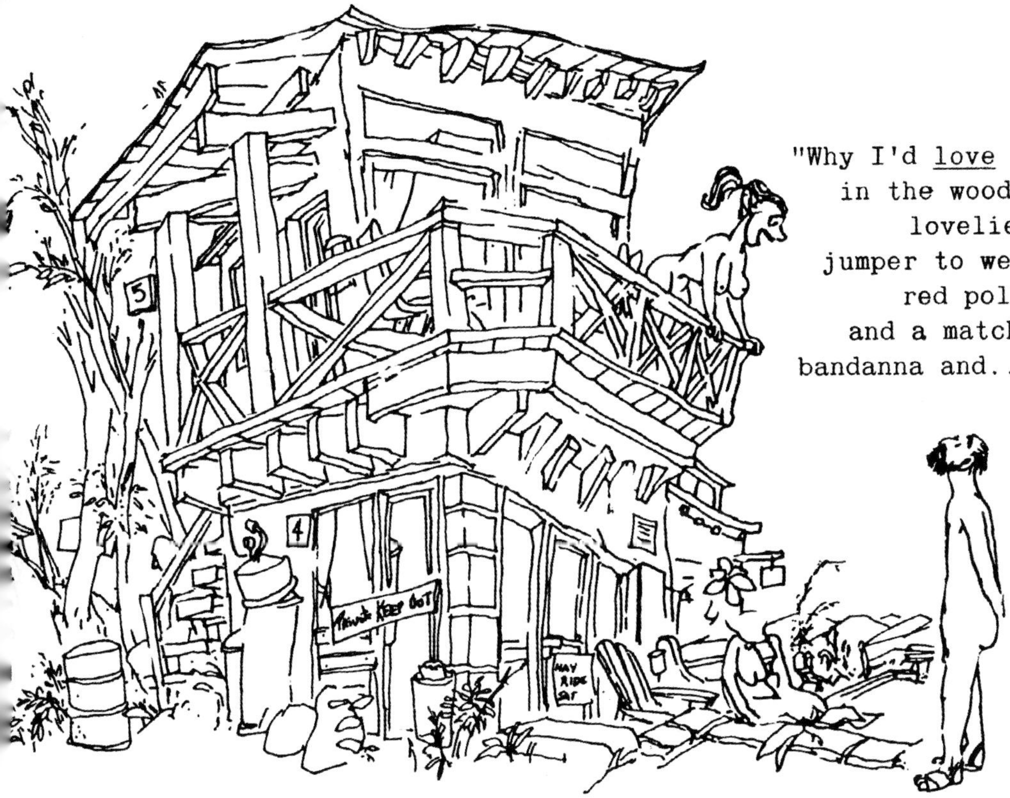

"Why I'd love to go for a walk in the woods! And I have the loveliest blue-denim jumper to wear...with a red polka-dot blouse... and a matching bandanna and..."

"You see, it's clothing that stimulates the imagination. Now if I were wearing lace panties, you'd probably be all excited, but instead you see me completely natural and that's the reason you're not in the least affected, Mr. Silverstein... Mr. Silverstein..."

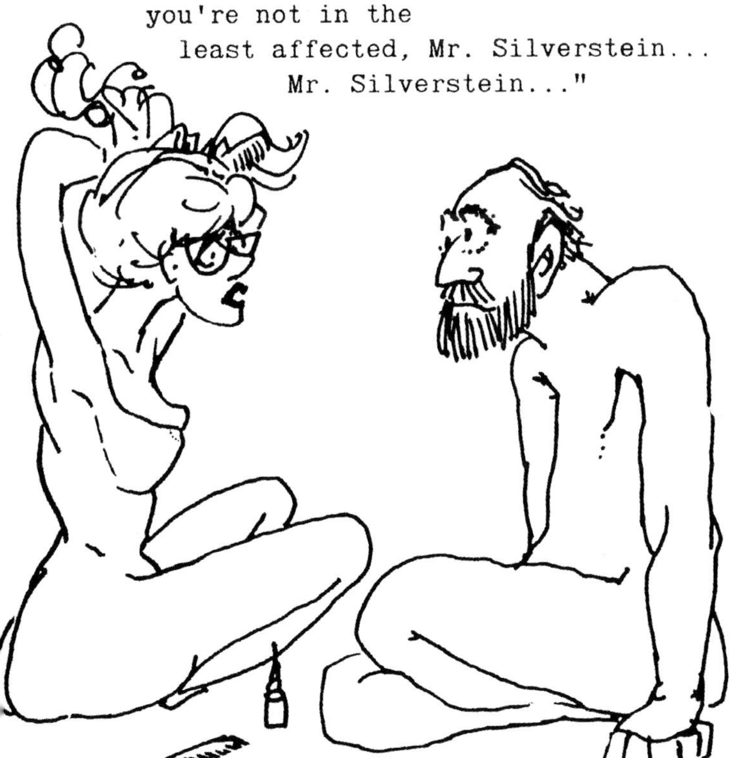

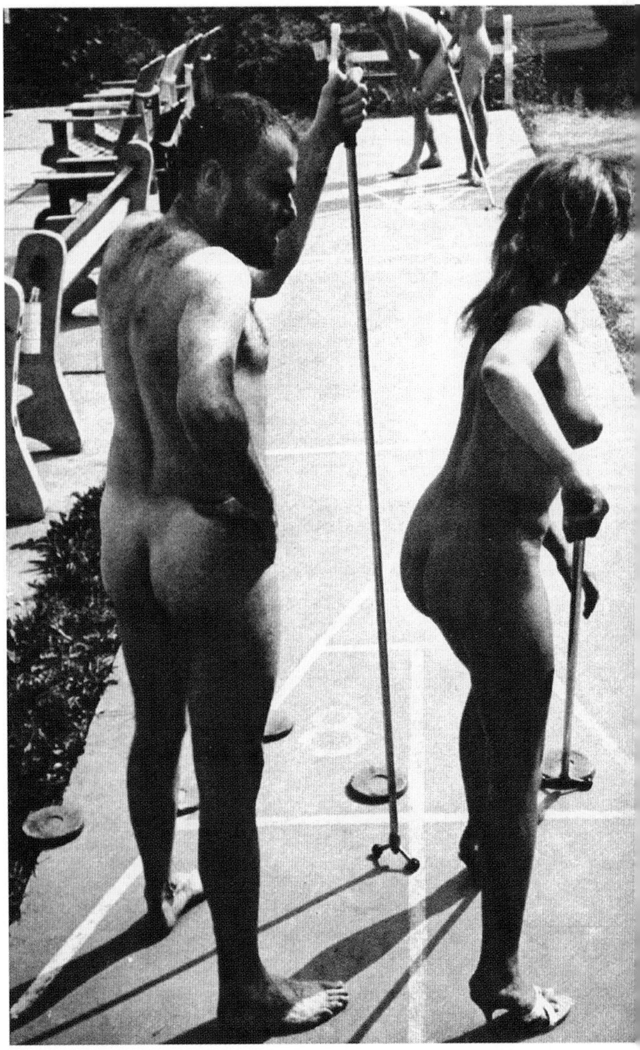

Caught up in the spirit of camp life, our barefoot boy with cheek admires the form of a fellow shuffleboarder.

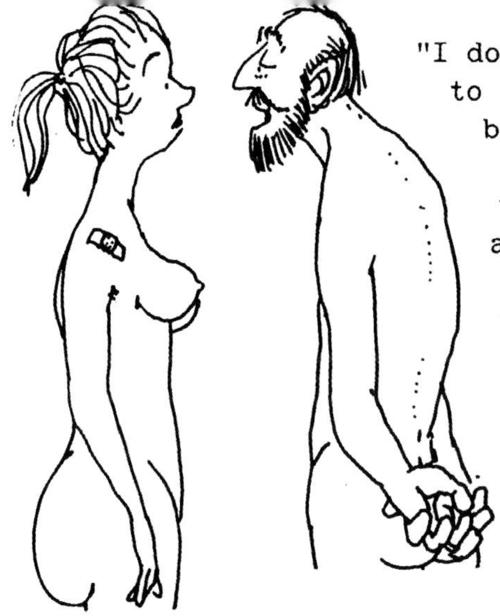

"I don't know how to ask you this, Laura, but could I...er... would you let me... uh...could I take a peek under that Band-Aid?"

"Well the <u>next</u> time anyone calls me up to come out for a part in the filming of a 'Naked City'...!"

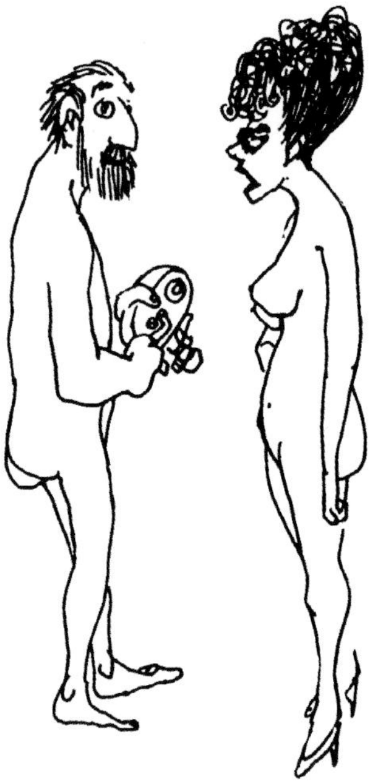

"After a while you'll get the hang of it. You put your money inside your watch band. You put your cigarettes behind your ear. You put your driver's license inside your shoe. But that fountain pen..."

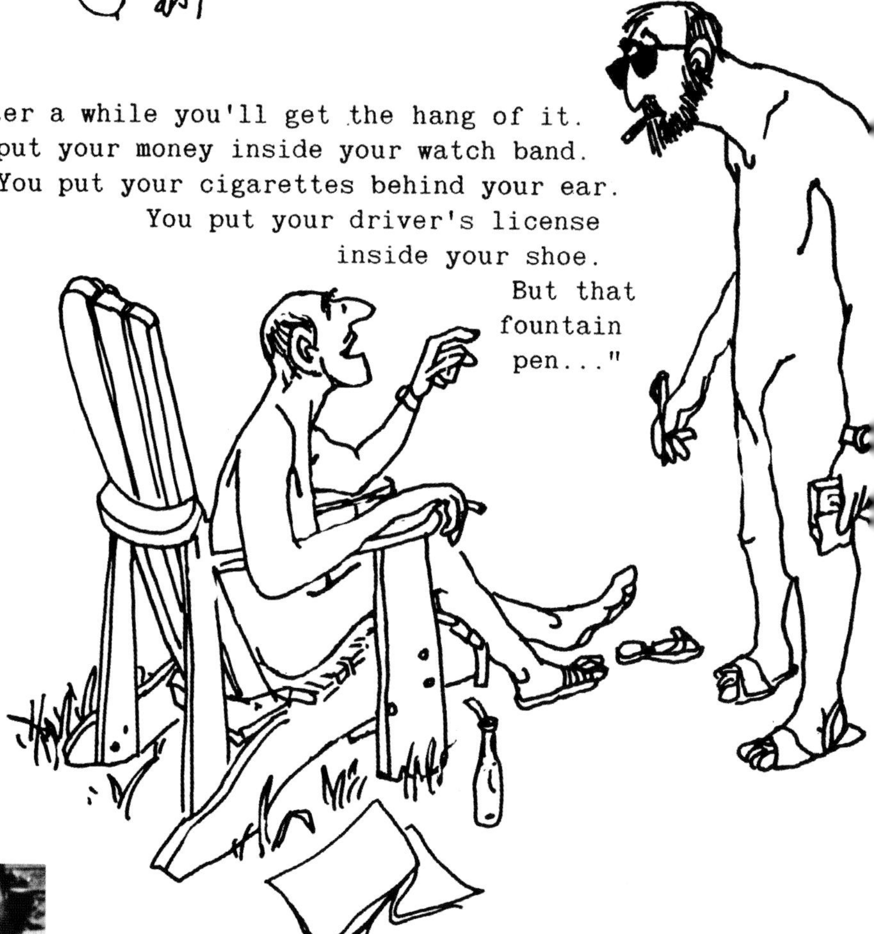

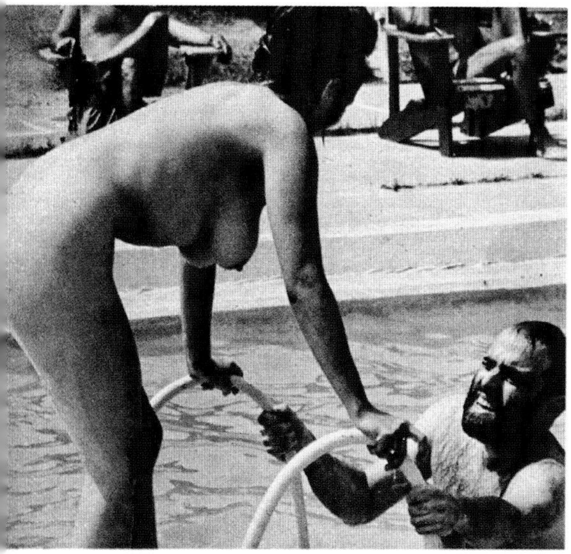

The apprentice *au naturelist* takes time out from an afternoon swim to chat with a comely comrade.

"...And I never have to worry about my shoulder straps falling down.

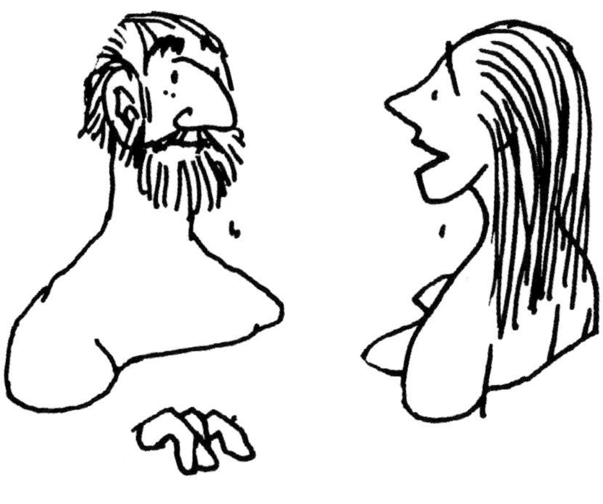

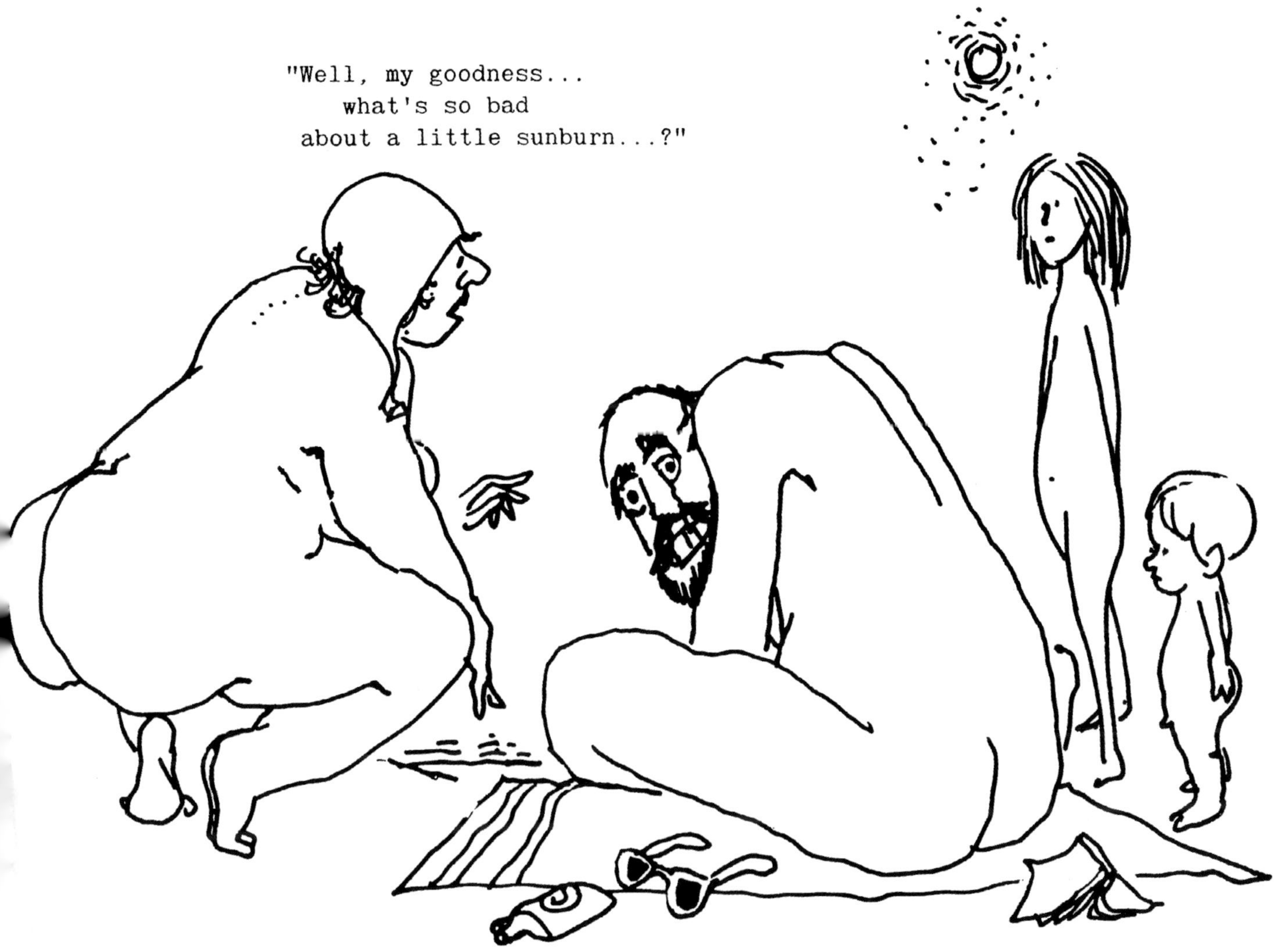
"Well, my goodness...
what's so bad
about a little sunburn...?"

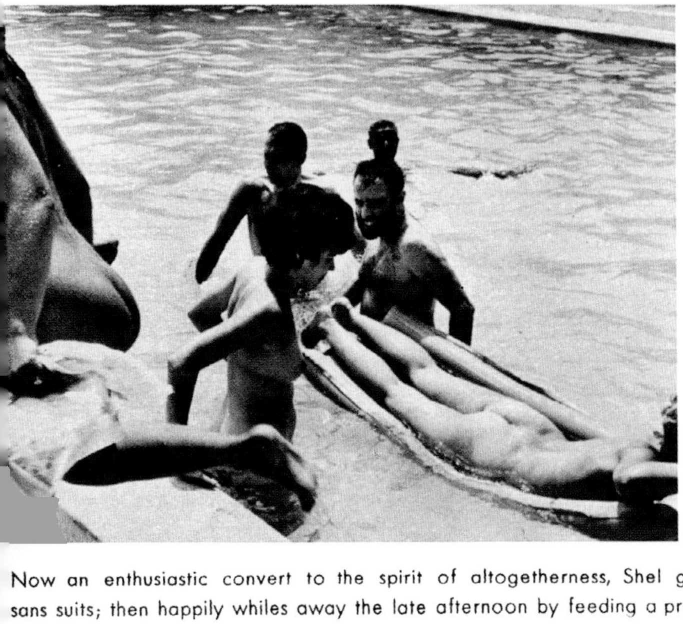

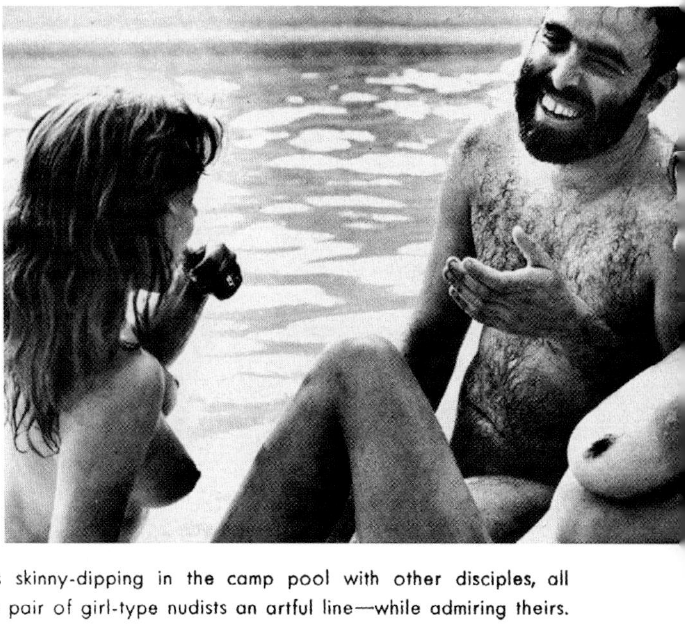

Now an enthusiastic convert to the spirit of altogetherness, Shel goes skinny-dipping in the camp pool with other disciples, all sans suits; then happily whiles away the late afternoon by feeding a pretty pair of girl-type nudists an artful line—while admiring theirs.

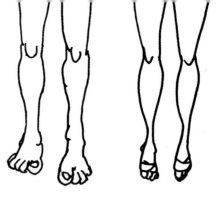

"You see, my dear,
if any other cartoonist
tried to draw a man
and woman completely
nude like this —
front view —
no magazine would
print it.
But I draw it —
and they print it!!"

"I think he
must be
a famous movie star...
I'm sure I've seen
him in films,
but I just
can't remember
his name..."

"You know, nudism is such a
wonderful institution, it's a
shame that it has to be confined
to summer camps! Now I have this
big apartment back in the city and...

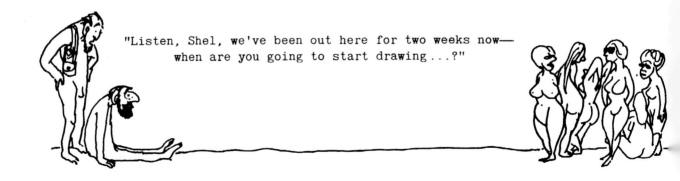

"Listen, Shel, we've been out here for two weeks now—
when are you going to start drawing...?"

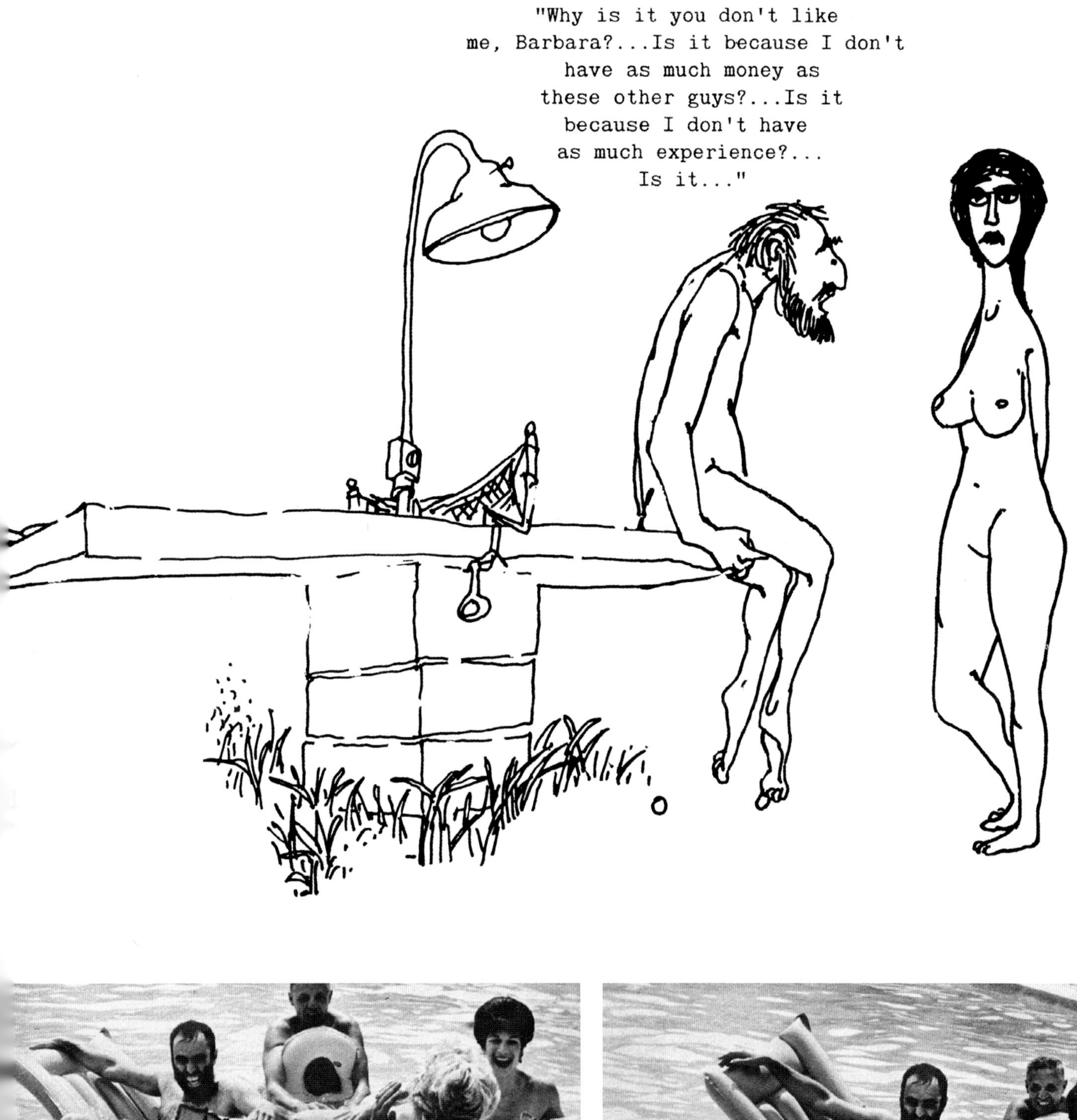
"Why is it you don't like me, Barbara?...Is it because I don't have as much money as these other guys?...Is it because I don't have as much experience?... Is it..."

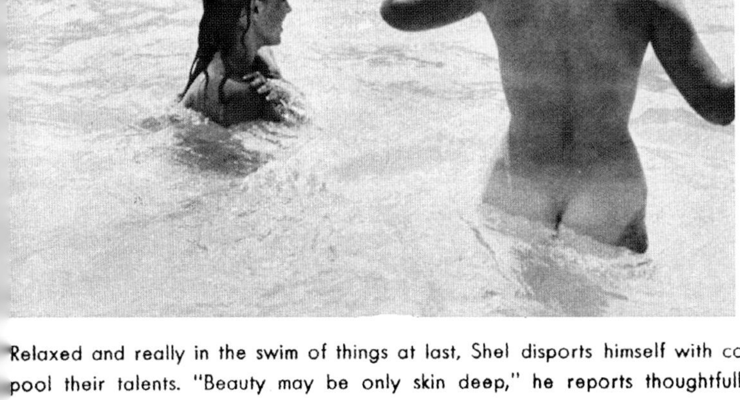

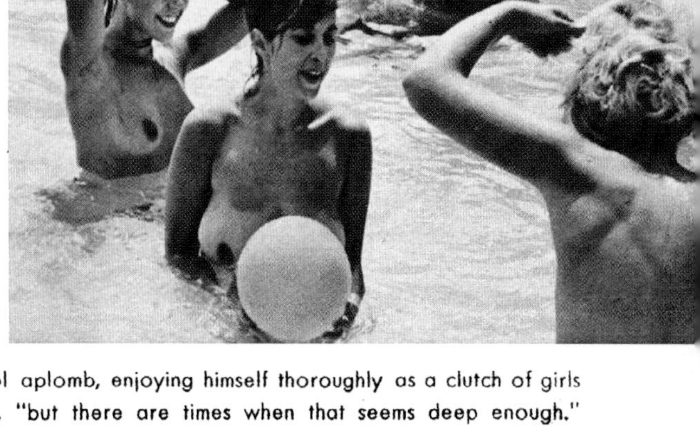

Relaxed and really in the swim of things at last, Shel disports himself with cool aplomb, enjoying himself thoroughly as a clutch of girls pool their talents. "Beauty may be only skin deep," he reports thoughtfully, "but there are times when that seems deep enough."

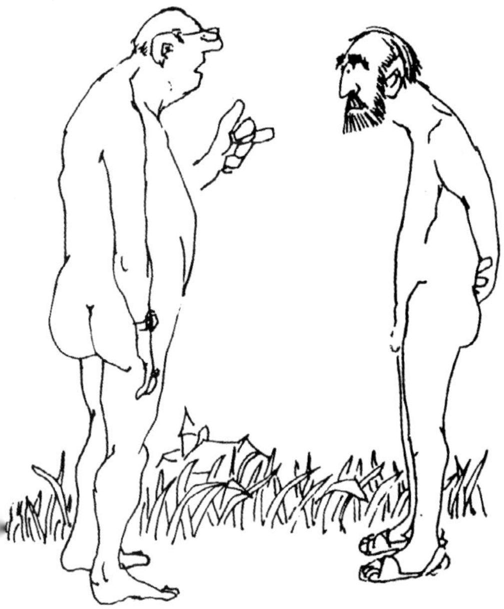

"The great thing about a nudist camp is that here, without your clothes, everyone is equal! For instance, you'd never know that I am the president of a large corporation! You'd never know that I am worth over $2,000,000!! You'd never know that I own a $100,000 home in Philadelphia, three cars, and..."

"Please, Shel... I've already put on my shoes... and I've put on my bra...! Don't ask me to put on any more...!"

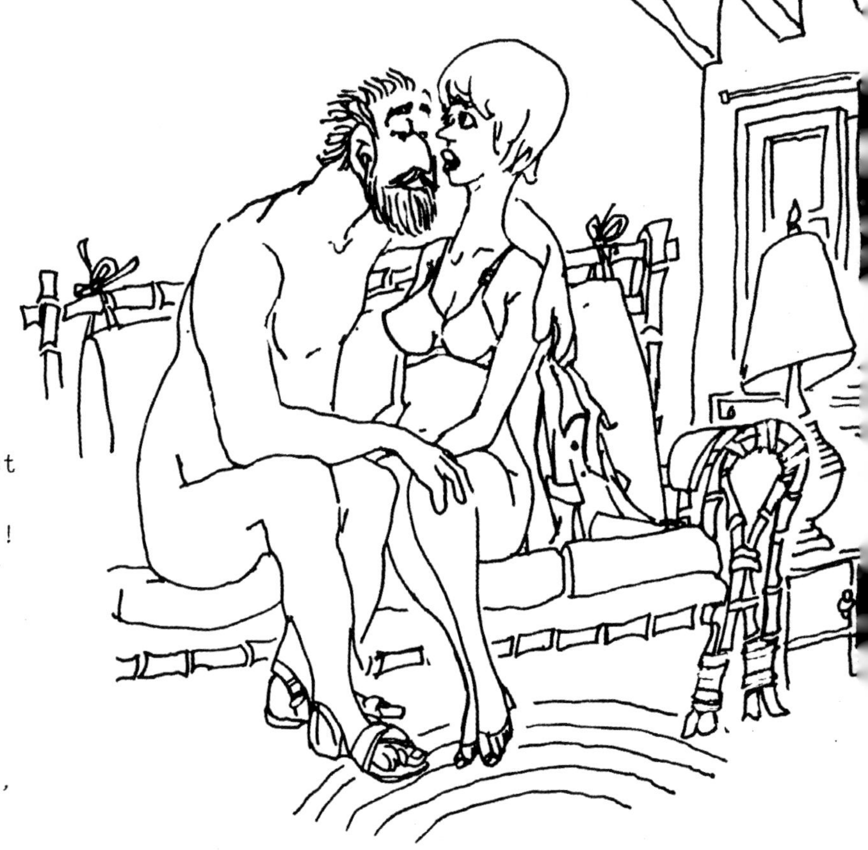

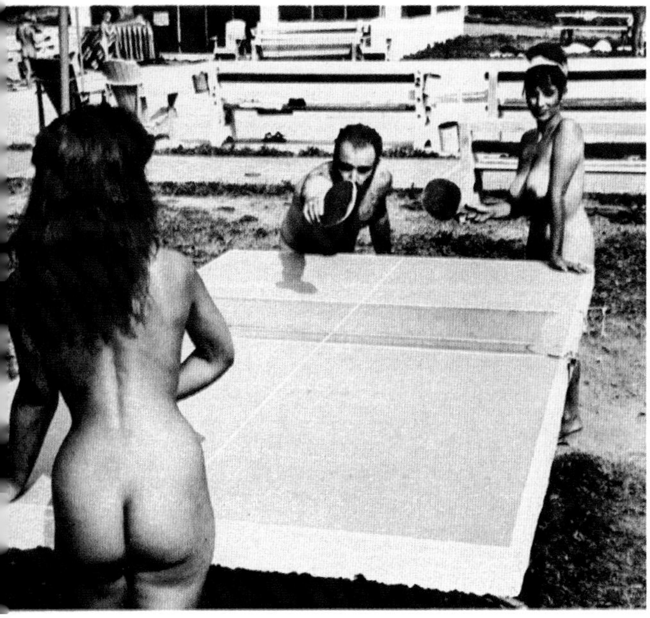

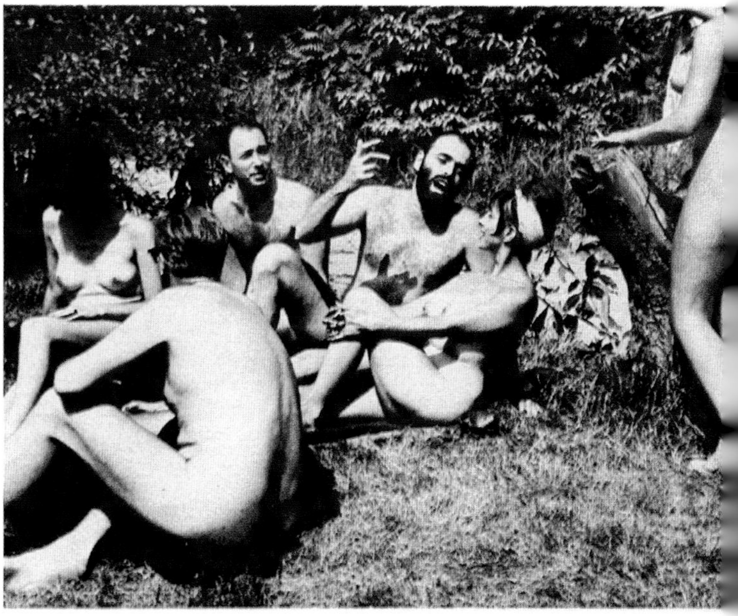

Left: sportsman Silverstein plays Ping-Pong, tries manfully to keep his eye on the ball. "Winning," he says, "never seemed less important.' Right: at eventide, PLAYBOY's vagabond cartoonist amuses his new-found Sunny Rest friends with clad tidings from the outside world.

"...And very few men used to ask me out, so I thought
it was because I was flat-chested, so I began
wearing falsies and a lot of men began asking me out,
but I realized they just liked me for my large chest,
so I began telling them I was wearing falsies
and then not very many of them asked me out, so I came
to this nudist camp and lost my self-consciousness
about my figure, but not very many of the men
here asked me out, so I went back to the city and told
everyone where I'd been and a lot of men began
asking me out, but I realized
it was just because
they associated nudism
with promiscuity,
so I began telling
them first that
I was definitely
not going
to sleep with
them... and
now nobody
asks me
out...!"

"They ask me to take off
my coat, so OK! Then they ask
me to take off my shirt and
pants, so I go along with them!
Then they ask me to take off
my shorts and shoes and socks,
so all right, I cooperate!
So then they tell me to..."

"Now here is the way I figure it...Sally leaned against the poison ivy and
got it on her leg...the dog brushed up against her leg and got it on
his back...Mrs. Hansen petted the dog and got it on her
hand...then she slapped Mr. Heinrich on the back and gave it to him...
Mr. Heinrich scratched his back and then shook hands with Bob Coogan...
who patted Jeanie on the behind...and then..."

IN MEXICO

MARCH 1965

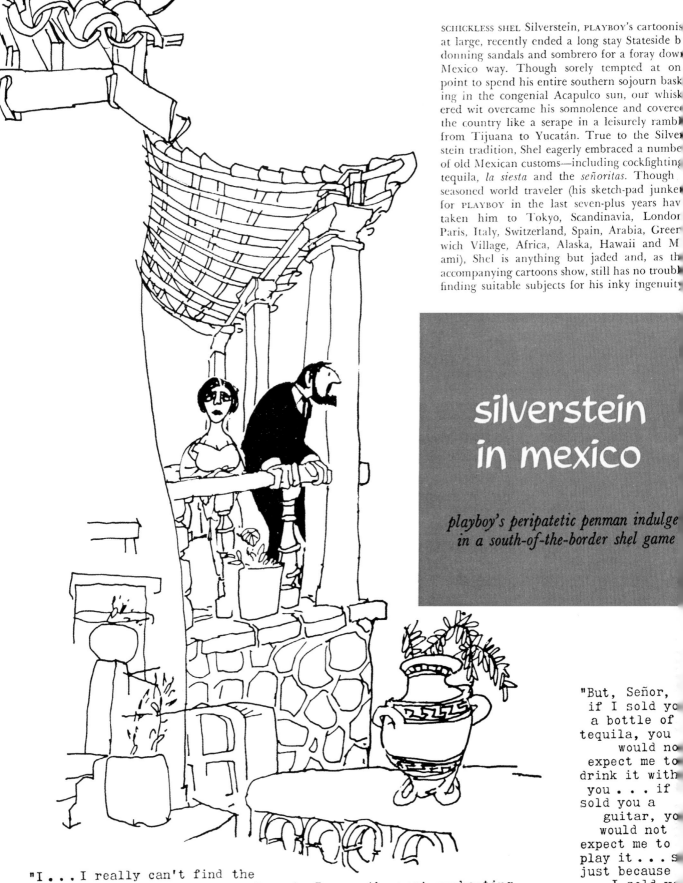

SCHICKLESS SHEL Silverstein, PLAYBOY's cartoonis at large, recently ended a long stay Stateside b donning sandals and sombrero for a foray dow Mexico way. Though sorely tempted at on point to spend his entire southern sojourn bask ing in the congenial Acapulco sun, our whisk ered wit overcame his somnolence and covere the country like a serape in a leisurely rambl from Tijuana to Yucatán. True to the Silver stein tradition, Shel eagerly embraced a numbe of old Mexican customs—including cockfighting tequila, *la siesta* and the *señoritas*. Though seasoned world traveler (his sketch-pad junke for PLAYBOY in the last seven-plus years hav taken him to Tokyo, Scandinavia, Londor Paris, Italy, Switzerland, Spain, Arabia, Greer wich Village, Africa, Alaska, Hawaii and M ami), Shel is anything but jaded and, as th accompanying cartoons show, still has no troubl finding suitable subjects for his inky ingenuity

silverstein in mexico

playboy's peripatetic penman indulge in a south-of-the-border shel game

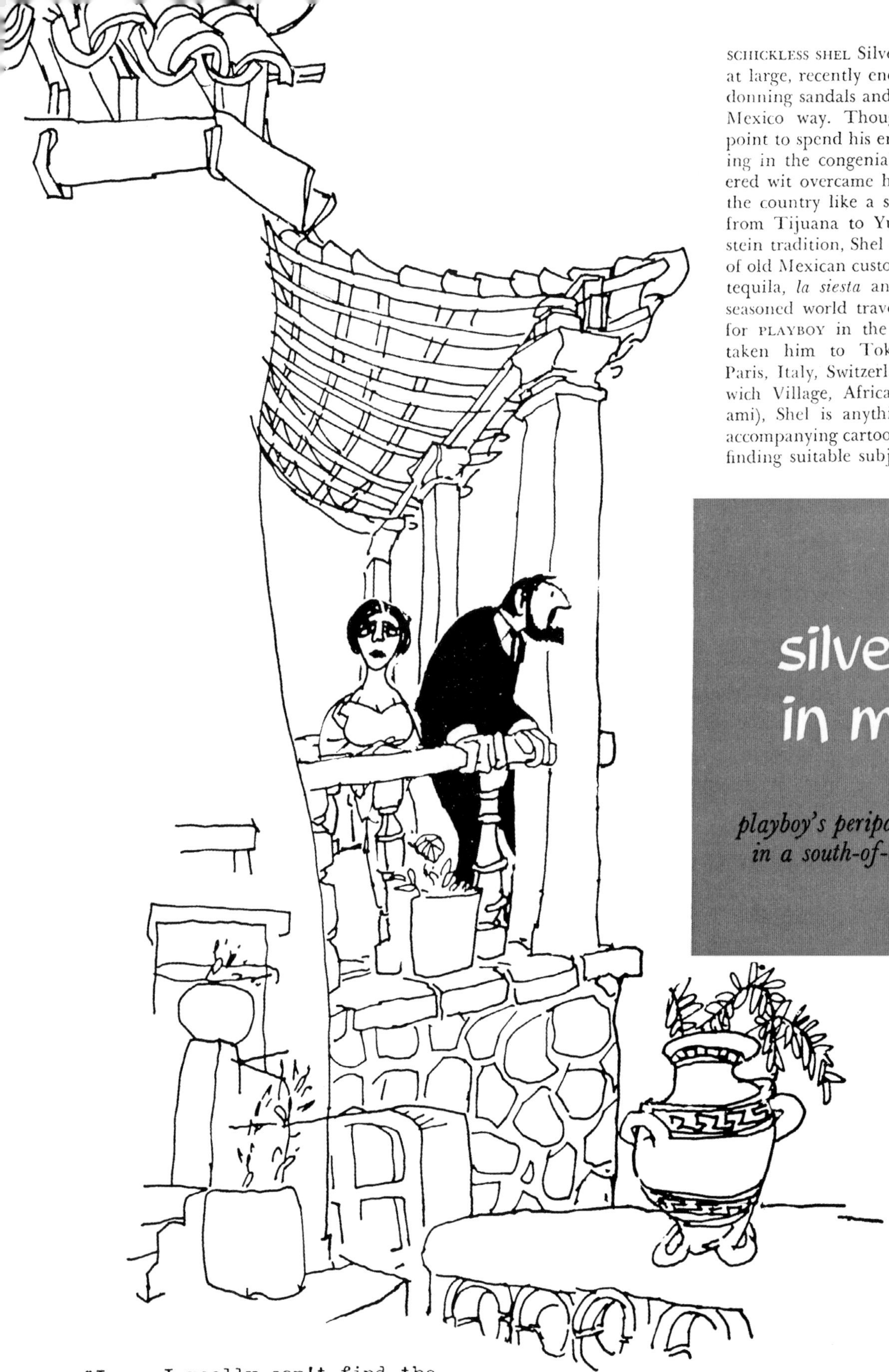

"I . . . I really can't find the words to express it. Here I am in Taxco, the most enchanting city in the world . . . a beautiful girl at my side . . . an orange sun burning in the clear azure sky . . . the rows of picturesque adobe houses set along a lazy street . . . a gentle breeze caressing our hot bodies . . . the romantic sounds of a guitar being played in the distance . . . and I think I'm getting diarrhea . . ."

"But, Señor, if I sold yo a bottle of tequila, you would no expect me to drink it with you . . . if sold you a guitar, yo would not expect me to play it . . . s just because I sold yo a blanket . . .

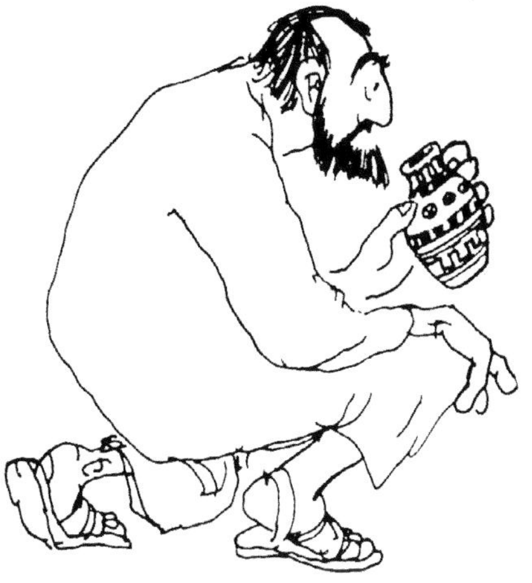

"OK, so you're hungry, but if I buy this for three pesos and it's only worth two pesos, then you'll become materialistic and lose your simplicity, so for your own sake, with your own best interests in mind, I'll give you one peso!"

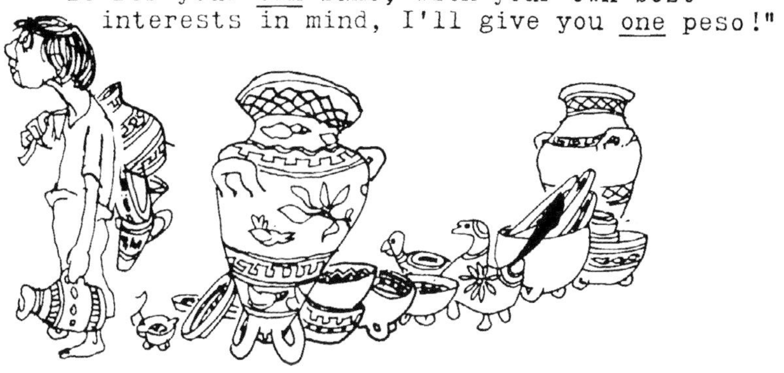

Below left: Shel finds a spot of shade from which to sketch a local peon at work, later shares a smoke with a *caballero*.

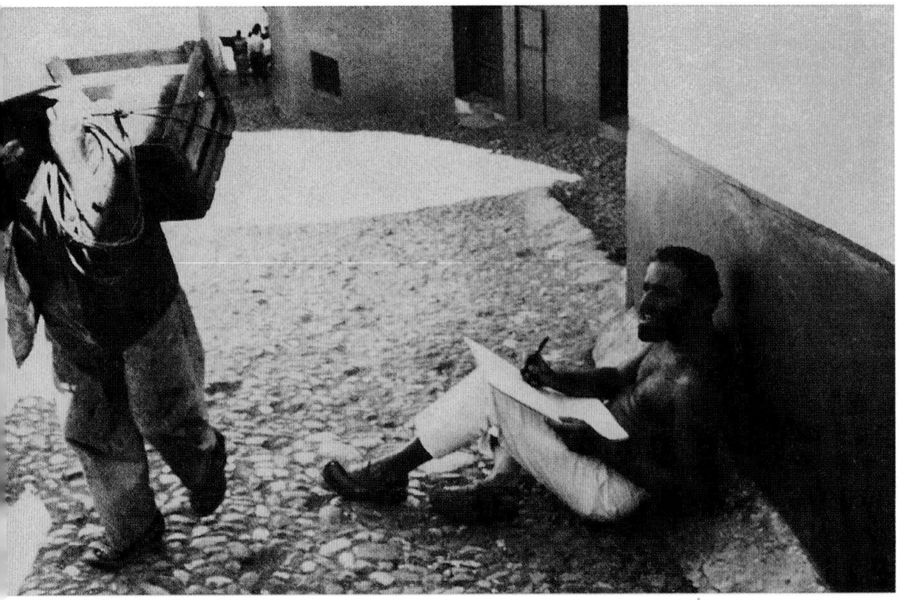

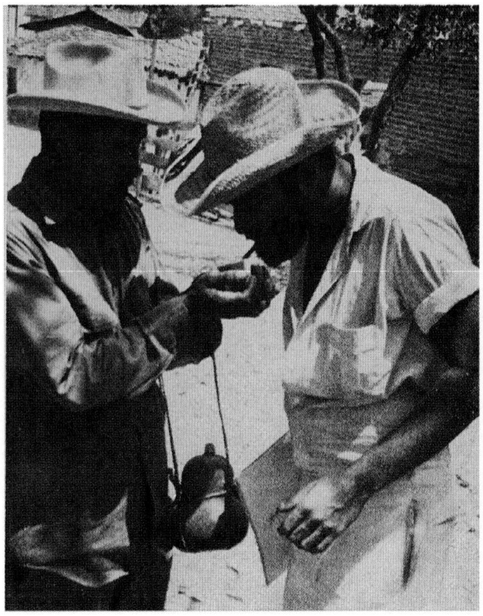

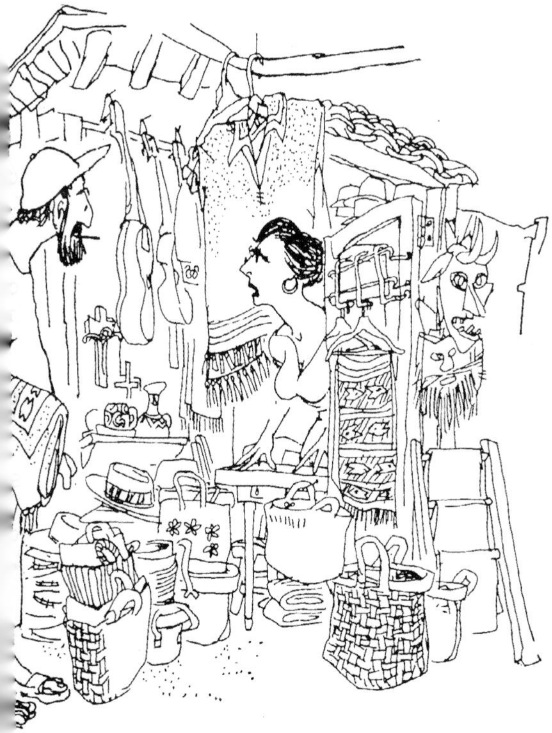

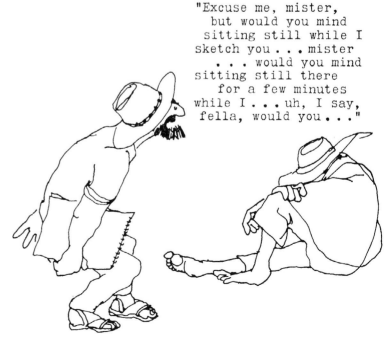

"Excuse me, mister, but would you mind sitting still while I sketch you . . . mister . . . would you mind sitting still there for a few minutes while I . . . uh, I say, fella, would you . . ."

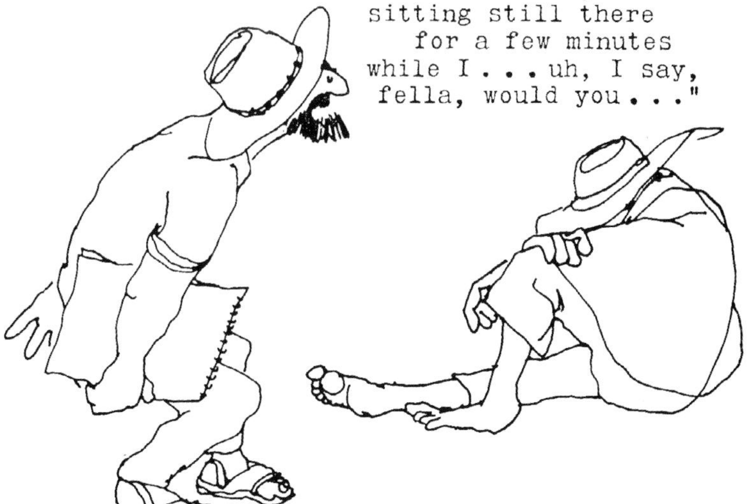

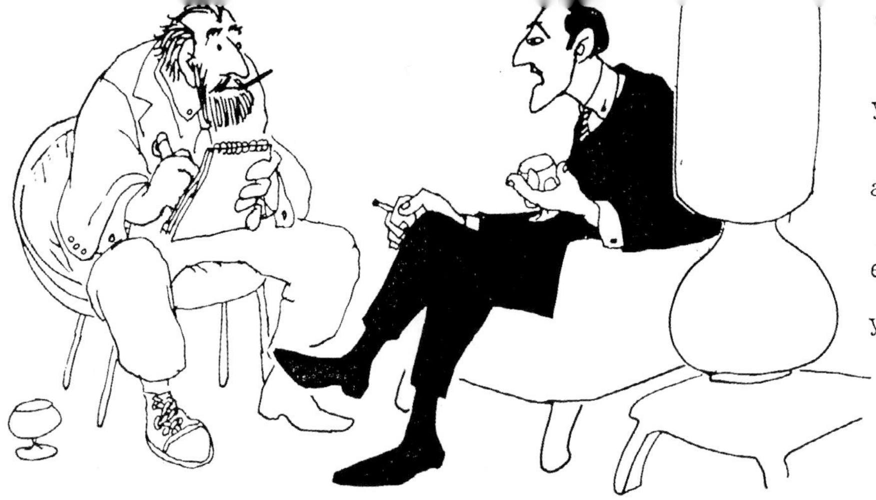

"You see, you Americans have a stereotype concept of Mexicans--you picture us as lazy peons, in big sombreros, living in adobe huts! But there is a modern Mexican --an educated, urbane, enterprising . . . well, I'd explain more to you, but it is time for my siesta . . . !"

Below left: Feathers fly and a Mephistophelean Silverstein almost jumps into the pit himself. ("Ixcapuzalco" is the name of a fighting-cock ranch.) Center: Shel adorns monastery wall. Right: In Acapulco's *zona roja*, he discusses America's balance of payments with local economist.

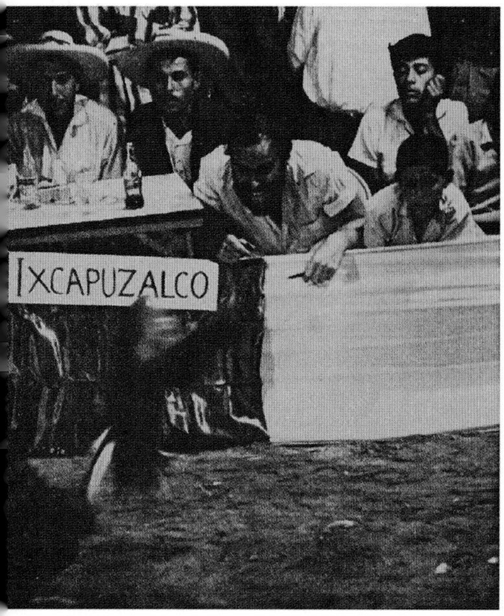
IXCAPUZALCO

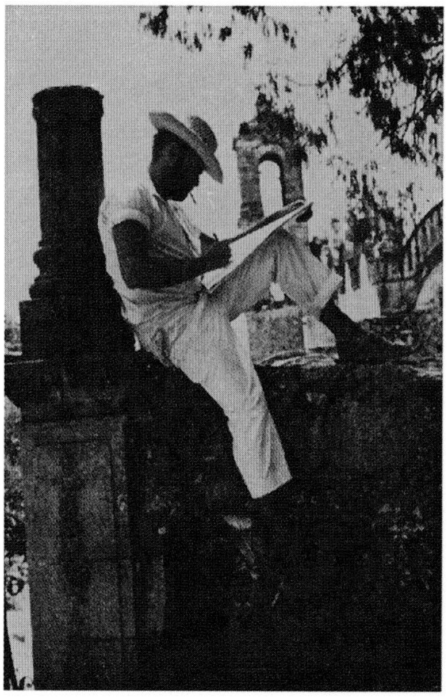

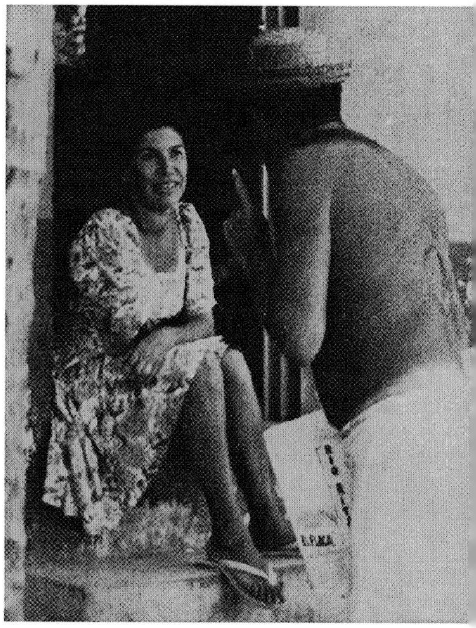

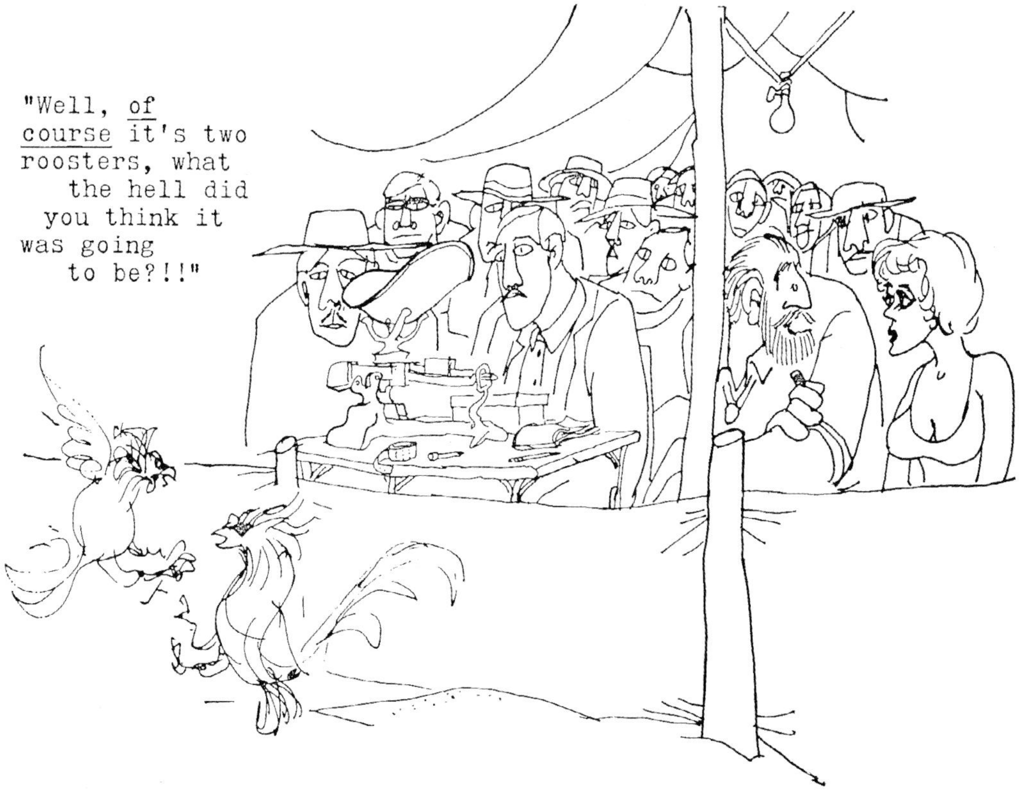
"Well, of course it's two roosters, what the hell did you think it was going to be?!!"

"Well, if you've got no television, no radio, no night clubs and no movies, what in the world do you do for entertainment?"

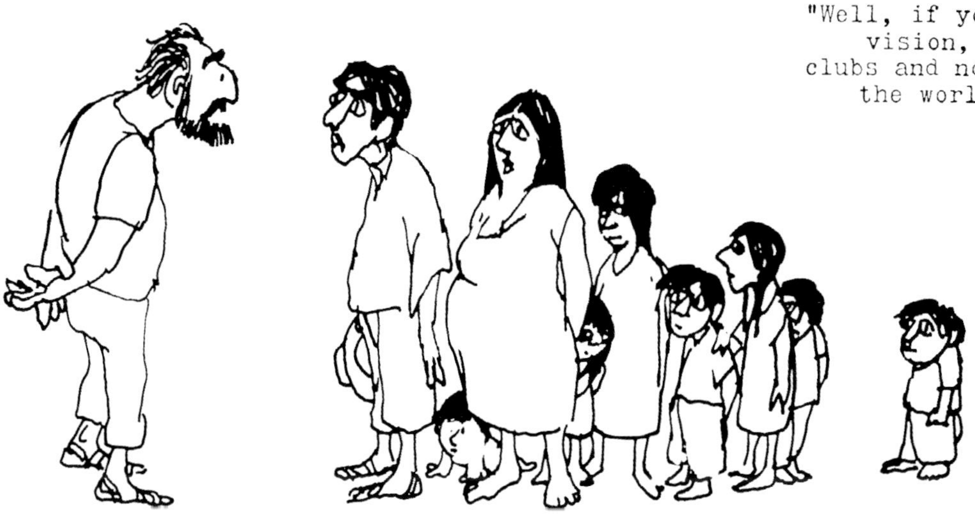

"I can't understand it . . . it couldn't have been Maria--she's much too sweet . . . it couldn't have been Dolores--she was a virgin . . . it couldn't have been Luisa--she . . ."

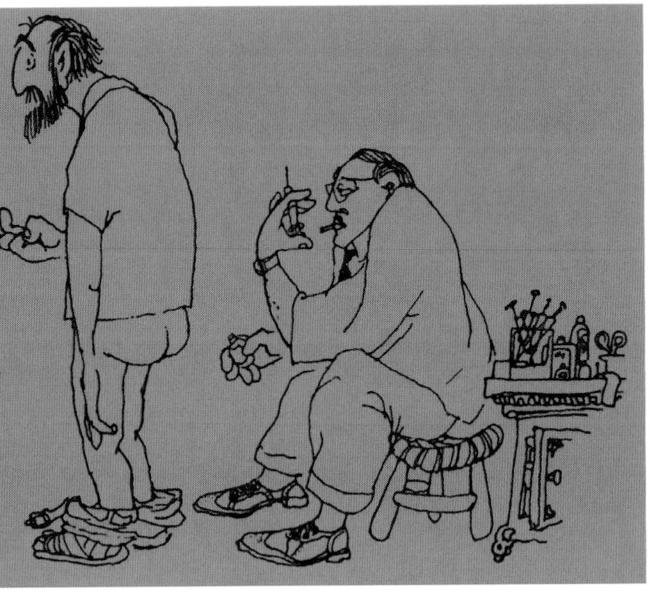

"But if you just had a little ambition, you'd move to the city and get a job and work hard and, in time, there'd be promotions and by saving and investing wisely, you'd be financially secure and then every year you could afford to come here on a two- or three-week vacation . . . !"

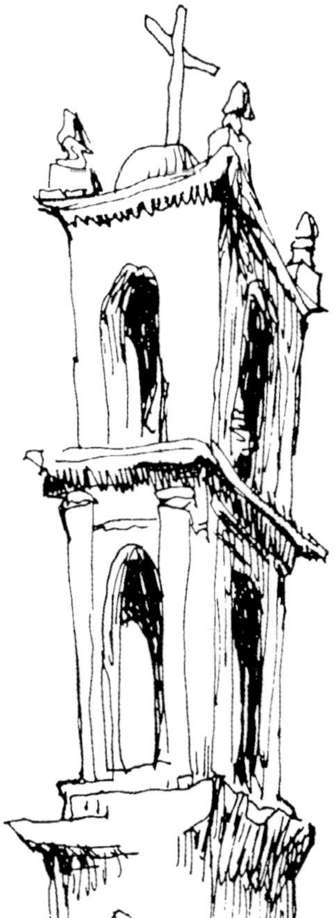

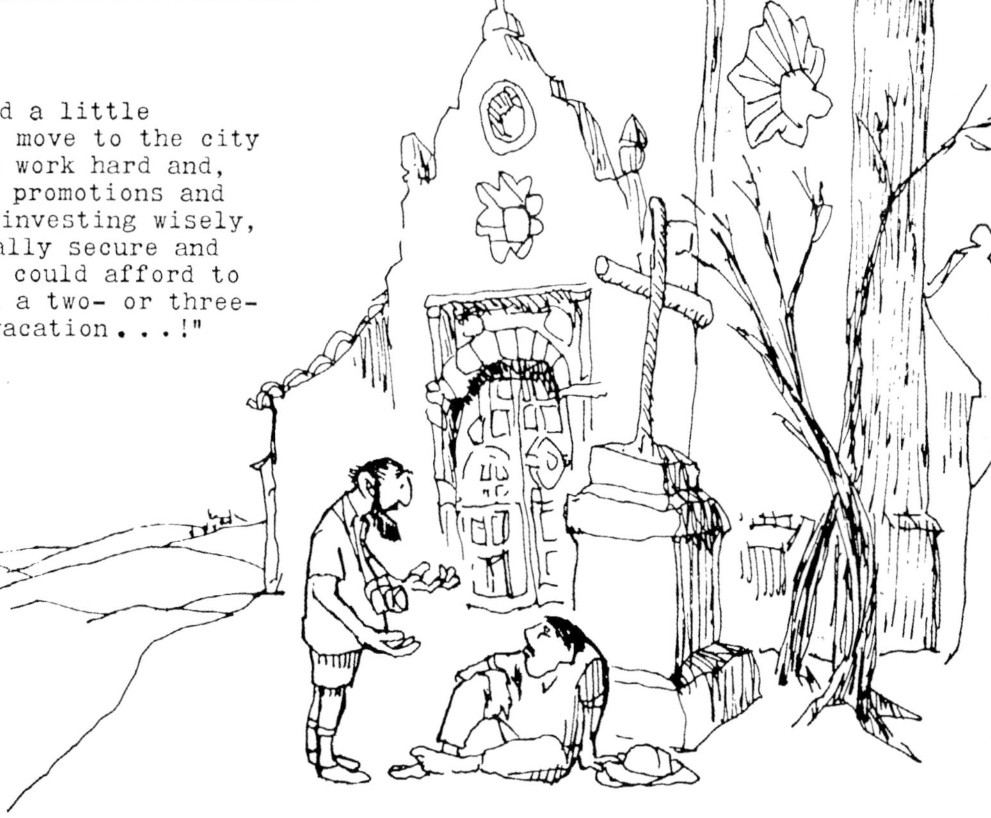

"I have a terrible confession to make, Señor Silverstein . . . I have been using you just to learn English!"

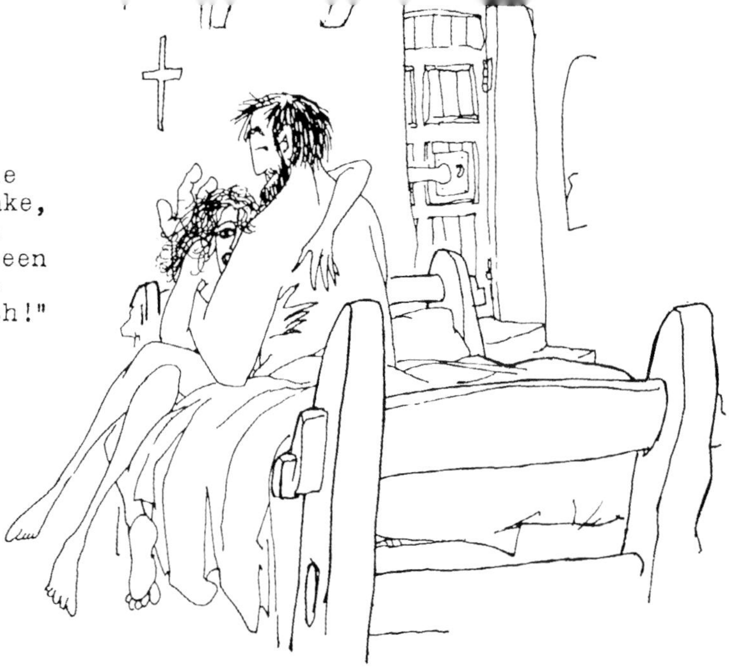

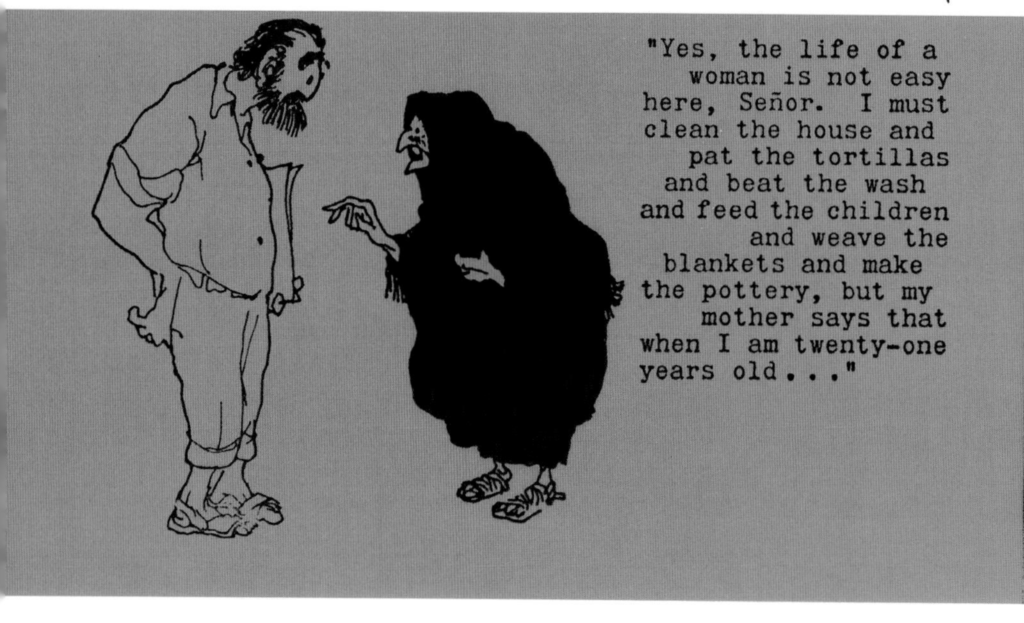

"Yes, the life of a woman is not easy here, Señor. I must clean the house and pat the tortillas and beat the wash and feed the children and weave the blankets and make the pottery, but my mother says that when I am twenty-one years old . . ."

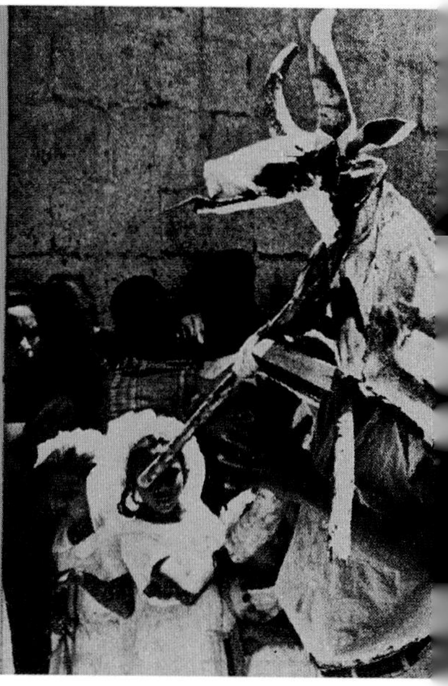

"But how do you know you can't make a kosher corned beef enchilada if you don't try to make a kosher corned beef enchilada?!"

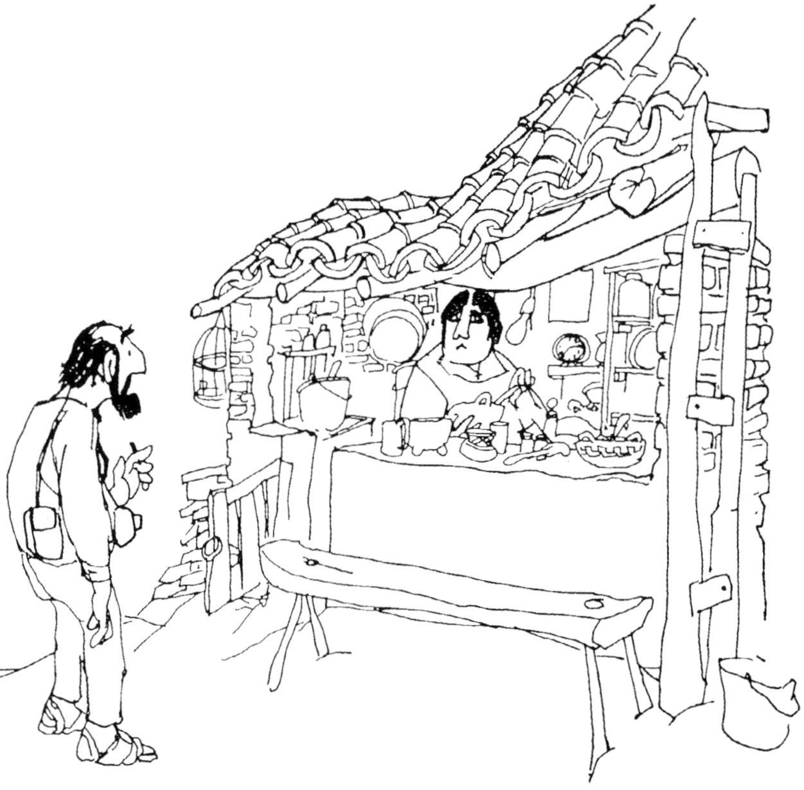

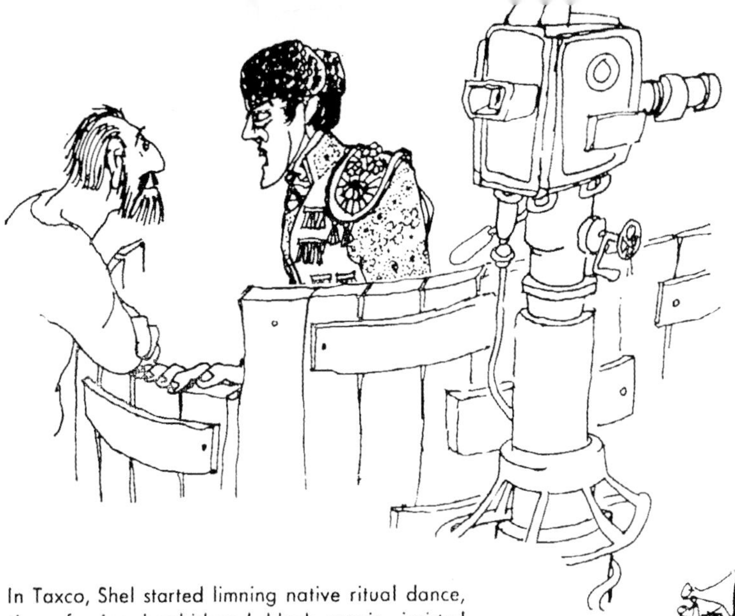

"In the old days, Señor, a matador had only to worry about the horns of the bull. Now we must concern ourselves with not turning our backs to the camera, with wearing the colors that will pick up well, with staying out of the late-afternoon shadows at the edge of the ring and--most importantly --remembering never to make the kill during the commercial!"

Below: In Taxco, Shel started limning native ritual dance, and natives, fearing bewhiskered black magic, insisted (right after photo was taken) that he set aside his sketch pad.

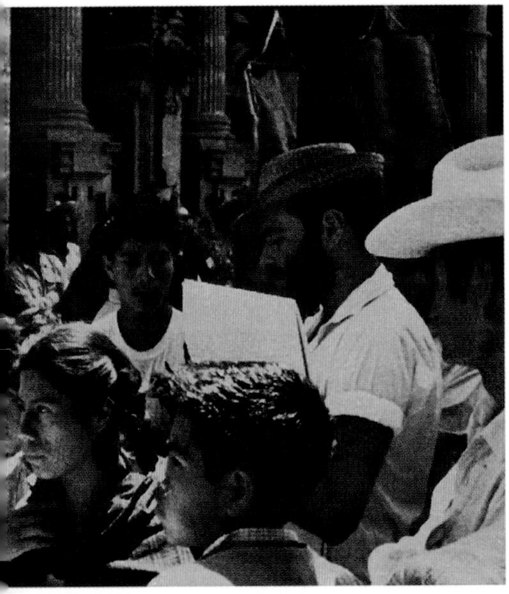

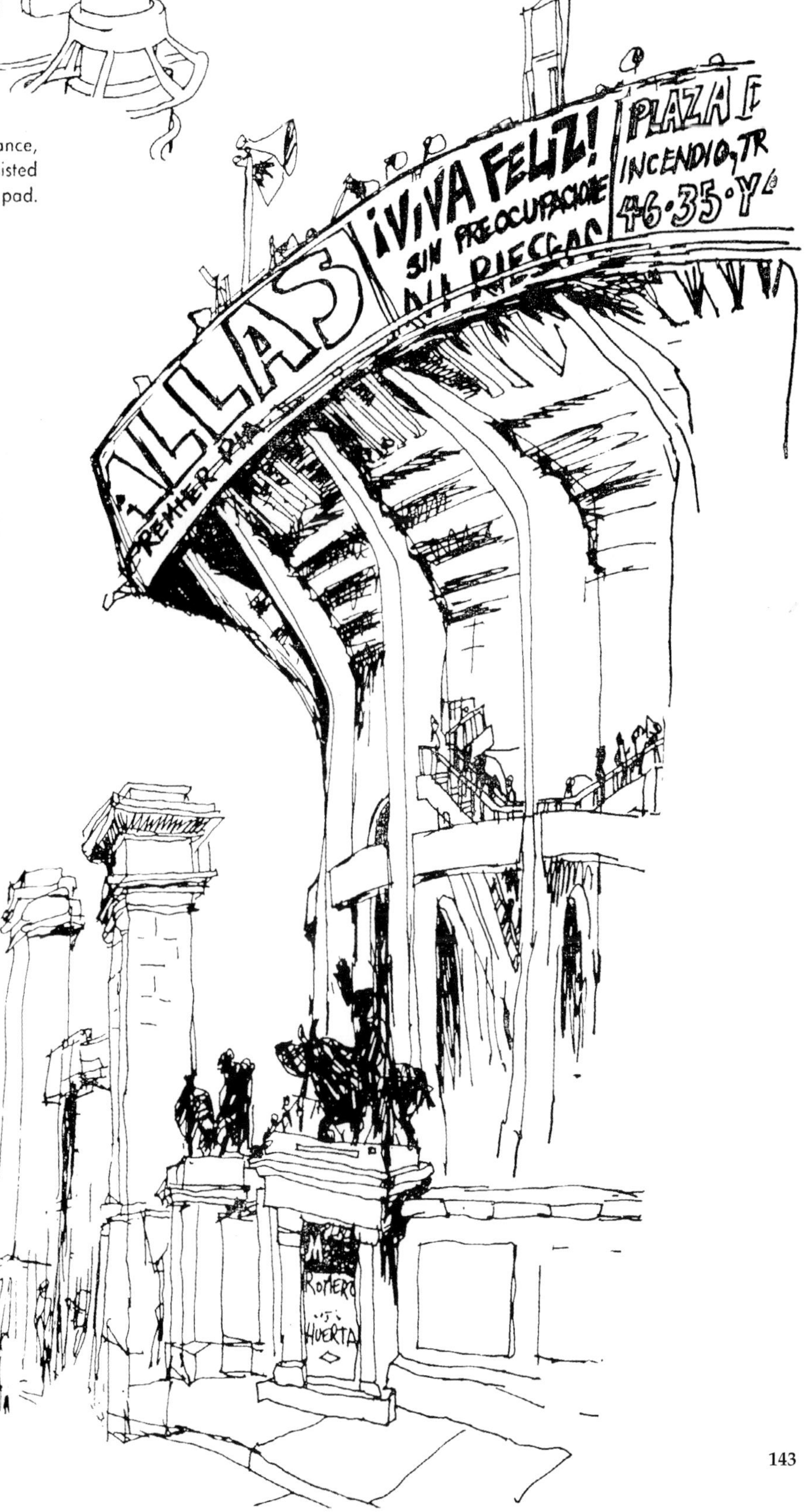
PLAZA
¡VIVA FELIZ!
LLAS
ROMERO
HUERTA

"You Americans are never satisfied! I get us two good seats for the corrida and you complain because we're in the sun . . . so we exchange them for seats in the shade and you complain that we're not close enough to the bulls . . . so we get the closest seats possible, but now you <u>still</u> complain!!"

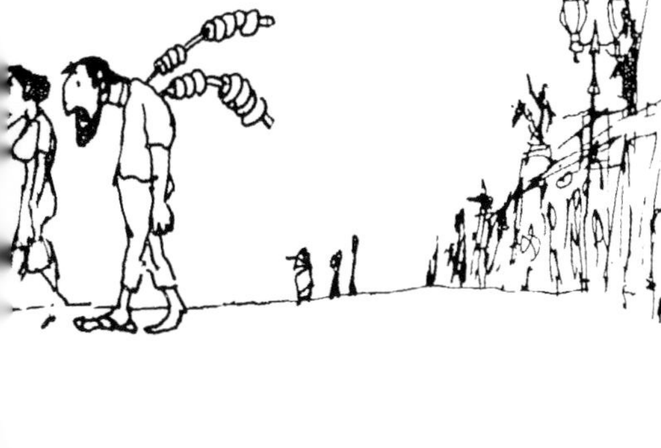

ON FIRE ISLAND

AUGUST 1965

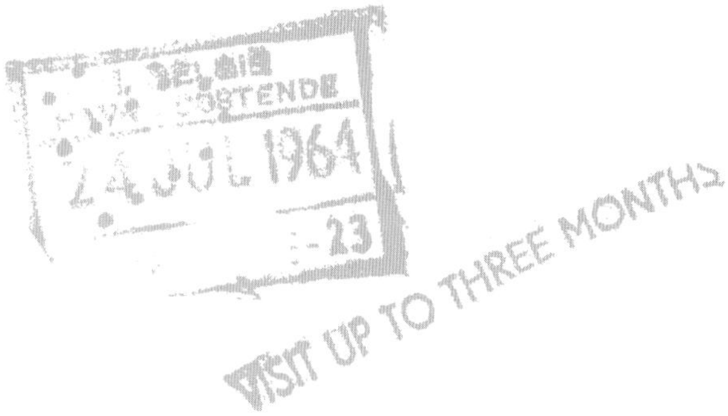
24 JUL 1964
VISIT UP TO THREE MONTHS

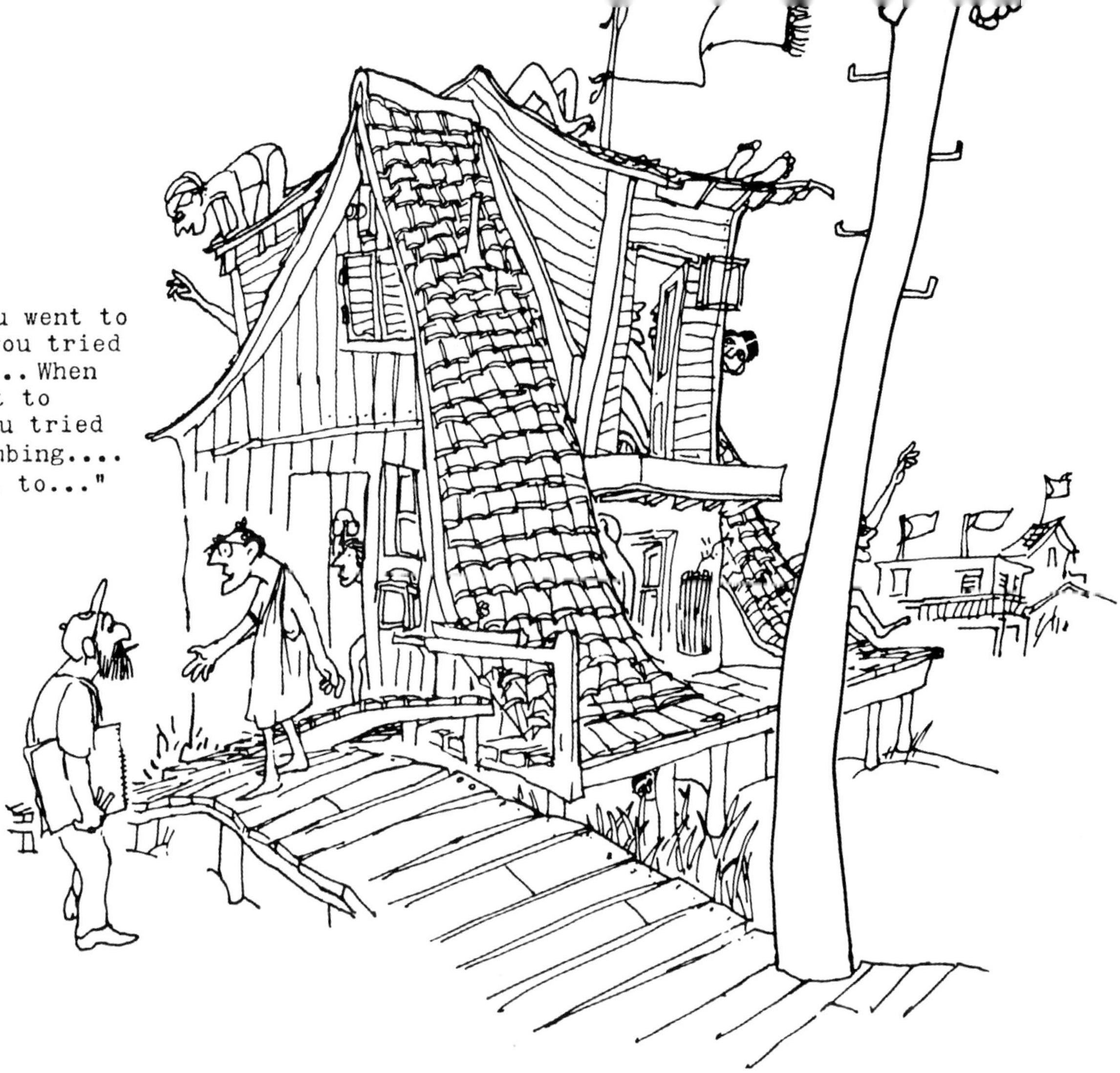

"But when you went to
Spain, you tried
bullfighting.... When
you went to
witzerland, you tried
mountain climbing....
When you went to..."

Silverstein
on
Fire Island

foot-loose shel visits the gay side of gotham's offshore bohemia—where the fruits are unforbidden

"Fifty years ago it was something special to be a homosexual: people were prejudiced against us...we were persecuted...we were social outcasts...we couldn't find work! Now we're everywhere: in positions of importance in Hollywood...of prominence in New York theater...of prestige on the national literary scene. Homosexuality is openly discussed and defended in the mass media--in major magazines, on radio and television; we also have our own publications, and national organizations and societies--we even have our own lobby in Washington. Today we're accepted in most liberal, upper-level sections of society; and in sophisticated circles, we're considered chic! We're not controversial any longer!...We don't shock anybody anymore!...And as a result, I'm seriously considering going straight!!"

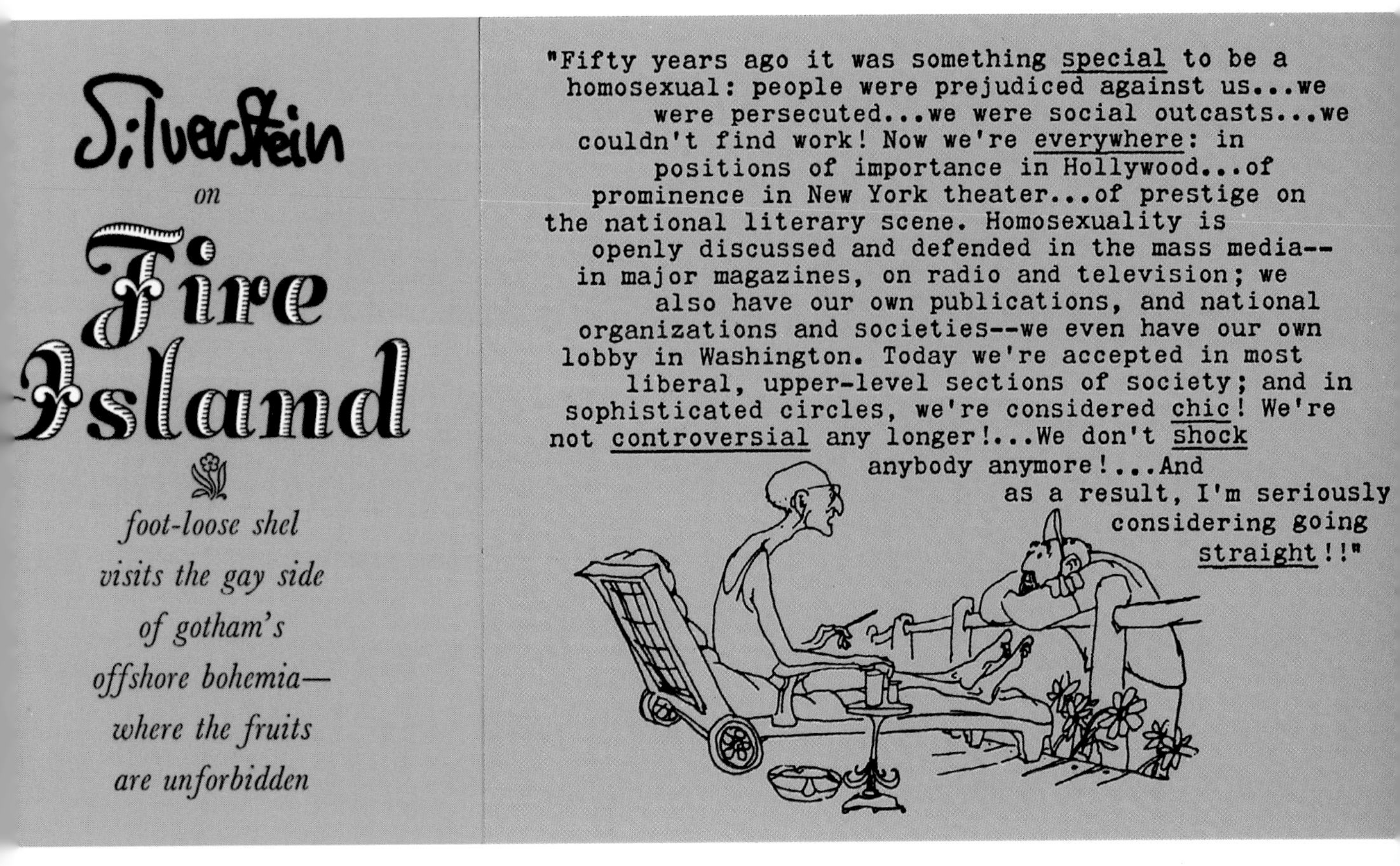

"Look, fella, in the first place, I'm trying to draw that building over there.... Secondly, I don't have anything to do with choosing the Playmate of the Month.... Thirdly, the Playmate is <u>always</u> a <u>girl</u>...! Fourthly..."

IN THE EIGHT YEARS he's been reporting PLAYBOY, roving cartoonist Shel Silverste has worked his inky wit in the four corners the globe. In the line-drawing of duty he h been gored in a Spanish bull ring, badly injur on safari in Uganda, knocked off the mound spring training with the Chicago White Sox, sunburned all over at a New Jersey nudist can All these high adventures pale by comparison however, with Shel's most recent (and most u usual) PLAYBOY assignment: to relax, as best could, for a week at a high-camp summer reso In the last few years homosexuality as a soc phenomenon has emerged from the shadows, the extent that today there are clearly recogniz gay enclaves in most big cities. Near New Yo City, off the south coast of Long Island, ther Fire Island's incongruously yclept Cherry Gro community, a small section of the free-swingi island resort traditionally (and almost exclusi ly) the province of Gothamites who would rath switch than fight. Here, sans stares, homosexu of every stripe gayly enjoy the amenities of thriving vacation community. And here, throu this summer fairyland, strolled our straight Joh bewhiskered, bare-pated and bewildered, reco ing for posterity his walk on the Wilde side.

"Look, Charlie, I'm no psychiatrist, but it seems to me that if you want to function as a <u>man</u>, you're going to have to stop wearing women's clothes, and walking and talking funny, and dating guys.... On the other hand, if you want to make it as a <u>girl</u>, you're going to have to shave off that mustache!"

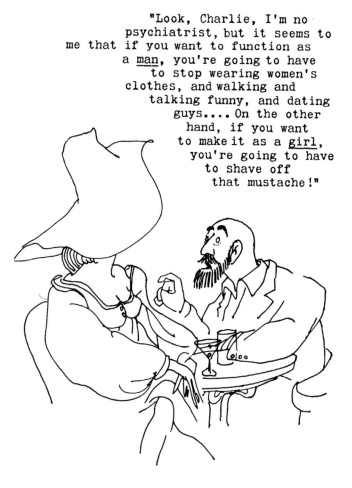

"You say this guy walked up to you whil you were sketching, started getting frien told you you had beautiful eyes, and th tried to make a pass?! Well, that's th way these fagots <u>are</u>, buddy--and <u>I</u> got patrol this damn beach all summer, and k these screaming queens in line, and wat them swishing, and listen to their screeching, and now that you mention it buddy, you <u>do</u> have beautiful eyes...!"

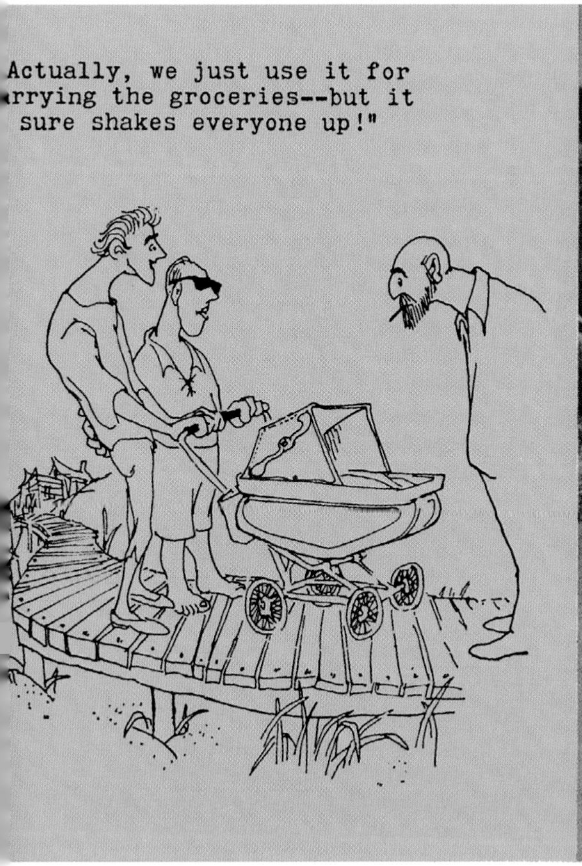
Actually, we just use it for
rrying the groceries--but it
sure shakes everyone up!"

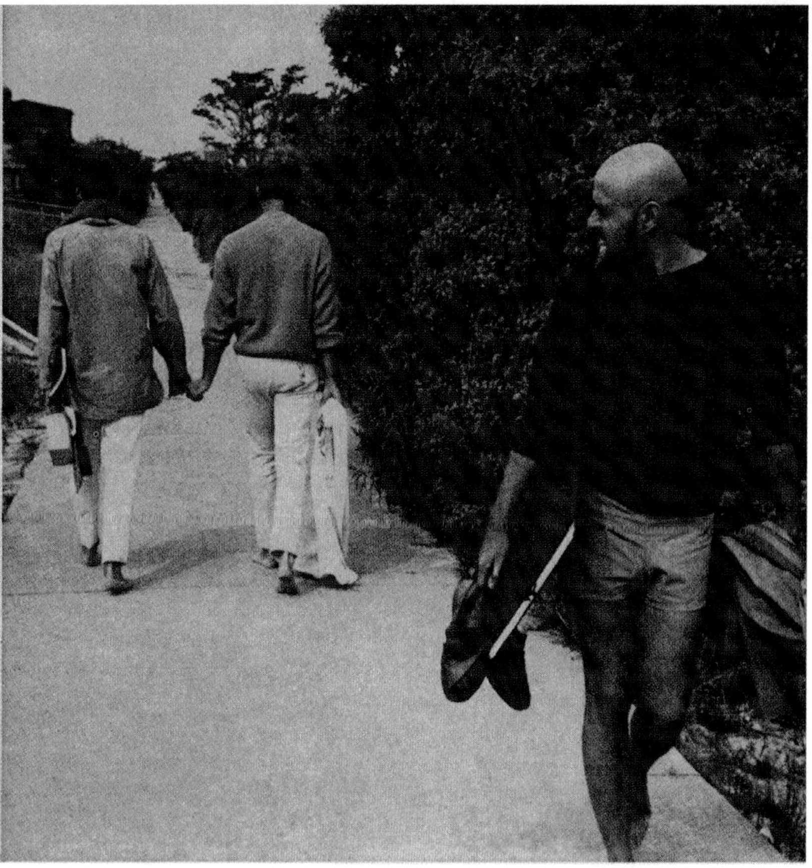

Above: A stranger in paradise, our outcast islander ponders *status quo*.

v: Sketching Shel hears bold new solution to population explosion.

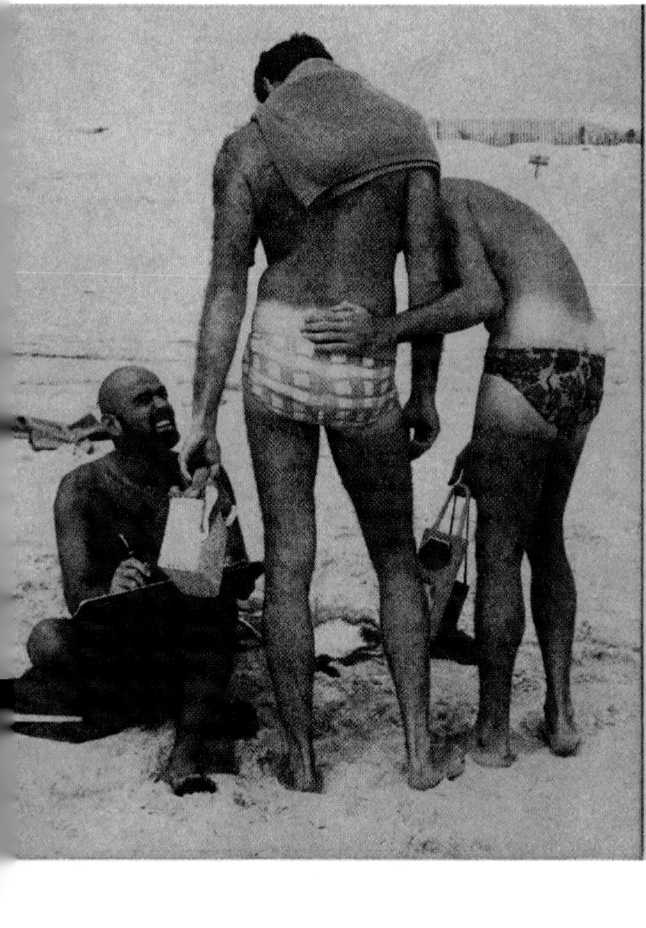

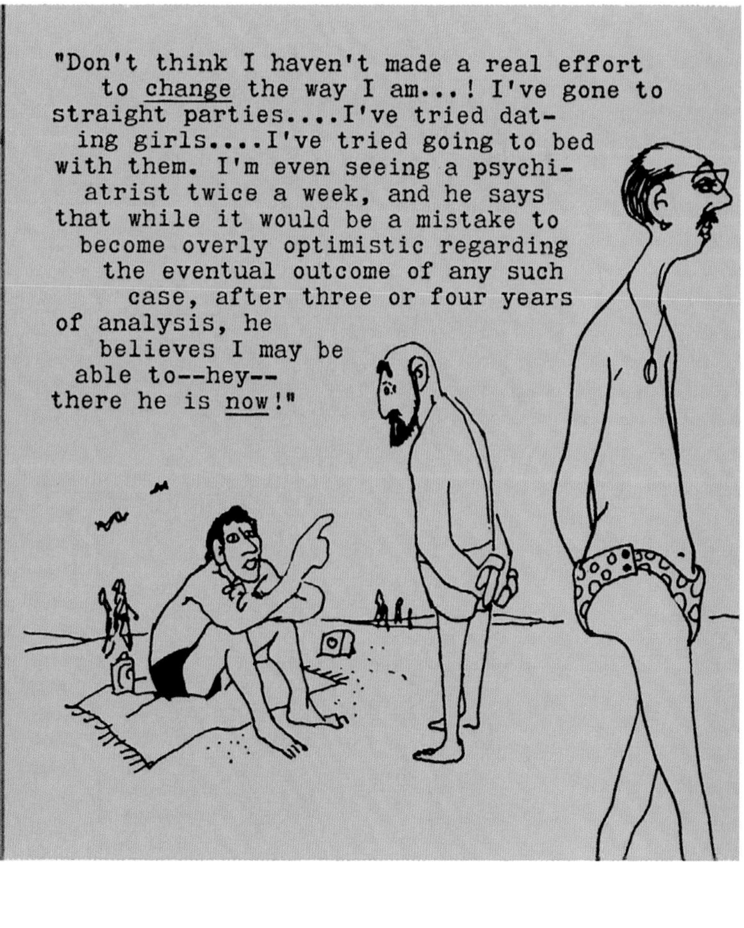
"Don't think I haven't made a real effort to change the way I am...! I've gone to straight parties....I've tried dating girls....I've tried going to bed with them. I'm even seeing a psychiatrist twice a week, and he says that while it would be a mistake to become overly optimistic regarding the eventual outcome of any such case, after three or four years of analysis, he believes I may be able to--hey--there he is now!"

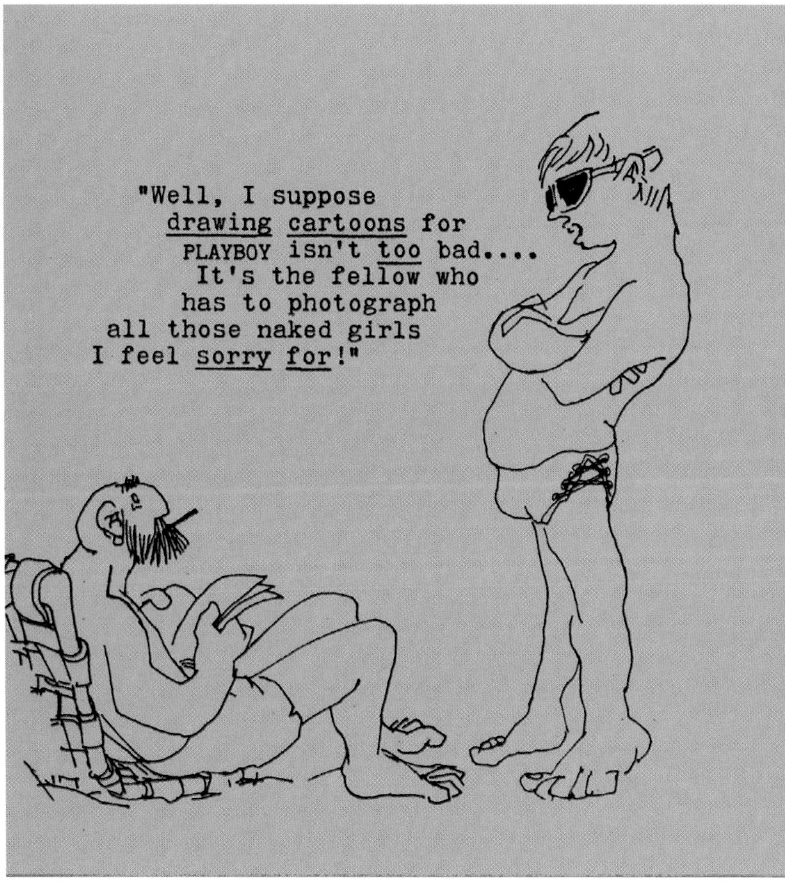
"Well, I suppose drawing cartoons for PLAYBOY isn't too bad.... It's the fellow who has to photograph all those naked girls I feel sorry for!"

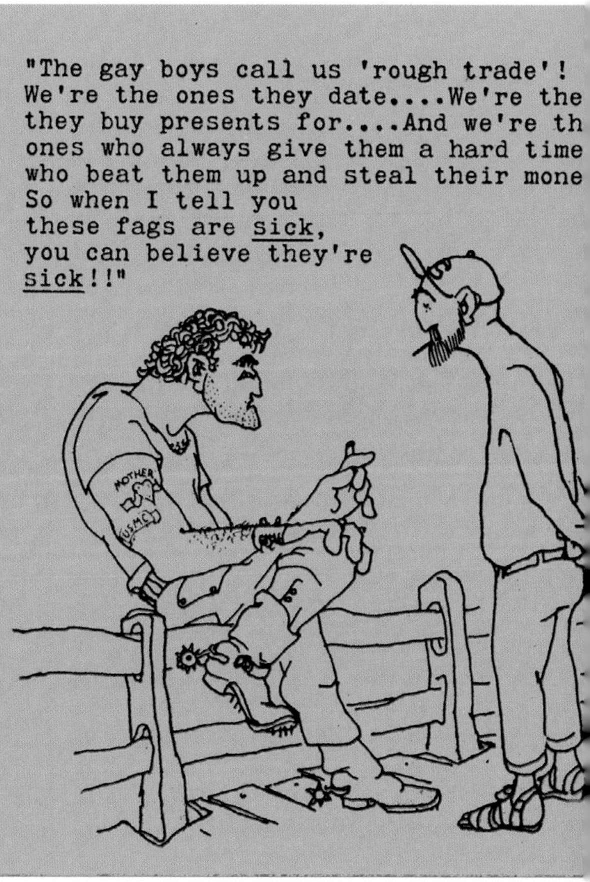
"The gay boys call us 'rough trade'! We're the ones they date....We're the they buy presents for....And we're th ones who always give them a hard time who beat them up and steal their mone So when I tell you these fags are sick, you can believe they're sick!!"
MOTHER
USMC

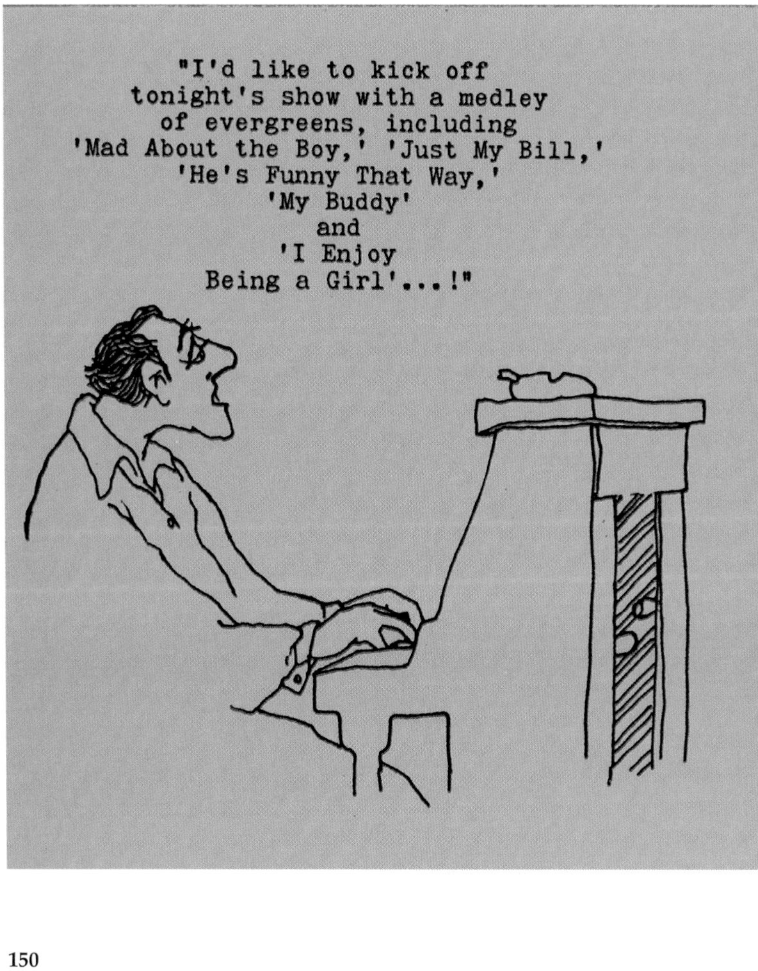
"I'd like to kick off tonight's show with a medley of evergreens, including 'Mad About the Boy,' 'Just My Bill,' 'He's Funny That Way,' 'My Buddy' and 'I Enjoy Being a Girl'...!"

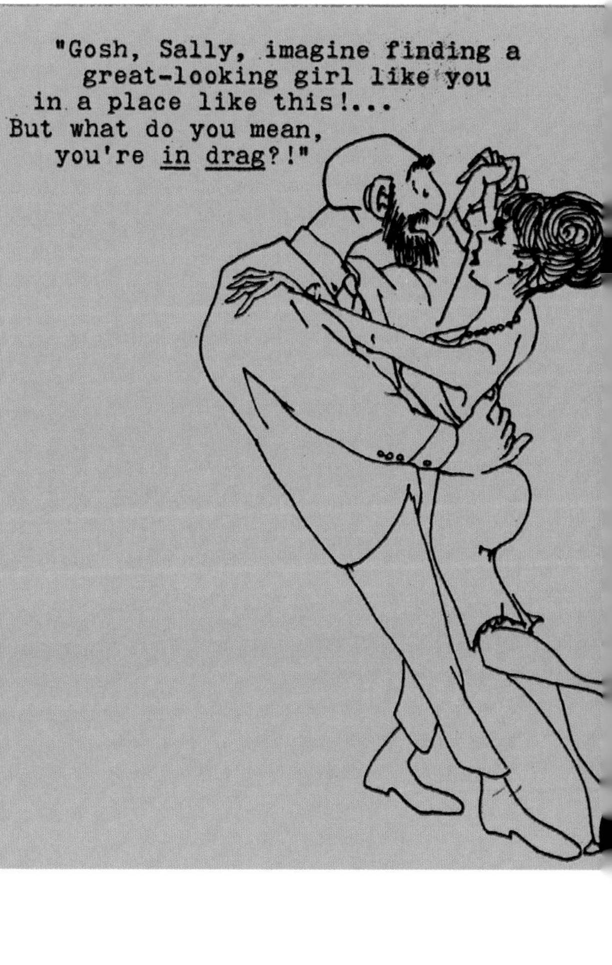
"Gosh, Sally, imagine finding a great-looking girl like you in a place like this!... But what do you mean, you're in drag?!"

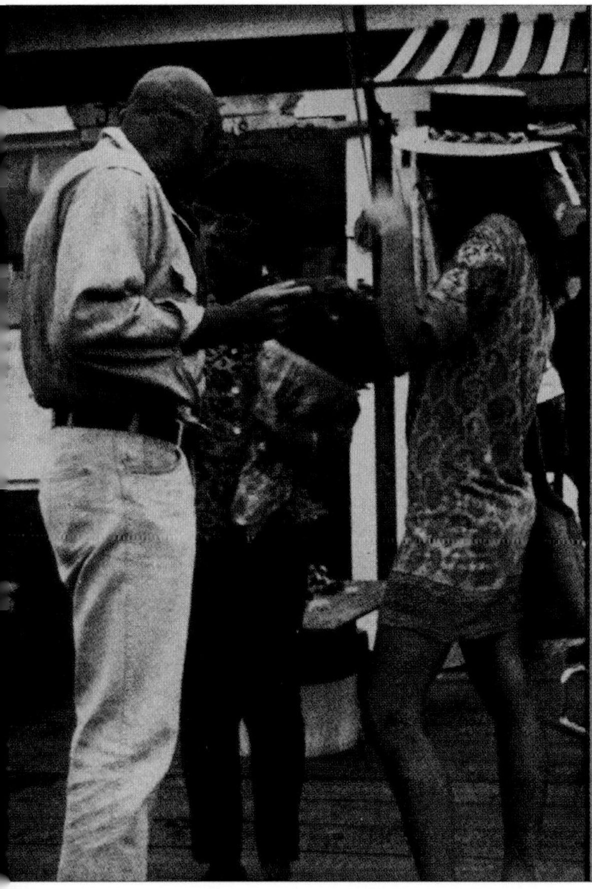

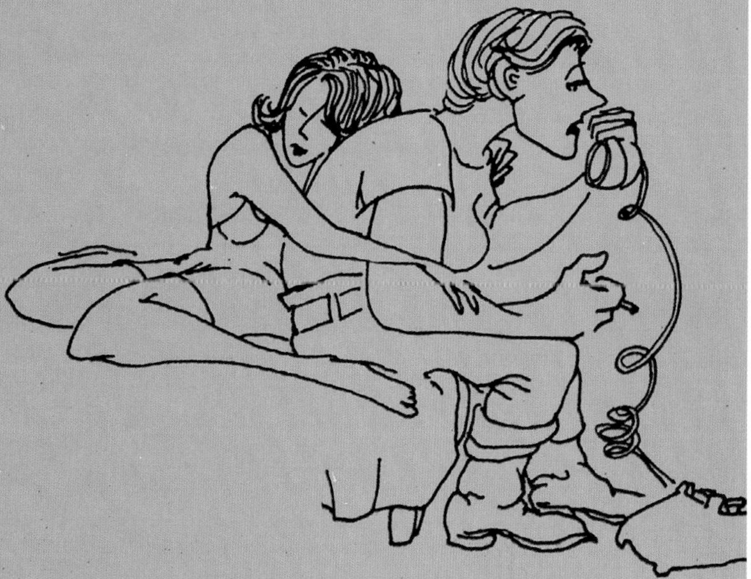

"Hello, Mom, this is Betty....Yeah, I had a nice trip, Mom....No, the motorcycle didn't give me any trouble....Yes, Mom, I'm staying with a girlfriend....No...I didn't take my pink chiffon gown, because I don't have any use for it here....Well, sure, Mom...sure there are lots of nice Jewish boys around, but..."

ove: Shel extols virtues of heterosexuality to skeptical couple.

low: Gay deceiver pouts provocatively for our amused cartoonist.

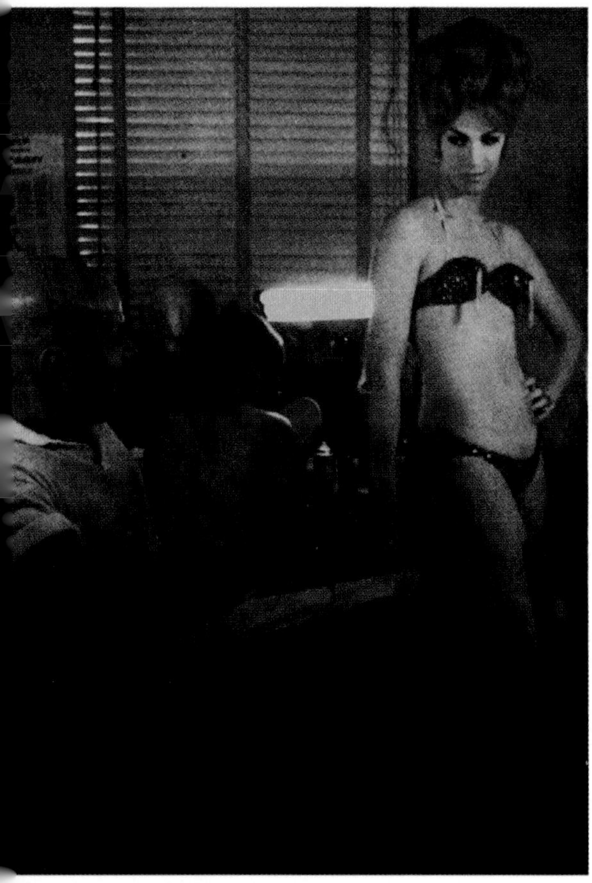

"...I'm relaxing in my cottage yesterday afternoon, when the doorbell rings--and me--thinking it's Philip, I run and put on my best cologne, I put on my garter belt, I put on my nylons and spike heels, I put on my black negligee, I put on my wig and make-up, and I run to the window and peek out--and it's my <u>parents</u>!! So I run back into the other room, I wipe off my make-up, pull off my wig, slip out of the negligee, kick off the heels, remove the nylons and take off the garter belt--put on a pair of blue jeans, a flannel shirt and a pair of loafers, and run back to the door--and they're <u>gone</u>! So I stroll back into the other room, take off the blue jeans, the shirt and the loafers--put on my garter belt..."

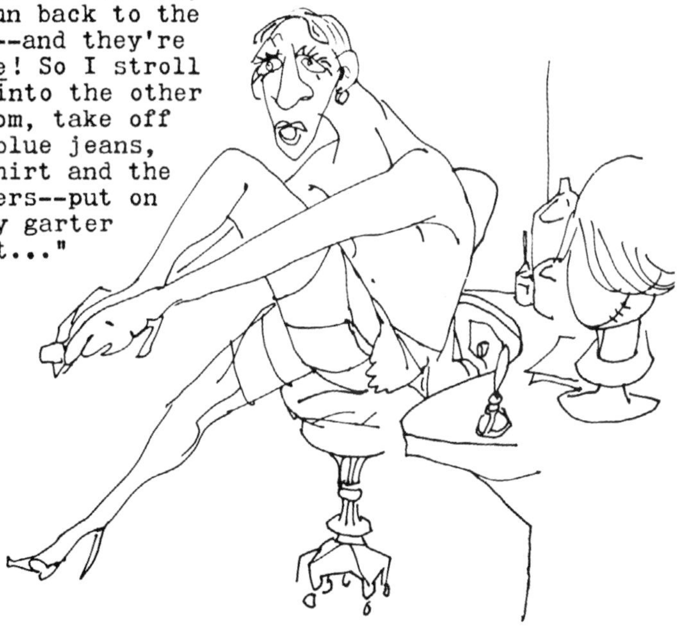

IN LONDON

JUNE 1967

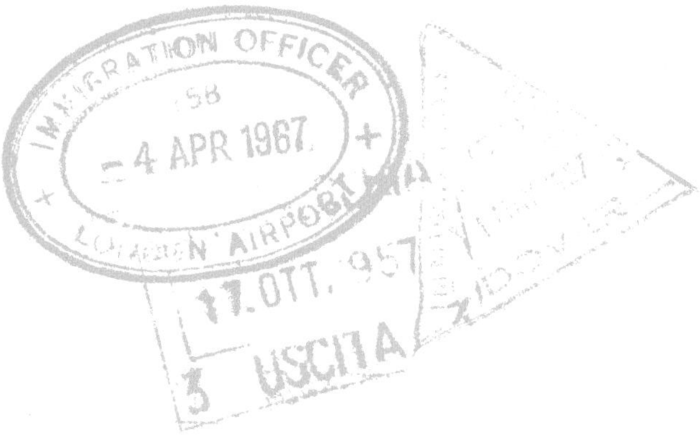
IMMIGRATION OFFICER
4 APR 1967
AIRPORT
17. OTT. 957
USCITA

SILVERSTEIN IN LONDON

our switched-on beard catches the mod show in a return visit to swingsville-on-thames

TEN YEARS AGO, Shel Silverstein, our bawdy bard of the satiric sketchbook, portrayed for PLAYBOY a London that was venerated and venerable. England's capital has since become the West's prime example of urbane renewal; today, titled nobility is bypassed in favor of a closely knit coterie of miniskirted mannequins, pop-music groups, fashion photographers, dress designers and *disco*-technicians. Shel's second sortie into Londontown finds him caught up in the storied city's new-found spirit. In a word: Modness.

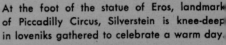

At the foot of the statue of Eros, landmark of Piccadilly Circus, Silverstein is knee-deep in loveniks gathered to celebrate a warm day.

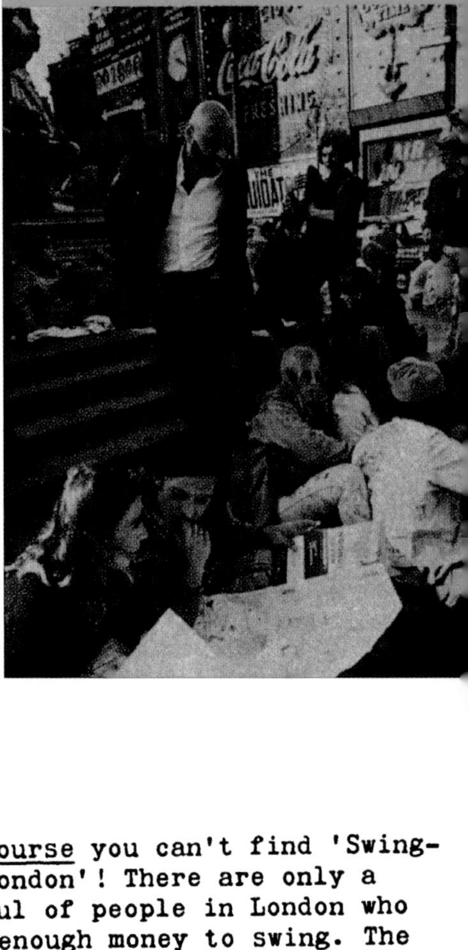

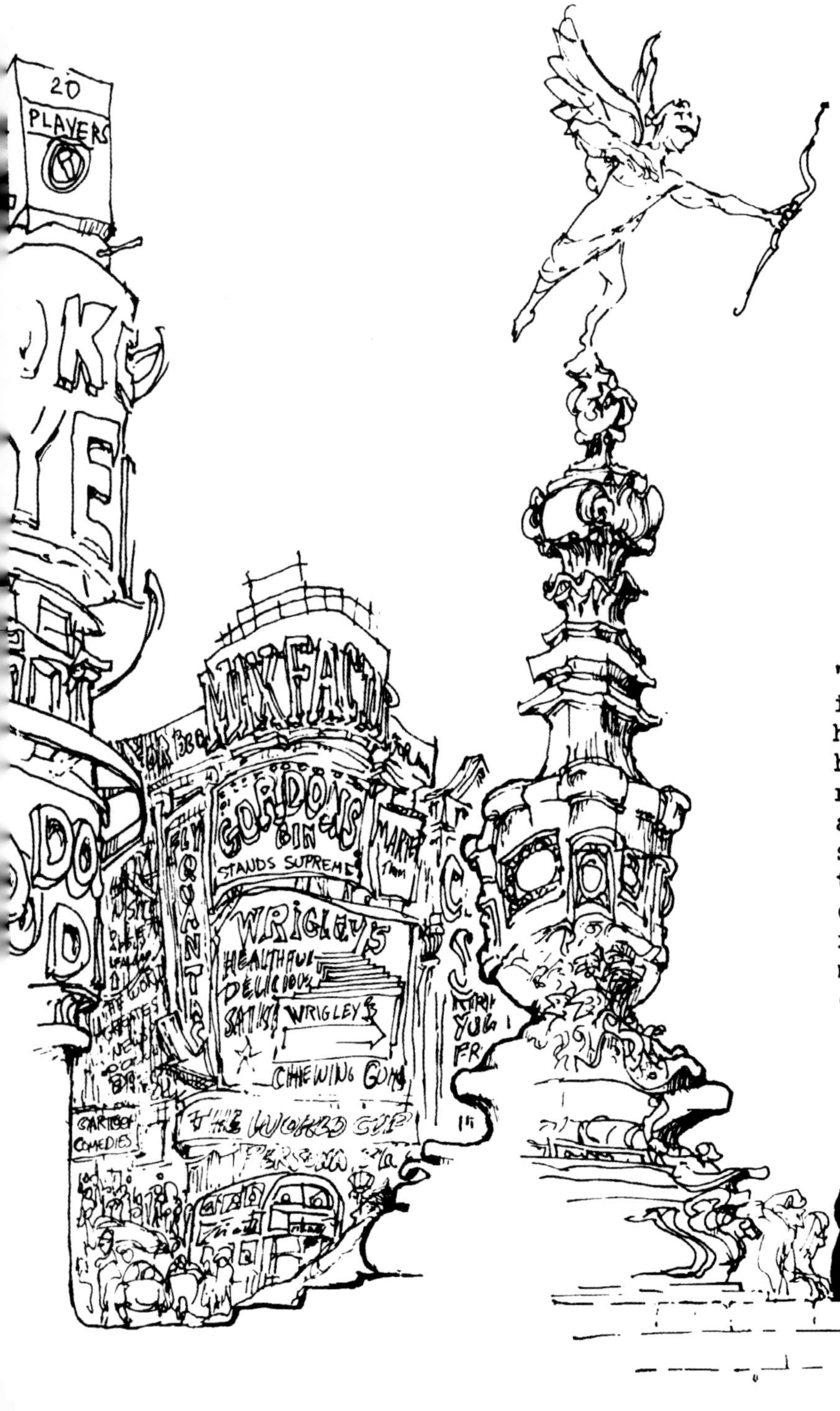

20
PLAYERS
GORDON'S
GIN
STANDS SUPREME
WRIGLEY'S
HEALTHFUL
WRIGLEY'S
CHEWING GUM
CARTOON
COMEDIES

"Of course you can't find 'Swinging London'! There are only a handful of people in London who have enough money to swing. The rest of us are busy doing articles and picture stories and television shows on 'Swinging London,' so that you desperate Americans will come swarming over here looking for the action, and spend enough money to beef up our economy so we can afford to swing a bit!"

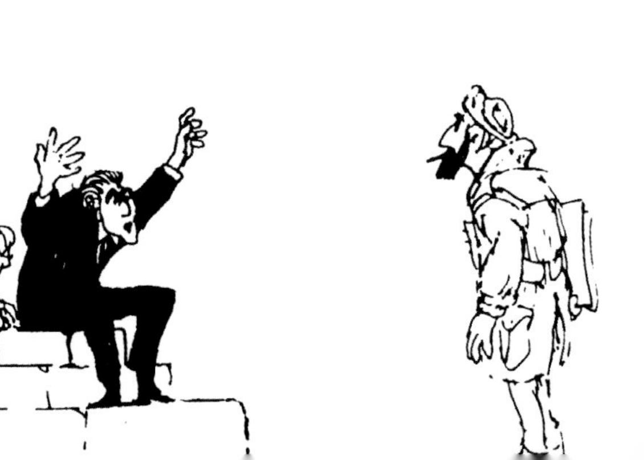

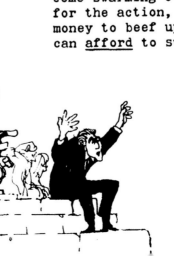

"Well, Mr. Silverstein, you passed the physical, but did poorly on the mental exam, only average in the personality tests, language proficiency, art and literature, but you'll be pleased to learn that your over-all grade was a passing one, so we will consider tailoring you a suit!"

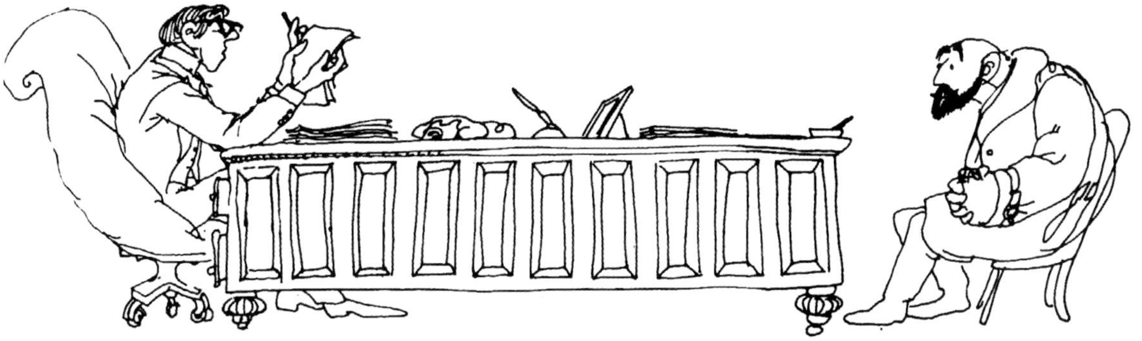

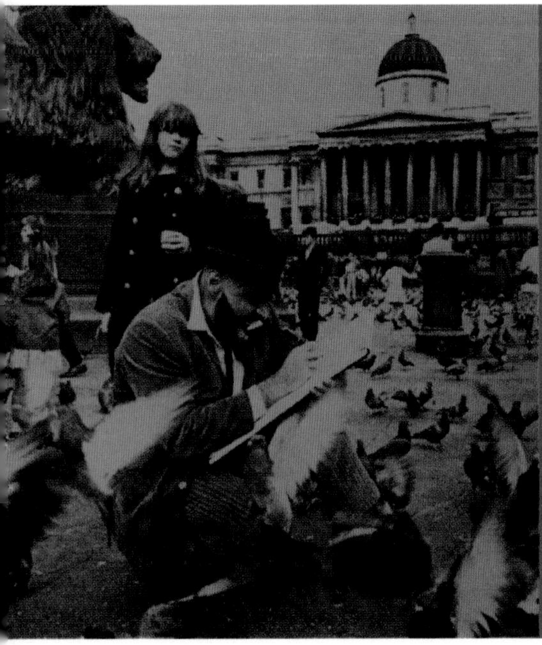

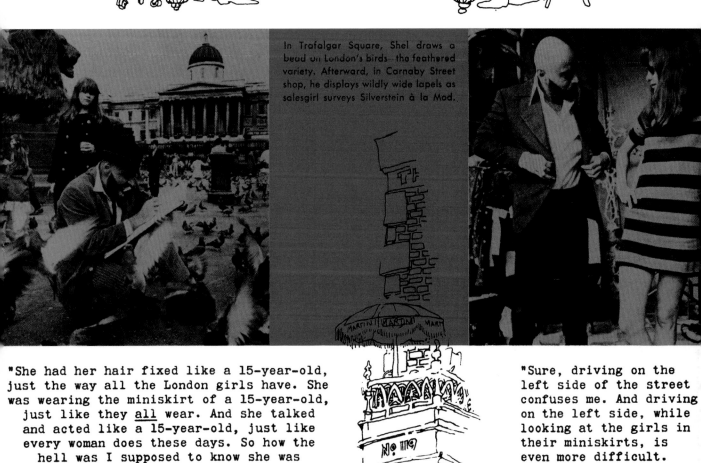

In Trafalgar Square, Shel draws a bead on London's birds—the feathered variety. Afterward, in Carnaby Street shop, he displays wildly wide lapels as salesgirl surveys Silverstein à la Mod.

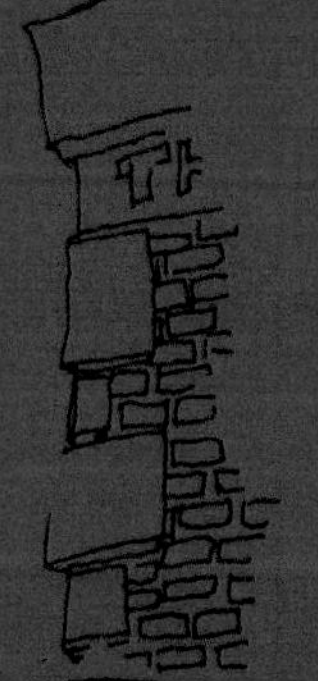

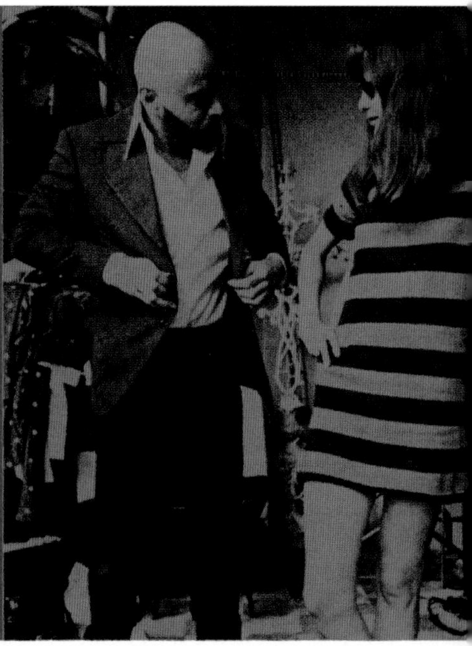

"She had her hair fixed like a 15-year-old, just the way all the London girls have. She was wearing the miniskirt of a 15-year-old, just like they all wear. And she talked and acted like a 15-year-old, just like every woman does these days. So how the hell was I supposed to know she was actually a 15-year-old?!!"

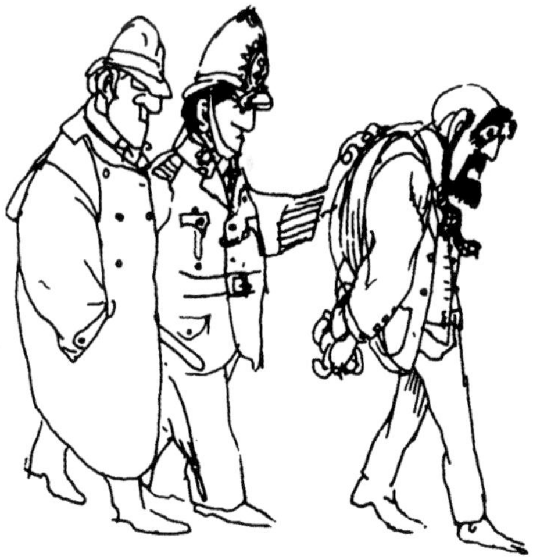

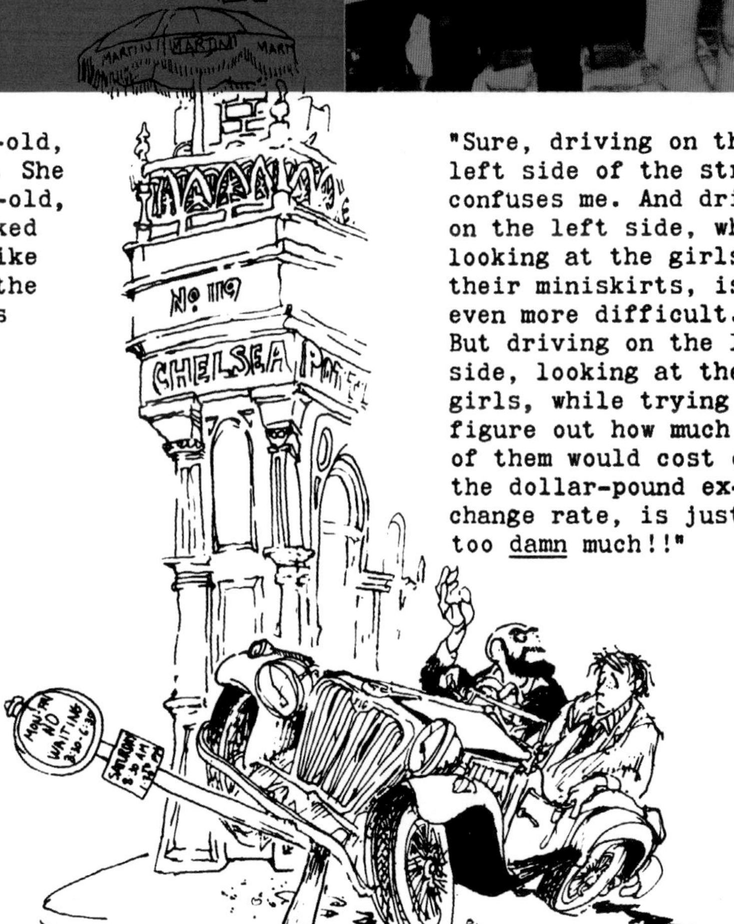
MARTINI
No 119
CHELSEA
NO WAITING

"Sure, driving on the left side of the street confuses me. And driving on the left side, while looking at the girls in their miniskirts, is even more difficult. But driving on the left side, looking at the girls, while trying to figure out how much one of them would cost on the dollar-pound exchange rate, is just too damn much!!"

"Actually, all this publicity about the sexual promiscuity of London girls is highly exaggerated, and you'll find after you've been here a while, Mr.... Mr.... what did you say your name was again...?"

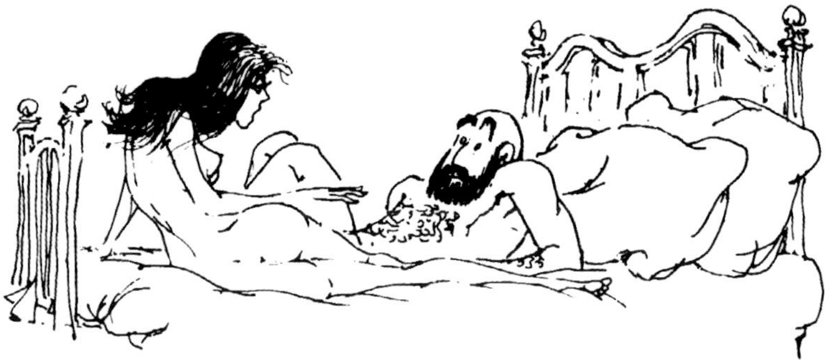

Twiggy, London supermodel and an international celebrity at 17, oversees lunch date Shel sketching away at Alvaro's, mecca for rich young Britons. Later, he digs the threads worn by busbied Buckingham Palace guard.

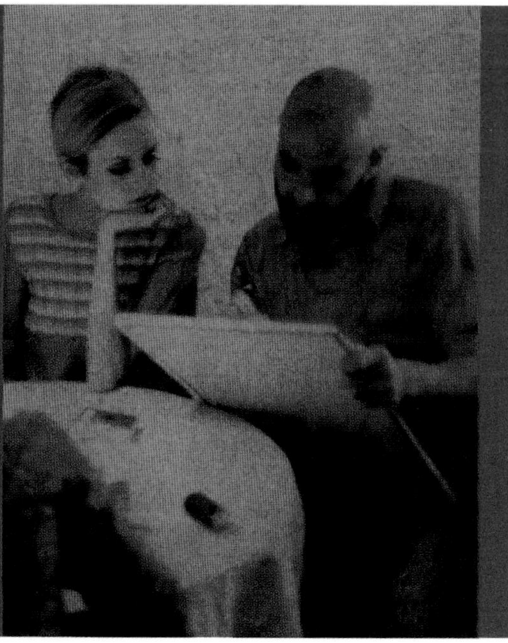

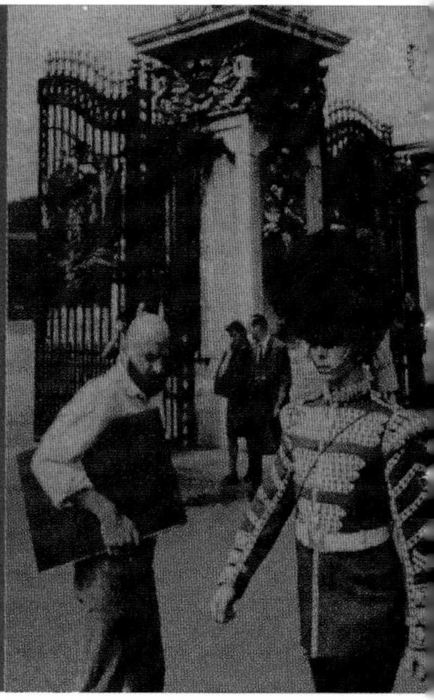

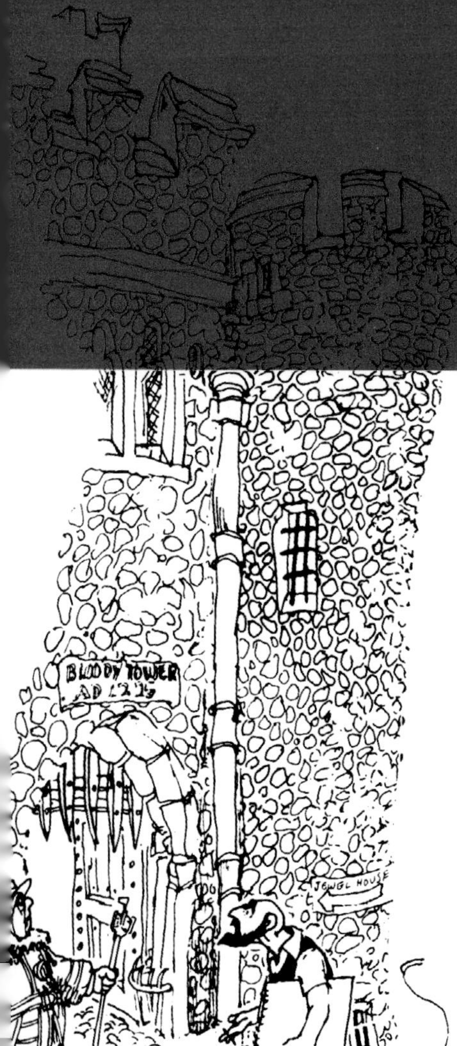
BLOODY TOWER

"No cameras or drawing pads allowed in the crown jewel chamber? Well, what the hell do you think I'm gonna do--steal 'em? I happen to be a well-paid cartoonist--with an international reputation--and besides, how could anybody steal the crown jewels--from an electrified glass case, with three guards, in a stone tower with a barred window?! It's impossible! Unless, of course, you could find a way to lower yourself to the window from the parapet above, which would require 18 feet of rope, a grappling hook, and a blowtorch for the bars. But then you'd be faced with the problem of the electrified case, for which you'd need a jumper wire and a pair of alligator clips--to disconnect the alarm without interrupting the circuit. But even then you'd need somebody on the inside to take care of the guards, and how would you like to meet me at the pub down the street a little later for a friendly drink...?"

"Well, they don't call them sentry boxes where I come from...! But it was an honest mistake ...and I said I was sorry... and I will clean it up...!"

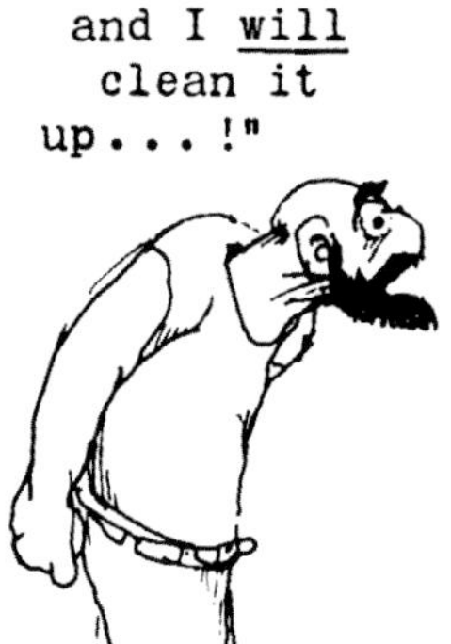

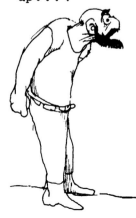

"I remembered the odds, I remembered the amounts of the natural bets, I remembered to clear the layouts and pay the outside bets first, I remembered the pay-offs, I remembered to offer the bank, and I forgot to take my pill...."

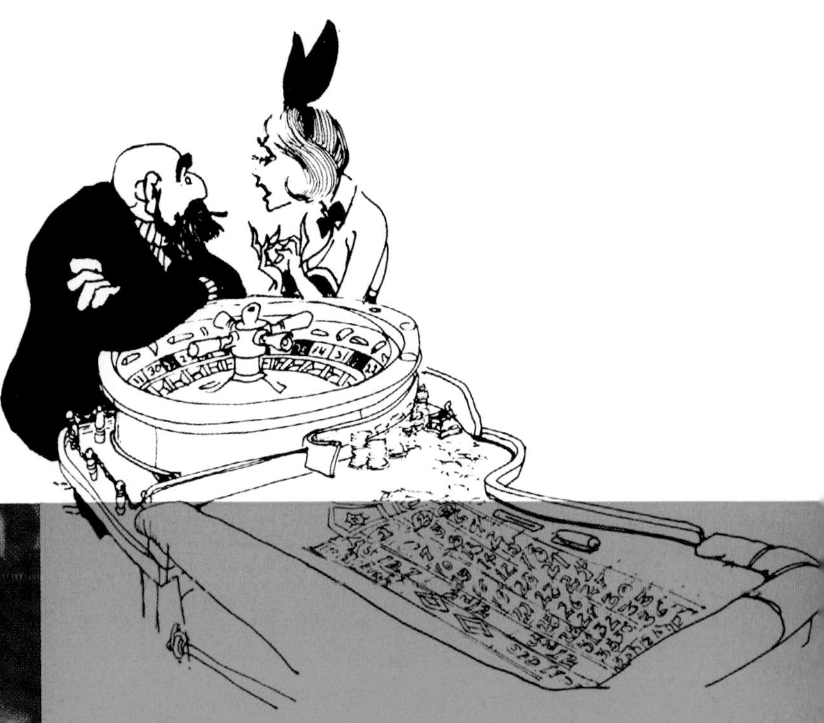

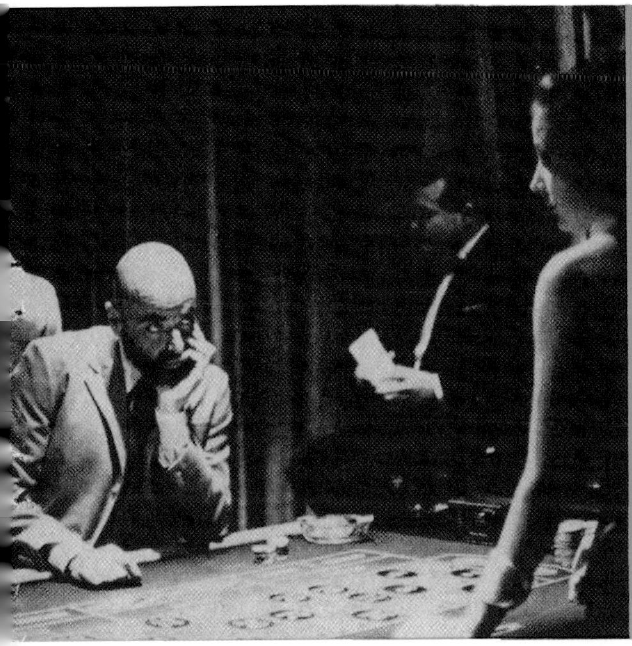

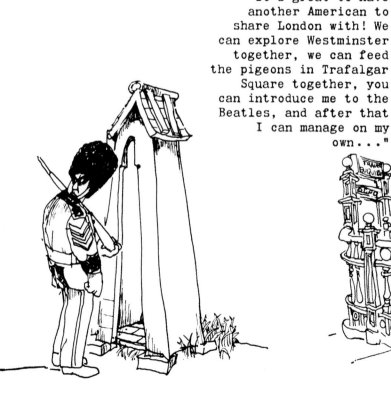

Visiting the London Playboy Club's gaming rooms, Silverstein concentrates his betting on roulette, his attention on the Croupier Bunny.

"It's great to have another American to share London with! We can explore Westminster together, we can feed the pigeons in Trafalgar Square together, you can introduce me to the Beatles, and after that I can manage on my own..."

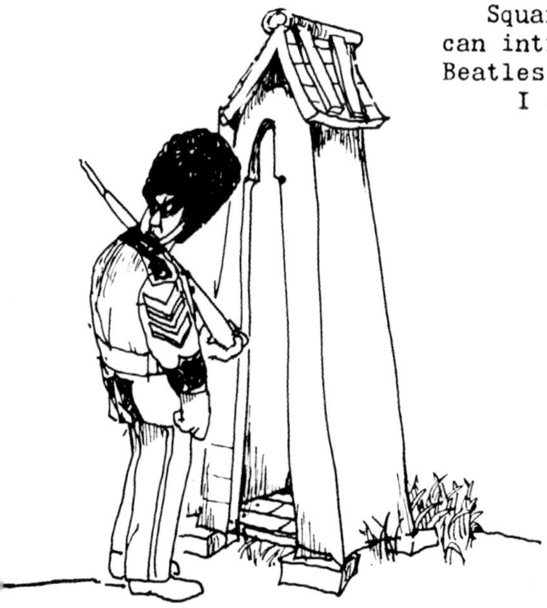

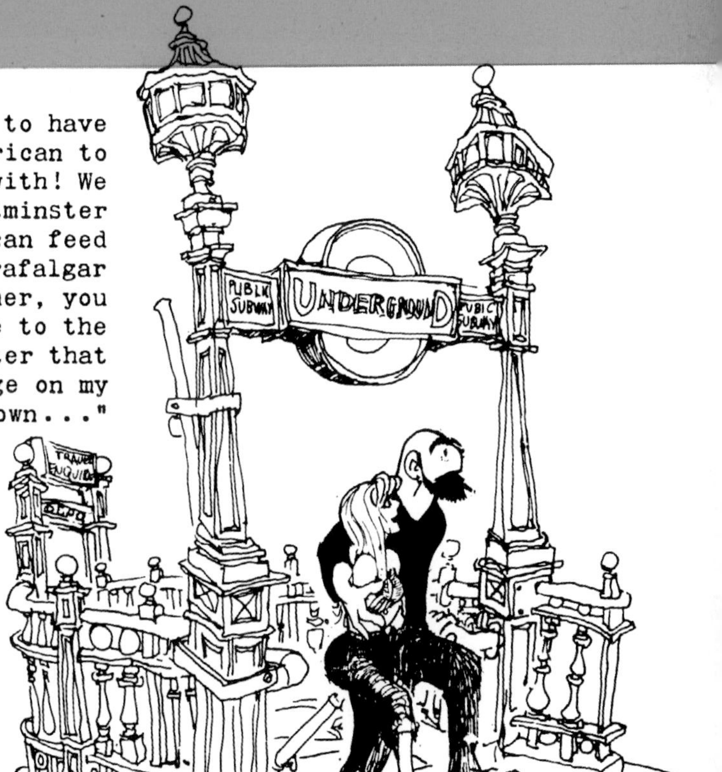
UNDERGROUND

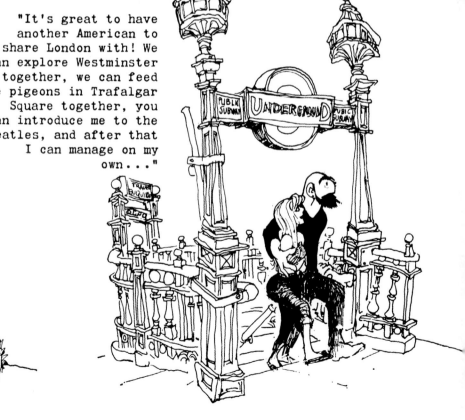

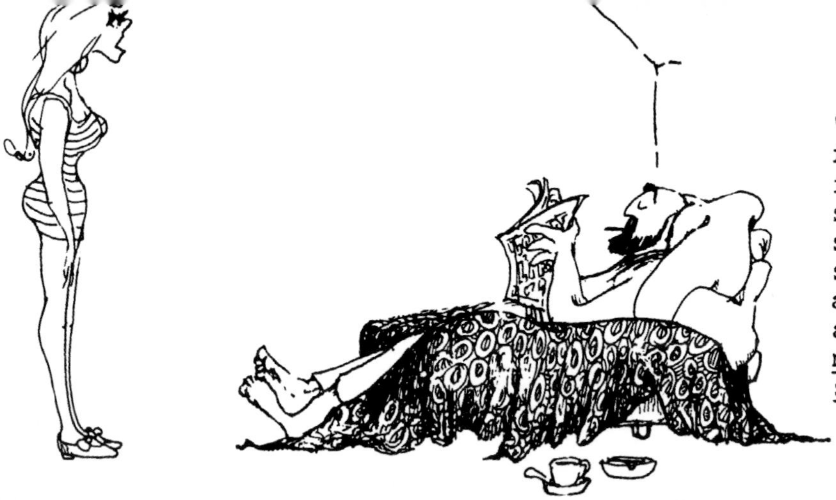

"When you first arrived in London, you said my mini-skirts were sophisticated and smart--now all you say is my ass is showing!"

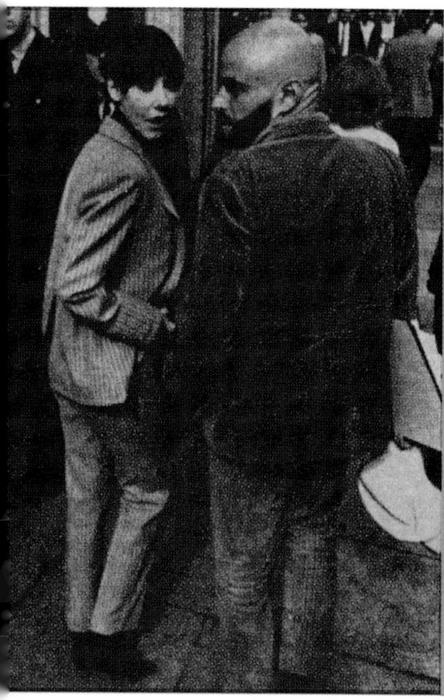

American mannequin Peggy Moffitt leads Shel on a shopping safari in Knightsbridge area. Silverstein then repairs to a nearby pub, where he downs a pint with playwright Herb Gardner and film maker Jerry Farrell.

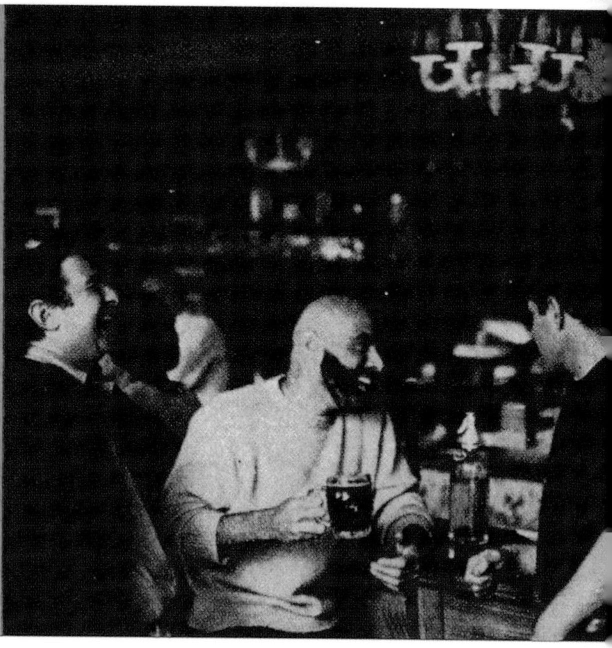

"That's old Betsy, and you've been introduced to Spot and Judy, so I guess you've met the entire family.... Oh, and, of course, I also have a wife and three children...."

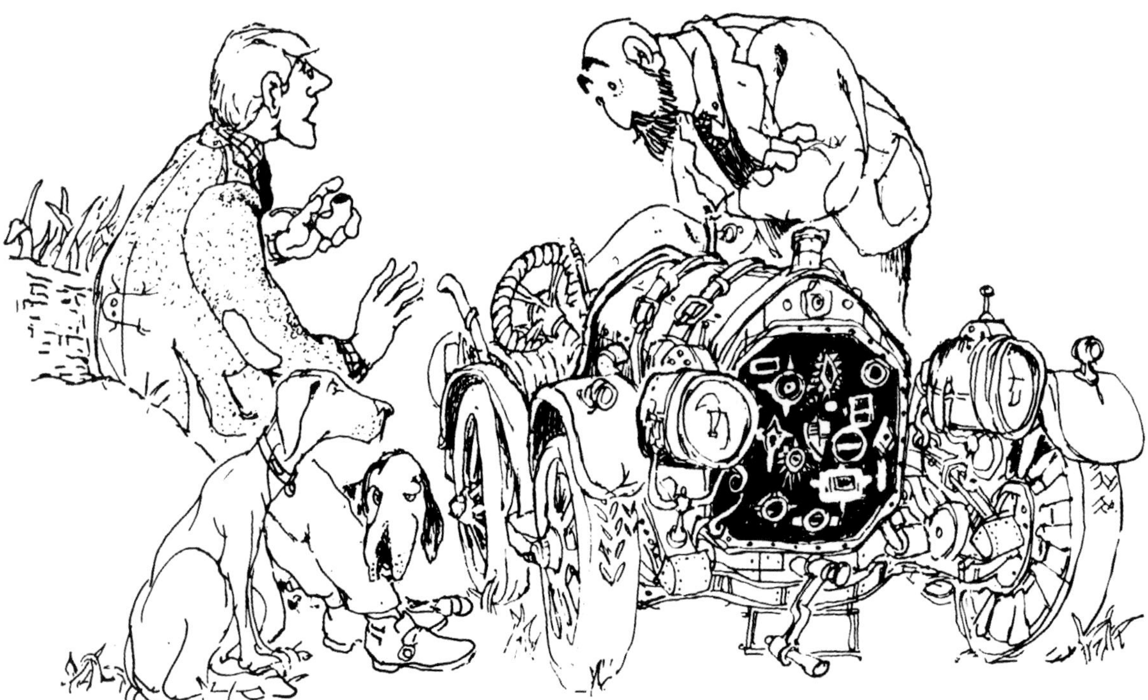

"Through libera
legislation ou
antiquated se
laws are bein
modernized
Homosexuality
for example, wa
once a majo
offense, then i
became a mino
infraction;
few months ago
it was mad
legal and I, fo
one, shan't b
satisfied unti
it become
mandatory!

Neither rain nor fog can stay the hand of PLAYBOY's penman: Silverstein, with brolly unfurled, camps out on Westminster Bridge for a moist morning of drawing historic Big Ben.

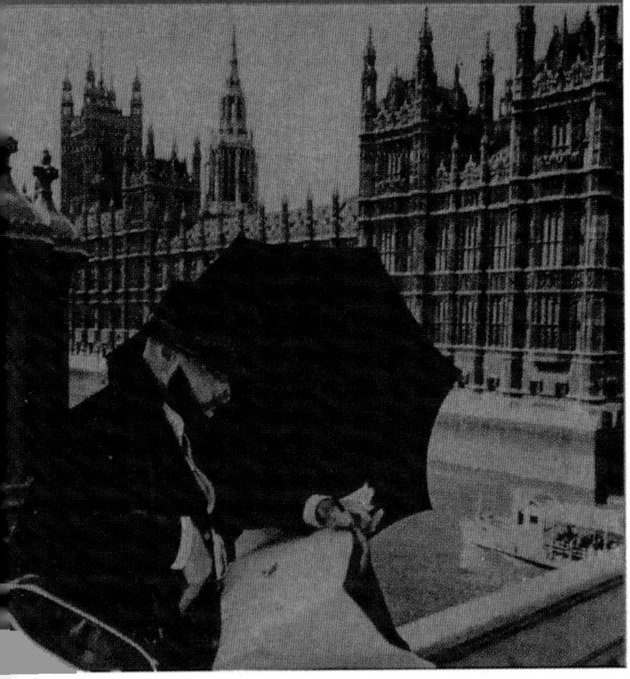

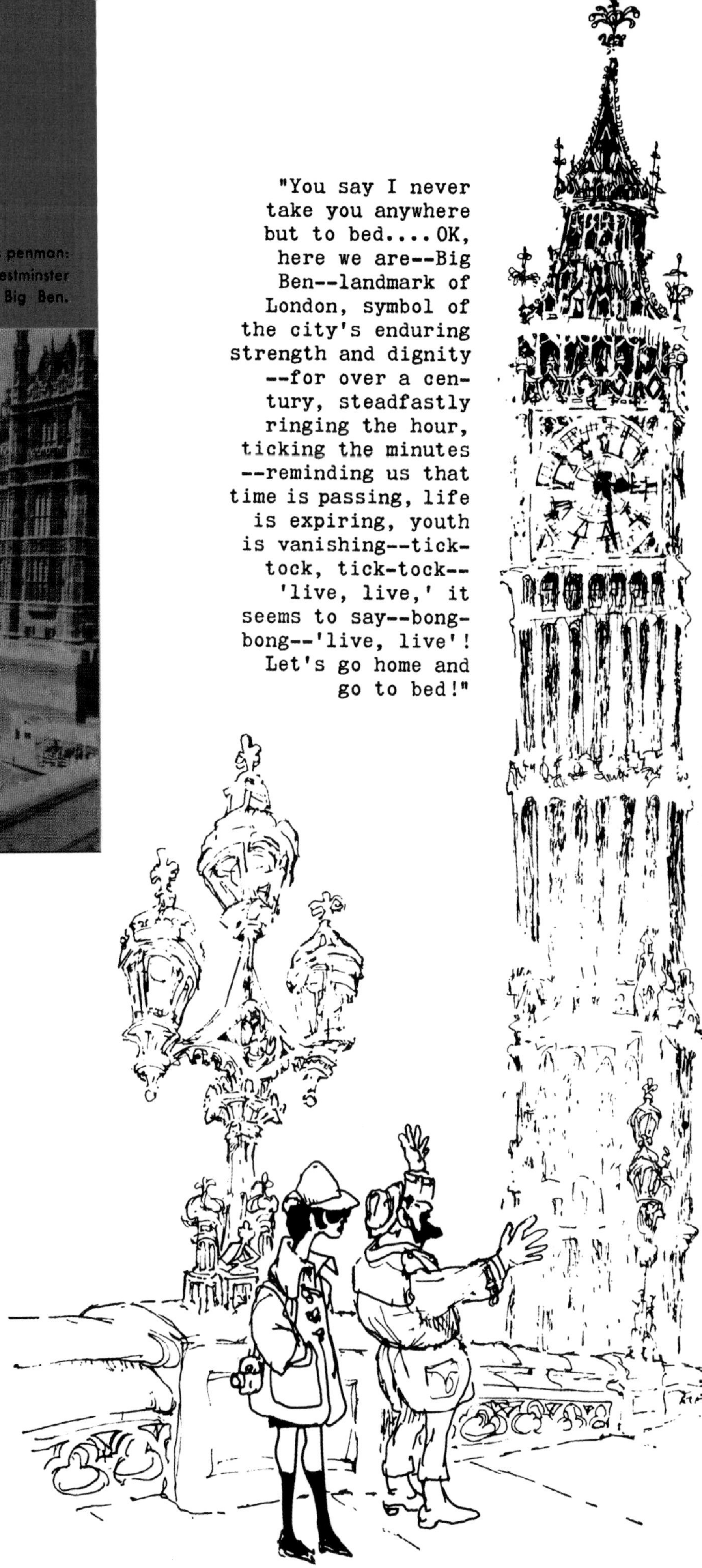

"You say I never take you anywhere but to bed.... OK, here we are--Big Ben--landmark of London, symbol of the city's enduring strength and dignity --for over a century, steadfastly ringing the hour, ticking the minutes --reminding us that time is passing, life is expiring, youth is vanishing--tick-tock, tick-tock--'live, live,' it seems to say--bong-bong--'live, live'! Let's go home and go to bed!"

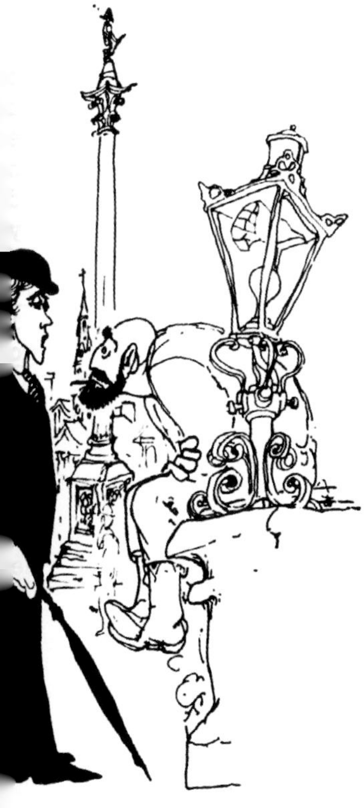

3 JULI 1967

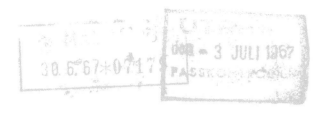

IN HOLLYWOOD

JANUARY 1968

Silverstein

IN HOLLYWOOD

playboy's roving cartoonist laureate sets his sights on the exotic fauna flourishing in and about tinseltown

FOR MORE than a decade now, PLAYBOY's bewhiskered cartoonist, Shel Silverstein, has risibly illuminated for us many of the nation's odd corners, including Fire Island and Greenwich Village; he has toured the Middle East, the Far East and Africa, gone bird watching in London and embarked on his own mission to Moscow. Yet his star had never led him to Hollywood—an omission that is rectified herewith, as Shel dispels the golden haze and peeks under assorted halos to portray the producer-hunting starlets, the status-hunting executives, the goggle-eyed tourists, the fast-talking guides and the fast-moving youth of the world's dream capital. Not even the secrets of such sanctified figures as Mickey Mouse and Goofy escape Shel's quest for truth. "It's all true: It *is* a town of phonies," says Shel. "lazy, shallow guys, desperate girls and smalltime hustlers—I feel completely happy and at home there!"

"This is it, folks, Hollywood and Vine, the heart of movieland, crossroads of the stars, where at any moment-- Hi ya, Frank! That was Frank Sinatra who just drove by in that sports car, folks. Hey, Marlon, baby--how's it goin'?! That was Marlon Brando who just looked out of that window up there. And, if I'm not mistaken, that's the Tony Curtis limousine coming down the street--and who's that riding with Tony? Why, it's Natalie Wood and Rock Hudson and Kim Novak and Cary Grant --and they're heading this way. Oops, too bad--they turned off--yessir, folks, you're really seeing the great ones today...!"

"Wait till you see it tonight... lights flashing across the sky... stars and starlets arriving in chauffeur-driven limousines...police fighting to hold back the cheering crowds...! I tell you, it's going to be the greatest SUPERMARKET OPENING this town has ever seen!"

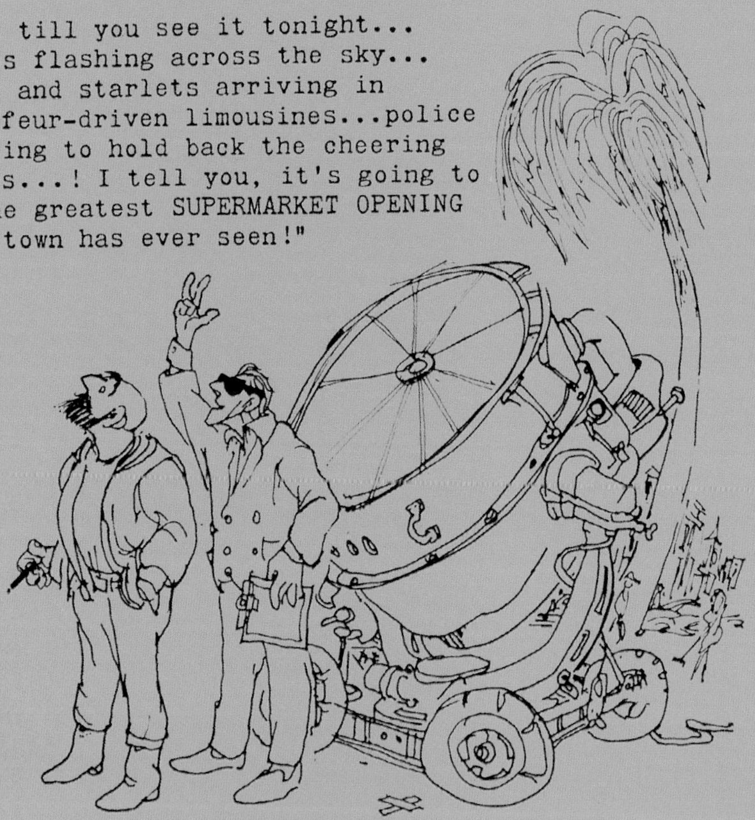

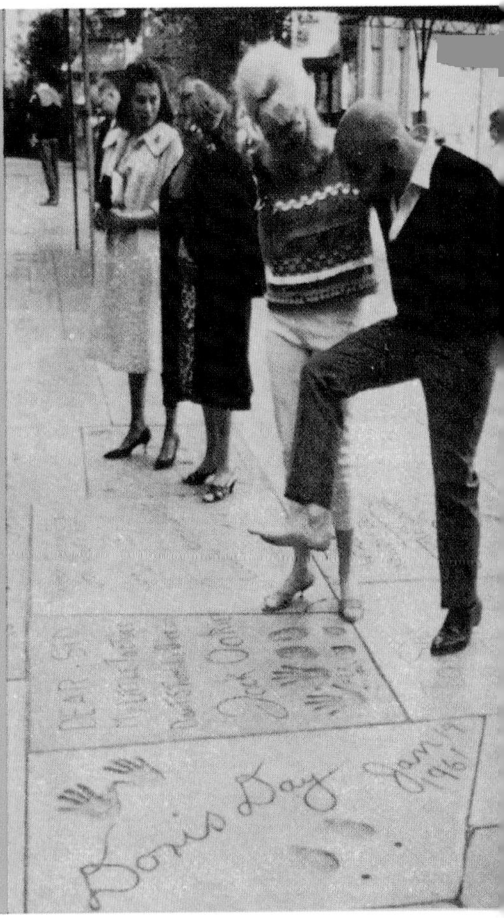

Doris Day

At Grauman's Chinese Theater, Shel plays arch-tourist, tries to fill Jack Oakie's footprints.

"In Hollywood, it's all a matter of being *discovered*. I was originally discovered parking cars at Dino's on the Strip--got myself a contract at Paramount. Then I was discovered sitting in the studio commissary--got a small part in a TV Western. Then I was discovered by a major producer--got an important role in a big-budget picture. And finally, I was discovered in a motel with the producer's wife--and that's why I'm back parking cars!"

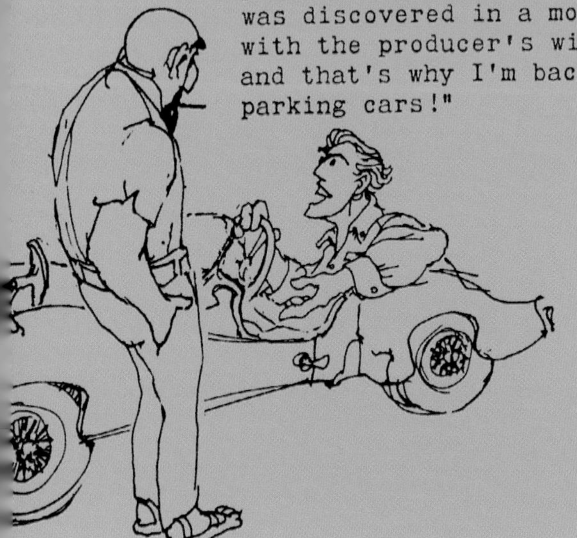

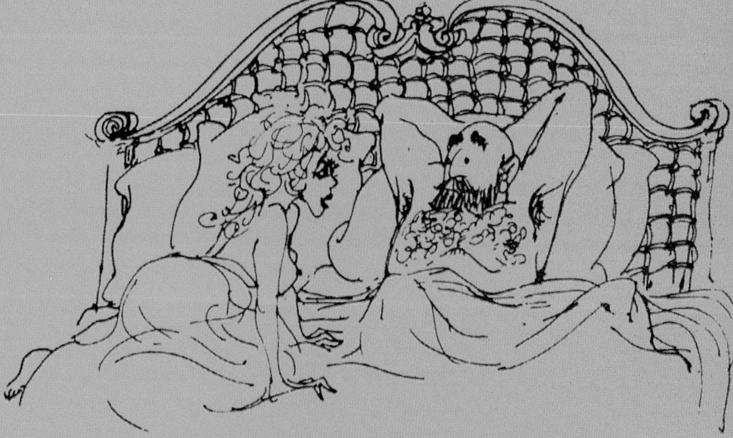

"*Of course* I'm going to be a *big star*!...you noticed me on that crowded dance floor at P.J.'s--that proves I have *personal magnetism* ...you propositioned me--that proves I have *sex appeal*...I did everything you told me to do--that proves I can *take direction*...and I convinced you that you're a great lover--that proves I can *act*!"

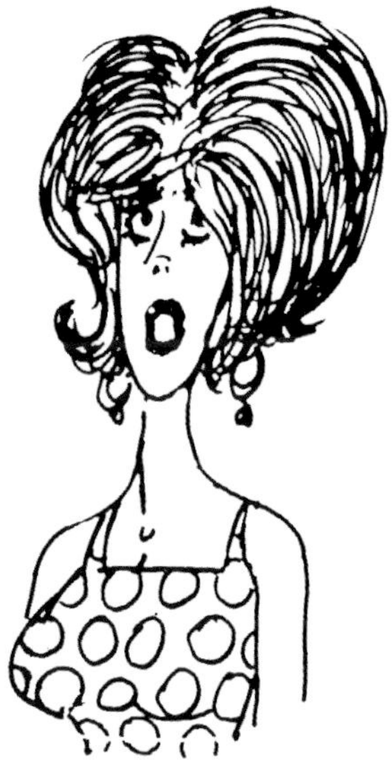

"So my agent asks me if I want to make a TV pilot, and I say, sure... and the next thing I know, I'm in a hotel room with a naked guy in aviator goggles...."

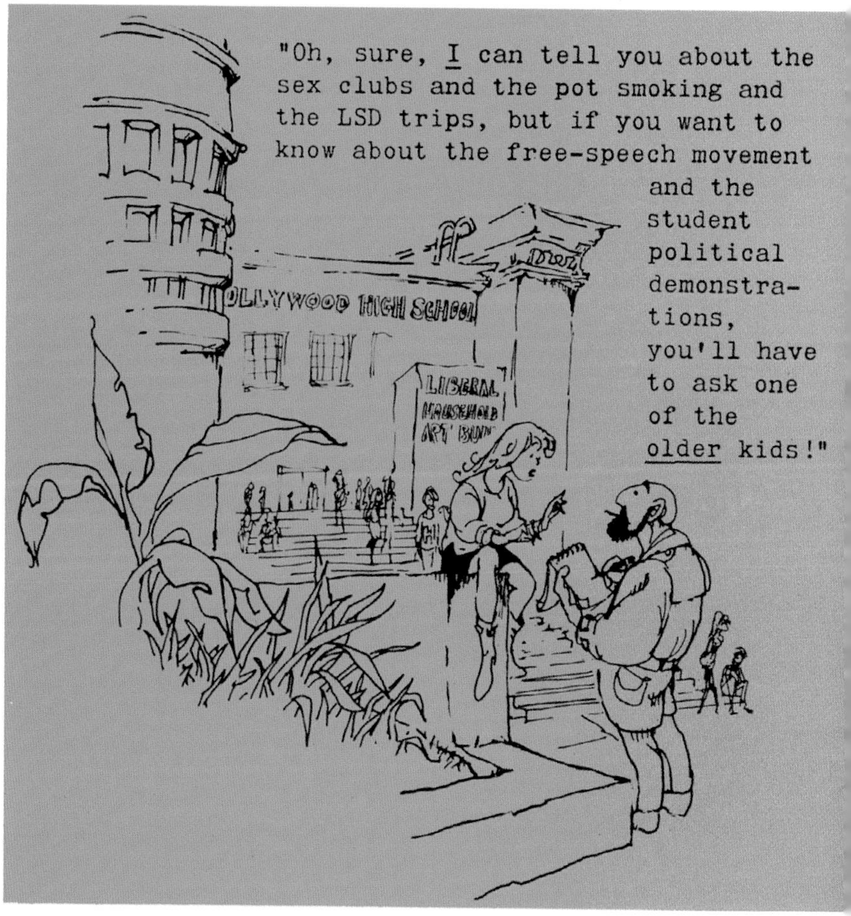
"Oh, sure, I can tell you about the sex clubs and the pot smoking and the LSD trips, but if you want to know about the free-speech movement and the student political demonstrations, you'll have to ask one of the older kids!"
OLLYWOOD HIGH SCHOOL
LIBERAL

At Muscle Beach, Shel draws th
tissimus dorsi but eyes the pecto

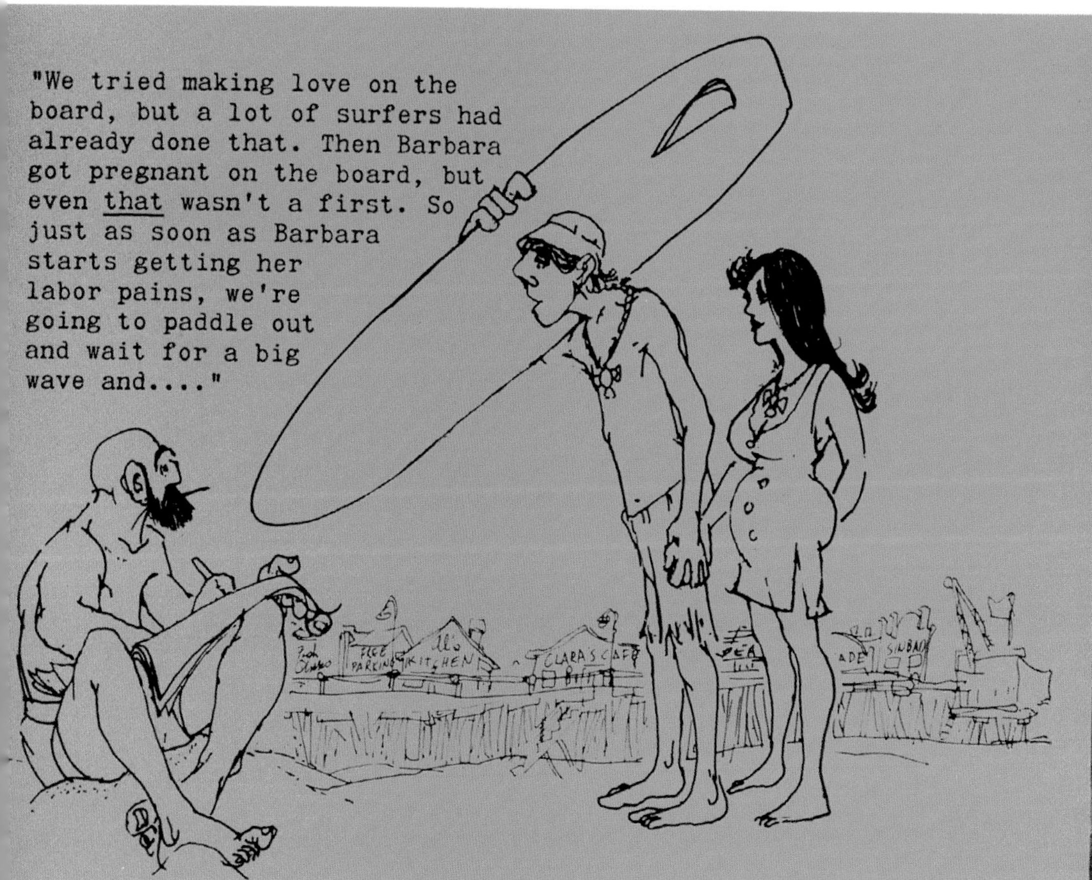
"We tried making love on the board, but a lot of surfers had already done that. Then Barbara got pregnant on the board, but even that wasn't a first. So just as soon as Barbara starts getting her labor pains, we're going to paddle out and wait for a big wave and...."
FREE PARKING
KITCHEN
CLARA'S CAFE

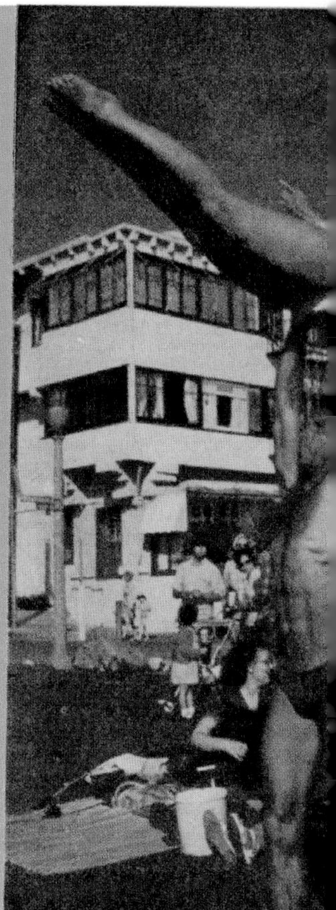

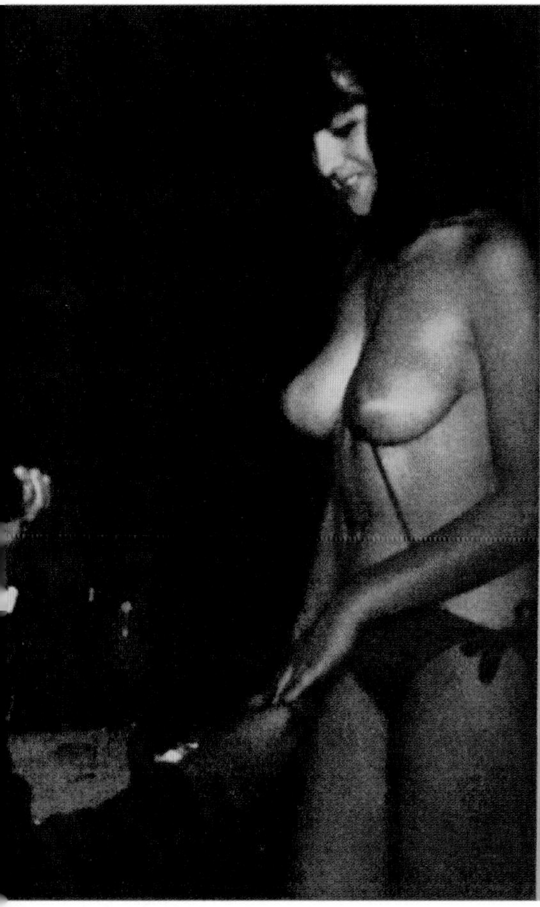

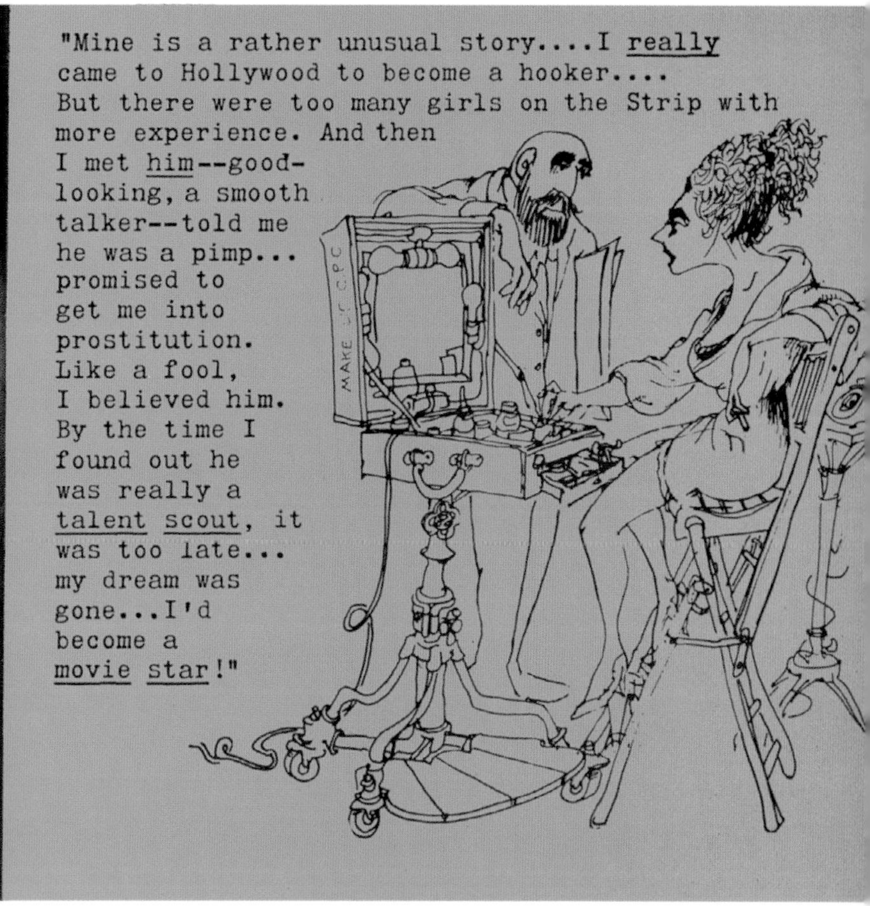
"Mine is a rather unusual story....I really came to Hollywood to become a hooker....
But there were too many girls on the Strip with more experience. And then I met him--good-looking, a smooth talker--told me he was a pimp... promised to get me into prostitution. Like a fool, I believed him. By the time I found out he was really a talent scout, it was too late... my dream was gone...I'd become a movie star!"
MAKE-UP

verstein can't decide what to order at The Ball, a topless tro. Shel's appraisal: "The beef Stroganoff was just fair."

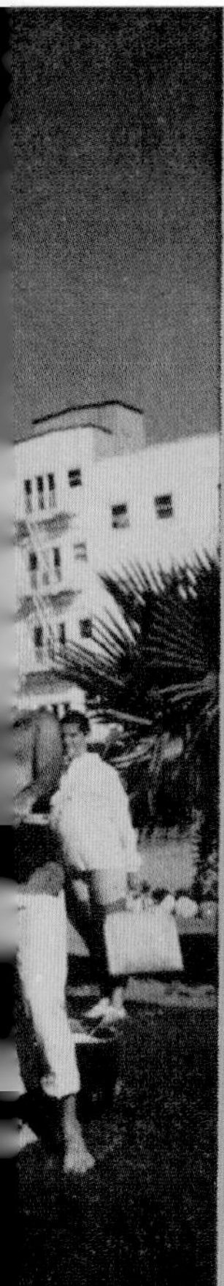

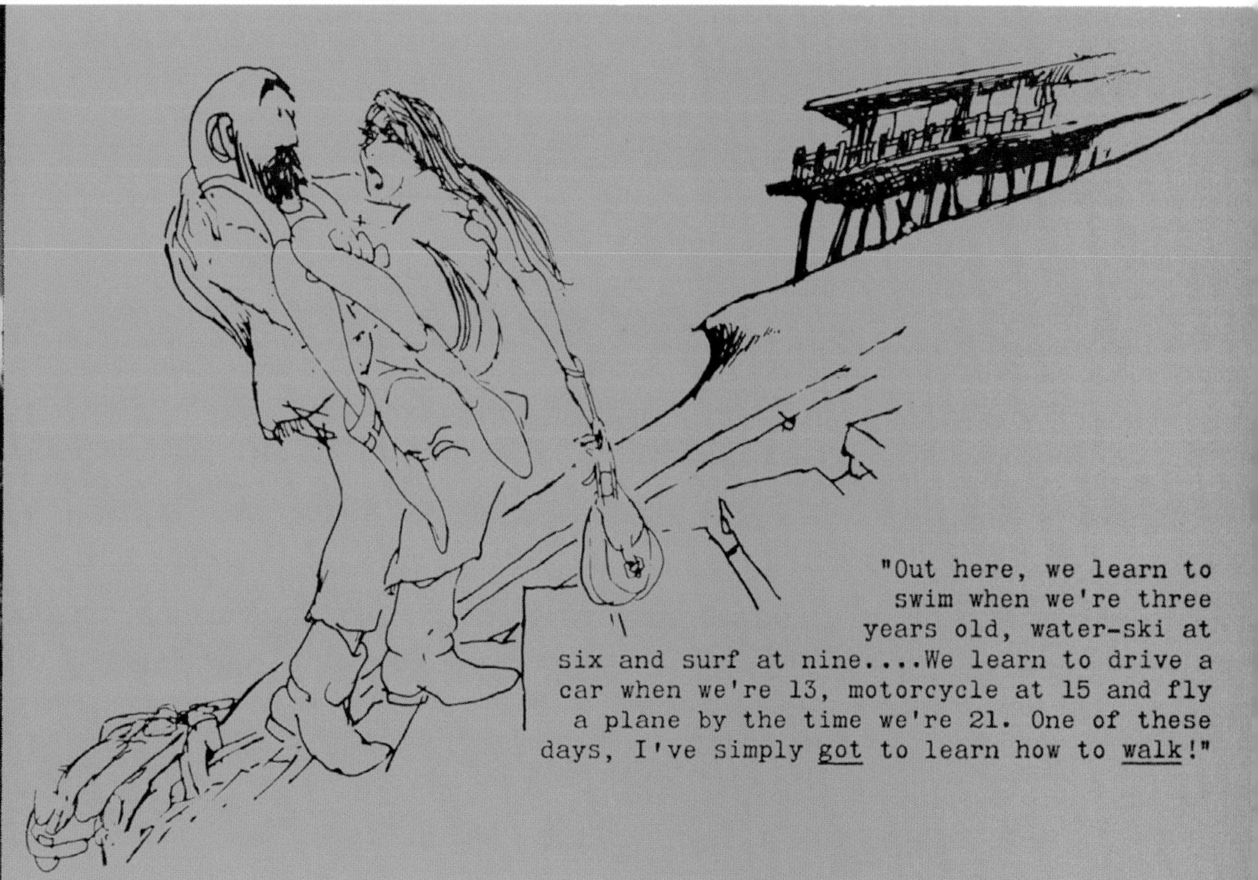
"Out here, we learn to swim when we're three years old, water-ski at six and surf at nine....We learn to drive a car when we're 13, motorcycle at 15 and fly a plane by the time we're 21. One of these days, I've simply got to learn how to walk!"

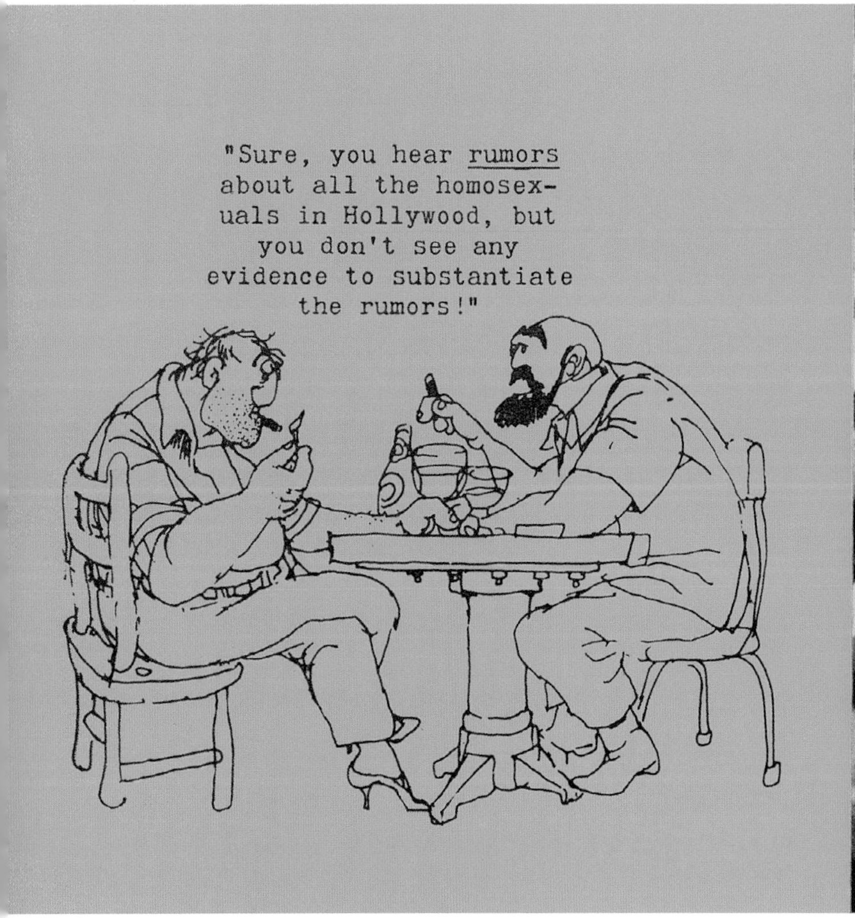
"Sure, you hear rumors
about all the homosex-
uals in Hollywood, but
you don't see any
evidence to substantiate
the rumors!"

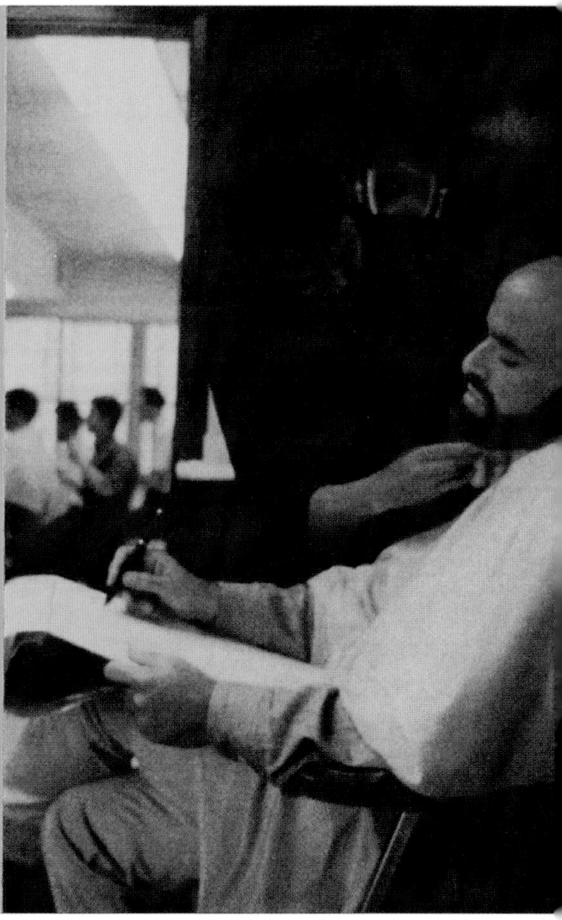

Faced with a glossy pate, Jay Sebring, tonsorial artist to the stars, settles for trimming Shel's beard.

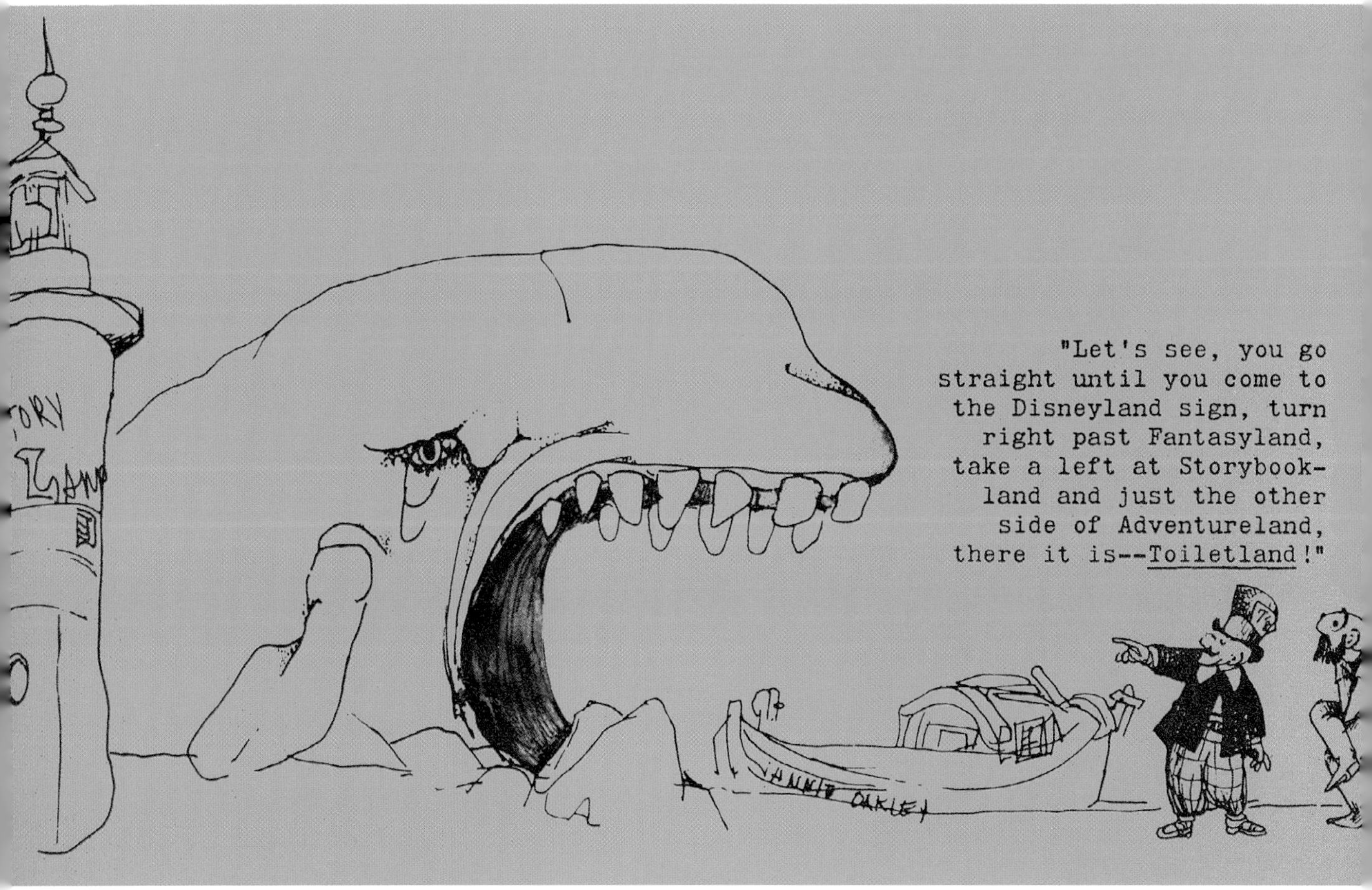
"Let's see, you go
straight until you come to
the Disneyland sign, turn
right past Fantasyland,
take a left at Storybook-
land and just the other
side of Adventureland,
there it is--Toiletland!"

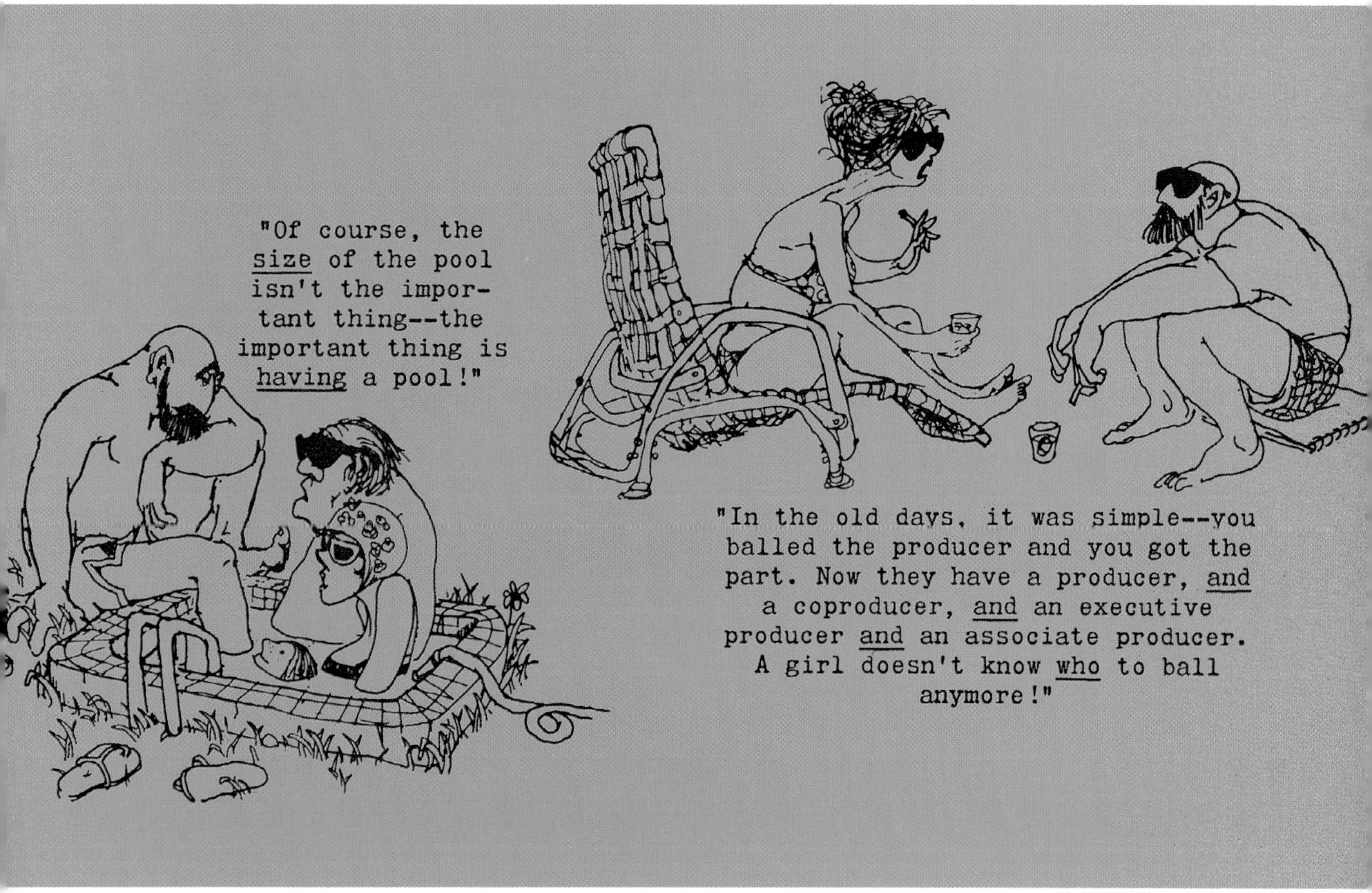
"Of course, the size of the pool isn't the important thing--the important thing is having a pool!"
"In the old days, it was simple--you balled the producer and you got the part. Now they have a producer, and a coproducer, and an executive producer and an associate producer. A girl doesn't know who to ball anymore!"

sizes up the pleasure-domed gold mine built by a
d fellow cartoonist, dreams of his own Silversteinland.

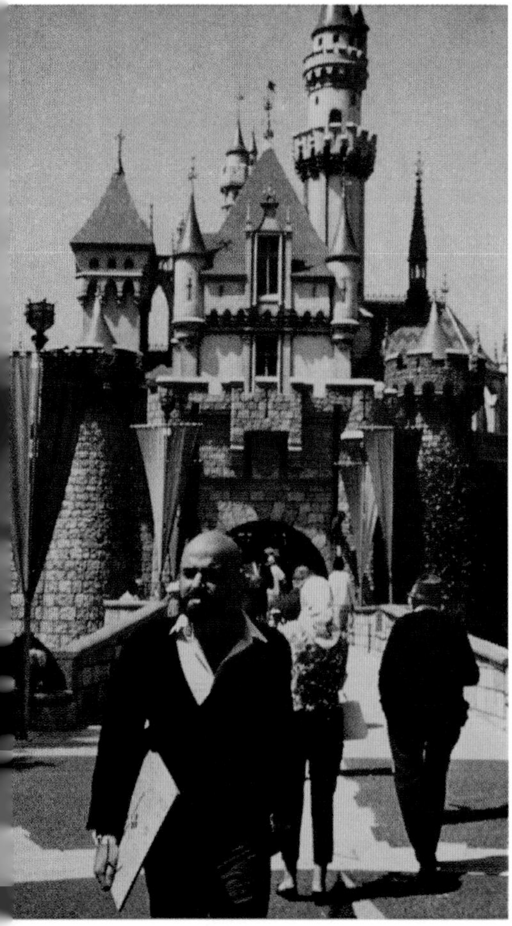

"Sure, it's hot wearing these costumes, but the gig is really sort of groovy; I mean, like last week these two crazy-looking chicks start following me around the park and, when it gets close to closing time, one of them says, 'Mickey, baby, how would you like to take a real trip to Fantasyland?' Well, I can see they have eyes to make a scene, so we pick up Bob, here--I mean Goofy--who also grooves with the idea, and the four of us split for the chicks' pad, where we settle back and smoke some Acapulco gold and...."

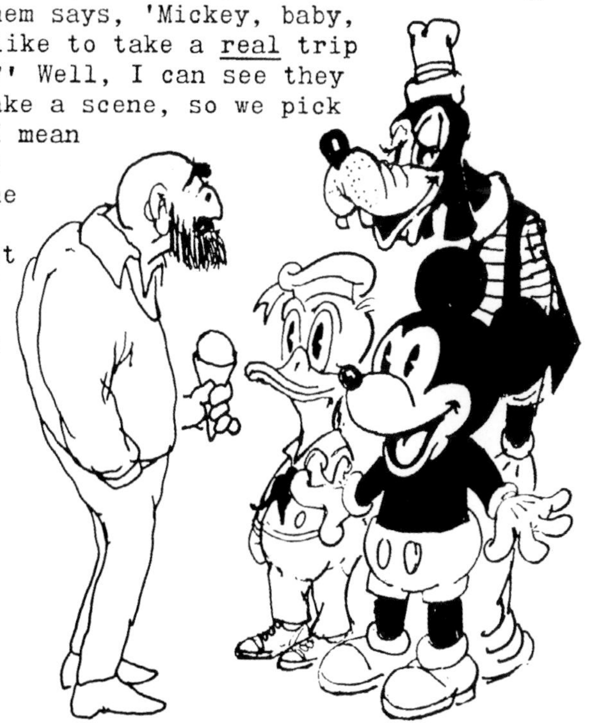

AMONG THE HIPPIES

JULY 1968 | AUGUST 1968

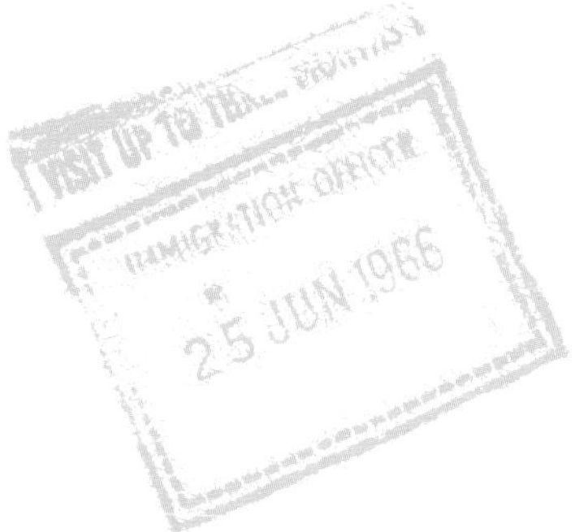
IMMIGRATION OFFICER
25 JUN 1966

Silverstein AMONG THE Hippies

playboy's grand guru roams the hashbury with pen and flower in hand

"I TELL MYSELF I'll start drawing today and head down Haight Street toward Hippie Hill," says our bearded Shel Silverstein. "Three people sit in a doorway smoking grass. A guy in a monk's robe asks me for some spare change. Electric rock comes from a basement window. The girls line up at the free clinic to get their birth-control pills—a sign says DON'T GIVE THE CLAP TO SOMEONE YOU LOVE. The tourists drive by with their windows rolled up. 'Wanna buy a lid?' The Diggers ladle out free beef stew and apples. Beads, pot pipes, posters, underground newspapers for sale. Written on a psychedelic-painted truck, DON'T LAUGH, YOUR DAUGHTER MAY BE IN HERE! A hand reaches out of some bushes and gives me a roach. A long-haired girl takes my hand and leads me up a path through some trees, where we lie down. Afterward, she smiles and says, 'Welcome to Haight-Ashbury.' I think I'll wait and draw tomorrow."

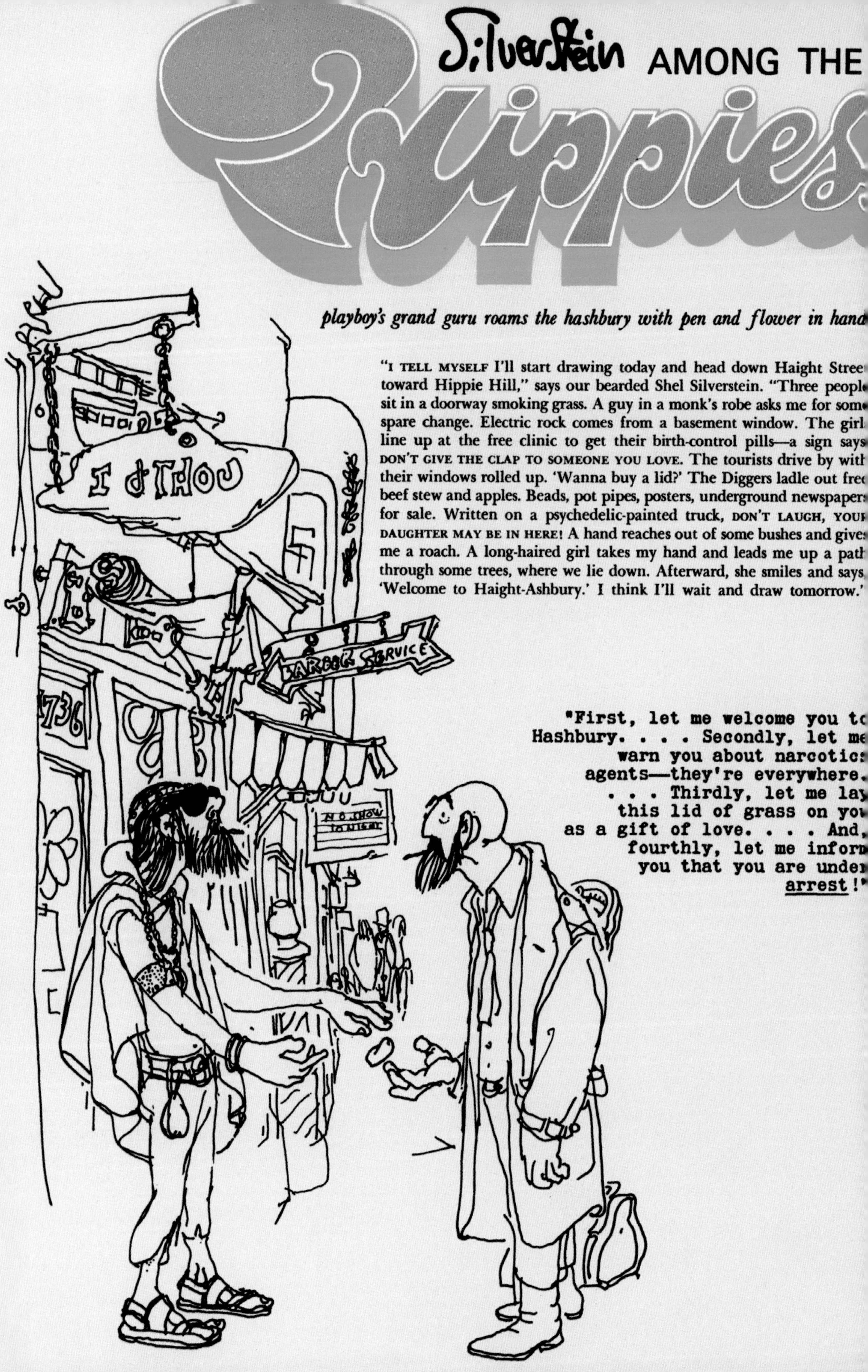

1736
NO SHOW TONIGHT

"First, let me welcome you to Hashbury. . . . Secondly, let me warn you about narcotics agents—they're everywhere. . . . Thirdly, let me lay this lid of grass on you as a gift of love. . . . And, fourthly, let me inform you that you are under arrest!"

"Of course, there's a lot more to see in San Francisco than just Haight-Ashbury. There are the opium dens of Chinatown . . . the pot parties on Telegraph Hill . . . and there's Fisherman's Wharf, which is a gas when you're tripping on acid . . .!"

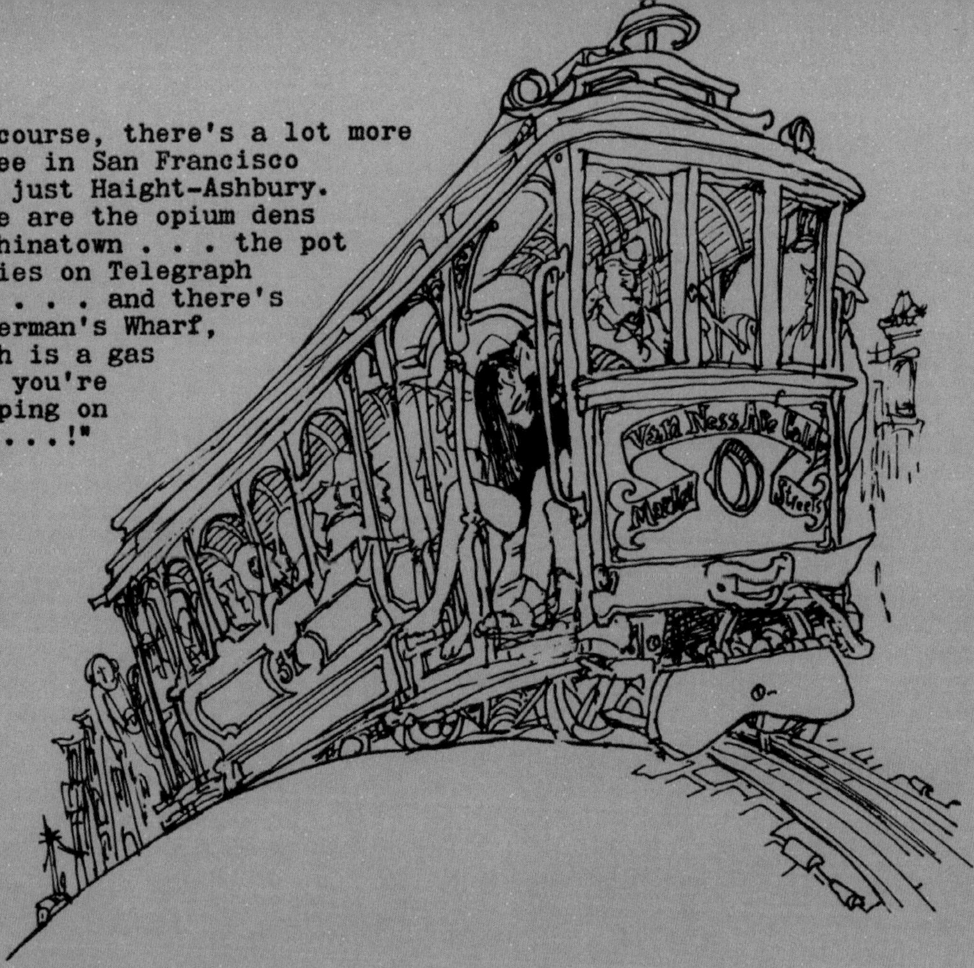
Market
Streets

"Gee, Shel, I'd invite you to stay in our commune, but I'm already sharing my bedroom with four pot smokers. . . . We keep away from the living room, because it's full of speed freaks who are very paranoid about the two smack junkies living in the closet. . . . And the acid heads never come out of the kitchen, because the opium eater in the bathroom brings them down. . . . So I wouldn't know where to put a guy who doesn't use anything!!"

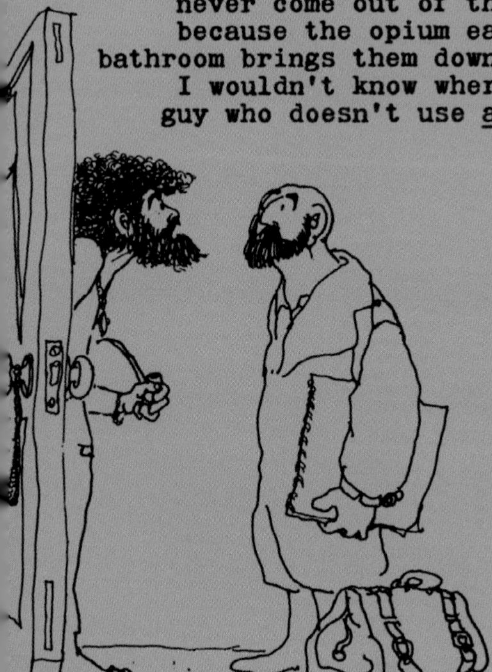

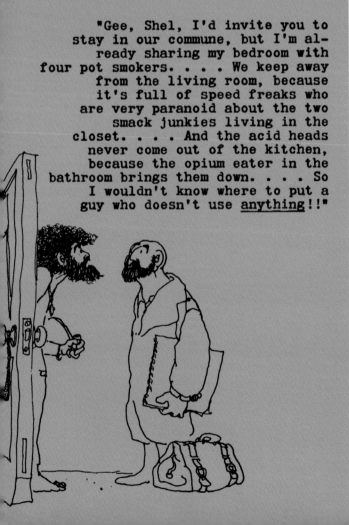

"There's no such thing as prostitution here. . . . This is a land of love! I give you my body because I love you. . . . And then you give me some money because you love me!!"

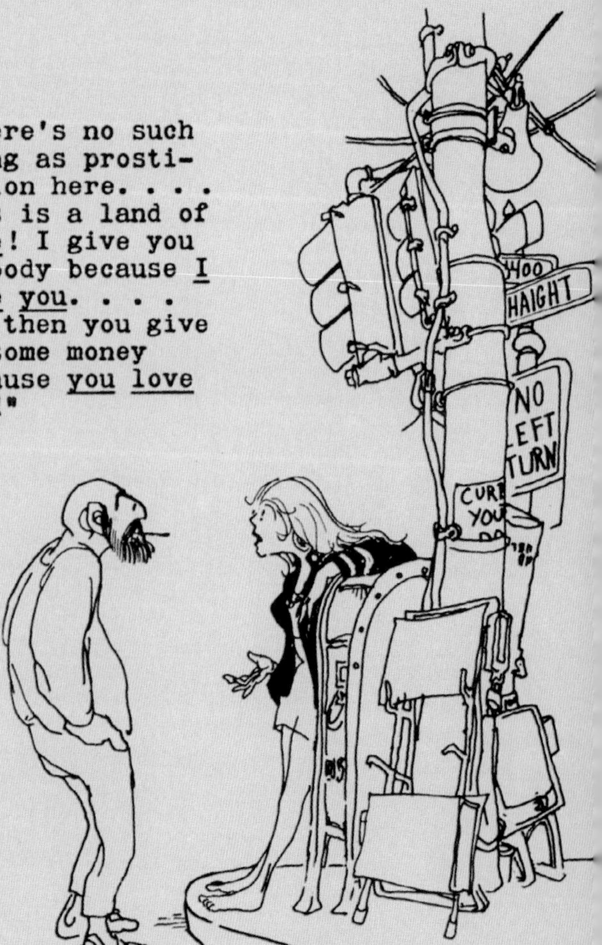
HAIGHT
NO LEFT TURN

"Well, I guess this destroys the myth about hippies never <u>bathing</u>!!!"

"It's <u>almost</u> a <u>perfect</u> psychedelic poster . . . except I can still read three of the words!"

Silverstein sizes up the panhandlers in front of the Drog St the Boulevard of Brotherly Love (Haight Street to nongro

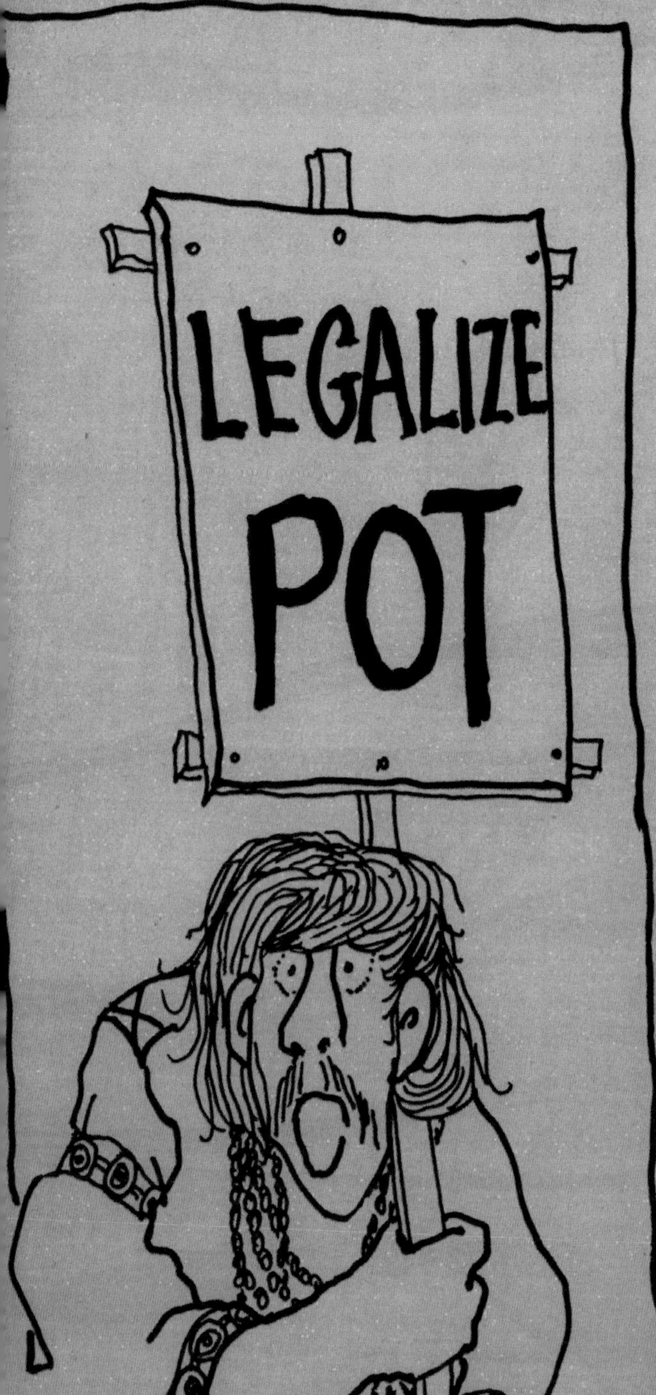
LEGALIZE
POT

Vell, first we pass
round a whatchamacallit
. . and get everybody to
ign it . . . and then we
ake it to the . . . uh . . .
ne House of Whoeverthey-
re . . . and get them to
ass a . . . y' know . . . and then
show that to
e . . . uh . . . the . . . uh. . . ."

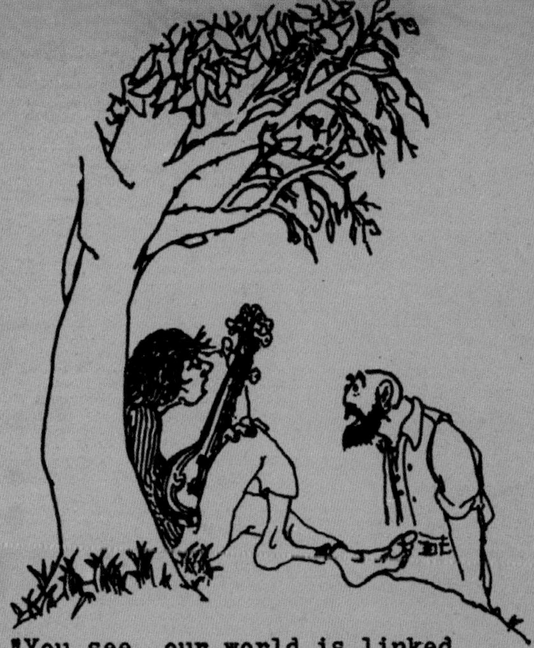

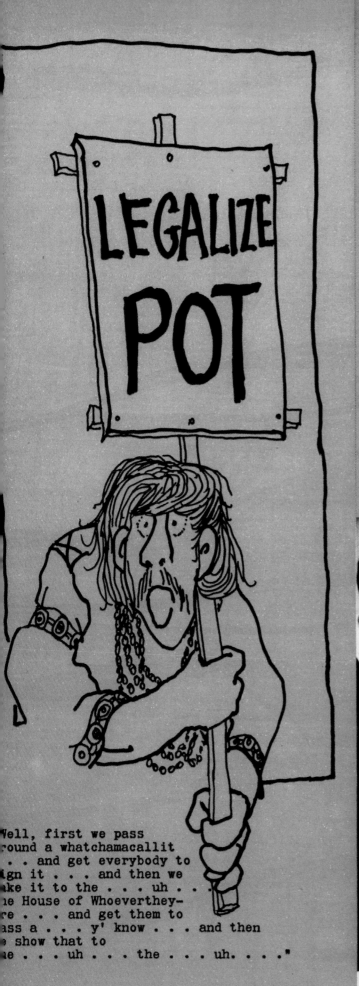

"You see, our world is linked to music. This sitar is over one hundred years old. It's made of Indian cedar, and the neck is inlaid with black pearl, and trimmed in hammered silver. . . . The pegs are hand-carved ivory, and the strings have a history of. . . ."

"But you can't <u>play</u> it!"

"Man, you don't understand. This sitar is over one hundred years old. It's made of Indian cedar, and. . . ."

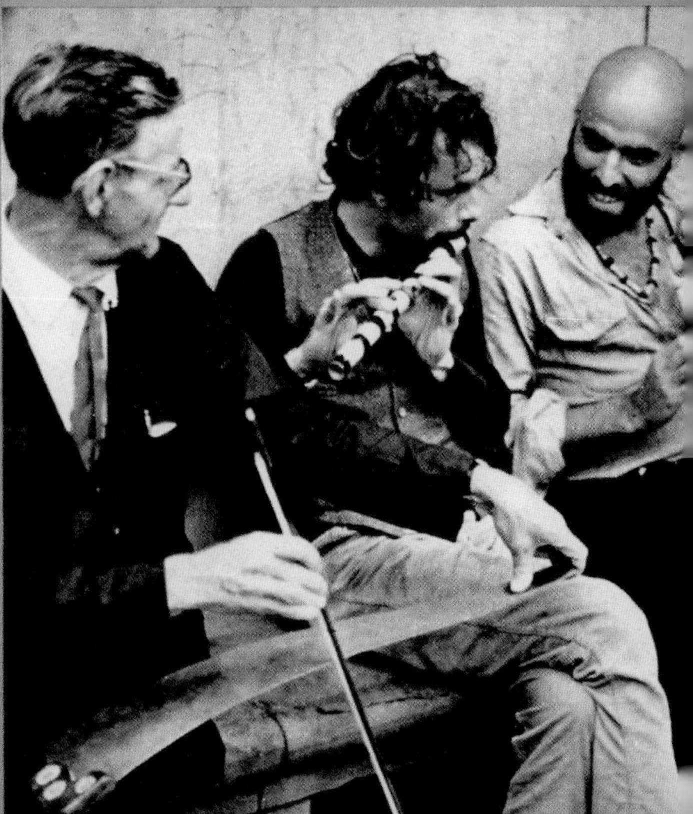

Shel, blowing recorder, joins friend Tony Price, on flute, and saw-playing Golden Gate Park regular for a musical session.

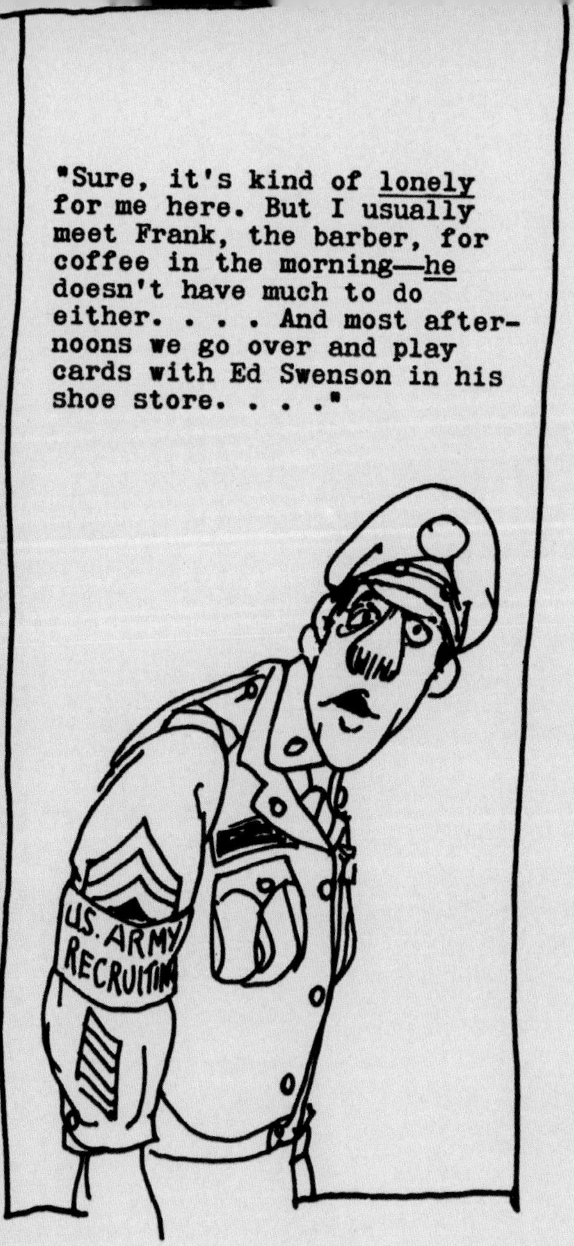
"Sure, it's kind of lonely for me here. But I usually meet Frank, the barber, for coffee in the morning—he doesn't have much to do either. . . . And most afternoons we go over and play cards with Ed Swenson in his shoe store. . . ."
U.S. ARMY RECRUITING

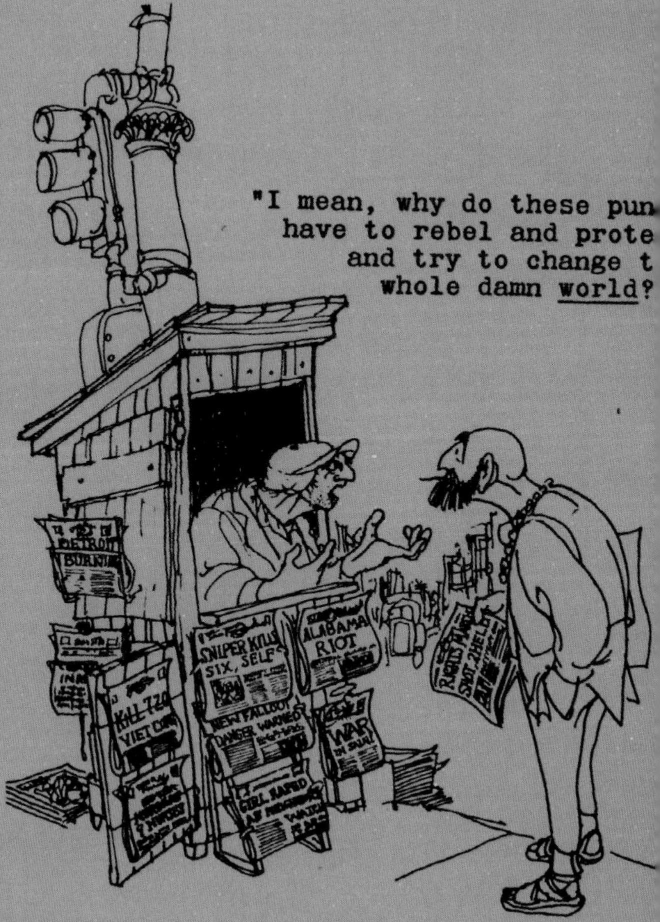
"I mean, why do these pun
have to rebel and prote
and try to change t
whole damn world?
SNIPER KILLS SIX, SELF
ALABAMA RIOT
NEW FALLOUT DANGER WARNED
WAR

Temporarily abandoning sketchbook and clothes, Shel applies his artistic talents to a hippie body-painting party.

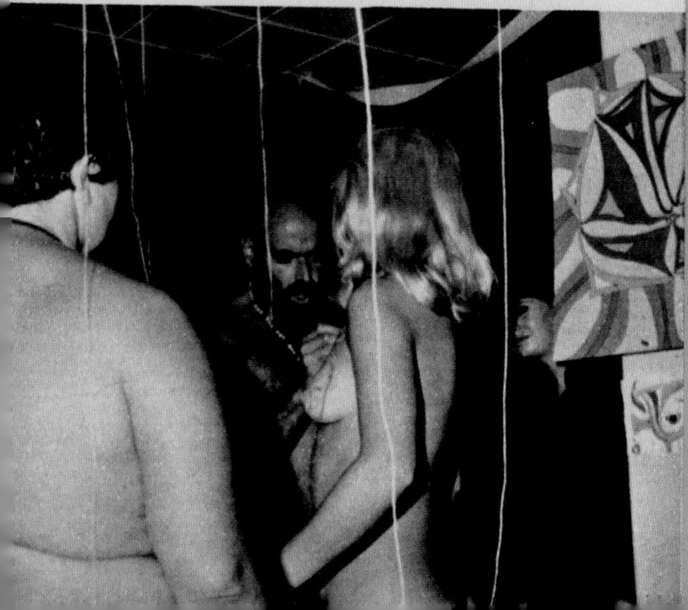

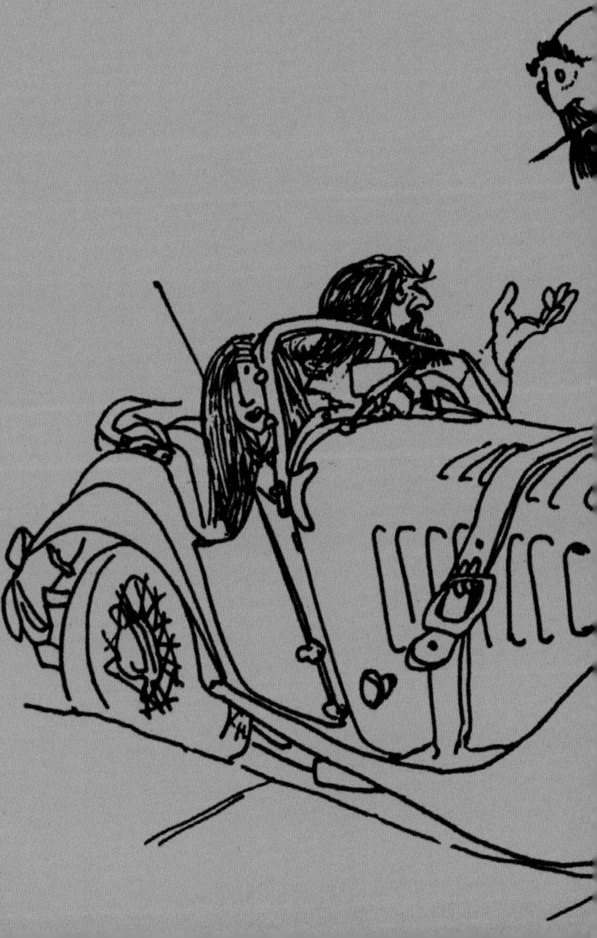

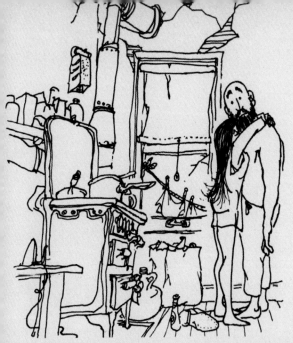

sn't it groovy living together like this
-free from the middle-class conventions
and obligations of marriage! Listen,
upper won't be ready for another twenty
minutes, so why don't you take out the
garbage and go pick up the laundry and,
oh, yes, stop by the grocer's and get
some coffeecake—I've invited Francine
and Bill to come over later and watch
television."

FREE CLINIC
558
HAIGHT ASHBURY MEDICAL CLINIC
LOVE
FUCK
HATE
560
PAX
MAKE LOVE NOT WAR

"Well, sure . . . lots of hippies have
rs. I need a car. I mean, how else would
I be able to get home weekends. . . .
Not that I want to go home, but that's
the only way I can get my allowance,
man. . . . I mean, not that I want an
allowance, but how else could I
pay the rent on a seven-room
apartment. . . . Not that I. . . ."

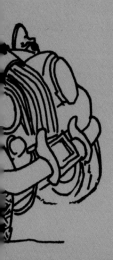

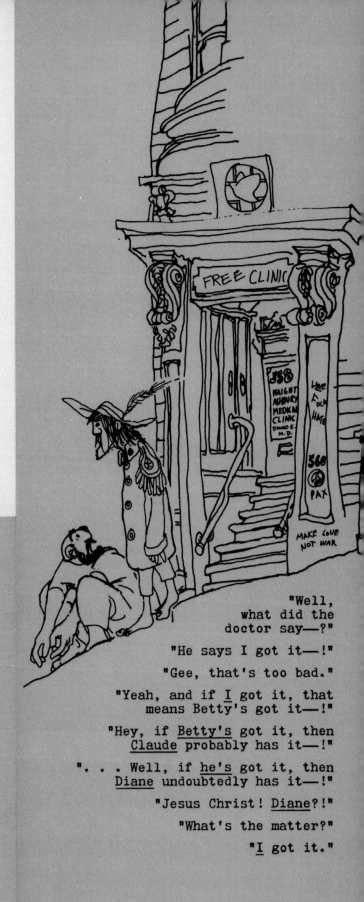

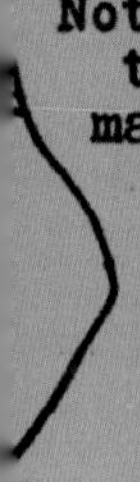

"Well,
what did the
doctor say—?"

"He says I got it—!"

"Gee, that's too bad."

"Yeah, and if I got it, that
means Betty's got it—!"

"Hey, if Betty's got it, then
Claude probably has it—!"

". . . Well, if he's got it, then
Diane undoubtedly has it—!"

"Jesus Christ! Diane?!"

"What's the matter?"

"I got it."

NEXT MONTH: MORE OF
SILVERSTEIN AMONG THE HIPPIES

MORE Silverstein AMONG TH

Hippies

the further adventures of truth seeker shel in darkest hashb

"A GUY IN A BLANKET panhandles on the corner with a sign, IT'S DEBBIE'S BI DAY—HELP ME GET HER HIGH," Shel reports, recalling his Hashbury highlig "The other night, some guys sneak into the zoo, shoot a buffalo, drag it and the Diggers have meat for their free food line. A beaded girl takes me ho makes 'like' to me and never speaks a word. An old man on a soapbox: 'Yo tried pot, you've tried LSD—now how about giving Jesus Christ a chan And everyone talks about the 'death of the hippies' and they stage a hi funeral and some people who were just sitting in doorways getting sto march to the park carrying a giant coffin, and they set it on fire and d dance around it and everybody says, 'Well, the hippie thing is dead.' then they all go back to Haight Street and sit back in the doorways and s getting stoned again. And the funeral is over, but the corpse is still groovi

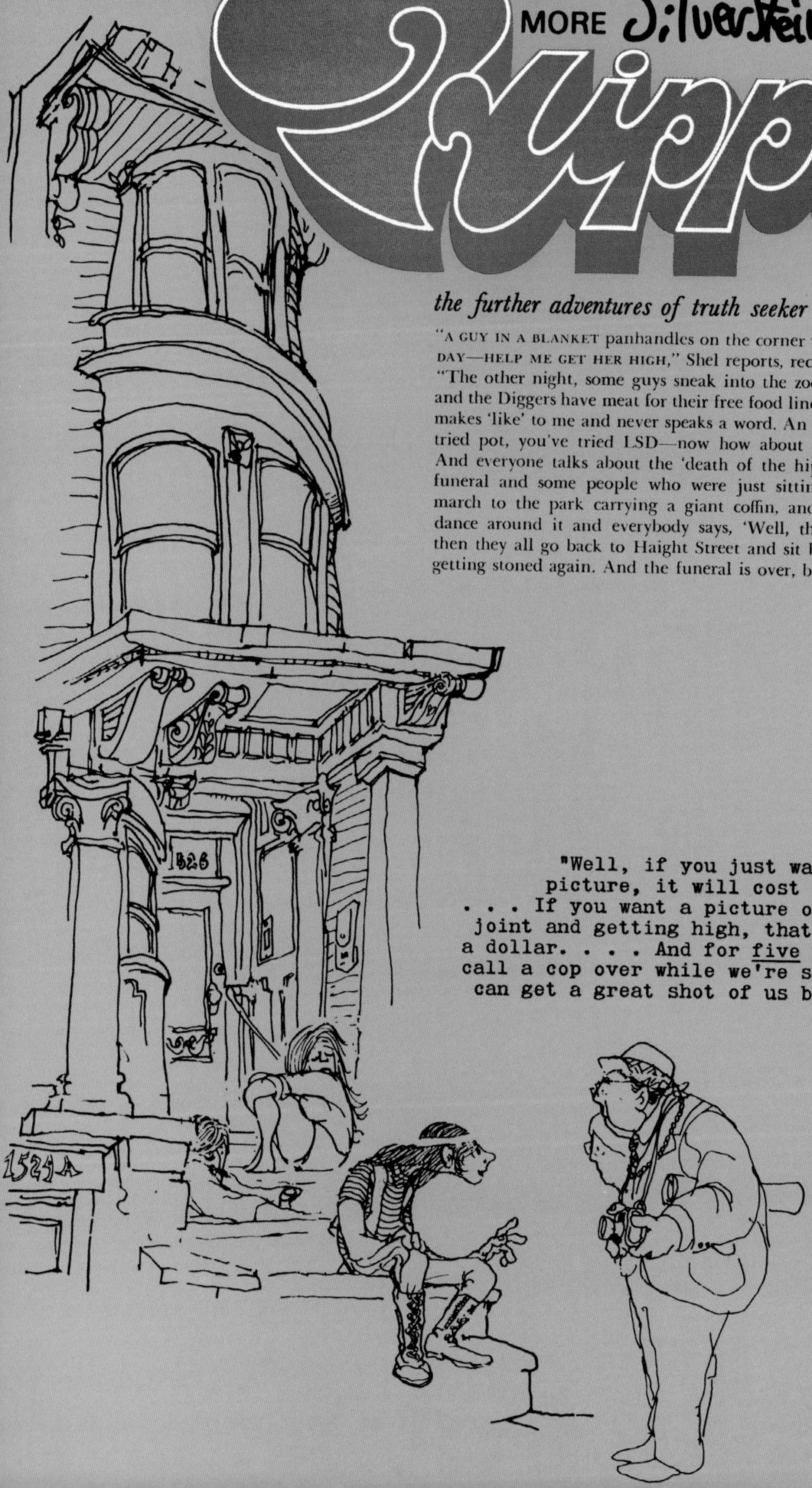
526
1529A

"Well, if you just want to take our picture, it will cost you a quarter. . . . If you want a picture of us rolling a joint and getting high, that will cost you a dollar. . . . And for <u>five</u> dollars, we'll call a cop over while we're smoking and you can get a great shot of us being <u>busted</u>!!"

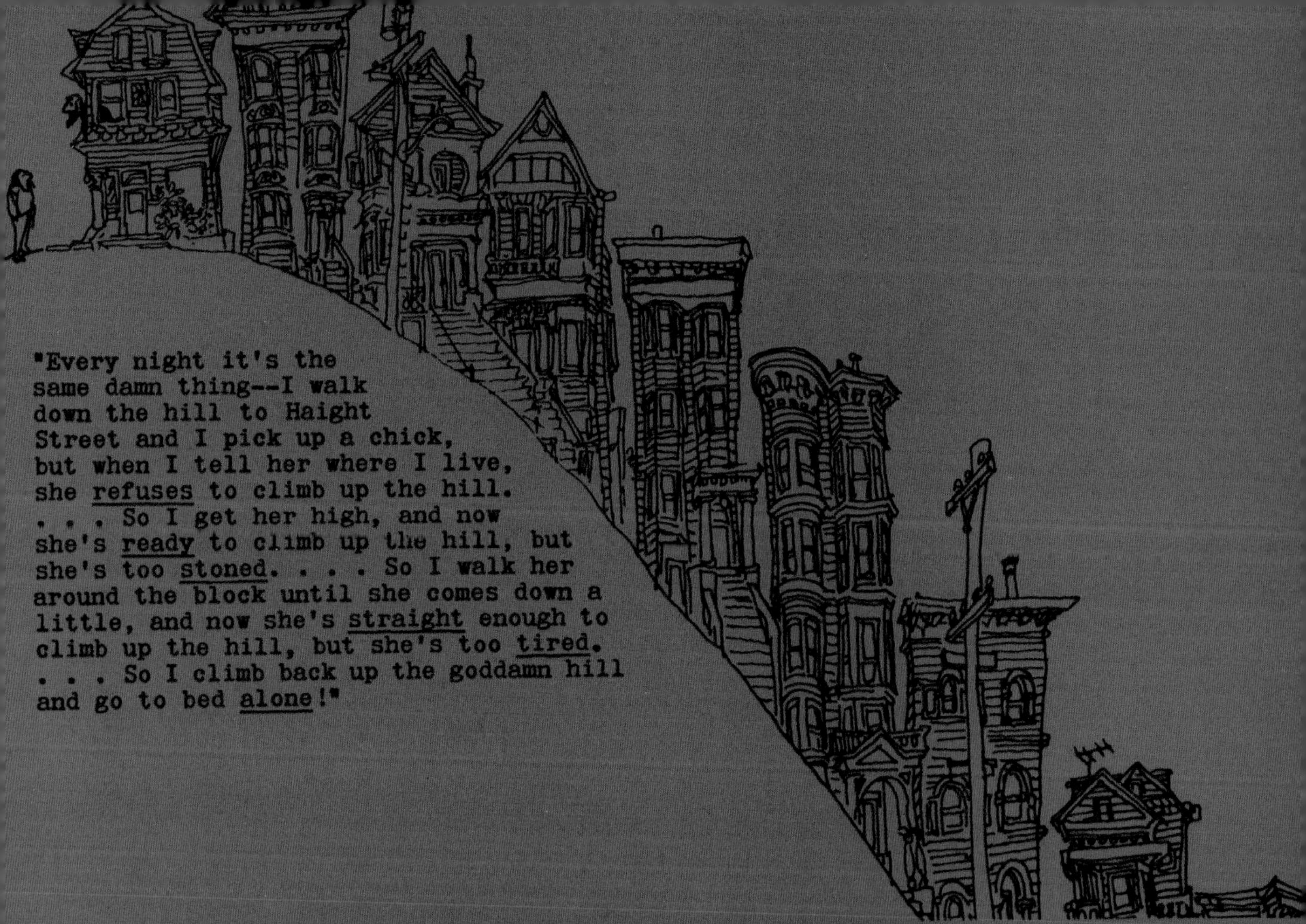
"Every night it's the same damn thing--I walk down the hill to Haight Street and I pick up a chick, but when I tell her where I live, she refuses to climb up the hill. . . . So I get her high, and now she's ready to climb up the hill, but she's too stoned. . . . So I walk her around the block until she comes down a little, and now she's straight enough to climb up the hill, but she's too tired. . . . So I climb back up the goddamn hill and go to bed alone!"

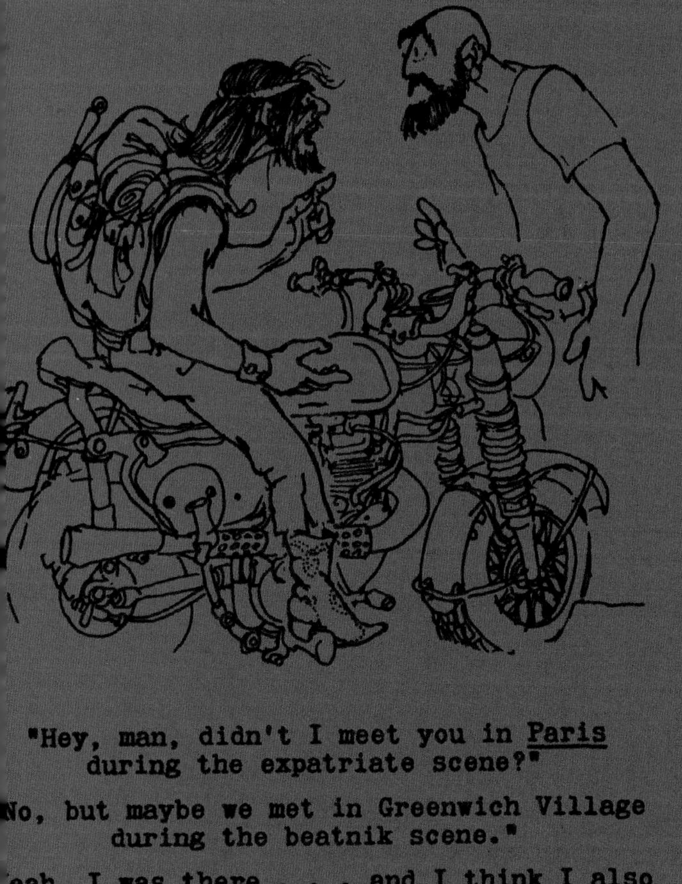
"Hey, man, didn't I meet you in Paris during the expatriate scene?"
No, but maybe we met in Greenwich Village during the beatnik scene."
eah, I was there . . . and I think I also sed to see you in Big Sur during. . . ."

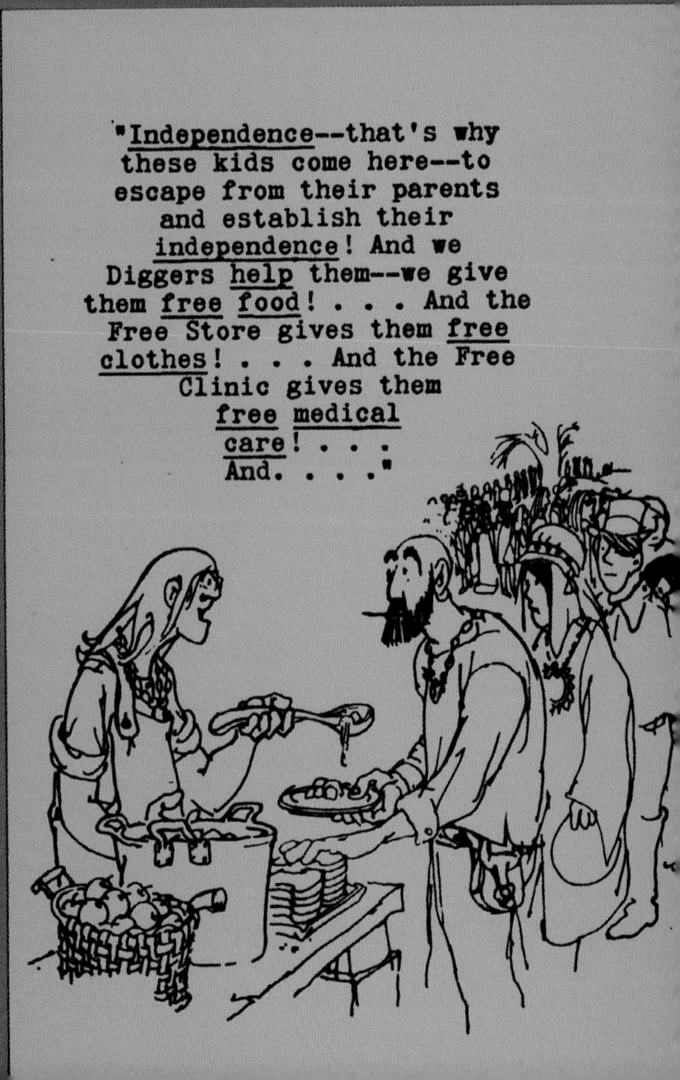
"Independence--that's why these kids come here--to escape from their parents and establish their independence! And we Diggers help them--we give them free food! . . . And the Free Store gives them free clothes! . . . And the Free Clinic gives them free medical care! . . . And. . . ."

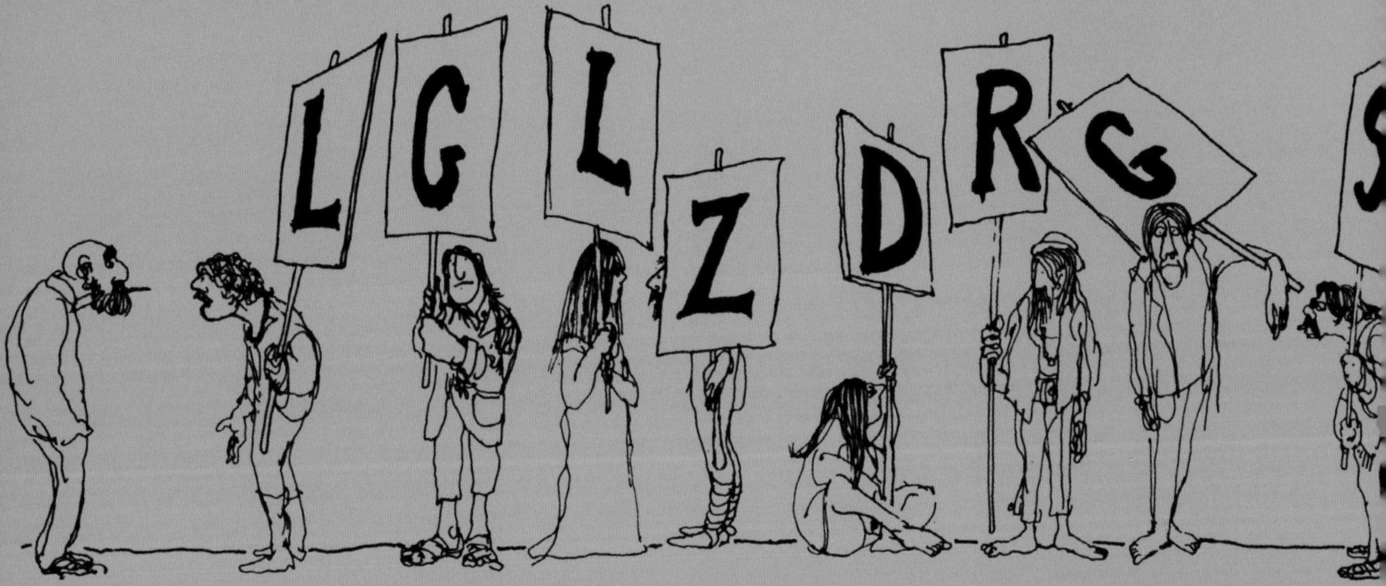
L
G
L
Z
D
R
G
S

"It was supposed to say '<u>LEGALIZE</u> <u>DRUGS</u>' . . . but <u>E</u> is out trying to score, <u>A</u> and <u>I</u> are on an acid trip, the other <u>E</u> just got busted, and <u>U</u> was simply too strung out to show up!"

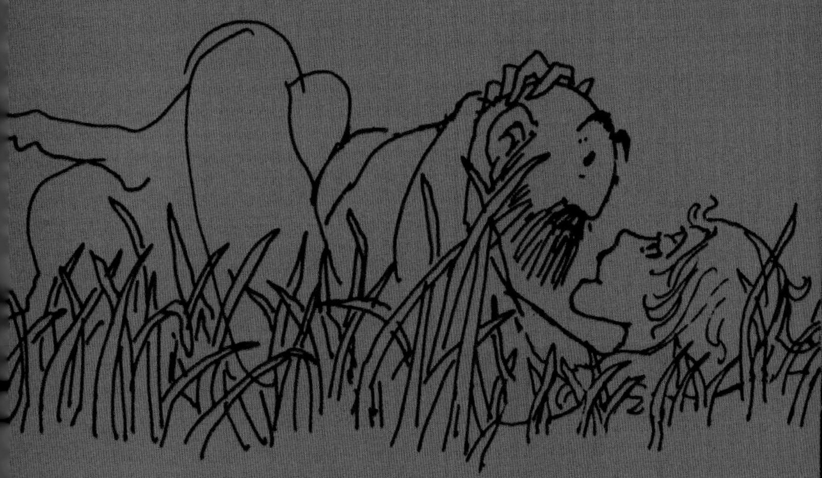

"I'm doing this as a statement of independence, a rebellion against my parents and a protest against outdated puritanical morality. Why are *you* doing it?"

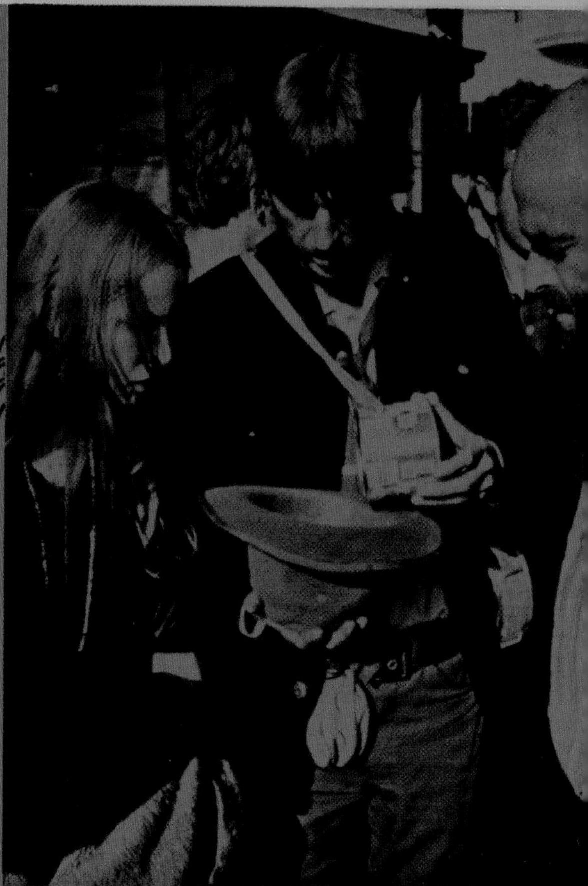

Silverstein looks on as Haight resident passes the h
mind-blowing donations to be doled out to the n

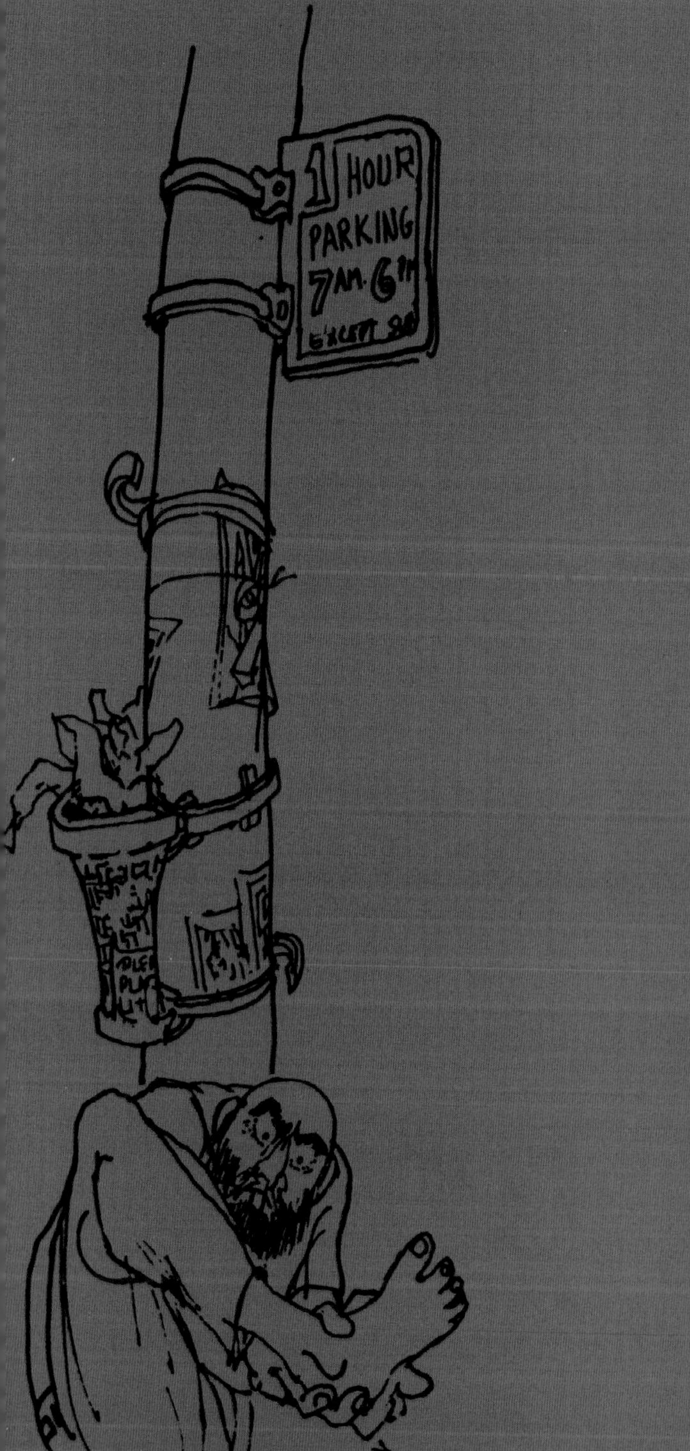
1 HOUR
PARKING

"Sure, they shout about the
freedom of going barefoot--
but they don't shout about
the broken glass, and the
dog shit, and the. . . ."

". . . And while you were out
all night getting high, did
you ever think about your
wife and children waiting for
you here at home . . . did you
ever consider bringing a little
something home with you,
so that we could get
high, too?! Oh,
no . . . !"

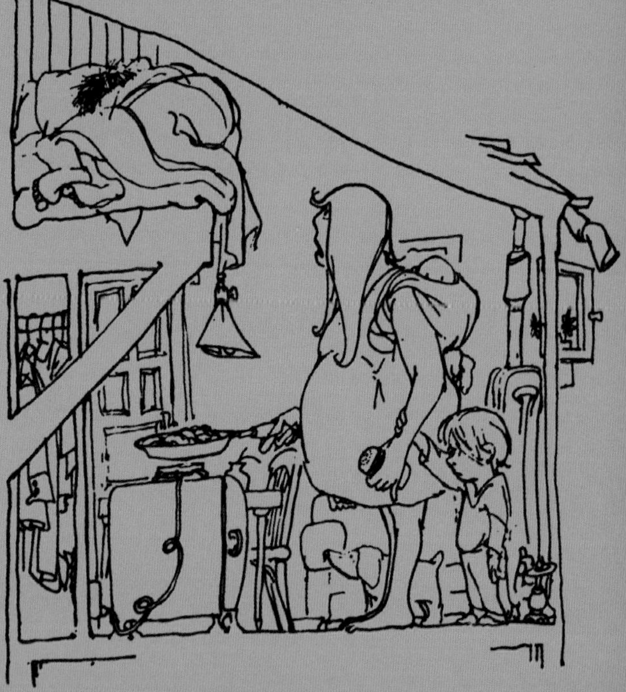

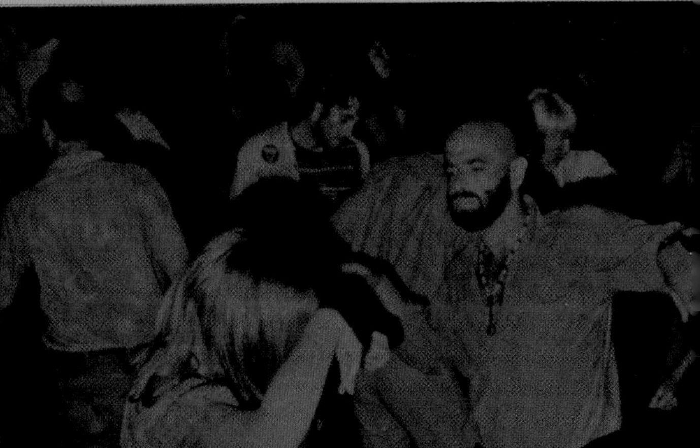

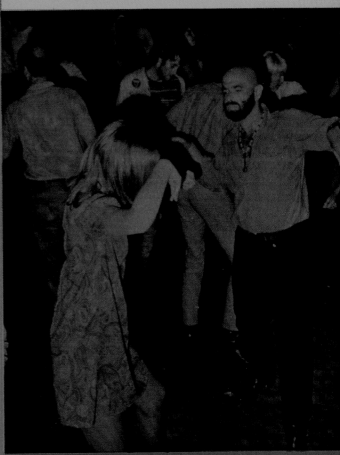

With swinging teeny-bopper friend, Shel plugs into the Fillmore Auditorium's high-voltage electric-rock scene.

"Long hair is hard to manage . . . earrings are expensive . . . shawls are uncomfortable . . . beads are a bother . . . ! Sometimes I wish I'd been born a <u>girl</u>!"

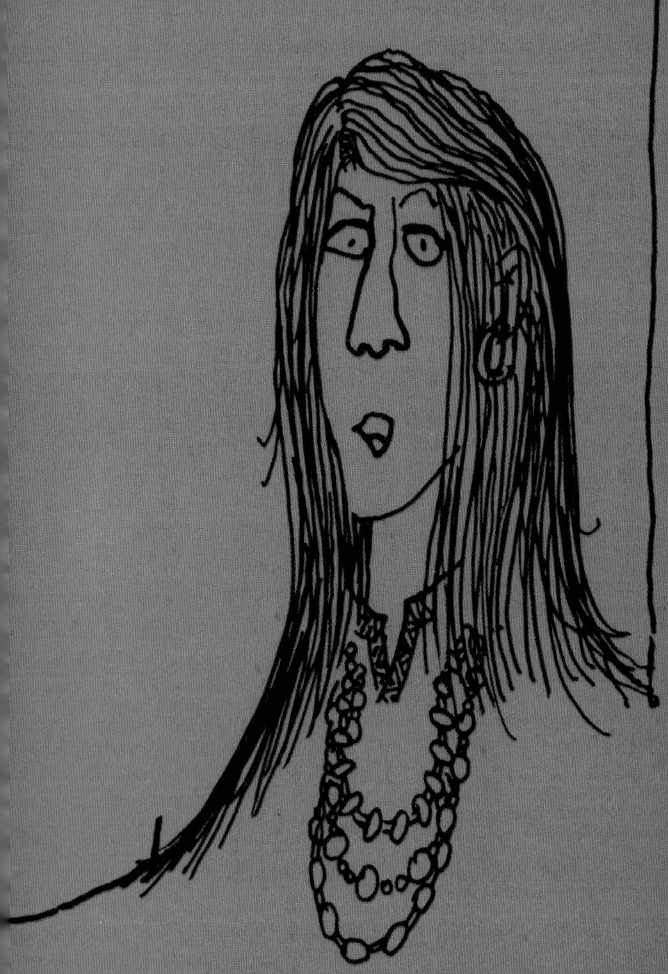

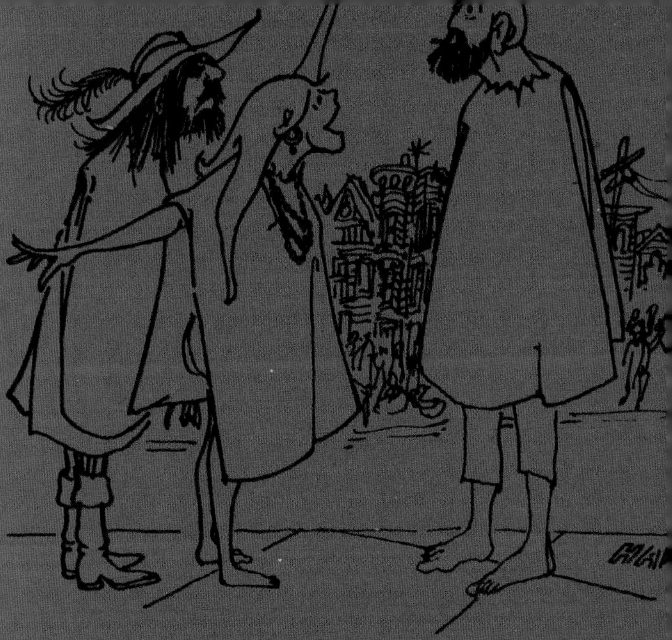

"Shel--you're wearing a <u>blanket</u>! Now you're one of <u>us</u>--liberated from the senseless restrictions of clothing, no longer governed by the inane rules of fashion . . . ! Of course, it <u>is</u> a little too short . . . and it's the wrong color . . . and. . . ."

Silverstein hangs out with sun-grooving nature children at the Morningstar Ranch just outside of San Francisco.

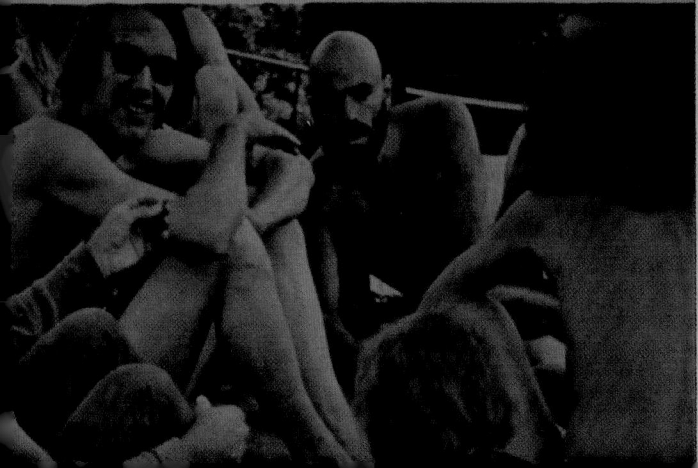

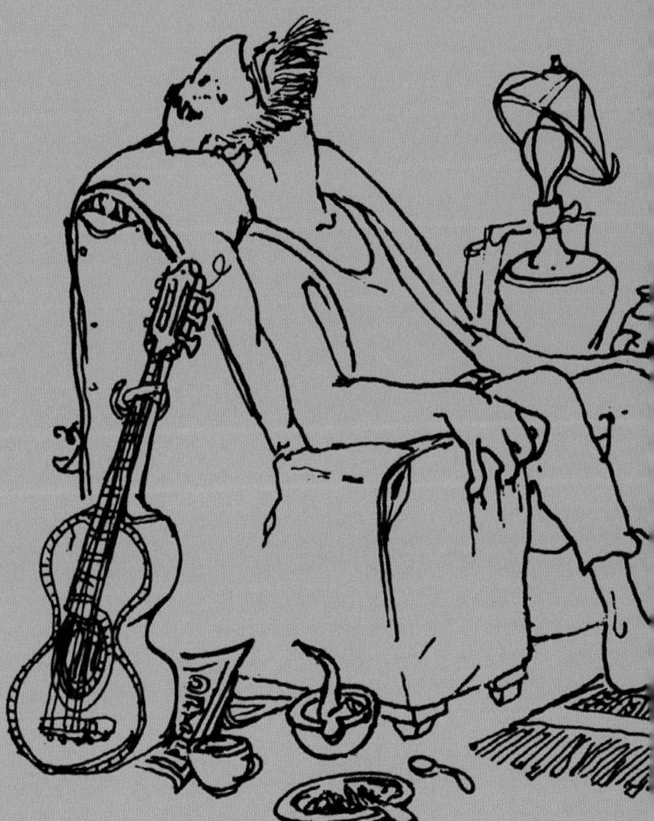

"Sure, I can feel it, but I don't think it's affecting my drawing style!!"

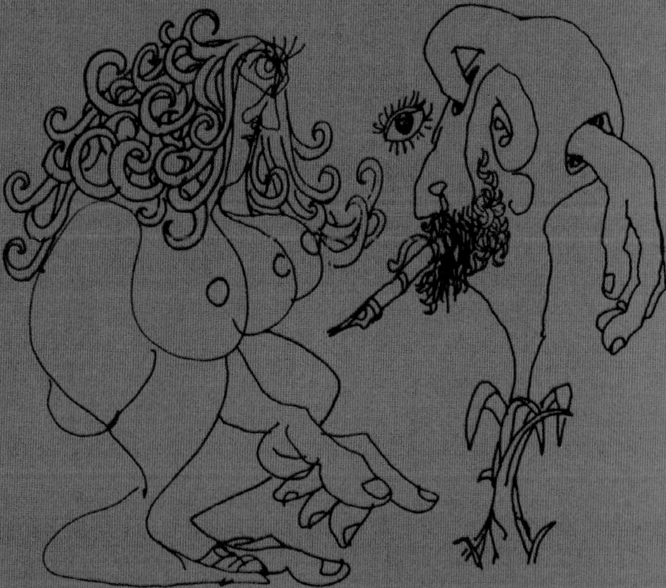

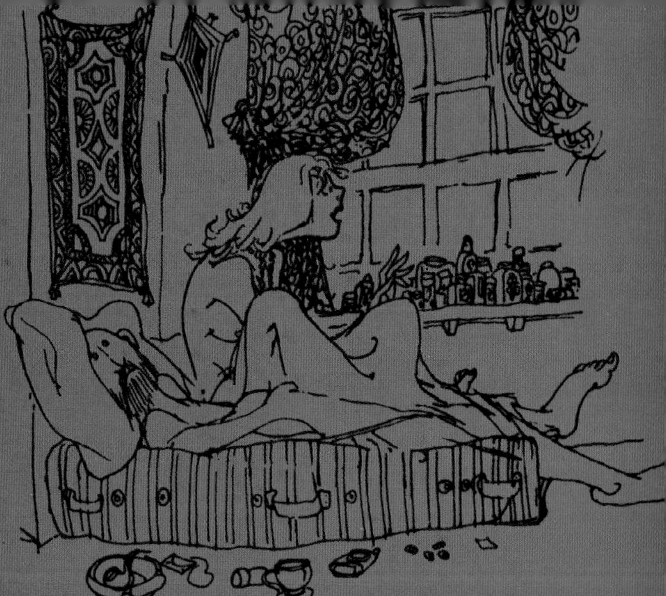

"Oh, Shel, what a beautiful day! We'll take some Dexi to get us going . . . smoke some pot to make breakfast taste better . . . then we'll take that acid trip I've been promising you . . . and tonight we'll sniff coke to help us make love . . . and take some Seconal. . . ."

"But I didn't mean to go to bed with him, Shel--I was standing in the psychedelic shop, when he walked up and showed me his 'LSD' button, so I showed him my 'Better Living Through Chemistry' button, then he showed me his 'Get Out of Vietnam' button, so I showed him my 'Make Love, Not War' button, and then he showed me his 'Let's Fornicate for Freedom' button and I didn't have any button to reply, so I didn't know what else to do . . . !"

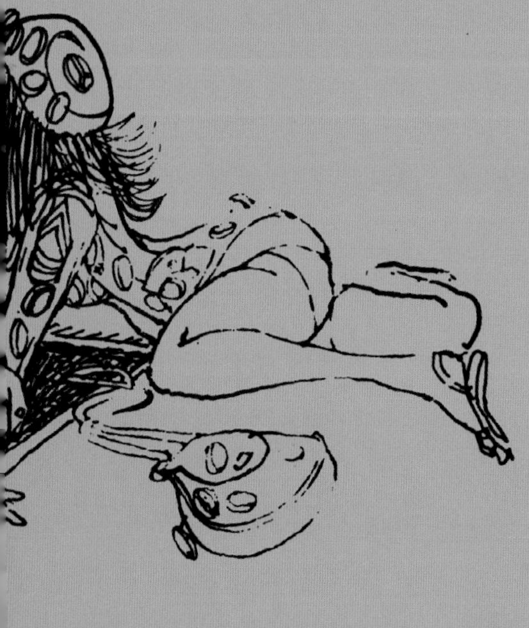

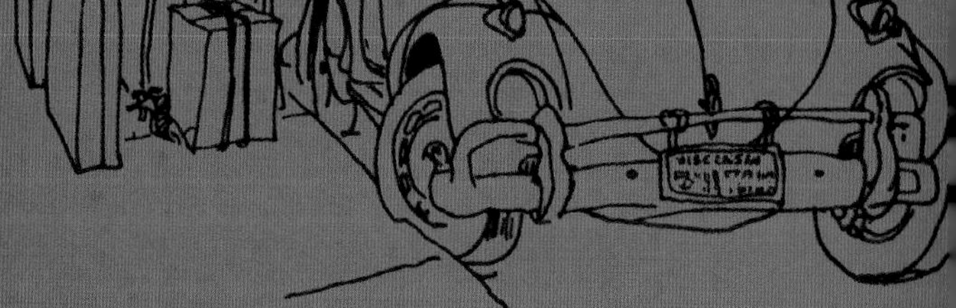

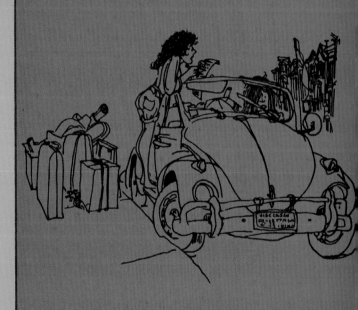

"OK, let's check the list. Let's see. . . . Smoke pot--check. . . . Take LSD trip--check. . . . Go to a love-in--check. . . . Panhandle in the street--check. . . . Join a protest movement--check. . . . Get arrested--check. All right, Susie, I guess we can go back to Milwaukee now!"

ACKNOWLEDGMENTS

Special thanks to Hugh M. Hefner, LeRoy Neiman, Larry Moyer, Victor Lownes and Art Paul for the interviews, images and insights. Gracious thanks to Hef, Leopold Froehlich, Tom Staebler, Mary O'Connor, Bradley Lincoln, Aaron Baker, Gene Snyder and everyone at *Playboy* for making this collection possible. Humble thanks to the Silverstein family for the opportunity. Big thanks to Michael Carr, Ali Benis and Ellen Philips for their professional assistance. Added thanks to Joy Kingsolver and Jerry Foust for their archival efforts. Finally, thanks to Jack Romanos, Mark Gompertz, Trish Todd and everyone at Simon & Schuster.